Visual Reference Guides

Philosophy

STEPHEN LAW

METRO BOOKS
New York

"MAN IS A ROPE STRETCHED BETWEEN THE ANIMAL AND THE SUPERMAN— A ROPE OVER AN ABYSS."

Friedrich Nietzsche, *Thus Spoke Zarathustra*

"PHILOSOPHERS... ARE IRRESISTIBLY
TEMPTED TO ASK AND ANSWER
QUESTIONS IN THE WAY SCIENCE DOES."

Ludwig Wittgenstein, *The Blue Book*

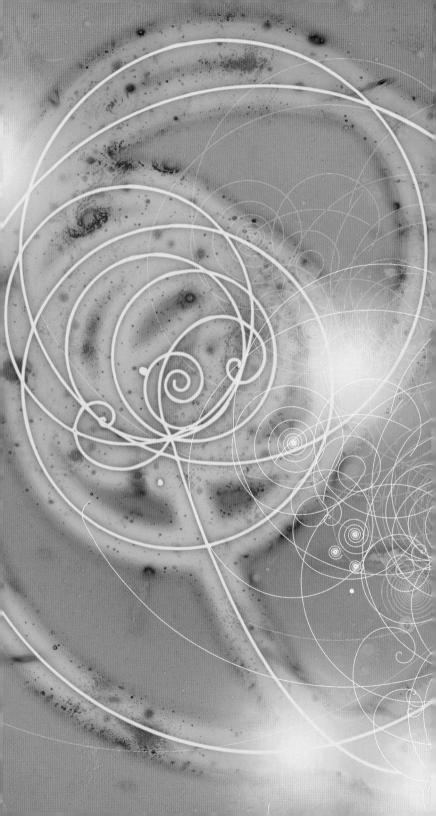

"THE WISEST HAVE THE MOST AUTHORITY."

Attributed to Plato

METRO BOOKS
New York

An Imprint of Sterling Publishing
1166 Avenue of the Americas
New York, NY 10036

METRO BOOKS and the distinctive
Metro Books logo are trademarks of Sterling Publishing Co., Inc.

© 2007 by Dorling Kindersley Limited

Project Editor	Sam Atkinson
Project Designer	Victoria Clark
Production Controller	Rita Sinha
DTP	John Goldsmid
Managing Editor	Debra Wolter
Managing Art Editor	Karen Self
Art Director	Bryn Walls
Publisher	Jonathan Metcalf

**Additional text contributions by Daniel Cardinal,
Michael Lacewing, and Chris Horner.**

Produced for Dorling Kindersley by

cobaltid

The Stables, Wood Farm, Deopham Road,
Attleborough, Norfolk NR17 1AJ, UK
www.cobaltid.co.uk

Editors
Marek Walisiewicz, Kati Dye,
Louise Abbott, Jamie Dickson, Maddy King

Art Editors
Paul Reid, Lloyd Tilbury, Pia Ingham,
Darren Bland, Claire Oldman, Annika Skoog

ISBN 978-1-4351-3894-0

Color reproduction by GRB, Italy
Manufactured in China by L. Rex Printing Co. Ltd.

10 9 8 7 6 5 4

www.sterlingpublishing.com

Foreword 10

Chapter One
**INTRODUCING
PHILOSOPHY**

What is philosophy? *14*

Chapter Two
**THE HISTORY
OF PHILOSOPHY**

The Ancients *24*

The medieval world *30*

The early moderns *34*

The modern age *40*

CONTENTS

Chapter Three
BRANCHES
OF PHILOSOPHY

Introduction *46*

KNOWLEDGE 48
Scepticism *50*
What is knowledge? *58*
Reason and
experience *66*

METAPHYSICS 74
Plato and the Forms *76*
Mind-dependence *82*

MORAL
PHILOSOPHY 100
What should I do? *102*
So what is morality? *112*

PHILOSOPHY OF
MIND 122
The consciousness
puzzle *124*
Could a machine
think? *132*

PHILOSOPHY OF
RELIGION 138
Does God exist? *140*
The problem of evil *153*
Faith and reason *157*

POLITICAL
PHILOSOPHY 160
The liberal ideal *162*
The common good *172*

PHILOSOPHY OF
SCIENCE 178
The problem of
induction *180*
Falsificationism *186*

Chapter Four
PHILOSOPHY
TOOLKIT

Introduction *192*
Reasoning *194*
Fallacies *198*
Thinking tools *212*

Chapter Five
WHO'S WHO IN
PHILOSOPHY

Introduction 228
Directory 230

Index 346
Acknowledgments 352

THINKING PHILOSOPHICALLY IS AN ADVENTURE. IT IS A JOURNEY TO THE OUTER LIMITS OF THOUGHT AND UNDERSTANDING. MANY ARE FASCINATED BY PHILOSOPHICAL QUESTIONS AND ISSUES, BUT ARE UNSURE WHERE TO BEGIN. THIS BOOK AIMS TO GIVE THOSE NEW TO PHILOSOPHY A CLEAR AND NON-TECHNICAL GUIDE.

This companion guide to philosophy is written for the interested layperson, though it will also be of value to students beginning a degree in philosophy. Within these pages you will discover some of the most extraordinary, baffling, inspiring, and in some cases downright peculiar thoughts ever entertained by humankind. Many of the questions addressed in Classical times by Plato, one of the greatest philosophers of all time, are questions with which philosophers are still grappling today.

This is not a book to plow through from cover to cover. You will no doubt find yourself delving into its pages in a piecemeal way. That is exactly what is intended. Feel free to jump from one chapter to another as you explore connections between different thinkers and ideas.

The best way to engage with any philosophical text is to approach it actively, not passively. Think critically about what you have read as you go along. Be prepared to read one or two of the trickier passages a second time or even a third time. And do regularly take time out to reflect.

It is worth stressing that this book is a "taster." No attempt has been made to cover everything. The book offers readers a carefully chosen selection of questions, thinkers, and ideas. While most of the main areas of Western philosophy are included, one or two selections, such as the mirror puzzle, are rather more idiosyncratic. The precise selection of topics explored in the book reflects to some extent the tastes and interests of the authors and what they happen to most enjoy writing about, and should not be taken to be definitive of what is of greatest philosophical importance.

Plato

> "*The safest general characterization of the European philosophical tradition is that it consists of a series of footnotes to Plato.*"
>
> **Alfred North Whitehead**

Stephen Law

When we start to think philosophically, we take a step back and begin to question even those things that we ordinarily take for granted—such as if anything exists at all.

INTRODUCING
PHILOSOPHY

WHAT IS PHILOSOPHY?

Philosophical questions include some of the most exciting, puzzling, and important questions ever asked. They can challenge our most fundamental beliefs. This chapter asks: what are philosophical questions, and how do philosophers attempt to answer them?

We all hold philosophical beliefs

Philosophy is sometimes dismissed as a wholly "head in the clouds" discipline with no relevance to everyday life. The truth is that philosophy can be, and very often is, very relevant indeed.

Though we may not realize it, we all hold philosophical beliefs. For example, I am sure that you, like me, suppose that the past is a fairly reliable guide to the future. That is a philosophical belief. We may believe that God exists. Or we may believe that he doesn't. Again, these are philosophical beliefs. Some believe we possess immortal souls, while others suppose we are purely material beings. Many believe things are morally right or wrong independently of whatever we might happen to suppose, while others claim that right and wrong amounts to nothing more than subjective preference. We believe that the world we see around us is real, and that the world continues to exist even when we are not observing it.

Where did the universe come from? Why, indeed, is there anything at all? Philosophy asks fundamental and often unsettling questions about life.

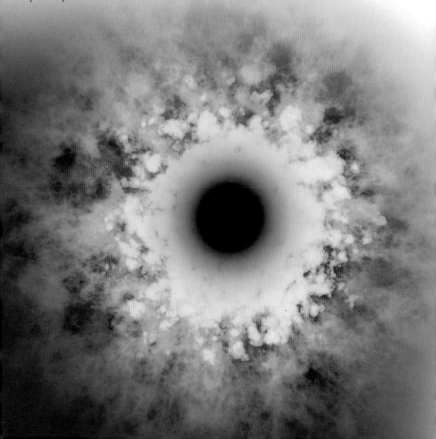

Goya's etching *The Sleep of Reason Brings Forth Monsters* captures the spirit of the Enlightenment and its emphasis on the role of reason in dispelling fear, uncertainty, and superstition.

Again, these are philosophical beliefs, and they have both been subjected to much scrutiny by philosophers.

Clearly, these beliefs can have a significant impact on our day-to-day lives. Someone who believes morality amounts to nothing more than subjective preference may end up behaving very differently from someone who believes that the wrongness of stealing or killing is a matter of objective fact. There is also a philosophical aspect to many contemporary moral and political debates. Questions about abortion, animal rights, waging war, and freedom of speech—all of these have an important philosophical dimension.

Someone who has never really thought about such issues, or who is ill-equipped to think about them, is therefore at a serious disadvantage when it comes to figuring out what is, or is most likely to be, true.

FUNDAMENTAL QUESTIONS

As we all know, children tend to ask "Why?" over and over again. It need not take long for them to dig down to some of our most fundamental beliefs. Philosophers have this same childlike tendency to question fundamentals—

in philosophy. It is not surprising that so many of us prefer not to think about such issues or consider such questions. We prefer to stay where we feel safe.

Yet the risk is worth taking. Questioning fundamentals can be fruitful. Some of the greatest scientific developments have come about through scientists asking just such questions. Einstein remarked that one of his

"PHILOSOPHY IS A BATTLE AGAINST THE BEWITCHMENT OF OUR INTELLIGENCE BY MEANS OF LANGUAGE."

Ludwig Wittgenstein, *Philosophical Investigations*

to ask those basic questions that, in our day-to-day lives, may simply not occur to us because they pertain to what we usually take for granted.

While thinking philosophically can be exhilarating, it can also be disturbing. When we start to think philosophically, we begin thinking without a safety net. The firm ground we thought lay beneath our feet can quickly dissolve away, leaving us hanging over a void. This feeling of intellectual vertigo is common

greatest inspirations came from reading the 18th-century philosopher David Hume, who got him to start questioning what others had just assumed to be true.

It is not just scientists who can benefit from questioning fundamentals. Some of the most important moral and political developments have come about through people being willing to question, and in some cases reject, what almost everyone else simply assumed to be true. Not so long ago it was considered "obvious" across much of the West that slavery was morally acceptable and that the proper role of women was in the home. Moral and political progress in these areas was brought about by those willing to take a step back and question what others took for granted. Western civilization owes a very great deal to those who have been prepared to think and question what others considered "given."

PHILOSOPHY AND RELIGION

Many of the questions tackled by philosophy are also addressed by religion. Religions typically attempt to provide an answer to the question of why the universe exists and why, indeed, there is anything at all. Some religions suppose God created

Like many other cultures, the Ancient Egyptians had creation myths. Philosophy also tackles questions about ultimate origins.

everything. Many religions also tackle the questions of whether we possess some sort of non-physical essence, or "soul," and what makes things right and wrong. Indeed, many of the greatest religious thinkers have been philosophers, and some of the most important philosophers have been theologians.

Given this overlap between philosophy and religion in terms of the questions they address, how do philosophy and religion differ? One way in which philosophy and religion can differ is in the emphasis they place on the role of reason. Obviously, we should acknowledge that reason has its limits. Reason may not be able to solve all philosophical puzzles. Philosophy

The Mayans, like numerous other ancient peoples, had complex structures of belief interweaving religious, mathematical, and cosmological ideas.

"THE UNEXAMINED LIFE IS NOT WORTH LIVING."

Attributed to Socrates

simply encourages us to apply our own powers of reason as well as, and as far as, we can.

Religion, too, may encourage the application of reason. But religions usually also insist on the importance of other roads to the truth, including revelation and scripture. Some even go as far as discouraging the application of reason to certain questions. Where that is the case, philosophy and religion part company. In the Western philosophical tradition, the important thing is to subject claims to critical scrutiny, and to attempt to justify your position rationally: to try to provide at least fairly good grounds for supposing it is true.

PHILOSOPHICAL REASONING

It is worth noting that the kind of "reasoning" engaged in by philosophers is not of a special, rarefied sort. It is, for the most part, everyday, common-or-garden reasoning of the kind you already apply when trying to figure out what is wrong with your car, whether someone is

telling you the truth, or how to get from A to B by the most efficient route. As I say, it would be a mistake just to assume that reason is able to answer all our most important questions. However, reason undoubtedly does have the power to illuminate at least some of them. And even when it cannot provide definitive answers, it can often reveal why certain answers will not suffice. That is one of the reasons why thinking philosophically can still be a valuable exercise, even when no solution is found.

A. J. AYER ON PHILOSOPHY

"It is by its methods rather than its subject matter that philosophy is to be distinguished from other arts or sciences. Philosophers make statements which are intended to be true, and they commonly rely on argument both to support their own theories and to refute the theories of others; but the arguments which they use are of a very peculiar character. The proof of a philosophical statement is not, or is only seldom, like the proof of a mathematical statement.... Neither is it like the proof of a statement in any of the descriptive sciences. Philosophical theories are not tested by observation."

A. J. Ayer, *The Problem of Knowledge*

PHILOSOPHY AND SCIENCE

Philosophy addresses questions that, in many cases, seem to reach beyond the point where science might provide us with answers. For example: why is there anything at all? How can I know that I am not trapped inside a virtual reality? Do we have immortal souls? What makes things morally right or wrong? Do human beings possess free will?

One reason why science can, in many cases, offer little help in answering such questions is that science itself presupposes certain answers to them. Take the question: how can I know that I am not trapped inside an illusory world? Those who have seen the film *The Matrix* will be familiar with the idea that the world we seem to inhabit could be unreal—a computer-generated virtual reality, perhaps, into which we are all plugged from birth: a deception fed into our nervous system by a central machine. Because empirical science simply presupposes that our five senses do provide us with access to reality, it cannot settle whether we are the victims of such an elaborate illusion.

Or consider the question: why is there anything at all? Scientists explain the existence of the universe by positing a "big bang" that took place some thirteen and a half billion years ago. This extraordinary event produced not just all matter and energy, but even time and space. Does this scientific explanation ultimately remove our sense of mystery? Does it explain why there is something rather than nothing? No. For we can now ask—why was there a bang rather than no bang? The mystery of why there is anything at all has not been solved, only postponed. While science has much of interest to say about the origin of the universe, it seems the fundamental mystery of why there is anything at all reaches beyond the point where science might ever provide us with an answer.

Religion addresses many of the same questions as philosophy. But, unlike philosophy, religion sometimes emphasizes the importance of faith over the application of our powers of reason.

Particle physicists try to identify the fundamental particles that make up the universe, and understand how they interact together. But they cannot tell us why those particles exist, since it is not possible to answer this question by experimentation.

probability toward or away from God, even if such evidence cannot conclusively settle whether or not God exists (though perhaps it can). Empirical investigation and evidence is not irrelevant when it comes to belief in God, despite the fact that the existence of God remains a philosophical question.

DIFFERENT APPROACHES

While most philosophers stress the importance of reason, they can still differ dramatically in terms of their approach to philosophical questions. The most obvious method of applying reason to a philosophical question is to try to "figure out" the answer, much as you might try to figure out the solution to any logical puzzle. Even if you cannot establish which answer is correct, you might still be able to show that a certain answer is not, or is unlikely to be, correct (in much the same way that, even when Sherlock

Another reason why science alone is incapable of answering these questions for us is that they are often at least partly about meanings and concepts. If we wish to answer the question "Do human beings possess free will?" we need to get clear about what "free will" means: what the concept involves. Even when all the scientific facts are in, the puzzle about whether we possess free will will remain if we remain unclear about what "free will" means. This sort of clarification of meanings and concepts is one of the central activities of the philosopher.

A ROLE FOR SCIENCE

None of this is to say that science, and empirical evidence, is always irrelevant to answering philosophical questions. In some cases, science, and certainly the evidence of our senses, can have a major bearing. Take arguments about the existence of God. Some believe contemporary science has uncovered evidence of an "intelligent designer." Others believe that the sheer quantity of suffering found in the world provides overwhelming evidence against the existence of an all-powerful, all-good God. In both cases it is held that observation of the world reveals evidence that can dramatically shift the balance of

BERTRAND RUSSELL ON PHILOSOPHY

"What is the value of philosophy and why ought it to be studied? It is the more necessary to consider this question, in view of the fact that many men, under the influence of science or of practical affairs, are inclined to doubt whether philosophy is anything better than innocent but useless trifling, hair-splitting distinctions, and controversies on matters concerning which knowledge is impossible.... If the study of philosophy has any value at all... it must be only indirectly, through its effects upon the lives of those who study it. It is in these effects, therefore... that the value of philosophy must be primarily sought."

Bertrand Russell, *The Problems of Philosophy*

Holmes cannot yet figure out exactly who committed a crime, he may be able to establish that the butler didn't do it). This "head-on" approach to tackling philosophical questions is commonplace. But there are alternatives.

A rather more radical approach is to try to show that there is something wrong with the question. Here is an illustration: we might approach the question "Why is there something rather than nothing?" head on and try to figure out the answer. Alternatively, we might try to show that, though the question would seem to make sense, actually it doesn't. When we ordinarily consider a situation in which there is "nothing," we mean there is nothing there: there is, say, a tract of space that is empty, such as when we say "There is nothing in this box." But the kind of "nothing" we are asked to envisage when we consider the question "Why is there something rather than nothing?" is far more radical— it involves the absence of even time and space. But does this notion of *absolute* nothing even make sense? A number of philosophers have argued that it does not. And if the notion of absolute nothing does not make sense, then neither does the question. In which case, the question does not require an answer.

When faced with an apparently intractable philosophical problem, it is always worth considering this type of alternative approach.

THINKING SKILLS
There is a further reason why thinking philosophically can be a valuable exercise. The activity of philosophizing can help to foster important thinking skills, skills we all need if we are to remain sensitive to the truth. They are often highly transferable skills that never go out of date. The ability to spot a logical howler, cut through waffle, be relevant, make a point clearly and

precisely, and so on are all abilities that always come in handy, whatever your walk of life. Certainly these skills are often of use to professionals, which is why many businesses place great value on an academic qualification in philosophy.

The critical skills developed by philosophy are of practical benefit in other ways, too. They help to immunize us against the wiles of politicians, medical quacks, second-hand car salesmen, Holocaust deniers, lifestyle gurus, and the many other purveyors of snake oil. There are certain basic mistakes we are all prone to make when it comes to weighing up probabilities and drawing conclusions, and even a little exposure to philosophical and critical thinking can contribute toward making us less vulnerable.

Indeed, there is growing evidence that encouraging collective philosophical debate in the classroom can have measurable educational benefits for children, enhancing not just their intellectual intelligence, but their social and emotional intelligence, too. It seems that even a little exposure to philosophy early on can be a profoundly life-enhancing thing.

One useful value of a little training in critical thinking is that it can help you to see through the claims of dubious salesmen and political spin.

NAVIGATING THIS BOOK
The brief History of Philosophy which follows provides a map on which the major movements and developments in philosophy can be located. In Branches of Philosophy, seven of the most important subdivisions are introduced, and selected topics are examined in more detail. But this book aims to provide not only knowledge of what questions philosophers have asked and what philosophers have said, but also some skill in thinking for yourself. The Philosophy Toolkit contains some key thinking tools: how to apply, for example, the techniques of argument and

reasoning that philosophers deploy, and how to spot common logical errors. Finally, in Who's Who in Philosophy, you will find concise introductions to many of the major figures in the history of philosophy, as well as briefer entries on some less well-known thinkers.

THE VERDICT OF SOCRATES

The Ancient Greek philosopher Socrates, when charged with corrupting the youth of Athens and facing a possible death sentence, is reported to have commented: "The unexamined life is not worth living." Socrates believed it better to die than to give up thinking philosophically. That might be an exaggeration. But I believe that a good case can be made for saying that a society in which there is little if any philosophical reflection is an unhealthy society. A philosophy-free society in which there is little critical thought about fundamentals is a society perilously close to atrophy.

"WE MUST NOT MAKE A PRETENCE OF DOING PHILOSOPHY, BUT REALLY DO IT; FOR WHAT WE NEED IS NOT THE SEMBLANCE OF HEALTH BUT REAL HEALTH."

Epicurus, quoted in *Hellenistic Philosophy* (A. A. Long)

When we start to think philosophically, we may start to walk against the crowd: we begin to question, and sometimes even reject, what most people ordinarily take for granted.

THE HISTORY OF
PHILOSOPHY

THE ANCIENTS

Aristotle said that philosophy begins in wonder; if so, its origins must lie as far back as humanity itself. But as far as we know, before *ca*.600 BCE, reactions to the puzzles that characterize the human condition were mythical and religious, involving tradition and the supernatural.

Ancient Greece

The first person about whom we have records of recognizably philosophical thinking, from 585 BCE, is Thales, who lived in the Greek colony of Miletus on the coast of Asia Minor. What is characteristic about him and the Milesian thinkers that followed is their concern to deploy reason in search of naturalistic explanations for observable phenomena. A central theme in their speculations concerned the substance from which the universe is made. And while they disagreed about what this substance is, their basic conviction that everything must be made of just one type of stuff has endured into contemporary physics.

Early philosophers debated the composition of the universe. Thales thought it was all made of water, in many different forms.

Their philosophical spirit soon spread through the Greek world. In southern Italy, Parmenides and Zeno argued that nothing can be created or destroyed: all that exists is one undifferentiated and unchanging reality, and the appearance to our senses of multiplicity and change is therefore an illusion. Early sources report that Pythagoras (*ca*.570–495 BCE) was advised by Thales to visit Egypt to learn about mathematics. Pythagoras then set up his influential school in Croton in southern Italy. The importance of the Pythagoreans lies in their conviction that numbers hold the key to grasping the nature of reality. The impact of this idea on the development of science is difficult to overestimate.

Leucippus may have been the first "Atomist," with his thesis, in the 5th century BCE, that the universe is composed of an infinite number of minuscule, indestructible particles of matter, which, through their combinations and movements, produce all phenomena. Elaborated by Democritus and later by Epicurus, Atomism was forgotten in the Middle Ages, only to be resurrected in the modern era.

After the Atomists, philosophy turned toward human nature and ethics, especially in Athens in Greece, where philosophy entered a golden age. Skill in debate and argument was prized in Athens's direct democracy, where political success was won by swaying the crowd. In this atmosphere, users of

KEY DATES

563 BCE Siddhartha Gautama, founder of the Buddhist religion, is born in Nepal, 12 years after the birth of Confucius in China.

ca.427 BCE Plato is born. His metaphysical theories later form the foundations for much Western philosophical thought.

600 BCE　　　　　　　　　**400 BCE**　　　　　　　　　**200 BCE**

ca.570 BCE Pythagoras, the father of modern scientific and mathematical thought, is born on Samos, an island off the coast of modern-day Turkey.

221 BCE The Great Unification marks the beginning of imperial China, which is ruled by successive dynasties until 1912, when China becomes a Republic.

ca.100 BCE The opening of the Silk Road between China and the West permits exchange of trade and ideas.

effective argumentation flourished. Chief among these was Socrates. He would engage anyone in discussion in the hope of acquiring knowledge of moral concepts, and his dialectical method of question and answer had a lasting impact.

According to his student, Plato, Socrates met Parmenides; Plato himself certainly inherited the latter's distrust of the senses as a route to true knowledge. Plato, whose writings exploited his

Under the rule of Pericles, 5th-century BCE Athens, the dominant Greek city-state, enjoyed a golden age of art, architecture, and philosophy.

changing physical objects we perceive around us. Plato, an aristocrat, attacked Athenian democracy, on the grounds that the people are not the best judge of policy, blaming it for defeat in the Peloponnesian war and for condemning Socrates to death in 399 BCE. Plato's student Aristotle was the first to try to present philosophical

"ALL MEN BY NATURE DESIRE TO KNOW."

Aristotle

teacher's dialectical method, crystallized in his dialogs a body of work with which all philosophers have had to contend to the present day. He is best known for his Theory of Forms—the idea of a world of eternal ideas that is more real than the

ideas in a truly systematic way and also the first to tackle logic and categorize valid forms of argument. Both Plato and Aristotle set up schools which, with gaps, endured for centuries, carrying on the Socratic tradition of free critical inquiry.

49 BCE Julius Caesar and his forces cross the Rubicon river to seize power in Rome.

121 CE Roman Emperor Marcus Aurelius studies Greek philosophy, and commends the Stoic ethos in his influential *Meditations*.

205 CE The Neo-Platonist philosopher Plotinus is born in Egypt. His explication of Plato's works informs the development of Christianity, Islam, and Judaism.

| 0 | 100 CE | 200 CE | 300 CE |

30 CE Christ dies by crucifixion. The exact year of his death is still disputed and 33 CE has also been proposed as a likely date.

150 CE Ptolemy of Alexandria, a Greek scholar of astronomy and mathematics, proves that the world is round.

Ancient Eastern thought

While Socrates and Plato were laying the foundations for Western philosophy, Confucius and Lao Tzu ushered in the classical era of Chinese philosophy, which lasted for 400 years and was enriched by such thinkers as Mozi, Mengzi (Mencius), and Han Feizi. These thinkers were all concerned primarily with social and political issues and established the four principal schools of Chinese thought.

SHAPING SOCIETY

The first such school is Confucianism, an enduring influence on government within China and the official philosophy of the Han Dynasty.

The "three wise men" of the East: Lao Tzu, Buddha, and Confucius. Chinese philosophy is shaped by the influence of a few key thinkers.

Confucius emphasized the value of traditional social roles and structures, arguing that rulers needed to foster a natural moral sense in their subjects.

The second is Daoism, which began with the *Dao De Jing*, a work attributed to Lao Tzu, and was later developed by Zhuangzi. Daoism argues for minimal interference from government in order to allow society to return to an unforced condition that is more in tune with nature. Lao Tzu himself rejected all artificial social distinctions, and eventually left the civilized world, never to be heard of again.

The third strand of Eastern philosophical thought begins with Mozi, who founded a community based on mutual support in the 4th century BCE. Mohism, like Confucianism, argues that the inherent moral virtue in people must be allowed to flower.

Opposed to this view is the fourth school, Legalism, founded by Han Feizi, which stresses the need for strict laws in order to ensure conformity to moral codes of behavior among an inherently immoral populace. Legalism was the guiding principle of the autocratic and ruthless Qin Dynasty that oversaw the first Great Unification of China into a single imperial state in 221 BCE. From the classical era (which came to its conclusion at the end of the Qin Dynasty) onward, Chinese philosophy is essentially a working through and development of the various themes of these four main schools of thought.

THE VEDAS

Indian philosophy grows out of what are essentially a set of ancient religious writings, the Vedas, which date back as far as the 14th century BCE. Little is known of their authors. The concerns of the Vedas are primarily cosmological, metaphysical, and religious: for example, in one section, sages dispute the question of what the origin of the universe was. Several schools of thought grew up in reaction to the Vedas, either accepting their authority or questioning their tenets. Buddhism, founded by Siddhartha Gautama, represents one of the nine schools within this tradition and one that is sceptical of the Vedas. It urges that spiritual enlightenment can only be gained once an individual is free of the shackles of earthly desires.

Deities, not philosophers, are the vehicles of wisdom in the Vedas. Here, an effigy of one such deity, Ganesh, undergoes ritual immersion during a Hindu festival.

From Greece to Rome

Throughout most of the Golden Age the Greek city-states remained independent. It was only in 330 BCE that they were united as one nation by the Macedonian leader, Alexander, who went on to conquer most of the known world, from Greece and Egypt in the west to China and India in the east. This empire ensured that Greek culture would have a lasting influence on the world. One of Alexander's greatest achievements was the construction of the port of Alexandria in Egypt, which became a center for Western and Eastern culture and thought.

Meanwhile, on the other side of the Mediterranean, a small state was steadily growing. Rome, initially a crossing point over the Tiber River, had grown into an Empire that had begun to dominate Western trade routes. Having defeated and razed the rival trading power Carthage, they turned their attention to Greece. By 146 BCE Rome had brought the Greek

mainland under its control, finally ending the Golden Age of Greek culture. Although the Roman Empire went on to new heights, the Greeks still gained a victory, for Rome held up Greek culture as a standard for its Empire. And so the traditions of Plato, and to a lesser extent Aristotle, found their way into Roman intellectual life.

"I AM A CITIZEN OF THE WORLD."

Diogenes

THE ERA OF "SCHOOLS"

There were many philosophical sects that sprang up in Greece after the death of Aristotle and found their way to Rome. The first philosophical school of this new era was formed by the Cynics. Antisthenes (*ca.*445–360 BCE) was a contemporary of Plato who, after Socrates's death, abandoned the aristocratic life of leisure and began to live and work among the poor. He rejected the trappings of civilization in order to embrace a more natural way of being. Diogenes (*ca.*400–325 BCE), his better-known disciple, was more radical still, rejecting all artificial

The Roman emperor Marcus Aurelius followed the Stoic school of thought. His own writings stressed the fleeting, ephemeral nature of human life.

distinctions based on social convention, such as between naked and clothed, public and private. He gave up washing and dressing and lived in a barrel. This gave him the nickname of "cynic" or "dog."

The Stoic school was founded by Zeno of Citium in 300 BCE in Cyprus and became the dominant philosophical outlook of the Roman Empire. Denying Atomism (*see p.24*), they taught that the universe was a continuum governed by a "world soul:" it conformed to rational principles discoverable by human reason. Since we are ourselves part of this natural order, there is no transcendent reality and therefore no spiritual dimension to reality, no afterlife. The natural order, being the proper way of things, is something we should not try to resist, and so we should calmly accept what befalls us—hence the word "stoic." The later stoics, Seneca and Marcus Aurelius, a Roman emperor, produced important works defending Stoicism.

Diogenes is the best-known Cynic philosopher. On meeting with Alexander the Great, he snubbed him, being unimpressed by earthly achievements.

EPICUREANS AND SCEPTICS

At around this time Epicurus set up his own school, known as the Garden. The Epicureans were Atomists and argued that the gods had no concern with mankind. Since death is the end, we have to make the most of this life by maximizing worldly happiness. Epicurus argued for the empiricist view that all knowledge comes to us via the impact of atoms on our sense organs. Inevitably the denial of the involvement of the gods and of personal survival after death made Epicureanism unattractive to Christianity, and Epicurus was to be denounced as the

Antichrist in the Middle Ages. The Roman poet Lucretius's 1st-century CE masterpiece *On the Nature of Things* is an exposition of Epicurus's philosophy.

In around 80 BCE Aenesidemus founded the Sceptic school, which looked back to the scepticism of Pyrrho (360–272 BCE) as its inspiration and argued that positive knowledge is impossible since all information gleaned from the senses is subject to inconsistency. They concluded that the only rational course is to withhold assent from any belief and believed that by suspending belief we can achieve peace of mind. Such scepticism has its origins at least as far back as Socrates and his claim that he had no knowledge, yet before, knowledge had always been thought possible. Pyrrho himself seems to have been impressed by the great diversity of different opinions among peoples of different cultures which he encountered while serving in Alexander's army. Since that day, scepticism has retained a vital if often destructive role at the heart of the philosophical enterprise.

NEO-PLATONISM

The founder of Neo-Platonism is Plotinus (*ca.*205–270 CE). From their base in Alexandria, the Neo-Platonists came to exert an enormous influence on the intellectual traditions of Rome and, later, Christianity. With his doctrine of the trinity (The One, The Intellect, and The Soul), Plotinus bridges the gap between Plato's Theory of Forms (the One is the ultimate form equivalent to the Good, the world has reality only because it shares in the Forms) and Christian theology. What Christian scholars took from Plotinus was the idea that the body is essentially unimportant. What matters is the nurturing of the Soul, with the aim of reaching God, the One. Attaining the One was a kind of ecstatic revelation.

THE MEDIEVAL WORLD

The philosophy of what is called the medieval period, from the decline of classical pagan culture to the Renaissance, is characterized by the concern among Jewish, Christian, and Muslim thinkers to combine Greek and Roman philosophy with religious orthodoxy.

East versus West

The Roman Empire was genuinely pluralistic, and had been able to assimilate most religions into its culture. Christianity, though, was outlawed because of its ban on the worship of Caesar, and its adherents were persecuted. After three hundred years of struggle, however, it was eventually accepted by the Roman emperor Constantine as a legal religion. In 330 CE Constantine decided to move the capital of the increasingly large and unwieldy Empire from Rome to Byzantium, where he built the glorious city of Constantinople (modern Istanbul), and in 380, in a desperate attempt to unite the by then fragmenting Empire, Christianity became the official religion of the Roman Empire.

Throughout western Europe "barbarian" hordes drove out Roman colonists.

This had many repercussions. Most notably, the resultant power vacuum in Rome became swiftly filled by Christian bishops, electing Popes who were to be the dominant political force in Western Europe for the next fourteen hundred years. Christianity now needed a formal and coherent doctrine that could be written and taught; scholars such as Augustine (354–430) first formulated the intellectual traditions of the Christian Church, and were the first to deal with the theological problems that Christian intellects have struggled with ever since. Augustine stands on the cusp between Greek and medieval Christian thought.

THE FALL OF ROME

In 476 the western wing of the Roman Empire collapsed, its borders too weak to stand against the hordes of barbarians, and from around 500 to 1000, northern and western Europe were plunged into the Dark Ages, so called because intellectual and cultural activity lost its vibrancy, and little of philosophical interest survives. By the year 800 the Church had established a strict hierarchy of control emanating from the Pope and reaching across Europe through a network of bishops. Opinion that differed from the orthodox was quickly crushed either by imprisonment, excommunication, or torture. At this time, literacy in Europe was confined to

KEY DATES

410 The Goths sack Rome, leading to the decline of the Roman Empire in Western Europe, and its general collapse there after 476.

480 Ancius Manlius Severinus Boethius, author of the *Consolations of Philosophy*, is born in Rome.

570 Birth of the Islamic prophet Mohammed, in Mecca. By 750, the Islamic empire stretches from Spain to central Asia.

300

500

700

380 Christianity becomes the official religion of the Roman Empire, now controlled from its new capital of Constantinople.

552 Buddhism spreads to Japan from Baekje (modern-day Korea). Its appearance is documented in the *Nihon Shoki*.

***ca.*700** Indian mathematicians calculate the value of pi and the length of the solar year.

clerics so Papal control of intellectual writings was almost complete, and philosophical speculations had to conform to church dogma.

ISLAMIC PHILOSOPHY

Meanwhile, in Constantinople and the Byzantine Empire, the study of the philosophies of the Ancient Greeks was continuing through Europe's Dark Ages, and by the 9th century the Islamic world, which now stretched from India to Andalusia in Spain, became aware of them. Early in this period Baghdad was the center of philosophical activity: the school known as the House of Wisdom, supported by the Caliphs, pursued scientific and philosophical inquiries relatively free from political interference. This was the beginning of the period known in the Islamic world as the golden age of scholarship, an era lasting until around the 13th century that was marked by a remarkable flowering of Islamic culture. Scientific inquiry was encouraged by both religion and state, and major advances were made in a wide range of disciplines including medicine, engineering, astronomy, and mathematics. The period would be brought to an end by the Crusades and the destruction wrought by the Mongols, but not before Islamic discoveries had paved the way for modern science.

Constantinople—modern Istanbul— became the center of power in the Near East after Constantine made it capital of the faltering Roman Empire.

1099 Christian crusaders capture the holy city of Jerusalem. The city is later recaptured by Muslim forces in the year 1187.

1225 Thomas Aquinas, one of the great theologians of the Catholic church, is born in the Kingdom of Naples. His theories influence later thought on ethics and epistemology.

900   **1100**   **1300**

ca.1070 Anselm, a Christian theologian and philosopher, puts forward his ontological argument for the existence of God.

1126 The Islamic philosopher Averroes, an innovator in mathematical, medical, and theological thinking, is born in Cordoba.

1275 The Venetian explorer Marco Polo travels in Mongol China.

Like their brethren working in the Jewish and Christian traditions, Islamic scholars were concerned to harmonize the revealed truths of their faith with the flame of philosophical inquiry that had been carried from Greece and spread through the known world. Philosophers were concerned with the nature of God and his relation to the created world, human free will, and immortality. Importantly they identified and translated many Ancient Greek texts. They engaged particularly with Neo-Platonism and Aristotle in an attempt to reconcile the revealed truth of the Koran with reason. For example, they adopted the Neo-Platonist account of God as the source of all being and used Aristotelian concepts in identifying the essence and existence of God. They also updated Aristotelian arguments to prove God's existence in the Kalam argument.

While Al Farabi and Avicenna flourished in the East, developing these issues as well as their own versions of the ideal Platonic state, in Moorish Spain were found Averroes and the Jewish philosopher Maimonides (1135–1204), who argued that there could be

A statue of Maimonides in the city of Córdoba in Spain. This Jewish philosopher and physician produced important works on medicine and tried to reconcile Aristotle with Jewish theology.

The pharmacy of Ibn Sina, the 10th-century Persian philosopher known in the West by his Latinized name of Avicenna. A true polymath, Avicenna did important work not only in philosophy but in astronomy, mathematics, and medicine.

no contradiction between the discoveries of human reason as made by Aristotle and the teachings revealed by God.

CHRISTIAN SCHOLASTICISM

In Western Europe at this time, while Plato's works had been assimilated into Christian doctrine, the great scientific and philosophical works of Aristotle had been virtually lost to the West for over a thousand years. The intellectual climate was in stark contrast to that of Ancient Greece. In the writings of Plato and Aristotle there exists a sense of freedom: the discussions were capable of leading anywhere. In this, the Scholastic period, the conclusions to any philosophical

"YOU MUST ACCEPT THE TRUTH FROM WHATEVER SOURCE IT COMES."

Moses Maimonides

argument were determined in advance: all had to toe the official line of the Church. However, during the 12th and 13th centuries, Islamic translations of Ancient Greek texts began to become available in the West. Further original Greek texts of Aristotle were discovered when Constantinople was sacked during the Fourth Crusade (1202–04). The availability of these works revolutionized Scholastic philosophy. At first Aristotle was seen as a threat and the study of his works was banned by the Church, but one man was so deeply impressed by the Greek philosopher that he made it his life mission to bring Aristotle and the Church together. Thomas Aquinas, from northern Italy, sought to reconcile the writings of Aristotle with Platonized Christianity. The result, known as Thomism, is still the official line of the Catholic Church today, and must be studied by all trainee clerics. Aside from the writings of Karl Marx, no single person's philosophy has shaped the world we live in today more than Thomas Aquinas's.

GOOD AND GOD

In this way the philosophical projects of the Ancient Greeks found root in the former Roman Empire and the Catholic Church. Christianity had become a type of Platonism with its concern to downgrade life in this world by contrasting it with an ideal world to which we aspire. The body being only a temporary house for the soul, genuine knowledge is to be found only once our souls return to the other world. Plato's Good had become the Christian God, the source of being and knowledge and the ultimate object to which we aspire. This paradigm still holds despite the reconciliation of Aristotle's philosophy with Catholic doctrine. Aristotle's writings were enormously important for the Renaissance that

was to come. However, it is ironic that after vehemently disagreeing with Plato's Theory of Forms during his lifetime, Aristotle was finally reconciled with Plato fifteen hundred years after his death.

Philosophy had not died, but it was constrained by religion to such an extent that scholars found themselves exercising their intellectual energies on arid debates of increasingly marginal concern. However, within two hundred years Europe was to see an astonishing series of intellectual revolutions that were to change our world. In science, in the arts, in religion, and in philosophy, old ideas were thrown out and new models of thinking began to take their place. The Platonic and Aristotelian ideas that had held sway over the West for one-and-a-half millennia were questioned, examined, and often rejected as Europe experienced a period of intellectual growth unlike anything since Ancient Greece.

St Thomas Aquinas, one of the most influential scholars in the history of the Catholic church, wrote on issues of wide-ranging philosophical importance, including the existence of God.

THE EARLY MODERNS

As the Middle Ages drew to a close, a spirit of intellectual and artistic rebirth began to flourish in Europe. During this period of innovation and discovery, a new breed of thinkers emerged who challenged orthodox medieval views on how the universe and society were ordered.

Humanism and the rise of science

The Renaissance represented the emergence of a new humanism in the arts and a reinvigorated spirit of discovery in the sciences. It began in Italy in the mid-14th century and spread quickly to the rest of Europe. This period of growth and innovation took place against a backdrop of radical social and economic changes that occurred because of the rapid expansion of cities. As cities grew, the agricultural economy developed in response to increased demand, and new technologies helped to increase productivity. This, along with the enclosure movement (which sought to convert common land to private ownership), saw peasants and serfs forced off their land and into the cities. The feudal system was giving way to capitalism as a new class of wealthy merchants emerged.

Latin and Greek texts from antiquity were also becoming more available, and many of the thinkers of the day were

Galileo's revolutionary new *Systemate Mundi*, or "world system," acknowledged his debt not only to Copernicus and Ptolemy but also to Aristotle.

discovering an alternative heritage to the Aristotelian and Platonic tradition that had dominated intellectual life for so long. Through the elegant Latin verse of Lucretius and Cicero, the pagan philosophies of Stoicism and Epicureanism were brought back to life.

NEW SCIENCE

Renaissance thinkers were interested in alchemy and the occult, but also in science, and the end of the Scholastic era (*see pp.32–3*) was precipitated by an increased readiness among the scientists of the day to question received theories about the world—theories in which the Church often had a heavy investment. An English courtier, Francis Bacon (1561–1626), proposed a new approach to scientific endeavor that has become known as the method of induction (*see pp.180–5*). He advised scientists to begin with observations of the world and use them as a basis for producing general theories. This approach stood in stark contrast to

KEY DATES

1300 The Christian Neo-Platonist philosopher and mystic Meister Eckhart lectures in Paris.

1400 The burgeoning scientific and artistic achievements of the Italian Renaissance usher in a new era of progress and discovery in Europe.

1543 Nicolaus Copernicus publishes *On the Revolution of the Celestial Spheres*, proposing that the earth orbits the sun.

1300   **1400**   **1500**

1347 The "Black Death" plague pandemic begins in Europe, killing more than a third of the continent's population by the close of the century.

1445 Johannes Gutenberg invents the first printing press, enabling the mass-production of books and facilitating the spread of ideas throughout Europe.

the medieval thinkers' tendency to bow to the authority of traditional models of how the world worked.

This new approach found its clearest expression in the revolution in cosmology that followed the discoveries of Galileo at the turn of the 17th century. The traditional picture of the universe, one supported by Aristotelian physics and Neo-Platonist cosmology, placed the earth at its center with all the heavenly bodies in fixed orbits around it. Scholastic philosophers (*see pp.32–3*) had entrenched this cosmology and it was deeply entwined with their metaphysical

The new humanism saw intellectual debate spread beyond the Church and into daily life. *The Four Philosophers* by Rubens illustrates how intellectual and artistic endeavor had begun to intertwine.

views about the place of man, the Creation, and God. But Galileo, making observations with a telescope of his own manufacture (*see also pp.82–5*), saw that the sun had spots that changed position, suggesting the earth was moving around the sun. On the basis of this and other observations, he was able to put together a compelling case for the heliocentric (sun-orbital) model of the universe that had been proposed by Copernicus some

1596 René Descartes, the rationalist thinker and "father of modern philosophy," is born in La Haye en Touraine (now Descartes), France.

1751 The first volume of Denis Diderot's *Encyclopédie* is published, including contributions from the Geneva-born political and social philosopher Jean-Jacques Rousseau.

1600

1700

1800

1651 The English political philosopher Thomas Hobbes publishes his *Leviathan*, outlining theories on the ideal structure for society and government.

1748 The Scottish philosopher David Hume publishes his seminal work *A Treatise of Human Nature*.

1789 The storming of the Bastille prison in Paris marks the beginning of the French Revolution.

70 years earlier. This discovery more than anything else demonstrated that, on scientific matters at least, the Church and the Ancients had been wrong.

The Church was not sympathetic to Galileo's work and forced him to recant his view, under threat of torture. However, the tide was turning and the Church was ultimately powerless to resist the rise of the new critical spirit.

A NEW ERA

Under the influence of the ancient Atomists, Galileo, Gassendi, and Hobbes (*see p.275*) revived the mechanical view of the nature of the universe. Philosophers began to put human beings and the natural world, rather than God and the next world, at the center of their inquiries.

In Northern Europe, the Renaissance also produced the Reformation, when a series of religious thinkers rebelled against the Church, urging a return to the teachings of the Bible. Reformers like Erasmus, Calvin, and Luther questioned the teachings of Catholicism, and in 1517 the Reformation began in earnest, when Luther nailed his 95 theses challenging the Church's authority to the Castle Church in Wittenberg, Germany.

Martin Luther defied the Catholic church, burning a Papal Bull outside the walls of Wittenberg. Luther challenged the view that people could only have a relationship with God through the church.

Against the Catholic view that God could only be reached through the institution of the Church, Protestants emphasized the individual's personal relationship with God. The resultant schism within the Church further loosened the stranglehold of Scholastic thought.

Important though the Renaissance was in terms of the arts and science, the real impact on philosophy was still to come. By the early 17th century, the stage was set for a new breed of philosophers who would be free from religious dogma and intended to return to the spirit of Ancient Greece. In the front rank of these was the French philosopher René Descartes (1596–1650). Inspired by the scientific works of Galileo, he tried to apply the mathematical method to all areas of human understanding, and thus build a body of knowledge on certain truths obtained by pure reason. In doing so he broke with the past and put philosophy and science on a new intellectual foundation.

"I THINK, THEREFORE I AM."

René Descartes

The Enlightenment

The intellectual and social developments taking place in Europe reached their culmination in the 18th century with the Enlightenment. Thinkers after Descartes began to see themselves as emerging into a new Age of Reason, one that was finally throwing off the shackles of medievalism characterized by slavish adherence to tradition, authority, and superstition. Science became the champion of rebellion against the dogma of the medieval Catholic philosophers. Francis Bacon had called on scientists to determine for themselves the structure of the natural world, a structure he described, using a legal metaphor, as the "Law" of nature. Scientific advances, most notably those of Isaac Newton (1642–1727), fueled the optimism of Enlightenment philosophers concerning scientific and social progress, and they

styled themselves as free thinkers forging a bright new future. In France, the group of intellectuals known as the *philosophes*, including Voltaire, Rousseau, and Diderot, produced the vast collection of information called the *Encyclopédie*, the ambition of which was to catalog human knowledge in a spirit of the new science. Rousseau directly challenged the old order by declaring that everywhere man is born free, and social pressure for a more egalitarian system of government led to the French Revolution in 1789, followed by the Revolutionary and Napoleonic Wars that shook the established political order.

RATIONALISM

After Descartes, the development of philosophy can be seen in terms of two opposed tendencies: rationalist and

Science became the new god during the Enlightenment, and inspired awe in a new generation of thinkers.

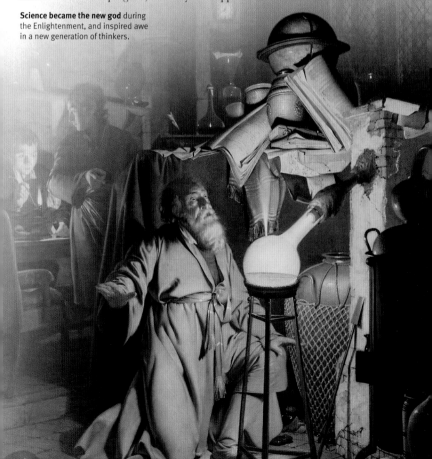

empiricist (*see pp.66–73*). Philosophers such as Spinoza and Leibniz exemplify the former tendency, while Locke, Berkeley, and Hume in Britain, together with the *philosophes* of Paris, represent the latter. The rationalists followed Descartes in treating reason as the proper avenue by which to establish knowledge. They were influenced by contemporary successes in the use of mathematics in science and felt it was possible, using the method of deduction from first principles, to build a grand theory that could explain everything, and so initiated a tradition of metaphysical system-building. Spinoza explicitly modeled his intellectual construction on the axiomatic method of Euclidean geometry. In this construction, those axioms and definitions held to be self-evident and recognizable through reason are first stated. From them are deduced a series of conclusions that tell you about the nature of the universe. God remains the central principle of these systems, knowledge of whom could be discovered rationally, and they retain elements of Aristotelianism in their understanding of key concepts, such as that of substance.

EMPIRICISM

The English reaction to the new science stressed not the role of mathematics, but rather of empirical observation, and was

suspicious of system-building. John Locke, the first of three great British empiricists of the era, adopted a more modest tone, claiming merely to describe how knowledge is acquired from experience. In this way, he tried to determine the limits of what humans are capable of knowing. Locke rejected the view, associated with the rationalist thinkers, that we have innate knowledge of abstract principles (*see pp.68–9*). Instead, he argued, all our knowledge must come exclusively through our senses.

"DARE TO THINK."

Immanuel Kant

Thus the empiricist project of "renewal" was more radical than that of the rationalists. In it, building a body of knowledge involved starting from scratch, and so was allied to the empiricists' rejection of all inherited conceptual distinctions from the Aristotelian tradition. It was this final rejection of orthodox teachings, particularly those still associated with the Church, that paved the way for modern liberalism and gave rise to new social and political ideals.

The second of the three British empiricists, George Berkeley, is best known for taking Locke's approach to its logical extreme and denying that we can have knowledge of anything beyond the mind. The very idea of a material world lying beyond one's perception of it was, he thought, a contradiction in terms.

The third, David Hume, attempted to apply to the mind the principles that Newton had applied to the world: in other words, to find an underlying law that would explain its workings. His sceptical conclusion is that something other than reason governs the operations of the mind and is the basis for our beliefs. Hume is also important for his devastating attacks on religious belief.

The German thinker Immanuel Kant is another key figure in Enlightenment philosophy. Kant regarded his work as a synthesis of both rationalist and empiricist tendencies, involving a Copernican revolution that placed the mind at the center of the acquisition of knowledge.

William Blake depicted Sir Isaac Newton as the "great architect." Newton's work sought to find general principles that governed the workings of the universe.

THE MODERN AGE

Kant's death in 1804 marked the culmination of a period that saw science and rationality as the route to both knowledge of the world and social progress. Western thinking was to take a new direction as political and technological change accelerated and faith in reason was eroded.

The 19th century

Rather than confine itself to a rational interpretation of reality, the Romantic movement that followed on the heels of the Enlightenment searched for an emotional and spiritual dimension in its response to the world and man's place within it. Underlying this development were the social and economic changes being wrought by industrial revolution—in particular, the emergence of a new class of impoverished industrial workers. The abject conditions in which these workers were trapped and the social divisions thus manifested were to provide the impetus for the development of socialist and utilitarian philosophies aimed at ameliorating the perceived ills of industrialization.

The Romantic movement in Europe sought to establish the supremacy of the human spirit within the natural world.

ABSOLUTE IDEALISM

The early part of the 19th century was dominated by the absolute idealist movement in Germany. German idealists were imbued with the metaphysical spirit and recovered some of the ambitions of the great 18th-century system builders, Spinoza and Leibniz. The three great figures of the school—Fichte, Schelling, and Hegel—were all sons of protestant pastors and had studied theology, and the religious influence on their thought is clear to see. Following Kant, they regarded human consciousness as the primary metaphysical fact, but rather than simply imposing a form upon reality, mind or spirit was regarded as constitutive of it. If the universe is identified with thought, by reflecting on the self, we can come to knowledge of the absolute mind or spirit that characterizes reality.

The inevitable backlash to such metaphysical optimism was a renewed respect for empirical investigation as the basis for knowledge. In France, the Positivism of Auguste Comte rejected any claims to knowledge not grounded in scientific investigation and regarded religious and metaphysical thinking as antiquated. He argued that society should be treated as an object of scientific study, and coined the word "sociology." In England, Mill defended

KEY DATES

1802 Napoleon Bonaparte proclaims himself emperor of France, ending the country's status as a revolutionary republic.

1848 Karl Marx publishes his *Communist Manifesto*, calling for an end to the capitalist system and for the creation of a classless society.

1905 Albert Einstein publishes his *Special Theory of Relativity*, ushering in a new era of scientific understanding.

1800   **1825**   **1850**   **1875**

1804 Immanuel Kant, perhaps the greatest of the Enlightenment philosophers, dies at the age of 80.

1859 Charles Darwin publishes his *Origin of Species*, which puts forward the theory that life on Earth, including humankind, evolved through natural selection.

1886 Nietzsche's critique of morality, *Beyond Good and Evil*, is published.

a comparable empiricist project and tried to work out an inductive logic of discovery. In politics Mill was a liberal, and developed the utilitarian ethics of his father James Mill and Jeremy Bentham with a view to effecting social reforms. More radically, Marx, in the *Communist Manifesto* of 1848, called for the overthrow of the capitalist system and class society.

Another important strand of 19th-century philosophy is represented by Schopenhauer, Nietzsche, and Kierkegaard, who, in different ways,

stood against faith in reason and science. Schopenhauer accepted Kant's idea of the existence of an unknowable reality lying behind appearances, but embraced a wild, irrational core to human experience. Nietzsche also opposed the Enlightenment idea of reason as the key force in life, and Kierkegaard stressed the reality of individual subjective consciousness.

Throughout Europe, social inequalities led to unrest and revolt. Emile Zola's novel *Germinal* (here in a scene from the 1995 film version) explored this theme through the story of a bitter miners' strike in France.

1914–18 Europe is plunged into conflict during WWI. In 1917, a popular revolution overthrows the Czarist autocracy in Russia, eventually leading to the creation of the Soviet Union under a Communist system of government.

1969 Astronauts from the Apollo space program become the first explorers on the Moon.

2003 Scientists announce that the mapping of the human genome is "essentially complete."

1925 **1950** **1975** **2000**

1921 Ludwig Wittgenstein publishes his *Tractatus Logico-Philosophicus*, concerning the relationship of language to reality and philosophical inquiry.

1939–45 Hitler's invasion of Poland sparks the outbreak of WWII, during which millions die. Heidegger, author of *Being and Time*, supports the Nazi party.

1989 The collapse of the Soviet Union heralds the decline of Communism in Europe.

The 20th century

By the turn of the 20th century, heirs to Comte's Positivism (*see p.40*) were addressing the foundations of mathematics and questioning the Aristotelian categorization of logical argument. Frege tried to show that logic and math are interrelated aspects of the same domain of human thought; Russell argued that all philosophical difficulties might be resolved by clarifying the true logical structure of language that lies beneath its surface.

The new-found interest in language later moved away from the search for an ideal language of complete scientific clarity, toward a greater respect for ordinary discourse. Wittgenstein and others came to believe that philosophical confusions are the result of the misuse of ordinary language. What remained in this development, however, was a focus on questions of meaning and rigorous attention to the detail of philosophical argumentation. These tendencies came to characterize what became known as analytic philosophy, which dominated in the English-speaking world during the 20th century. Its influence on the style of philosophizing by contemporary thinkers is still clearly in evidence today.

PHENOMENOLOGY

Meanwhile, in Germany, the foundations for an alternative tradition were being laid. Husserl returned to Descartes's idea that philosophy should begin with the thinking subject. He coined the term "phenomenology" to describe an approach to philosophy that confined itself to describing what was directly apparent to consciousness. Heidegger, through his critique of Husserl, developed the theory of being that had

Modern science raises new and challenging ethical issues, such as the use of animals in scientific and medical research.

Dasein, the abstract human being and the manner in which it finds itself in the world, as its center-point. Heidegger's influence on later thinkers has been immense, especially on the existential phenomenology of Sartre.

MARXISM

Two world wars, the Holocaust, Communist revolutions in Russia and China, all had their impact on the political philosophy of the age. Based in Marx (*see p.311*) and pursued in the socialist East, Lenin's materialist version of Marx was geared toward practical issues such as the role of the Communist party in effecting change. Like Marx, he saw philosophy as a tool for changing the world, not a disinterested description of it, and looked upon it as a weapon in the struggle. However, by the latter part of the 20th century adherence to grand narratives, such as the Marxist vision of history, was on the wane.

POSTMODERNISM

A number of 20th-century thinkers became increasingly suspicious of the earnest search for systematic, complete accounts of reality and the optimistic visions of human progress prevalent since the Renaissance. Since the end of World War II, their views have gradually coalesced to form the movement known as postmodernism. In its stance it is heir to the strand of 19th-century philosophy that was critical of Enlightenment values, as exemplified by the philosophy of Kierkegaard and by Nietzsche's suspicion of the notion of objective knowledge or a single "truth." Nietzsche saw the idea of truth as a disguise for power, and rationality as an imposition of human distinctions on an irrational world. Twentieth-century philosophers such as Lyotard and Foucault have been profoundly influenced by these views.

The overthrow of old orders characterized the first half of the 20th century. Bold new political ideals proposed alternative structures for society.

BRANCHES OF PHILOSOPHY

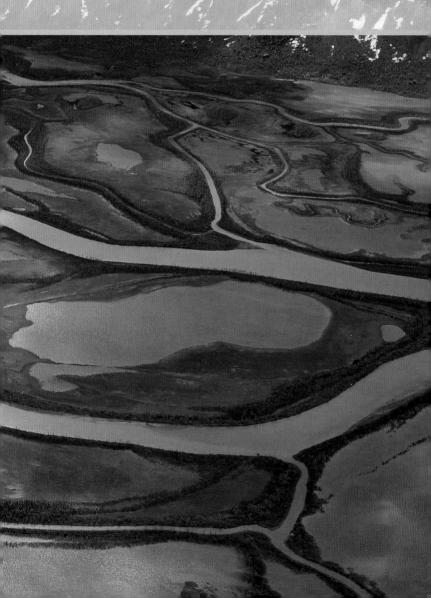

PHILOSOPHY HAS MANY SUBDIVISIONS AND
SCHOOLS. THE SEVEN BRANCHES OF PHILOSOPHY
DISCUSSED IN THIS SECTION INTRODUCE SOME
OF THE MOST IMPORTANT ARGUMENTS AND
IDEAS, TAKEN FROM THE ENTIRE SWEEP OF
THE HISTORY OF PHILOSOPHY, FROM ANCIENT
GREECE RIGHT UP TO THE PRESENT DAY.

While there are other areas philosophy addresses, such as mathematics, language, and aesthetics, a guide of this type must necessarily be selective. In fact, the discipline called "philosophy" once encompassed much more than it does now. It included "natural philosophy" (what we now call natural science—including physics, chemistry, and biology). As our understanding of the universe has progressed, so certain areas of enquiry that once fell under the umbrella of philosophy have developed into disciplines in their own right. This raises the question whether the same thing might yet happen to other parts of philosophy.

Early philosophers, like Democritus (*above*), were concerned with the natural sciences too – subjects that are now separate disciplines with their own methods and practitioners.

It would be a mistake to view the seven areas of philosophy covered here as hermetically sealed areas of enquiry. They overlap. Metaphysics, in particular, subsumes many of the questions addressed within the philosophy of religion, moral philosophy, and philosophy of mind. Even where the branches don't overlap, they remain heavily intertwined. The way in which we answer a question in one branch of philosophy may well have repercussions for other branches. For example, answers to metaphysical questions about what, ultimately, exists outside our minds will raise difficulties concerning how knowledge of the physical world is possible. And an answer to the question "Does God exist?"—from the philosophy of religion—might well inform how we answer questions in moral philosophy about how we should live.

While one or two philosophers have lived out their intellectual lives within a single branch, they are very much the exception rather than the rule. Descartes, for example, is a pivotal figure in both the philosophy of mind and the theory of knowledge, as well as having important things to say within other branches too.

Some of the most important issues raised in philosophy have a tendency to lead the questioner from one branch of the subject to another.

KNOWLEDGE

Knowledge has a claim to be the most important subject in philosophy. The questions of what we can know, how we can know what we know, and what knowledge is are central to philosophy as a whole. This is because other branches of philosophy must take for granted the possibility of knowledge in order to have anything to discuss at all.

There are several different types of knowledge. They include acquaintance knowledge (for example: I know Oxford well), ability knowledge (I know how to ride a bike), and propositional knowledge (I know that eagles are birds). The first two types of knowledge are interesting, but philosophy has chiefly been concerned with the third: what it is to know a proposition.

A proposition is a declarative statement that makes a claim, such as: "elephants are gray." In everyday life, we take it for granted that we can "know" such propositions by, for example, relying on the immediate evidence of our senses, or by recalling what we have learned in the past. But do we, in fact, know as much as we think we do?

In philosophy, the question of what we can know is of fundamental importance, and it is often approached via the challenge of scepticism: the view that our claims to knowledge are rarely, if ever, justified. Scepticism supposes that

reality could be very different from how it appears—not in the sense that physics reveals it to be different, but in the sense that appearances—the appearance of a world existing outside the mind, for example—could be utterly misleading. Scepticism then challenges us to say how we know that reality is, by and large, as we experience it.

It is also important to define what we mean by knowledge. In the *Thaetetus*, the Greek philosopher Plato (*see pp.244–7*) argued that knowledge is justified true belief: in other words, beliefs must be both true and supported by strong evidence to qualify as knowledge. But this definition came under attack in the 20th century, and the last 40 years have witnessed a vigorous exploration of developments and alternative theories.

A further debate tries to establish whether pure reason can yield knowledge on its own (the rationalist view), or if we must depend on sense-experience for all knowledge, as empiricists believe. Such questions have a direct bearing on some of the oldest problems in philosophy, including the search for proof of the existence of God.

The search for what we can know often starts with a very fundamental question: are appearances a good guide to reality? Sometimes we can be deceived by things that are happening in plain sight.

SCEPTICISM

Scepticism is the view that while we may have any number of beliefs, in fact we know very little, if anything—and certainly far less than we usually think we know. Some of the world's greatest philosophers have championed scepticism, presenting powerful arguments in its favor.

Belief and knowledge

We intuitively make a distinction between belief and knowledge. People can have false beliefs. But if you *know* some proposition, *p*, then *p* must be true. For example, if you claim that elephants are pink, and you think you know this, you are mistaken. If elephants are not pink, but gray, then you can't know that they are pink. You can, at best, merely believe it.

Even true belief is not sufficient for knowledge. People can have true beliefs without having any evidence or justification for them. For example, someone on a jury might think that the person on trial is guilty just from the way they dress. Their belief that the person is guilty might be true. But how someone dresses isn't good evidence for whether they are a criminal. So, if this is the reason why they believe the accused is guilty, their belief is unlikely to be knowledge, even if it is true.

Or again, I know that there is a lot of evidence that astrology does not make accurate predictions. Suppose I read my horoscope and believe a prediction, in spite of what I know about astrology. And then the prediction turns out to be true. Did I know it was right? No, because I possessed no good grounds for supposing the prediction was true.

Knowledge, then, needs some kind of support, some reason for thinking that a proposition we believe in is true—in short, it needs to be justified.

Astrology claims to be a system of knowledge. But even if some astrological beliefs turn out to be true, they aren't knowledge unless they are justified.

But what is justification? A standard answer involves "evidence." To have evidence for a belief, you need some grounds, aside from the belief, that justify what you believe to be true. For example, you believe the rose is red because you see the rose, and it looks red. Or you remember where you left your keys: you put them down on the dresser. Which is why you believe that is where they are now.

USING LOGIC

Sometimes the relationship between a piece of evidence and what it is evidence *for* is logical. For example, if you see the dog behind the cat, that logically entails that your belief that the cat is in front of the dog is true.

But evidence doesn't usually logically entail that for which it is evidence. Normally, a given piece of evidence merely provides grounds, perhaps very good grounds, for supposing the belief in question is true. Notice that you might possess excellent evidence for believing something, yet still be mistaken. A piece of evidence does not normally provide us with a logical guarantee that our belief is true.

The peculiarity of philosophical doubt

Philosophical doubt arises when we start to reflect on how we know what we think we know. Take my belief that I have two hands. Why do I believe this? Well, I can feel them, and I can see them. However, couldn't my experience be deceptive? After all, exactly the same patterns of electrical stimulation being fed into my brain by my eyes, ears, and other sensory organs could instead be fed in by a supercomputer running a sort of virtual reality program. If these patterns of stimulation received by my brain really were exactly the same, the experiences I had as a result would presumably be the same, too. I would not be able to tell the difference. What I took to be the real world would actually be an elaborate computer-generated illusion, just as in the film *The Matrix*. Even the body I seemed to possess would be virtual.

So how can I know that I am not actually wired up to such a computer? In fact, how can I know that a world exists outside my mind at all? But if I don't know that, how can I know that I really do have two hands? Scepticism raises these doubts as a philosophical challenge.

BEYOND ORDINARY DOUBT

Philosophical doubts are peculiar. They aren't the sort of doubt we normally raise. For example, if I've just left my house but can't remember locking the door, I might well have the panicky worry that the door is still open, and that burglars could get in while I am out. The sceptic is not asking you to consider that sort of doubt. They are raising a doubt that is to apply even in those cases in which we would not ordinarily dream of doubting. Suppose I seem to see a book in front of me and have no grounds for doubt of the ordinary sort. But still the sceptic's doubt can be raised. For how do I know that what I see is a good guide to how things really are? True, it appears that there is a book before me. But how do

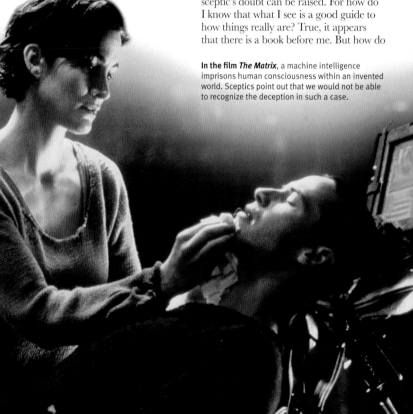

In the film *The Matrix*, a machine intelligence imprisons human consciousness within an invented world. Sceptics point out that we would not be able to recognize the deception in such a case.

"IF YOU WOULD BE A REAL SEEKER AFTER TRUTH, YOU MUST AT LEAST ONCE IN YOUR LIFE DOUBT, AS FAR AS POSSIBLE, ALL THINGS."

Descartes, *Discourse on the Method*

I know such appearances are actually a reliable guide to reality? Scepticism challenges our most basic assumptions about the nature of the world around us.

Is this sort of doubt legitimate? True, it rarely has any practical consequences. Even those philosophers who are officially sceptical about the external world will, as soon as they leave their study, immediately carry on behaving just like the rest of us. Their philosophical doubt evaporates the moment they step outside. There is a sense in which philosophical scepticism about the world around us is untenable. Even if it is true, we cannot really make ourselves believe that it is true: certainly not in a sustained way. But of course, it might still be true, despite that. Indeed, it might still be the only genuinely rational position to adopt.

SUMMARIZING SCEPTICISM

The conclusion drawn by the sceptic is not: "We can't be certain of our everyday judgments, although they are probably true." Rather, the sceptic typically points out that we really have little, if any, reason for supposing these judgments to be true. It seems that if the sceptic is right, we possess no more grounds for supposing that the world around us is real than we do to suppose that it is an elaborate illusion. The sceptic claims it is just as sensible for us to believe that the world we think we see is illusory, as it is for us to believe it is real. This is obviously a far more radical conclusion than that we cannot be completely certain that what we are experiencing is real.

It is important to note that the sceptic is not claiming to know that they, or you, are being deceived by a supercomputer. Their point is that you have no way of knowing, one way or the other, whether or not you are experiencing genuine reality. For the sceptic, that you are experiencing a real world is hardly any more likely than that it is all an illusion.

DIFFERENT KINDS OF SCEPTICISM

The kind of scepticism most often discussed by philosophers is called scepticism about the external world. It throws into doubt our knowledge of physical reality, of the world outside our minds. But that is not the only sort of knowledge claim about which you might be sceptical. Some are sceptical about mathematical or logical claims, while others are sceptical about memory. It is also possible to embrace a more restricted form of scepticism about the external world. You might claim, say, that while some knowledge of the external world is possible, we cannot have knowledge of those portions of the world we have not actually observed. This would, of course, include knowledge of the future.

Explorers at the North Pole embody humanity's instinct to gain knowledge at first hand. But much of the universe lies beyond direct observation.

NOT TRUSTING THE SENSES

In his *Thaetetus*, Plato (*see pp.244–7*) presents the view of the Greek philosopher Protagoras: "Things are to you such as they appear to you, and to me such as they appear to me.... The wind is cold to him who is cold, and not to him who is not." Faced with disagreement, how can I be sure that what I experience is how the world is? Don't such disagreements reveal our five senses to be highly untrustworthy?

FINDING AGREEMENT

Disagreements about the evidence of the senses are not widespread. At the least, people agree that air is a gas, not a liquid. And people commonly agree on whether or not there is a breeze (even if they disagree on how warm it is). In fact, our disagreements on such issues actually presuppose a lot of agreement in our perceptions, which supports the claim that perception can provide knowledge after all. Another worry about the reliability of our senses is raised by optical illusions. For example, water can give straight objects that pierce its surface a bent appearance. Don't such illusions reveal our senses to be highly unreliable? Again, no. These kinds of perceptual errors are correctable, or at least predictable, given knowledge of the behavior of light and so on. What I have previously experienced (the object being straight; the effect of water on how things appear) can be used to correct what I seem to see now. So, illusions do not present good grounds for supposing our senses to be *generally* unreliable.

Optical illusions demonstrate that the senses are not always the best guide to reality and can sometimes be fooled quite easily.

Doubting memory and reason

Can we extend our sceptical doubts further? On closer examination, the hypothetical possibility of being wired up to a supercomputer that deceives us with an imitation of reality (*see p.51*) would seem to bring memory, as well as sense-experience, into doubt. For, by affecting what goes on in a person's brain, such a computer might generate "memories" of things that never happened. Perhaps that red bicycle I seem so vividly to remember having been given for my fifth birthday never actually existed. Indeed, perhaps all my memories are fake. I seem to have no way of establishing that they are not.

If that is true, it appears that just as I cannot know anything of the world around me, so I can know nothing of my past, including whether it happened at all.

It also seems that, for all I know, I might have existed for only a very short time. Perhaps I popped into existence just a few minutes ago.

It is not just sense experience and memory that the supercomputer hypothesis throws into doubt. The ability of reason to reveal the truth also seems vulnerable. For what if my thoughts are being fed to me by a supercomputer? What if I think "$2 + 2 = ?$" and the computer makes me think "4" when the answer is actually 5? Or that whenever I try to think through the consequences of my beliefs about the world, it makes me arrive at illogical conclusions?

It is beginning to look as if all my judgments about matters of logic and mathematics are thrown into doubt too, even in the simplest of cases.

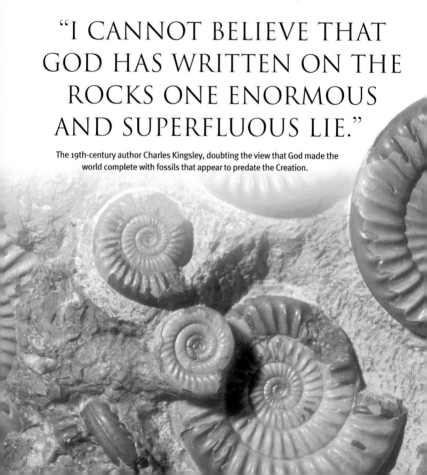

"I CANNOT BELIEVE THAT GOD HAS WRITTEN ON THE ROCKS ONE ENORMOUS AND SUPERFLUOUS LIE."

The 19th-century author Charles Kingsley, doubting the view that God made the world complete with fossils that appear to predate the Creation.

Reliabilism

How might we respond to the sceptic, and counter their arguments? The sceptic points out that our belief that appearance is a good guide to reality is not justified. But perhaps we don't need to justify it.

Reliabilism claims that a belief (that a rose lies before me, for example) counts as knowledge if and only if it is true and is produced by a *reliable* process: one that produces a high percentage of true beliefs. Usually, what makes a process reliable is a causal connection between what the belief is about (the rose) and the belief. In this case, the connecting process is vision. Vision is indeed a fairly reliable process for producing true beliefs (it sometimes leads us astray, of course, but not that often). So, my belief that a rose lies before me does indeed qualify as knowledge for the reliabilist.

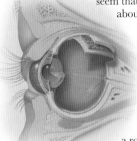

Reliabilism says that if the mechanisms by which beliefs are formed (such as sight) are reliable, then they constitute knowledge.

DEEPER INTO DOUBT

Of course, it is debatable whether reliabilism's definition of knowledge is true. Nonetheless, it does seem that if the reliabilist is correct about what knowledge is, then the sceptic's objections can be countered.

But of course, even if the sceptic is defeated, another problem arises. Perhaps the sceptic is mistaken. Perhaps I can know that there is a rose before me. But can I *know* that I know that there is a rose before me? In order to know that I know, I would also need to know that I am indeed in possession of reliable senses. But actually there is no reliable way of establishing this. After all, even if my senses were unreliable, and my brain were at the mercy of a deceiving supercomputer, I would still trust in my senses, because the computer would deceive me into thinking they were reliable.

So it seems that even if the battle against scepticism has been won, a deeper worry remains. I don't just want to know that there is a rose before me; I want to know that this is something I know. And that kind of knowledge is something even the reliabilist must concede that I cannot have.

ALVIN GOLDMAN

The American philosopher Alvin Goldman (*b.* 1938) first presented his "causal theory of knowing," in which he outlined the reliabilist thesis, in 1967. In response to criticisms of the theory, he later argued that knowledge also requires the ability to discriminate between relevant alternatives. Goldman then turned his attention to the links between theories of knowledge and cognitive science, and then to situating knowledge in a social context, including law and education. He is also known for his work in the philosophy of mind.

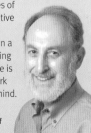

Alvin Goldman has explored many aspects of knowledge in his work.

The incoherence of scepticism

One response to scepticism claims that it doesn't make sense, and in fact contradicts itself.

For example, we might argue that what "knowledge" and "know" mean is determined by how we usually use the terms. If so, the sceptic's claim that, say, "I don't know I'm reading this page," makes no sense. For it is precisely through cases like this that we learn what "know" means.

Can such an appeal to "everyday language" be made to work against scepticism? It seems not. Sceptics argue that even in such typical cases of "knowledge," we are making an unjustified assumption. They claim it is a condition of knowing things about the world that we know appearance is a good guide to reality. We ordinarily just assume that this condition is satisfied, which is why we then typically say I "know" that there is a rose before me, and so on. The sceptic then points out that this condition is not satisfied: for all I know, I might be experiencing a virtual reality that has been created to deceive me. In which case, I have no grounds for supposing appearance to be a good guide to reality. So, even if we do learn the meaning of the word "know" by having typical "ordinary language" cases pointed out to us, it remains an open question whether the word is applied correctly in such cases.

Taking a different tack, the British philosopher Gilbert Ryle (*see p.331*) argues that the very idea of "error" raised by scepticism presupposes that we sometimes "get it right." Without

The Venus de Milo perhaps represents a being of perfect beauty. But can we possess the concept of imperfection only if perfect things exist?

correctness, the idea of error makes no sense, just as counterfeit art would make no sense if there were no genuine art.

But do our notions of "error" and "correctness" function in a similar way? Or do they perhaps function more like the terms "perfect" and "imperfect?" True, we can't have the idea of imperfection without that of perfection. But it doesn't follow that in order for us to have the idea of imperfection, something perfect must actually exist.

Likewise, we cannot infer that we *do* know some things simply because scepticism raises the possibility that we are often in error.

DOUBTING DOUBT

The Austrian philosopher Ludwig Wittgenstein (*see pp.326–7*) develops a more sophisticated version of the ordinary-language approach. He believes the sceptic is wrong to suppose it makes sense to doubt beliefs such as "There is an external world" and "I have two hands." These sort of beliefs he calls "background assumptions." Wittgenstein argues that many such fundamental beliefs are not in fact knowledge claims at all.

Take my claim to know that this is a hand that I am holding up before my face. True, there are occasions when the sentence "This is a hand" can be used to make a knowledge claim (an authoritative statement of belief): on an archaeological dig, perhaps, when rummaging among small bones. But if I hold up my hand in broad daylight and say, "This is a hand," am I then making a knowledge claim? Not according to Wittgenstein. Notice that holding up your hand under such circumstances and saying, "This is a hand" is something you would do if you were teaching others the meaning of the word "hand." The sentence, under these circumstances, is used, not to make a claim, but to show what the word "hand"

Without real coins, counterfeits couldn't exist. Ryle argued that, similarly, we must have some knowledge of truth to make sense of being mistaken.

means. It functions as a definition, in much the same way as does "Vixens are female foxes." Just as it doesn't make sense to ask "But do we know all vixens are foxes?" (someone who doubts that simply shows that they don't understand what "vixen" means), so someone who asks "How do I know this is a hand" under these circumstances is not expressing a genuine doubt.

So, rather than trying to defeat the sceptic by showing how the claim "This is a hand" can be justified, Wittgenstein attempts to show that the sceptic's request for justification makes no sense. Under such circumstances, no knowledge claim is made. So no justification is required.

FLAWED SOLUTION?

Wittgenstein's solution is contentious. One problem is that even if we accept that the statement "This is a hand" is not usually used to make a knowledge claim,

it doesn't follow that it can never be used to make a claim under such circumstances. And if it *is* used to make a claim, then the sceptic's challenge to justify it returns. It seems the sceptic may be able to resist Wittgenstein's argument.

> ## "IF I WANTED TO DOUBT WHETHER THIS WAS MY HAND, HOW COULD I AVOID DOUBTING WHETHER THE WORD 'HAND' HAS ANY MEANING?"
>
> Ludwig Wittgenstein, *On Certainty*

Wittgenstein argues that someone who asks: "How do I know this is a hand?" needs to be reminded how words are learned and used.

WHAT IS KNOWLEDGE?

Knowledge is not the same as unsupported belief, even if what you believe happens to be true. But is knowledge the same thing as true belief that is well justified (*see p.50*)? If so, just how "justified" does a belief need to be to qualify as knowledge?

Does knowledge require certainty?

If knowledge consists of true beliefs that are justified by evidence, then how strong does the justification need to be? We usually require only that we possess pretty good grounds for supposing a belief to be true. And to possess pretty good grounds for supposing that a belief is true is certainly not entirely to rule out the possibility of error. You can be justified in believing something and yet still be mistaken. If I hear water drops hitting the window, and see them trickling down the glass against the background of a dark sky, and if my friend enters shaking a wet umbrella and leaving wet footprints across the floor while complaining about the rain, then I possess excellent grounds for believing it is raining. Yet it is still possible I am mistaken—perhaps my friend has placed a lawn sprinkler

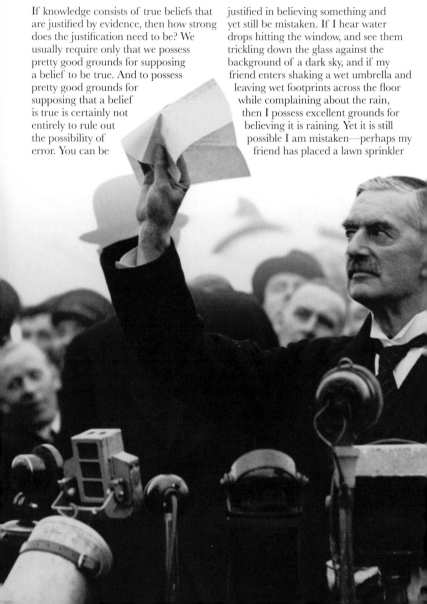

against the glass in order to trick me into thinking that it is raining.

INFALLIBILISM

Given that normal standards of justification can lead to mistakes, must we be absolutely certain that a belief is true before we can call it knowledge? The view that a belief can only qualify as knowledge if it is impossible for us to be mistaken about it is known as infallibilism. But how plausible is this view? If knowledge is only possible in those situations where we are immune to error, then there will be very few, if any, things that we can know. Even setting sceptical worries (*see pp.50–3*) to one side, it remains clear that, when it comes to our judgments about the external world, even if we happen to possess extremely good grounds for supposing that something is the case, it still remains possible that we are mistaken about it.

Surely any workable definition of knowledge would have to accept this, and allow for at least the possibility of error? Students new to philosophy often assume otherwise. One thing that can lead them astray is the following sort of argument. One cannot know what is not true. So, if I know that it is raining, then I cannot be mistaken that it is raining. But then, if I am to know that it is raining, I must be infallible about the fact that it is raining. I must

Theatrical illusions can be utterly convincing. They demonstrate that there is always some room for error when we trust the evidence of our senses.

be in a position such that I can't possibly be mistaken. The infallibilist may then conclude that, as I can never be in such a position—there is always some possibility, no matter how remote, that I am mistaken— so I can never know that it is raining.

However, this argument won't do: it trades on a deceptive slide from a reasonable claim about knowledge to a highly contentious one (*see box, below*).

NEW DEFINITIONS

Knowledge involves more than just true belief: it cannot be accidental or unsupported in the way that a true belief can be. But it seems equally wrong to suggest that a belief must be infallible before it can be classed as knowledge. In the following pages, we will look at some other definitions of knowledge that may avoid such problems.

A BAD ARGUMENT FOR INFALLIBILISM

Infallibilism claims that "if I know that *p* [any proposition], then I can't be mistaken about *p.*" But this claim can be read in two different ways, depending on how we understand "can't."

Reading 1: "It can't be the case that though I know that *p,* I am mistaken that *p.*"

We should agree with this. By definition, you cannot know what is false.

Reading 2: "If I know that *p,* (I am in a position that) I can't possibly be mistaken that *p.*"

This is what infallibilism claims. It is a much bolder claim than the first reading, because it says that if I know that *p,* then not only am I not mistaken about *p,* I must be in a position such that I am immune to error about *p.* The argument in the main text trades on this ambiguity. It begins by getting us to agree to Reading 1—which is true—but then concludes with Reading 2, which is certainly not entailed by Reading 1.

Neville Chamberlain confidently declared "Peace in our time" after signing the Munich agreement with Hitler in 1938. Feelings of certainty can be misplaced.

Looking for foundations

How does justification work? One historically popular theory argues that all knowledge ultimately rests on certain basic beliefs that support other beliefs, as foundations support a building.

Many of our beliefs rest on, and derive their justification from, others. For example, I believe that Napoleon was Corsican because I also believe that the historical sources that make this claim can be trusted. Now if my belief that Napoleon was Corsican is justified, my belief that the historical sources are trustworthy should also be justified. From this we can draw the general principle: to be justified in believing some proposition on the basis of evidence, one must be justified in believing the evidence.

We must trust historical documents and images in order to know whether historical events, such as Napoleon's Egyptian campaign, really took place.

But notice that if every belief is only justified on the basis of some other belief, we have an infinite regress (*see p.213*). The justification for my beliefs must come to an end somewhere, with beliefs that are not justified on the basis of other beliefs. Otherwise, how am I ever justified in believing anything?

Foundationalism claims that if we trace the chain of justification back far enough, we arrive at "basic" true beliefs that do not need to be justified by appeals to yet other beliefs. These basic beliefs form the foundations upon which all knowledge rests. But if the foundational beliefs are not justified by being inferred from other beliefs, how *are* they justified?

One of the most popular theories says that the foundations of knowledge lie in sense-experience. Many empiricists, including Locke (*see pp.282–3*) and Hume (*see pp.290–1*), argue that all knowledge is

It is not hard to accept that you see a brown-and-white dog in the picture on the right; but what concepts apply to what you see in an abstract painting? Does all perceptual experience involve concepts?

founded on what we experience. True, a sensory experience is not itself a belief; just seeing a chair isn't yet to believe that there is a chair in front of you. But provided that you do not suspect that you are hallucinating or dreaming, you can infer such a belief from sense-experience. These beliefs that are directly inferred from sense-experience constitute our "basic" beliefs. They are justified, despite not being inferred from other beliefs.

ILLUSORY FOUNDATIONS

This form of foundationalism has a certain initial plausibility. But it does face objections. Beliefs are structured by concepts. Believing that "the brown dog was scared by a loud car" involves the concepts: dog, brown, scared, loud, and car. I cannot have that belief if I do not possess these concepts. But is experience itself structured by these concepts? Do I see a brown dog or hear a loud car? Or do I have sensory experiences and then apply these concepts to them? Wilfrid Sellars (*see box, right*) says that either way, foundationalists face a problem.

Suppose we say that experience is itself structured by concepts. Is this true of all experience? Children, for example, need to learn concepts. If a baby doesn't know what a dog is or what brown is, it can't experience "a brown dog." Clearly, it does experience something, but whatever experience the baby has is not structured

by these concepts. During our childhood, we learn how to apply concepts correctly (for example, "This is a dog" and "This is not a dog") by trial and error, or other forms of reasoning. Therefore, our concept of what a dog is has been formed by making inferences.

So, argues Sellars, if experience is itself structured by concepts, experience can't be the foundation of knowledge, because it would still depend on knowledge gained by inference.

But what if we assume that experience is *not* structured by concepts? Now the problem is that we can't move from experience on its own to any beliefs about experience, because beliefs are structured by concepts. To move from experience to belief, we will need to apply concepts to what we experience. But this again makes use of inferential knowledge.

So, Sellars concludes, whether experience is or is not structured by concepts, beliefs based directly on sense-experience will involve concepts, and so depend on inferences from other things we know. For this reason, they cannot be the foundational beliefs on which all knowledge rests.

WILFRID SELLARS

The American philosopher Wilfrid Sellars (1912–89) is one of the best-known critics of foundationalist views on knowledge. He put forward his attack on the traditional appeal to experience as the foundation of knowledge in his essay "Empiricism and the Philosophy of Mind" in 1956. Sellars argued that we must process experience before we can glean knowledge from it. The question he addressed is how this is done. His attempts to reconcile scientific models of reality with our sense of ourselves as free and rational agents set the agenda in discussions of knowledge and philosophy of mind for the rest of the 20th century.

Is knowledge "justified true belief?"

Some philosophers believe that knowledge of propositions (such as that elephants are gray) involves having a true belief that is justified. But is this a complete analysis of knowledge? If it is, then you *know* a given proposition if and only if:

The proposition *p* is true
You believe that *p*
Your belief that *p* is justified

The "justified true belief" theory of knowledge claims these are the "necessary and sufficient conditions" (*see p.218*) for knowledge. The claim that knowledge is justified true belief is initially plausible. First, we cannot know what is false. If a proposition is false, then,

while we may think we know it, it turns out we don't. Second, it seems we must *believe* that *p* in order to *know* that *p*. How can I be said to know that it is raining if I don't even believe it? Third, it seems that knowledge involves more than true belief. The requirement that knowledge be justified explains why a lucky guess is not knowledge.

BEYOND BELIEF

In 1963 the American philosopher Edmund Gettier published *Is Knowledge Justified True Belief?*—a paper that famously presented cases in which it appears that someone has justified true belief but not knowledge. Here is an example of a "Gettier case." Suppose

Looking at the front, we might well be justified in believing that this is a real house on fire, not a fake building on a film set.

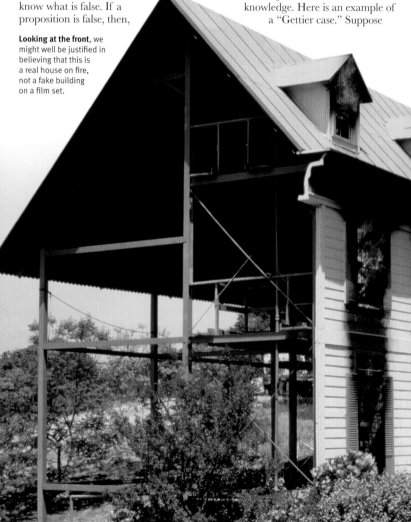

I'm driving through an area where, unknown to me, a film is being shot. Many of the "houses" around me are actually facades. A number of them are on fire. I think "that house is on fire." If I were looking at a facade, my belief would be false, so not knowledge. By pure chance, I'm looking at the only building that is a real house, not a facade, so my belief is true. And it seems to be justified: it looks like a house, it looks to be on fire, and I have no reason to doubt my eyes are working well (to reject this is to move toward scepticism).

But although my belief is true and justified, Gettier argued, it isn't knowledge. The connection between the reasons why I have my belief (its justification) and that it happens to be true is, in this case, too accidental. In these circumstances, I could have been looking at a facade, and not known any different. If justified true belief isn't enough for knowledge in Gettier's case, then knowledge is never merely justified true belief. Something else must be required to turn it into knowledge,

We are very good at recognizing other people, but unless we know that someone has an identical twin, it is easy to mistake one for the other.

something that takes into account situations in which we might not be aware of all the relevant possibilities.

RELIABILISM AGAIN

Certain Gettier objections can also be applied to reliabilism (*see p.55*). It is true that, on the whole, a belief won't be accidentally true if the process that produces it is reliable. But consider this Gettier case: you see a friend, Judy, and wave to her. But unknown to you, Judy has a twin sister, Anne, who lives nearby. If you had seen Anne across the street, you would have believed it was Judy. So your belief that you have seen Judy is only accidentally true. Yet the process that produced that belief—seeing and recognizing—is reliable. So, reliabilism seems to say you do know when you don't.

Some reliabilists respond that to qualify as knowledge, a belief must not only be produced by a process that is reliable; you must also be able to discriminate between relevant possibilities in the actual situation. If Judy doesn't have a twin sister, you can discriminate between possibilities (whether it is Judy or someone else) to know it is Judy. If Judy *does* have a twin, you only know that you are waving at Judy if you can tell her apart from Anne.

Even the evidence of our senses can be shaped by what we expect to see. In the first report of "flying saucers" in 1947, the witness actually reported boomerang-shaped craft that "skipped like saucers on a lake." But other people immediately began reporting saucers, and have done so ever since.

REASON AND EXPERIENCE

To what extent is knowledge dependent upon our senses? We discover things about the world through both reasoning and experience. A differing emphasis on one or the other has produced two schools of thought about the source of knowledge: rationalism and empiricism.

Two ways of knowing

Before discussing knowledge, reason, and experience, we need to introduce some terminology. The term "a priori" is derived from Latin and means literally "from what comes before." In philosophy, it refers to knowledge based on claims that do not require sense-experience to be known to be true. To know that "all bachelors are unmarried," we don't need to go around finding bachelors to check if they are unmarried. We can know it is true just by knowing what it means. On the other hand, claims that can only be established through our five senses are called "a posteriori."

The a priori/a posteriori distinction is about how we check or establish that a certain claim is true. It is not concerned with how we acquire the concepts or words involved in understanding the knowledge claim in the first place. Yes, of course we first have to learn what "bachelor" and "unmarried" mean before we are in a position to understand what "all bachelors are unmarried" says. This knowledge is clearly based on experience—but once I have grasped what the statement means, it seems I need no further experience in order to establish that what it says is true. If so, my knowledge that all bachelors are unmarried is a priori knowledge.

Some ways of describing how someone is related to you (in terms of other full-blood relations), are not obvious—but are still true by definition.

This contrast between two types of knowledge should be distinguished from another contrast, between "analytic" and "synthetic" propositions. A proposition is analytic if it is true or false just by virtue of the meanings of the words. Because "all bachelors are unmarried" is analytic, it is also a priori. But not all a priori truths are analytic. For example, I can surely know, a priori, that I exist, yet "I exist" is not analytic. Many analytic truths, such as "all bachelors are

in some definitions of the terms they are not mutually exclusive. Still, there is at least one standard way of contrasting rationalism and empiricism that does make them exclusive. Rationalism claims that we can have synthetic a priori knowledge of how things stand outside the mind. In other words, rationalists argue that it is possible for us to know (some) facts about how the world is outside our own minds, about morality, metaphysics, or even the material world,

"THE THINGS WE CONCEIVE VERY CLEARLY AND VERY DISTINCTLY ARE ALL TRUE."

René Descartes, *Discourse on the Method*

"ALL OBJECTS OF HUMAN REASON OR ENQUIRY MAY BE DIVIDED INTO TWO KINDS... RELATIONS OF IDEAS, AND MATTERS OF FACTS."

David Hume, *An Enquiry Concerning Human Understanding*

unmarried," are perfectly obvious, but some are not, such as: "your mother's brother's father's niece's sole female cousin is your mother."

A proposition is synthetic if it is not analytic: it is true or false not just in virtue of the meanings of the words, but in virtue of the facts. So, for example, "There are no ostriches in Iceland" is synthetic.

OPPOSING VIEWS

Rationalism and empiricism differ, roughly speaking, on whether you can have knowledge of the world that is not based on experience. However, the distinction is not always clear-cut, and

without relying on our five senses. Empiricism denies this, arguing that all knowledge of the world outside the mind is based on sense-experience.

How might we know things about the world without relying on experience? Some rationalists suggest we have a form of rational "intuition" that allows us to grasp certain truths intellectually. This faculty operates independently of our five senses; it is a special "sixth sense" that allows us to detect certain external moral, mathematical, and other facts.

Other rationalists claim we know certain truths innately (*see pp.68–9*). True, you may not know anything when you are born, but the seeds of knowledge are planted within you at birth. Later, as you develop, these seeds grow and flower, providing you with a priori knowledge of how things stand outside your mind.

DESCARTES AND THE TRADEMARK ARGUMENT

Rationalists reject the empiricist view that a priori knowledge, if it exists at all, is restricted to knowledge of analytic truths and truths about what goes on within the mind (*see pp.66–7*). The rationalist insists that we can have synthetic a priori knowledge of how things stand outside our minds. René Descartes (*see pp.276–9*) was clearly a rationalist, as his arguments for the existence of God demonstrate.

Descartes provides two arguments for God's existence. One is the ontological argument (*see pp.140–1*), a classic attempt to prove God's existence a priori. The other argument, the so-called "trademark argument," is what we focus on here. In the trademark argument, Descartes tries to prove that God exists just from the fact that we have an idea of God. Every idea must have a cause, Descartes argues, and if the cause isn't experience or our own minds, it must be that the idea is "innate." Innate ideas are not ideas that we can necessarily access from

Descartes believed that because the idea of God is something perfect that flawed beings such as humans could not imagine by themselves, it must have been imprinted in us by God.

birth. But they are, nevertheless, already present within us in some sense. He argues that the cause of the idea of God can only be God.

Why must the cause of this idea be God? According to Descartes, a cause must have at least as much "reality" as its effect. The English philosopher Bernard Williams gives a common-sense example: if we discover a picture of a sophisticated machine, we automatically think it must have been the product of an advanced society or a highly fertile imagination, even though it is just a picture. If we actually found the machine working as it should, this would be even more impressive—the machine has "more reality" as a working machine than it does as a drawing.

God is infinite and perfect, and so has the highest degree of reality. This idea of God is not something I am able to invent myself. As an imperfect and finite being, I can be the cause of an idea of something that is "not finite" and "not imperfect." But this negative conception of infinity and

our minds could not have created it. Only God could create it. It is as if, in imprinting an idea of himself in our minds, God left his "trademark:" a tell-tale sign that we are his creation. Both Descartes's ontological argument and the trademark argument for the existence of God aim to establish God's

"IT WOULD NOT BE POSSIBLE... THAT I SHOULD HAVE IN ME THE IDEA OF A GOD, IF GOD DID NOT REALLY EXIST."

René Descartes, *Meditations*

perfection is not the idea of God, Descartes argues. The idea of God is a positive conception of infinity and perception, not just the absence of limits. It is the idea of something for which there could be no limits. So even though it is only an idea,

existence a priori. Descartes believes that, simply by reflecting on certain ideas or concepts, we can establish an important fact concerning how things stand outside the mind—the fact that God exists. This is one reason why Descartes is a rationalist.

Empiricists on a priori knowledge

Rationalists suppose that at least some of our knowledge of the external world is not based on experience (*see pp.66–7*). Descartes, for example, supposes we can know, a priori, that God exists. He also supposes that our knowledge that physical objects are *extended* (they possess physical dimensions) is not based wholly on experience either. Descartes denies that physical objects possess those properties of color, smell, and so on that our senses seem to reveal. And their genuine, geometric properties, says Descartes, are ultimately apprehended not by experience, but by reason.

By contrast, some empiricist philosophers, such as John Stuart Mill (*pp.308–9*), deny that we possess any a priori knowledge at all. But most empiricists allow for

The mathematical depiction of solid objects, as in a technical drawing, excludes all those properties, such as smell, color, and taste, that depend on particular ways of perceiving them.

at least some a priori knowledge. Why, then, do they still qualify as empiricists? Because they insist that what a priori knowledge we have is of a very trivial and limited sort; it is knowledge of "analytic" truths (*see p.67*) and how things stand inside one's own mind.

Hume, for example, allows for a priori knowledge, but insists it is restricted to knowledge of "relations between ideas." For example, on Hume's view, pointing out that all bachelors are unmarried

merely reveals a relationship between the ideas of being a bachelor and of being unmarried: that the one idea involves the other. According to Hume, when it comes to how things stand in the world outside the mind, facts must be acquired via the senses.

THE ORIGIN OF CONCEPTS

We have seen that empiricists claim that all substantive knowledge of the external world depends on experience (*see pp.66–7*). We gain knowledge by using observation and inductive reasoning (*pp.180–5*). The foundation of our knowledge concerning what there is external to the mind lies in what we experience here and now, or can remember from past experience.

Some empiricists also insist that all concepts are ultimately derived from experience, and Hume takes this view. He allows us to have the concept of a unicorn—something we have not experienced—but only because that concept is built out of concepts drawn from what we *have* experienced (horns and horses). Despite this claim, there is nonetheless some plausibility to the suggestion that someone who has never experienced color cannot grasp the concept of red.

Some rationalists, on the other hand, believe that not only is synthetic a priori knowledge of how things stand outside the mind possible; we also possess certain concepts independently of experience. Descartes, for example, supposes that we are pre-equipped with a concept of God (*see pp.68–9*).

Experiences leave impressions on our minds, like a stamp in molten wax, enabling us to build a store of knowledge. Empiricists argue that knowledge without experience is difficult or impossible.

Empiricism on morality and God

Empiricism is usually thought of as a theory about knowledge of the material world, since it focuses on knowledge that comes from the senses. But this may not be all the knowledge we can have. How have empiricists dealt with the question of moral knowledge and knowledge of God's existence, for example?

Empiricists deny that there is any substantive a priori knowledge of how things stand outside the mind.

Another empiricist strategy for dealing with moral knowledge is to recognize that it is not based on experience, and embrace subjectivism instead. Subjectivism says that when we make moral claims, such as "X is morally wrong" or "Y is morally right," we are describing how we feel about X and Y. We are saying that we disapprove of X and approve of Y. Hume appears (in places) to commit himself to this subjectivist view.

"HAPPINESS IS THE SOLE END OF HUMAN ACTION."

John Stuart Mill, *On Utilitarianism*

So for any area of knowledge, they have three choices:

To deny that we have any knowledge in that area.

To say that any knowledge we do have is based on experience.

To say that any a priori knowledge we have is analytic.

The empiricist John Stuart Mill (*see pp.308–9*) argues for moral knowledge on the basis of "observation and experience". He defends the claim that maximizing happiness for the greatest number of people should be our goal (*see also pp.102–3*.) Mill argues that the only evidence we have for what is good is what we desire. Everyone desires happiness, and so there is no better final aim for action than happiness. This argument doesn't establish that we should desire and aim at each other's happiness, since each person desires their own. But Mill assumes that morality is concerned with all persons equally, and that this is an analytic truth. We should all, therefore, aim for happiness.

Mill argued that everyone wants to be happy. More controversially, he argued that this is *all* everyone wants, as everything we want is part of happiness for us.

Subjectivism deals with the problem of moral knowledge by defining it as knowledge only of our own mental states. The empiricist has no difficulty with a priori knowledge of moral truths if they turn out to be about how things stand in our own minds.

A slightly different empiricist strategy is to deny that moral claims are really claims. The emotivist (*see p.115*), for example, insists that someone who says "*X* is morally wrong" is not making a knowledge claim. Instead, they are expressing how they feel—a bit like saying "Forget *X*!" Because such emotive utterances are neither true nor false, there is nothing to "know," and so morality can be excluded from the debate about knowledge.

What of knowledge of God's existence? How might the empiricist account for that? The theistically inclined empiricist can allow for knowledge of the existence of God, but will deny that this knowledge is a priori. Rather than relying on a priori arguments such as the ontological (*see pp.140–1*) or trademark (*see pp.68–9*) argument for the existence of God, the empiricist may point instead to signs of apparent design in

According to emotivists, when we refer to things as being morally "good" or "bad" we are merely expressing an emotional response, much as soccer supporters do when their team scores a goal.

nature, for example, and so conclude it is reasonable to suppose that God is the designer (*see p.147*). Or, starting with the empirical observation that the universe exists, they may then reason, via the principle (which may or may not itself be empirical) that the existence of such a thing requires some sort of cause or explanation (*see pp.142–3*), and conclude that God is that cause or explanation. Both of these arguments are based on empirical evidence.

RATIONAL INTUITION

Rationalists often appeal to a sort of sixth sense, dubbed "intuition," in order to account for our synthetic knowledge of the world outside our minds. Hume argues that many of the so-called "truths" that previous philosophers claimed were supposedly known by means of "rational intuition" were actually just assumptions. Take, for

Religious experience is often claimed to provide believers with non-empirical evidence for the existence of God. But might our five senses also provide good evidence for it, as some empiricists have argued?

example, the claim made by some rationalists that "rational intuition" reveals that every event must have a cause. Perhaps it is very difficult for us to believe there might exist an event without a cause, but this does not mean that we are rationally justified in supposing there can be no such event. Given this objection, it would be helpful if rationalists could supply an account of what intuition is and exactly *how* it can provide knowledge. That is not an easy thing to do.

Rationalism's best form of defense may be attack. Empiricism's account of knowledge of morality, God, and even the external world

Pierre de Fermat's "last theorem" took 357 years to prove. Mathematical truths can be complex, but some deny that they represent substantive knowledge.

can be challenged. If there are good objections to such empiricist accounts, then rationalism can claim that, if we are not to fall into scepticism (*see pp.50–7*), we must accept that we do have rational intuition, even if we don't know exactly

mathematics to work out how many tiles to buy, I will find they fit exactly. Use some other method, such as pure guesswork, and they probably won't fit. Doesn't this reveal mathematics to be a reliable source of information about how the world is structured? Yet math is an a priori discipline. So, on the face of it, mathematics seems to provide a straightforward counter-example to empiricism.

How do empiricists deal with mathematical knowledge? Some, such as Mill, deny that mathematical knowledge is a priori. Others, like Locke and Hume, accept that it is a priori, but deny that it provides us with substantive knowledge. This is because, in their view, mathematical knowledge is analytic. Locke and Hume argue that all mathematical knowledge is reached by developing a series of definitions (definitions of mathematical terms such

> ## "THE MIND... MUST BE TURNED AWAY FROM THE WORLD OF CHANGE [AND THE SENSES] UNTIL ITS EYE CAN... LOOK STRAIGHT AT REALITY."
>
> Plato, *Republic*

what it is or how it works. However, even if this response does cast doubt upon empiricism, it is far from conclusive.

MATHEMATICAL KNOWLEDGE

One of the areas that empiricists have traditionally focused on is mathematical knowledge. On the face of it, arithmetic and geometry are capable of providing us with substantive knowledge of how the world out there really is, which is why they are so useful when it comes to tiling a bathroom. Suppose I want to tile a floor of 33 × 26 ft (10 × 8 m) with 3 × 3ft (1 × 1 m) tiles. If I use the rules of

as "1," "plus," "equals," and so on). But then, if this is true, how can it be that mathematical "discoveries" are possible? How can we be *surprised* by something that is true by definition? Empiricists reply that analytic knowledge doesn't need to be obvious. Mathematical truths are very complex, so it takes work to establish that they are true (just as in the truth that your mother's brother's father's niece's sole female cousin is actually your mother). Whether or not mathematics can be shown to be "analytic," or at least ultimately trivial, remains controversial.

METAPHYSICS

Metaphysics—one of the oldest and most important branches of philosophy—overlaps with other major subdivisions, such as philosophy of mind and the philosophy of religion, and is difficult to define precisely. Perhaps the best characterization of metaphysics is that it seeks to answer fundamental questions about the nature of reality.

One of the earliest and most interesting metaphysical theories is Plato's Theory of Forms, which provides a fine example of just how radical and challenging to common sense this branch of philosophy can be. According to Plato, the world we think we observe around us is an illusion. True reality is hidden from our senses, and can only be known through reason.

Other philosophers of metaphysics have sought to define the extent to which the objects and properties around us are dependent on our minds. Take the property of being delicious. This is not a fully objective property, but is rooted in our personal reaction to what we experience. For those who find eggs delicious, they are delicious; for those who don't, they are not. That is because the deliciousness—or otherwise—of eggs is ultimately rooted not in the eggs, but in us. But what about other aspects of reality? Could other things that are routinely assumed to exist

Metaphysics poses far-reaching questions about the nature of reality, and tackles issues that are beyond the reach of scientific inquiry. Philosophers apply reason to the problems of metaphysics.

independently of our minds, such as color, causation, and even physical objects, be mind-dependent?

Metaphysics also contains one of the oldest conundrums in philosophy. Plato himself attempted to solve the puzzle of why mirrors reverse right to left, but not top to bottom. What is the explanation for this strange asymmetry? It may be that the solution to this puzzle offers clues as to how other metaphysical questions might be answered.

A RADICAL ALTERNATIVE

It is worth reminding ourselves that not all philosophers consider the pursuit of metaphysical questions fruitful. Some, like Kant, have argued that the ultimate nature of reality (what he calls the *noumenal*) is in principle unknowable. Others, such as A.J. Ayer and Wittgenstein, suggest there is something wrong with metaphysical questions themselves, and it is always worth bearing this radical alternative in mind. Perhaps, rather than seeking solutions to metaphysical puzzles, we should consider whether we are asking the right questions.

PLATO AND THE FORMS

One of the most dramatic and best-known theories in Western philosophy is Plato's Theory of Forms. The theory challenges some of our most basic assumptions about the nature of reality, calling into question the validity of day-to-day existence as we know it.

A realm of shadows

Plato believed that the world we seem to observe around us is an illusion. True reality is hidden, and is inaccessible to our senses. But what is this reality like?

According to Plato, it contains abstract entities known as the *Forms*. Suppose we observe a number of beautiful things: a sunset, a flower, a painting, and so on. These things differ in many obvious ways. But still, we suppose they all have something in common: they are all beautiful.

According to Plato, this common "something" is an entity: the Form of beauty. Similarly, Plato supposes that there is a Form of the horse, a Form of the mountain, a Form of the bed, and so on. In each case, the various individual instances of a thing (which he called "particulars") partake of a common Form. It is this shared Form that makes them all horses, mountains, beds, and so on. Nonetheless, Plato believed that the Forms themselves differ from particulars in important ways.

DEFINING THE FORMS

Plato argues that each Form is *perfect*; it perfectly exemplifies the property in question. No particular thing is ever perfectly beautiful. It could always be a little more beautiful than it actually is. The Form of beauty, on the other hand—beauty itself —is perfectly beautiful.

Plato also argues that the Forms are *eternal*. Beautiful particulars come and go. The beautiful flower blooms, but then quickly withers and dies. Beauty itself, by contrast, neither comes into existence nor ceases to be.

Thirdly, the Forms are *changeless*. Of course, our judgment as to what is beautiful does change over time. Fashions come and go. But according to Plato, the Form of beauty, beauty itself, does not alter. Fourthly, the Forms are also *more real* than the particulars that partake of them. The particulars are merely fleeting shadows or reflections of the Forms, which are what truly exist.

What is beauty itself? To Plato, it is an entity that exists *in addition* to all the beautiful particular things.

THE FORMS AND KNOWLEDGE

Plato also claims that we each possess an immortal soul that was once acquainted with the Forms (an experience we have since forgotten, of course). This soul returns to the realm of the Forms when we die. He goes on to suggest that all genuine knowledge is knowledge of the Forms, and offers the following argument in support of this claim. Our opinions constantly change. For example, we used to believe the Earth was flat, but now we don't. But genuine knowledge cannot change in this way. If something turns out not to be knowledge, then it never was knowledge to begin with. What is knowledge at one time cannot cease to be knowledge at a later date.

But if knowledge itself cannot change, then, argues Plato, knowledge itself must be *of* what cannot change. Because only the Forms are unchanging, it therefore follows that the only true knowledge must be knowledge of the Forms.

Our five senses are unable to provide us with knowledge of the Forms—they reveal only an ever-shifting shadow-world. Because of this, Plato believes it is only through philosophical reflection that we can arrive at true knowledge: knowledge of the eternal, changeless, and perfect Forms.

Plato believed that what we take to be "real" objects are in fact merely imperfect, fleeting shadows of the eternal Forms. Like images reflected in a distorted mirror, they can only hint at the true shape of things.

THE STORY OF PLATO'S CAVE

The Cave is one of the most dramatic philosophical images ever constructed. It vividly illustrates what Plato takes to be the human predicament. We are trapped inside a world of shadows. The real world is hidden from us. Just like the prisoners in his allegorical cave, we are seduced by an illusion. We mistake shadows for reality, but have no means of knowing that we are being deceived.

IMPRISONED BY ILLUSION

In the *Republic*, Plato presents an allegory that vividly brings his Theory of Forms to life. Suppose that deep within a cave, prisoners are chained. The prisoners face a wall and cannot turn their heads. Flickering shadows are cast upon the wall, and because that is all they can see, the prisoners mistake these shadows for reality.

Then one of the prisoners is released from his shackles and led away. To begin with, he is taken to the true source of the shadows. There is a bright fire behind the prisoners, and in front of this fire people are carrying various objects back and forth. As the prisoner's eyes adjust to the light, he begins to recognize how he has been fooled. What he had taken to be real objects were in truth shadows cast by these real objects that had been hidden from sight.

The prisoner is again led upward, finally reaching the outside world. Here he is confronted by the sun. Again, the prisoner is initially blinded by the light, but eventually he comes to recognize that the sun is ultimately

that which governs and is the true source of everything around him. The prisoner is then returned to the depths of the cave.

REJECTED WISDOM

Because his eyes have become accustomed to the bright light of the sun, he now stumbles and struggles to see. When he tries to explain to the other prisoners how they have been fooled, they shun him. They see him stumbling and insist that he is the one who is blind, not they. They remain convinced by what their senses seem to show them: by the shadow-play on the cave wall. They remain seduced by the illusion of reality, and consider the one wise person among them to be a fool.

The cave story helped Plato to explain his belief in the Forms, including the highest entity of all: The Form of the Good.

In this allegory, the shadows represent the fleeting "particulars" (Plato's term for any individual thing we see in our "reality"), while the real objects casting shadows represent their real and perfect Forms. The sun outside stands for the Form of the Good. This ultimate Form, says Plato, "appears last of all, and is seen only with an effort; and, when seen, is also inferred to be the universal author of all things beautiful and right, parent of light and of the lord of light in this visible world, and the immediate source of reason and truth in the intellectual. This is the power upon which he who would act rationally, either in public or private life, must have his eye fixed."

The cave allegory illustrates the hierarchical structure of Plato's theory, with the Form of the Good at the top, the other Forms further down, and the realm of shadows, the world of particulars, at the bottom. The prisoner's journey upward represents the journey toward true knowledge: knowledge of the Forms and, ultimately, the Form of the Good. Like Socrates (*see pp.242–3*) in Plato's imagined philosophical dialogs, the prisoner discovers the illusory nature of what we ordinarily take to be reality, and tries to help others discover the truth. The result is that he is mocked, while the prisoners remain shackled to their illusion.

The One-Over-Many Argument

Why should we suppose the Forms exist? One of Plato's key arguments for the existence of the Forms runs as follows. All beautiful things have something in common: namely, beauty itself. Now this "something"—beauty itself—must exist *in addition* to all the particular beautiful things that there are, for clearly, none of the particulars is beauty itself. After all, each of the particulars could always be more beautiful than it is, whereas that is not true of beauty itself. And while the particulars may change and even cease to be beautiful, beauty itself is changeless. The additional "something" is the Form.

This argument is often called the One-Over-Many Argument. If cogent, the One-Over-Many Argument can also

be applied to show that there is a Form of the horse, a Form of the bed, and so on for every property there is.

Interestingly, the One-Over-Many Argument can be applied to the Forms themselves. After all, they too have something in common: they are all Forms. Plato concludes there must be an over-arching Form: the Form of the Good. This supreme Form exemplifies what all the different forms have in common: existence and perfection.

THE THIRD MAN OBJECTION

Plato himself considered a number of objections to his theory. One of the most interesting, discussed in Plato's dialog the *Parmenides*, is known as the Third Man Objection.

The One-Over-Many Argument says that whenever things share a common property, we are justified in supposing

Ideas of what constitutes loveliness in the female form have changed constantly through time, from the era of Rubens to the present day. Plato argued, however, that beauty itself is eternal.

"IT'S ALL IN PLATO, ALL IN PLATO; BLESS ME, WHAT DO THEY TEACH THEM AT THESE SCHOOLS!"

Digory, speaking in *The Last Battle* by C.S. Lewis, whose idealized realm of Narnia (pictured above) lay beyond what he called the "Shadowlands" of day-to-day existence.

that there exists a common Form. But if, as Plato appears to think, the Form itself possesses the property in question (if the Form of beauty is itself beautiful), then the particulars and the Form share a common property. But then, by the same argument, we must conclude that there is a second Form to account for this commonality. But if this second Form also possesses that property, there must be a third Form, and a fourth, and so on without end. So the One-Over-Many Argument seems to generate a *regress (see p.212)*. Rather than establishing the existence of a single Form for each kind of thing, it seems to establish an infinite number of such Forms. Plato denies there is an infinite number of Forms for each kind of thing. But if he rejects that conclusion, must he not also reject the One-Over-Many Argument?

PLATO'S LEGACY

Plato's philosophy has had a huge impact on Western culture, and particularly on Christian thinking. Take, for example, the Form of the Good. This Form sounds a great deal like the modern Christian conception of God. The resemblance is not entirely coincidental. Philosophers such as Augustine (*see pp.256–7*) have borrowed and adapted Platonic ideas, weaving them heavily into the Christian philosophical tradition.

One 20th-century Christian thinker heavily influenced by Plato was C. S. Lewis, author of *The Lion, the Witch and the Wardrobe* and the other Narnia stories. Lewis referred to our world as the Shadowlands—a direct reference to Plato's allegory of the Cave. Lewis, like Plato, believed that our world is ultimately illusory: the real world is that to which our immortal souls pass over when we die. In Lewis's thinking, the Christian idea of an afterlife and Plato's realm of the Forms are merged together.

Today, few philosophers embrace Plato's Theory of Forms. But the questions Plato asked, and the methods he used in trying to answer them, continue to dominate the Western philosophical tradition.

MIND-DEPENDENCE

Many philosophical questions concern the extent to which various phenomena are "mind-dependent." Take color, for example. Do colors really exist "out there" on the surfaces of objects, or are they somehow dependent on the minds of perceivers?

The eye of the beholder

Most of us tend to think that the color of a ripe tomato is a mind-independent feature of the tomato – a quality that is "there anyway," independently of how the tomato might happen to strike us. But this view is not shared by everyone. According to many scientists and philosophers, the colors that objects seem to possess are not truly possessed by them—at least not in the way that we think. Color, they argue, is in large measure a product of the minds that do the observing. The same, many would add, is also true of tastes, smells, and sounds. In fact, many philosophers and scientists distinguish between "primary qualities," such as position, number, shape, size, and motion, which are held to be fully objective features of external reality, and "secondary qualities," such as color, taste, and smell, which are essentially tied to the minds of observers.

ALL IN THE MIND

One of the simplest versions of the theory that color is a secondary quality belongs to the philosopher and pioneering scientist Galileo, writing in 1623: "I hold that tastes, colors, smells, and the like exist only in the being which feels, which being removed, these qualities themselves do vanish". By Galileo's theory, color is very mind-dependent indeed. Indeed, color is not a feature of external objects at all. It exists in our minds. Remove all observers, and the colors immediately vanish. So do other secondary qualities such as tastes and smells. The only qualities that remain are the primary

> ## "TASTES, COLORS, AND SMELLS EXIST ONLY IN THE BEING WHICH FEELS."
>
> Galileo Galilei, *The Assayer*

According to Galileo and Locke, color is both mind-dependent and relative to perceivers. For aliens to whom grass looks red, grass is red. The aliens' color judgments are no less accurate than ours.

The colors things appear to have are, according to Galileo, illusory. In his view, color exists only in the mind of the observer.

qualities of shape, size, position, and so on. One interesting consequence of Galileo's theory of color is that it makes color relative. Perhaps beings with very different physiognomies—aliens, say—would see red where we see green, and vice versa. According to Galileo, their experience of color would be as "correct" as ours.

LOCKE ON COLOR

The 17th-century philosopher John Locke also distinguishes between primary and secondary qualities, though he offers a more sophisticated version of the theory. According to Locke, secondary qualities such as colors, tastes, and smells do not exist in the mind, as Galileo claimed. But still, colors are mind-dependent. Color, for Locke, consists of an attribute (he uses the term "disposition") belonging to an object that triggers a certain sort of experience or idea in the mind. So, for example, for an object to be red is just for it to be true that *if* an observer were to look at it under normal conditions, *then* it would produce in them a certain color-experience.

Locke's account makes color akin to other dispositional properties, such as being soluble. For a sugar cube to be soluble is just for it to be true that if it were placed in water, then it would dissolve. Of course, the sugar cube remains soluble even when it is not dissolving. In fact it is still soluble even if it is never dissolved, for it remains true that *if* it were placed in water, *then* it would dissolve. Similarly, in Locke's dispositional theory of color, an object can continue to be red even when no one is looking at it. A red tomato remains red if it remains true that if someone were to look at it, then they would have a certain color-experience. Locke extends the same view to sounds, tastes, smells, and certain tactile qualities.

physical objects are made up of tiny particles called corpuscles. Individual corpuscles have only primary qualities, such as shape, size, position, number, and motion. However, as part of an object's microscopic structure, they determine what secondary qualities it has.

Of course, something not wholly dissimilar to the corpuscular theory has turned out to be correct. We now know that physical objects are made up of molecules and atoms, which in turn have

"SUCH QUALITIES... ARE NOTHING IN THE OBJECTS THEMSELVES, BUT... PRODUCE VARIOUS SENSATIONS IN US."

John Locke, *Enquiry Concerning Human Understanding*

THE FABRIC OF EXISTENCE

Why do objects have these dispositions? Locke believed it was because of their microscopic makeup. Like many of his contemporaries, he maintained that

their own subatomic constituents. And it is true that the molecular and atomic structure of objects does indeed determine and explain why they have many of their "dispositional" properties, such as color and smell. For example, the fact that water is made up of atoms of hydrogen and oxygen combined in a particular way explains why it boils at

GALILEO AND THE ENLIGHTENMENT

The scientist Galileo was one of the most important thinkers in the run-up to the Enlightenment, the era of rational progress that flourished in 18th-century Europe. Prior to the Enlightenment, thinkers tended to defer to the authority of Aristotle and the Church when developing their theories. Galileo rejected such appeals to authority and set about applying his own powers of reason and observation. By constructing a telescope through which he could observe both the mountains of our moon and the movement of the moons of Jupiter, Galileo showed that Aristotle was wrong to claim that all heavenly bodies are perfectly spherical and that they all rotate about the Earth.

Galileo dared to apply his own intelligence and powers of observation. His ideas brought him into conflict with the Church and its doctrines.

The solubility of a sugar cube is a dispositional quality of the cube, which remains soluble even when it is not actually dissolving.

212°F (100°C), but also why it is colorless and odorless, and so on.

THE FOREST TEST

How would Galileo and Locke respond to the question: "When a tree falls in the forest, unobserved by anyone, does it make a sound?" Galileo would say "no"; sounds exist only in the mind. So if there is no mind present, then there can be no sound. Locke's dispositional analysis of secondary qualities, on the other hand, allows him to answer "yes" to this question. So long as it is true that if someone were present, then they would hear a sound, then there is a sound. Whether or not anyone actually hears it is irrelevant.

While Galileo and Locke give differing accounts of color, both make color mind-dependent and relative to observers. Locke agrees with Galileo that aliens that see red grass where we see green would be having a very different, but no less valid sort of visual experience. Both state that there is no mind-independent, objective fact of the matter as to what color grass really is.

PHYSICAL OBJECTS

Locke and Galileo believe, therefore, that colors, tastes, smells, and other secondary qualities are mind-dependent. Indeed, Galileo claims they exist only in the mind. It has been argued that modern scientific methodology supports their view (*see box, right*). But of course neither Locke nor Galileo believes that physical objects are mind-dependent. On their view, physical objects and their primary qualities constitute a mind-independent reality. However, some philosophers, such as George Berkeley (*see overleaf*), have extended the claim of mind-dependence even to physical objects themselves.

A SCIENTIFIC ARGUMENT

One of the most popular arguments supporting the claims of Galileo and Locke runs as follows: When scientists construct their theories, they do so only by appealing to the primary qualities of things, not their secondary qualities. Colors, tastes, smells, and so on do not feature in scientific explanations, and do not figure in their accounts of how the universe is organized. Doesn't this strongly suggest that colors, tastes, and smells are after all not fully objective properties of things? That these properties are not really "out there" independently of us? If so, then many features of the world we perceive around us are at least partly contributed by the mind.

God and the mind

John Locke believed that we experience the physical world indirectly, via mental items he calls Ideas. When I observe an orange on the table in front of me, I do not perceive the orange directly. Rather, I am internally aware of a certain sensory appearance, or Idea, that the object causes in me.

This theory of Ideas raises a famous problem. If all we have direct access to are our own Ideas, how can we know that there is a physical world lying outside them? Our Ideas seem to form a veil beyond which we cannot peek. For all we know, there may be nothing beyond our Ideas. So Locke's theory of Ideas appears to generate a form of scepticism: it seems to have the consequence that we can know nothing about the physical world. Philosophers call this the "veil of perception" problem.

Locke's near-contemporary George Berkeley was struck by the way that 18th-century scientific theories, which tended to view the physical world as a great machine governed by laws, largely pushed God to the periphery. Berkeley's Idealism aims to address both these concerns: the veil of perception problem and the peripheral role allocated to God in the science of the time.

According to Berkeley, physical objects do not lie beyond our Ideas. Rather, physical objects *are* Ideas. The orange I now see before me on the table is not the hidden cause of the experiences I have when I look at it. Rather, it just is those experiences. It just is the Ideas that I

am having. An immediate consequence of this view is that physical objects cannot exist unobserved. Ideas, being mental items, can exist only in the minds of observers. But then it follows that physical objects, being Ideas, can exist only in the minds of observers.

This all sounds very peculiar, of course. Surely physical objects do continue to exist when we are not observing them? Isn't it ridiculous to suppose otherwise?

DIVINE OBSERVATION

In fact Berkeley agrees that physical objects can continue to exist when we are not observing them. But that is only because he supposes God observes them all the time. It is God who sustains the physical universe in existence while our attention is directed elsewhere.

You can now see that Berkeley's Idealism does appear to address his two chief concerns. By identifying physical objects with Ideas, the veil of perception problem is immediately solved. We no longer face the problem of explaining how we can know there are any physical objects beyond our Ideas. And because Berkeley's Idealism invokes God to sustain the unobserved universe from

If we experience the world indirectly via Ideas, like images on a screen, how can we know that there is anything beyond this veil of perception?

According to Berkeley, a physical object such as a tree exists only in the minds of observers. Ultimately, all that exists are minds and what goes on in them.

PHENOMENALISM

The phenomenalist agrees with the Idealist that physical objects are mind-dependent. But they disagree about the way in which physical objects are tied to the minds of observers. Unlike Berkeley, the phenomenalist allows that physical objects can continue to exist even when not observed, by suggesting that statements about physical objects are actually conditional statements.

UNPERCEIVED OBJECTS

Conditional statements have the form "If..., then...." John Locke, in effect, gives a conditional analysis of color (*see pp.83–5*). He says that for an object to be red is just for it to be true that *if* someone were to observe the object, *then* they would have a certain color-experience. By giving such a conditional analysis of color-talk, Locke can allow for, say, a poppy growing on a remote hillside to be red even if it is never actually observed. All that has to be true is that *if* someone were to observe the poppy, *then* they would have a color-experience of such-and-such a sort.

A chair in an empty room can continue to exist in the absence of observers, according to phenomenalists.

The phenomenalist simply extends the same kind of conditional analysis to physical-object talk. For example, according to the phenomenalist, to say that there is a flower growing at a certain spot on the Moon is (roughly) to say that *if* someone were to observe that spot on the Moon, *then* they would have certain flower-type experiences. It doesn't matter whether or not anyone ever does travel to the Moon to witness the flower. Just so long as this conditional remains true, it remains true that the flower is growing there. For the phenomenalist, physical objects are what John Stuart Mill called "permanent possibilities of sensation," by contrast with the Idealist's claim that they cannot exist unobserved.

one moment to the next, Berkeley's philosophy brings God back to center stage.

KEY ARGUMENT

Berkeley's Idealism seems highly counter-intuitive. Why on earth should we suppose it is true? Berkeley's key argument for his theory turns on what we are able to conceive of. Berkeley thinks he can show that we cannot even conceive of physical objects existing unobserved. His argument takes the form of a challenge. Try, he asks, to imagine something that exists unperceived. Try to imagine a tree that no one is observing. You cannot succeed, for in imagining the tree, you imagine yourself looking at it.

Berkeley concludes that the hypothesis that there are physical objects that can exist unobserved by anyone is not so much false as empty. That there could be a tree or other physical object that might continue to exist even when no one observes it is not even a thought we are able to entertain, let alone a true thought.

ILLUSION AND REALITY

One problem facing Idealism concerns the distinction between illusion and reality. A real physical object is just a collection of Ideas, according to Berkeley. But then so is an illusory object, of course. So it seems that Idealism is unable to make a distinction between real and illusory

The eternal gaze of God does more than monitor humankind's peccadilloes, said Berkeley: it keeps our world in existence.

perspectives on the same object are possible. If I look at a vase from over here, and then over there, I have two quite different sets of Ideas. From here it looks large and red, but from over there it is green and much smaller-looking. And it appears a different shape too.

If we simply identify a physical object with an Idea or set of Ideas, it seems that, because I have two quite different sets of Ideas, so I must be confronted with two different physical objects, not one. Yet

"I REFUTE BERKELEY THUS"

Dr. Johnson, kicking a stone in his path (though Berkeley never claimed that stones do not exist).

things. How does Berkeley solve this problem? He suggests that imaginary objects – a dagger that I hallucinate, for example, like Shakespeare's Macbeth – exist in my mind alone. Ideas of real things, on the other hand, exist in the minds of others: at the very least they exist in the mind of God.

Another of the more obvious problems facing Idealism is that it has difficulty explaining how different

it is the same object that I see. The theory of phenomenalism manages to sidestep this problem, because it can accommodate the fact that the same object can appear differently depending on how it is observed. Phenomenalism does not identify a physical object with any particular Idea or set of Ideas. Instead it suggests that talk about physical objects is conditional in form (*see facing page*).

Cause and effect

While watching a game of pool, you see one ball run up against another. The second ball moves. We suppose that not only did one event follow the other, one event caused the other. Indeed, we suppose that the movement of one ball necessitated that of the other. Given the movement of the first ball, the second must move. But what is this necessary connection? Is it there at all? As the Scottish philosopher David Hume (*see pp.290–1*) points out, the more closely we look, the more elusive this mysterious connection seems to become.

Note, first of all, that there is no logical necessity involved. Nor is there any logical contradiction in supposing that when one ball strikes the other, the second will remain motionless, or move vertically upward, or even turn into a posy of flowers. It seems, then, that if there is some necessary connection between the two events, the connection must be revealed, not by logic, but through experience.

But, as Hume points out, we do not appear to have any such experience. When we see one ball strike the other, we do not see any "causing." We simply observe one event follow another. That the movement of the first ball brings about the movement of the second is not something that shows up in what we observe before us. To reinforce this point, Hume points out that if we did experience such a necessary connection, then we could know, on the basis of a single observation, that two events are causally related. Someone who had no previous

> ## "WHEN WE... CONSIDER THE OPERATION OF CAUSES, WE ARE NEVER ABLE... TO DISCOVER ANY... NECESSARY CONNECTION."
>
> David Hume, *Enquiry Concerning Human Understanding*

experience of how physical bodies behave could know, seeing the one ball move and then the other, that the first ball caused the second to move, for they would be able directly to observe the "causing" taking place. But the fact that two events are causally related is not something that can be established on the basis of a single observation. That one event followed the other might just be a coincidence, like

Hume considered not pool but billiards, an older game he played enthusiastically.

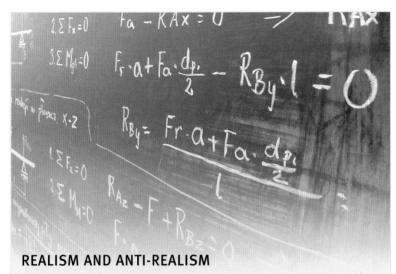

REALISM AND ANTI-REALISM

Disputes between realists and anti-realists can be found in almost every branch of philosophy, from morality to mathematics. In each case they disagree over the extent to which certain phenomena are mind-dependent. Realists, for example, hold that mathematical truths describe how things stand in a mind-independent mathematical reality. Anti-realists would say they are mind-dependent.

DRAWING THE LINE

Both Galileo and Locke are anti-realists about color (*see pp.82–5*). Both believe that colors, along with odors, sounds, and the other "secondary qualities," are mind-dependent properties. But of course Galileo and Locke remain realists about physical objects and their "primary qualities." Berkeley, on the other hand, is an anti-realist even about physical objects. Berkeley believes that they too are mind-dependent. So does the phenomenalist (*see p.88*).

Notice that it is possible to be more or less anti-realist. Locke and the phenomenalist, while respectively making color and physical objects dependent upon experience, nevertheless allow these phenomena to exist unperceived: that is, when there is no one there to experience them. Galileo and Berkeley, by contrast, embrace more extreme forms of anti-realism. Unlike Locke, Galileo places colors in the mind. According to Berkeley, even physical objects exist only in the minds of observers. Often, one of the things that drive philosophers in the direction of anti-realism is a concern about scepticism (*see pp.56–7*). That is true of Berkeley's anti-realism about physical objects, for example. Berkeley could not see how, if physical reality lies behind our Ideas, we could ever know about it. By embracing an anti-realist position, on which physical objects simply are Ideas, he solved that puzzle.

Does the light stay on when the refrigerator door is shut? Do objects continue to exist unperceived?

when the phone rings immediately after the kettle boils. In order to know that two events are causally related, you need to observe many such pairs of events. You are only in a position to know that *A* caused *B* if you have witnessed what Hume calls a "constant conjunction" of *A*s and *B*s in the past. Hume concludes we have no experience of any such necessary connection.

OUR CONCEPT OF CAUSE

Hume is an empiricist about concepts: he believes all concepts are derived from experience. So if we have a concept of causation, it must be derived from experience. But you can now see that we face a mystery. If, when we observe *A* cause *B*, there is no experience of any causal connection—if we observe no more than that *A* is followed by *B*— then from where does our conception of this necessary causal connection come? Why do I feel so strongly that such a connection is present? Why do I feel the second ball *must* move given the movement of the first?

Hume's answer to this question is: because of my prior experience of a constant conjunction. Suppose I see a pin moving toward a balloon. Whenever I have previously seen a pin pushed into a balloon, the balloon has popped. This constant conjunction produces in my mind an involuntary association—when

Hume claims that unicorns, and other imaginary entities, are merely a composite of ideas of things we have experienced (*see box, facing page*).

I now see the pin move toward the balloon, I have a vivid idea of a pop. I cannot help but expect a pop.

According to Hume, I mistakenly project this felt, internal, mental connection between my experience of the one thing and my idea of the other outward onto the objects themselves. I confusedly transform a connection between things in my mind into a connection between things in the world. This is the origin of my idea that the balloon *must* go pop. Again, something we believe to be "out there" in the world independently of us actually turns out to be rooted in ourselves.

A COSMIC FLUKE?

Hume argues that we have no conception of anything that might make the world behave regularly. It just has done, up to now. But if nothing makes the world behave regularly, if there is no necessary connection out there in nature, then those regularities we have observed up until now are down to sheer chance. It is just a coincidence that whenever a pin has pricked a balloon, it popped: like a dice having been rolled millions of times and, by pure chance, always coming up a six.

How plausible is this? Not very, surely. Aren't such cosmic coincidences too much to swallow? There must be some sort of objective necessity involved, some further

We think that one event leads to another by cause and effect—but does one event really necessitate the next?

> "WE HAVE NO OTHER NOTION OF CAUSE AND EFFECT, BUT THAT OF CERTAIN OBJECTS, WHICH HAVE BEEN ALWAYS CONJOINED TOGETHER, AND WHICH IN ALL PAST INSTANCES HAVE BEEN FOUND INSEPARABLE."
>
> David Hume, *A Treatise on Human Nature*

secret connection that *makes* the balloon go pop. But if Hume is correct about how our concepts are derived, it is difficult to see how we could even entertain the thought that there might be any such connection, let alone establish its existence.

HUME'S CONCLUSIONS

So what is a cause? Hume offers two definitions. On the first, one thing causes another when the first precedes and is "contiguous" with (for example, touches) the second, and there is a constant conjunction of such events.

On Hume's second definition, a cause is when one thing "always conveys the thought to that other." That is to say, your prior experience of a constant conjunction makes your mind move from the *experience* of one thing to the *idea* of the other (seeing the pin move toward the balloon leads you to expect a pop). On this second definition, unlike the first, causation is mind-dependent. With no mind to experience a constant conjunction, there can be no causes.

HUME ON CONCEPTS

Hume's empiricist position—that all concepts are ultimately derived from experience—still allows us to conceive of things we have never experienced, such as unicorns. Hume says this is because these concepts are built out of simpler concepts that are, in turn, derived from experience. If I have experienced both horned animals and horses, I can combine those two concepts to form a concept of a unicorn. Hume points out that we have no direct experience of any causal connection between events. Our conception of causation must therefore similarly be "built" out of those experiences we have had—such as our experience of constant conjunction. Both of Hume's two famous definitions of "cause"(*left*) define causation in terms of constant conjunction.

In the myth of Narcissus, according to the Greek poet Ovid, the youth becomes so absorbed by his reflected image that he is lost to the real world around him. But what if, as many philosophers have argued, the "reality" that we believe we experience is itself an illusion?

The mirror puzzle

Sometimes it is the things most familiar to us that turn out to be the most deeply puzzling. Take mirrors. How many times do you see yourself reflected in a mirror each day? Most of us never stop to think about what we see, but mirrors are philosophically mystifying things.

Take a look at yourself in a mirror. If the mirror before you were replaced by a sheet of glass, and you were to stand behind the glass in just the position your mirror-self seems to stand, then while your head would still be at the top and your feet at the bottom, your left hand would be over to the right, where your right hand appears in the mirror, and your right hand would be to the left, where your left hand appears.

Mirrors present an extremely accurate image of ourselves—except for one thing. Our right-hand sides are the left-hand sides of the person in the mirror.

That is the source of the puzzle: mirrors reverse the left–right orientation we would expect to see if we were standing in that position, but they leave top and bottom untouched.

What accounts for this peculiar asymmetry? Some of the world's greatest minds, including that of the Ancient Greek philosopher Plato (*see pp.244–7*), have struggled with and been defeated by this mystery. Notice that this left–right switch still happens no matter which way up you happen to be. Lie on your side in front of a mirror and see the result. It is still your left and right sides that are switched around, not your head and feet. Nor does it matter which way around the mirror is. Turn it upside down. The effect is exactly the same. Some people suppose that the effect must be due to our having a left and a right eye, rather than a top

A dancer resting beside a mirror demonstrates the puzzling behavior of reflections. Even when we are horizontal, the mirror still switches our left and right sides around, but not our heads and feet.

and bottom eye. But that is not the explanation. If you cover one eye, the asymmetric reversal remains, so we must look elsewhere for an answer.

A SCIENTIFIC APPROACH

Might science solve the mirror puzzle? In particular, is the explanation that light is reflected differently left-to-right than it is top-to-bottom? It seems not.

Suppose we hold a clock up in front of a mirror and draw arrows linking each number on the clock face with the same number reflected in the mirror (*see above*). The arrows show that the way the mirror reflects is entirely symmetrical in every direction. The arrows do not cross over top to bottom. But neither do they cross over left-to-right. It is not as if a mirror reflects rays of light differently depending on whether they are coming from your left and right sides rather than your top and bottom. The light is reflected in the same way no matter where it happens to land on the mirror.

So the puzzle has absolutely nothing to do with how light is reflected off the surface of the mirror. Indeed, the puzzle

Place a clock in front of a mirror and join the numbers with imaginary lines. The lines do not cross top to bottom *or* left to right.

is not a scientific puzzle at all. Even when we know all the scientific facts about how mirrors and light behave, that still leaves the mystery of *why* mirrors reverse one way and not the other. The more we grapple with this mystery, the deeper it seems to become, and the more mirrors seem to take on an almost magical quality. Just why do they do what they do? The profound sense of bafflement raised by this question is typical of that raised by philosophical problems more generally.

PROPOSING A SOLUTION

What follows is a suggested solution to the mirror puzzle (or at least part of a solution—one or two details need to be filled in). I should add, however, that this is my own answer to the puzzle. Whether or not it is a satisfactory one is something that you should judge for yourself.

As we have already seen, in a sense, mirrors don't reverse anything. But in comparing how your left and right sides

"RIGHT APPEARS LEFT AND LEFT RIGHT, BECAUSE THE VISUAL RAYS COME INTO CONTACT WITH THE RAYS EMITTED BY THE OBJECT IN A MANNER CONTRARY TO THE USUAL MODE OF MEETING."

Plato, attempting to explain why mirrors reverse left–right, in the *Timaeus*

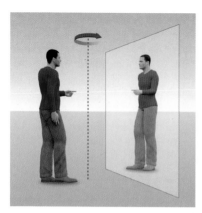

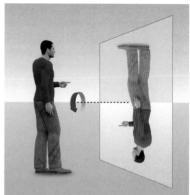

Rotated on a vertical axis (*above*) it is as if the man stands behind the glass, facing himself: his left hand is now on the right, and vice versa. Rotating him around a horizontal axis (*above right*), top and bottom are reversed, but not left and right.

would be oriented if you were rotated to stand across from yourself, and how mirrors actually reflect an image of you, we take something for granted. This is the axis about which we rotate you when we imagine you behind the mirror.

TURNING IT AROUND

When we turn something around, we rotate it on an axis. A spinning top, for example, rotates around a vertical axis. A car wheel rotates around a horizontal axis. When we imagine you over there in the position your mirror-self seems to be in, we mentally put you there by rotating you on a vertical axis, as in the above diagram. But what if we were to place you over there by rotating you around a horizontal axis instead? Then you would be standing on your head. And, compared to your mirror image, your left and right sides would not then be switched around. Your left hand (the one that is pointing in the diagram) would remain to the left. Which is where your right hand would appear if it were reflected in a mirror. But top and bottom are now reversed. Your head appears where your feet are in the image.

It seems the reason we say mirrors reverse left and right but not top and bottom is due to the fact that we take for granted a particular axis of rotation. But we could just as easily choose a horizontal axis. Then it would be true to say that a mirror reverses top to bottom but not left

to right. So yes, it is true to say mirrors reverse left to right, but only if we choose a vertical axis of rotation. Choose a horizontal axis and they then reverse top to bottom instead.

OVERLOOKING THE OBVIOUS

Of course, this explanation of why people perceive there to be something puzzling about mirrors raises the question of why we take the vertical axis for granted. The answer, presumably, is that we are not in the habit of somersaulting through the air and landing on our heads. We stand upright (most of the time), and when we rotate, it is almost always on a vertical axis. So this puzzle about why mirrors do what they do is generated by our not noticing what has been taken for granted.

WHEN ONLY PHILOSOPHY WILL DO

Notice that if this solution (or part solution) to the mirror puzzle is correct, we certainly didn't have to conduct any scientific research into how light and mirrors behave. Nor did we have to investigate how our brains work. Even if we had done that sort of scientific research, it still wouldn't have solved the puzzle. In order to solve this puzzle, we need to stop doing science and start doing philosophy. It is a puzzle that is solved by thinking. People sometimes assume all questions can be answered by science. They would assume that the mirror puzzle must have a scientific solution. But it turns out that the mirror puzzle is a puzzle that science cannot solve. It seems that, sometimes, only philosophy will do.

THE DOOR PUZZLE

Here is a conundrum related to the mirror puzzle. Walk through a door that opens on your left and turn around to come back through it, and the door now opens on your right. But pass through a door that opens at the top (like a cat flap) and turn to come back through it and the door still opens at the top. Why does passing through a door reverse the way it opens from left to right, but not top to bottom?

SOLVING THE MYSTERY

The solution to the door puzzle is much the same as for the mirror puzzle. When you pass through a left-opening door and turn around to come back through it, you would normally rotate on a vertical axis. But what if you were to rotate on a horizontal axis, and you floated back through upside down? Then the

Pass through this door, and it opens to the right. Return, and it now opens to the left.

door that opened on the left would still open on the left on the way back through it, but a door that opened at the bottom would now open at the top. We say that left and right are

reversed but not top and bottom only because we take for granted a particular axis of rotation. In the weightless environment of space, you could just as easily spin on a horizontal axis instead. So, after years in space, it might seem as natural to you to say that a door that opens at the top opens at the bottom when you come back through it, as it does to say that a door that opens on the left opens on the right when you return through it. For creatures that live in a weightless environment, where it is as easy to rotate on one axis as on the other, perhaps neither the mirror puzzle nor the door puzzle would even be puzzles.

For astronauts in a weightless environment, it is as easy to rotate on a horizontal axis as it is to rotate on a vertical one.

MORAL PHILOSOPHY

If any area of philosophy has a claim to be "practical," it is moral philosophy. It touches on some of the most emotive and controversial issues in life. But while philosophers have been concerned to discover how we should live, moral philosophy is best understood as the attempt to think critically and reflectively about right and wrong, good and bad.

There are three different ways in which we can think about morals. First, we can think about whether a particular action or type of action is right or wrong. Are abortion or euthanasia right or wrong? When is lying permissible, if ever? This type of thinking is called practical ethics, and anyone who has ever argued the case for or against a certain action on the basis of morality has engaged in it.

How are we to find the answers to these types of questions? Normative ethics, the second way to think about right and wrong, good and bad, develops general theories about what is right and what is good that we can use in practical cases. We can try to understand these ideas by looking at our actions themselves; or through examining the consequences of our actions; or by looking at the types of people we can be or become.

The third way to think critically and reflectively about morality is metaethics ("*meta-*" is a Greek word that means

Van Gogh depicts an example of moral goodness in his painting *The Good Samaritan*. But what makes such actions good, and is "goodness" anything more than a reflection of our emotional responses?

either "above," "beyond," or "after"). Metaethics is the study of the very ideas of right and wrong, good and bad—the concepts that ethics takes for granted. For example, if I say that euthanasia is wrong, am I making a statement that can be true or false in the same way that it is a true (or false) statement that you are holding this book in your hand? Or am I giving a command, such as "Do not commit euthanasia?" Or am I expressing a feeling, perhaps one that is shared with other people, but still just a feeling?

Of course, there are connections between these three approaches to morality, although just what the connections are is the subject of ongoing philosophical debate. For example, if moral judgments are simply expressions of feeling, rather than statements that can be correct or incorrect, is practical ethics pointless?

The idea that morality is grounded in human nature has been used in both normative ethics and metaethics. Morality relates not only to practical situations but to ideas about human nature and how "moral values" fit into our scientific conception of the world.

WHAT SHOULD I DO?

Morality presents itself as a guide to how we should live and act.
There are three main theories in normative ethics (which concerns
how people *should* behave, not how they do) that tell us what morality is
all about, and help to describe what is important about living morally.

Utilitarianism: be happy

The English philosopher and political
thinker Jeremy Bentham (*see p.300*) has
been described as the modern father of
utilitarianism. He defended the "greatest
happiness principle," which claims that
an action is right if, and only if, it leads
to the greatest happiness of the greatest
number of people it affects. As such,
actions are judged not "in themselves"
but in terms of what consequences they
have. For example, a lie that maximized
happiness would be morally good.
Bentham also argued that happiness is
simply pleasure and the absence of pain,
and that the total amount of happiness
produced by an action is the sum total of
everyone's pleasures produced, minus
the sum total of everyone's pains.

Commenting on this theory, John
Stuart Mill (*see pp.308–9*) argued that
human happiness is more complex than
Bentham thought. Pleasures and pains
are not all equally important; some types
of pleasure are "higher" than others and
more important to human happiness.
If everyone compares two pleasures and
agrees that the first is "more desirable
and valuable" than the second, then the
first is a "higher" pleasure. To make one
pleasure more valuable, people have to
prefer it even if having that pleasure
brings more pain with it.

HIGHER GROUND

As long as our basic needs are met, Mill
thought, people will prefer the pleasures
of thought, feeling, and imagination to
pleasures of the body and the senses,
even though our "higher" capacities also
mean we can experience terrible pain,
boredom, and dissatisfaction. For
example, the pleasure of being in love
carries the pain of longing and the
potential pain of breaking up. But
people still prefer being in love to
a delicious dinner. This isn't about
quantity of pleasure, but about
quality. Happiness is distinct from
contentment or satisfaction.

"BETTER TO BE A
HUMAN BEING
DISSATISFIED
THAN A PIG
SATISFIED."

J. S. Mill, *On Utilitarianism*

Mill argued that happiness
is partly about the quality
of our pleasures. Humans
have more valuable
pleasures than do pigs.

People often object to utilitarianism on the grounds that we can't foresee the consequences of an action, to discover whether it maximizes happiness or not. But we can easily reply that an action is right if we can reasonably expect that it will maximize happiness. Mill thought that we have a good sense of this from our inherited moral rules. These have developed as people have discovered which actions tend to produce happiness. Lying and stealing don't; keeping promises and being kind do.

ACTS OF EVIL?

A serious problem with utilitarianism is that it doesn't rule out any type of action. If torturing a child produces the greatest happiness, then it is right to torture a child. Suppose a group of child abusers only find and torture abandoned children. Only the child suffers pain (no one else knows about their activities). But the abusers derive a great deal of happiness. So more happiness is produced by torturing the child than not, so it is morally right. This is clearly unacceptable.

Utilitarians can reply that it is very probable that someone will find out, and then many people will be unhappy. But other people finding out isn't what makes torturing children wrong. Child abuse is morally bad in itself, we may argue.

Happiness is not always good, it seems, so morality can't be founded wholly upon the promotion of happiness.

Utilitarianism is often accused of ignoring the question of justice. The greatest happiness does not necessarily involve happiness being distributed fairly, or provide for the needs of the vulnerable few.

Furthermore, because we are aiming only to maximize happiness, the distribution of happiness—who gets happy by how much—is irrelevant. This fails to respect justice.

INDIVIDUAL NEEDS

Finally, utilitarianism does not consider the special relation we have to our actions and our lives. In the utilitarian society, my happiness doesn't count any more than anyone else's when I'm considering what to do. I am affected more often and more deeply by my actions than are other people—but that's all. The actions I take during my life are ultimately just a means of generating the greatest overall happiness.

Enjoying cruelty, as the Roman emperor Caligula did, is bad—other people suffer, and it is clearly wrong "in itself."

This is objectionable. Not only does it ignore the natural emphasis we place on our own wellbeing and that of those closest to us, it also makes morality too demanding. For example, every time I buy some music, I could have given the money to charity. That would create more happiness, since other people need food more than I need music. But because some people will always be in dire poverty, it will thus never be right for me to do something just for myself if I have more than the bare minimum I need to get by.

Doing one's duty

Deontologists believe that morality is a matter of duty (the Greek word *deon* means "one must"). Duties are usually understood in terms of particular actions we must do or refrain from. It is the action itself that is right or wrong: it is not made right or wrong by its consequences. Actions are understood in terms of intentions. For example, a person may kill someone else, but not all "killings" are the same type of action, morally speaking. If the person deliberately intended to kill someone, that is very different from an accidental killing or if the person was only intending to defend themselves against an attack. Deontologists propose that we should judge whether an action is right or wrong by the agent's intention. This does not make moral judgment subjective. What matters is the real reason why the person chose to act as they did. It may be difficult to know what the real reason was, but that is a different point.

We each have duties regarding our own actions. I may have a duty to keep my promises, but I don't have a duty to make sure promises are kept. Deontology claims that we should

Would it be wrong to torture someone if we thought we could prevent some disaster? Deontology suggests that some acts are wrong in themselves, regardless of the consequences.

each be most concerned with complying with our own duties, not attempting to bring about the most good. In fact, all deontologists agree that there are times when we should not maximize the good, because doing so would be to violate a duty.

Most deontological theories recognize two classes of duties. First, there are general duties toward other human beings. These are mostly prohibitions: do not lie, do not murder, and so forth. But some may be positive, such as helping people in need. Second, there are duties we have because of the particular personal or social relationships we have with particular other people. For example, if you are a parent, you have a duty to provide for your children.

OBJECTIONS TO DUTY

Utilitarians often object to deontology on the grounds that it is irrational. If it is my duty not to lie, this must be because there is something bad about lying. But then, if lying is bad, surely we should try to ensure that there are as few lies as possible. Utilitarianism views all reasoning about what to do as means-to-an-end reasoning: it is rational to do whatever brings about a good end. And surely more of something that is good is better. So, according to utilitarianism, I should prevent the proliferation of lies, even if that requires me to lie. Deontology rejects this view, and with it the means-to-an-end reasoning of utilitarianism.

Intuitionists (*see p.114*), such as the Scottish philosopher W. D. Ross, argue that there are several irreducible and distinct duties, and we have to use our moral intuition (an innate sense of the indefinable properties of goodness) to tell what these are. Other philosophers argue that our duty is to do what God commands (*see p.107*), which we may discover through scripture or by consulting our conscience.

CONFLICTS OF DUTY

Does deontology provide any guidance when our duties appear to conflict? Most deontologists hold that a real conflict of duties can never occur. If there appears to be a conflict, we have misunderstood what at least one duty requires of us. So either duties never conflict, which means that we have to formulate our duties very carefully, or duties can "give way:" in cases of conflict, one will yield and no longer be a duty in that situation. But then which duty should give way? Deontologists may reply that this lack of guidance is a strength of the theory. Choices in life are difficult and require insight.

Grounding morality in reason

Immanuel Kant (*see pp.294–7*) argues that moral principles can be derived from practical reason alone. If this is true, he thought, we could explain the characteristics of morality. Morality, he claimed, is universal: a set of rules that are the same for everyone. It must be possible that everyone could act morally (even if it is very unlikely that they will). Reason, too, is universal, the same in all rational beings. Morality and rationality are categorical; the demands to be rational and moral don't change depending on what we want. And we think that morality applies to all and only rational beings, not just human beings. Morality doesn't apply to beings that can't make rational choices, such as dogs and cats (pets may misbehave, but they don't act morally wrongly).

"MORAL LAWS HAVE TO HOLD FOR EVERY RATIONAL BEING AS SUCH."

Kant, *Groundwork to a Metaphysics of Morals*

MORAL MAXIMS

As rational animals, Kant argued, we make choices on the basis of "maxims." Maxims are Kant's version of intentions, our personal principles that embody our reasons for doing things, such as "to have as much fun as possible." If it is possible for everyone to act morally, and our actions are based on our maxims, then a maxim that is morally permissible must be one that everyone could act on.

Suppose you want to give a gift to a friend, but you can't afford it, so you steal it from a store. Your maxim is something like: "To steal something I want if I can't afford it." This can only be the right thing to do if everyone could do it. But not everyone can: if we all just helped ourselves to whatever we wanted, the idea of "owning" things would disappear. Because you can't steal

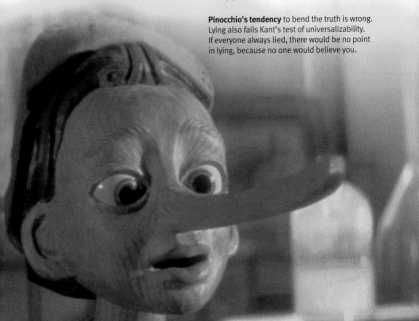

Pinocchio's tendency to bend the truth is wrong. Lying also fails Kant's test of universalizability. If everyone always lied, there would be no point in lying, because no one would believe you.

something that isn't owned by someone else it is logically impossible for everyone to steal things. And so stealing the gift is wrong, according to Kant.

We can discover our duties by testing our maxims against what Kant called the categorical imperative (an imperative being a command): "Act only on that maxim through which you can at the same time will that it should become a universal law." Kant does not claim that an action, such as stealing, is wrong because we wouldn't like the consequences if everyone did it. His test is whether we could choose ("will") for our maxim to be a universal law. His test is about what it is possible to choose, not what we like to choose. Choosing to behave in a way that it is impossible for everyone to follow is both immoral and irrational, and should be rejected.

Our ability to choose rationally gives us all equal dignity and value, whoever we are and whatever circumstances—affluent or poor—we are in.

Kant also argued that we should "act in such a way that you always treat humanity, whether in your own person or in the person of any other, never simply as a means, but always at the same time as an end." By using the word "humanity," Kant emphasizes our ability to rationally determine which ends to adopt and pursue. The ability to make free, rational choices gives human beings dignity.

To treat someone's humanity simply as a means, and not also as an end, is to treat the person in a way that undermines their power to make a rational choice themselves. Coercing someone or lying to them, and thus not allowing them to make an informed choice, are prime examples.

OBJECTIONS TO KANT

Philosophers have objected that Kant's categorical imperative is a flawed test. Couldn't any action be justified, as long as we phrase the maxim cleverly? In stealing a gift (*see p.105*), I could claim that my maxim is "To steal gifts when I am 30 years old." Universalizing this maxim, only people who are 30 can steal, and then only gifts. The case would apply so rarely that there would be no general breakdown in the concept of private property. So it would be perfectly possible for this law to apply to everyone. Kant's response is that his theory is concerned with my actual maxim, not some made-up one. If I am honest with myself, I have to admit that being 30 isn't one of my reasons at all. However, Kant's test delivers strange results. Suppose a hardworking sales assistant, who hates the work, wins the lottery and vows "never to sell anything to anyone again, but only ever to buy." This doesn't seem morally wrong, but it cannot pass the test. If no one ever sold things, how could anyone buy them? So perhaps it is not always wrong to do things that require other people to do something different.

BECAUSE GOD SAYS SO

One reason for believing that certain types of action are right or wrong in themselves is because God wills it and has commanded us to do or not to do them. Since the observance of God's commands is a fundamental part of many major religions, philosophers have tried to establish whether it is a good reason: however, it faces a famous objection, developed from an argument in Plato's *Euthyphro*.

DIVINE COMMAND

Is morality whatever God wills, or a set of values that God wishes us to adhere to because they are good? If goodness is independent of God, this places a moral restraint on God. However, if good is whatever God wills, then the idea of God being good doesn't say anything substantial about God; whatever God wills is by definition good. If goodness is whatever God wills, God invents morality. But if God has no independent reasons to will what he does, there is no rational structure to morality.

Are God's commands morally good simply because they are issued by God?

This would make morality arbitrary. Furthermore, it would then be right to slaughter innocent children if God willed it. Surely it is only right to do what God wills if what God wills is good? But how can we tell unless we have some independent standard of goodness? One response to this is to say that God's will is not arbitrary, because God is love. This doesn't make love the standard of morality by which to judge whether God's will is good, because the claim is not that the basis of morality is love, but that it is *God's* love.

If God is love and the source of morality, then, as Mother Theresa practiced, doing what is loving in God's eyes is doing what is good.

Virtue ethics

A virtuous person is someone who has morally good traits of character. We can argue that an action is right if it is an action that a virtuous person would take. A right action, then, will express morally good traits of character, and this is what makes it right. For example, telling the truth expresses honesty.

Character involves a person's dispositions that relate to what, in different circumstances, they would feel, how they think, how they react, and the sorts of choices they make and actions they perform. So someone is short-tempered if they are disposed to feel angry quickly and often, or intemperate if they get drunk often and excessively. A virtue of character is a character trait that disposes us to feel desires and emotions "well," rather than "badly."

Our main aim, therefore, should be to develop the virtues, because then we will know what it is right to do and we will want to do it. Aristotle (*see pp.248–9*) argues that virtues are qualities that help

a person to "live well:" an achievement defined by human nature. His term for "living well"—*eudaimonia*—has been translated as "happiness," but the idea is closer to "flourishing." We have an idea of what it is for a plant or animal to "flourish," and we can provide an analysis of its needs and judge when those needs are met. According to virtue theory, moral philosophy should concern itself with defining similar conditions for growth in the lives of human beings. Living involves choosing and acting as a central part, but also involves the nature of one's relationships with others and the state of one's "soul."

VIRTUE AND REASON

Because human beings are rational, for a human being to live well, he or she must live "in accordance with reason." If we feel emotions and desires, and make choices "well" (virtuously), we feel and choose "at the right times, with reference to the right objects, toward the right

Some people, such as Desmond Tutu, Gandhi, or the Dalai Lama, seem to demonstrate Aristotle's view that virtue is central to the "good life."

ARE VIRTUES RELATIVE?

Different cultures have thought different traits to be "virtues." The Victorians thought chastity was important, but it no longer has the same value in modern European culture. So, does virtue ethics entail relativism—the view that right and wrong are defined by culture alone? All human beings live in some culture or other, and the traits we need to be able to lead good lives in our own culture vary. However, many virtues are reflections of universal human nature: everyone needs courage, loyalty, temperance, and so on, because life throws the same challenges at us all. So some key virtues aren't relative.

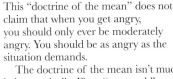

The honor of women in European cultures traditionally resided in chastity. Some virtues change status as cultures develop—but many do not.

people, with the right motive, and in the right way." The virtue of practical wisdom helps us know what is "right" in each case. This knowledge is practical knowledge of how to live a good life. I need to be able to understand my situation and how to act in it. Yet circumstances always differ, and so, Aristotle argues, ethical understanding is not something that can be taught, for what can be taught is general, not particular. Rules and principles will rarely apply in any clear way to real situations. Instead, moral knowledge is only acquired through experience.

THE MIDDLE WAY

Aristotle defends the idea that a virtuous response or action is intermediate: just as there is a right time at which to feel angry (or any particular emotion), some people can feel angry too often, about too many things, toward too many people, and so on. Other people may not feel angry often enough, or with regard to enough objects and people (perhaps they don't understand how people are taking advantage of them). The virtue is the intermediate state between the two vices of "too much" and "too little."

There are child prodigies in chess, math, and music, but never in morality. Aristotle argues that moral knowledge comes with experience.

This "doctrine of the mean" does not claim that when you get angry, you should only ever be moderately angry. You should be as angry as the situation demands.

The doctrine of the mean isn't much help practically. First, "too much" and "too little" aren't quantities on a single scale. Knowing the "right time, right object, right person, right motive, right way" is much more complicated than that. Second, there is no independent sense of "intermediate" that helps us answer the questions of how often we should get angry, and how angry we should get.

But virtue theory doesn't aim to provide an exact method for making decisions. Practical wisdom is not a set of rules, but it does provide some kind of guidance. It suggests we think about situations in terms of the virtues. Rather than ask "Could everyone do this?," as Kant suggests, or "What will bring about the best consequences?," as utilitarianism suggests, we can ask a series of questions: "Would this action be kind/courageous/loyal...?" If we think of actions as expressions of virtue, this approach could be very helpful.

AN EXERCISE IN PRACTICAL ETHICS

Stem cell research in its most controversial form involves removing an inner cell mass from, and so destroying, a five- to seven-day-old embryo. These cells have the potential to become any type of cell: brain, heart, liver, bone. Researchers believe stem cells may help them to treat diseases, so we have a strong reason to pursue this research. But is it morally permissible to destroy embryos for this reason?

A RIGHT TO LIFE

Deontologists (*see p.104*) might ask if embryos have a right to life. If the embryo has a soul—traditionally said to be acquired at conception—it has a right to life. However, two out of three embryos are rejected naturally by the uterus. If each has a soul, that seems a moral tragedy. Other grounds for believing human beings have a right to life—such as reason, the use of language, the depth of our emotional experience, our self-awareness, and our ability to distinguish right from wrong—are not things that an embryo has. But people with severe mental disabilities and senile dementia may also not have these characteristics, yet we do not normally think it is permissible to destroy them. One important characteristic they do have is sentience, the basic consciousness of perception, pleasure, and pain. However, embryos do not have this capacity in the earliest stages of their development. So if the right to life depends on sentience, then week-old embryos do not have a right to life.

A STOLEN FUTURE?

We may argue that the embryo has a right to life because it has the potential to become a person with a right to life in the future. However, it is not normal to treat potential as though it were already realized. Someone who has the potential to become a millionaire cannot spend the money yet. Furthermore, on

Many people are happy to eat meat, and yet believe humans have a sacred right to life. But are we different from animals? Stem cell research forces us to question our ethical assumptions.

its own, the embryo doesn't have the potential to become a person: we must implant it in a uterus first. Does it have a right to our help? A utilitarian (*see p.102*) may argue that we are depriving the embryo of future happiness. But the embryos used in stem cell research are the surplus embryos created in IVF (in vitro fertilization) programs, which would otherwise be disposed of. If this objection has any bite, then it is as an objection to IVF treatment, which creates the embryos in the first place. However, preventing IVF treatment will prevent many couples from becoming happy, and will not grant life or happiness to any extra human embryos. Virtue theory (*see p.108*) would

Advances in the field of genetic engineering have meant increased use of fertilized eggs for research and therapeutic purposes. But do we have the right to "tamper" with life in this way?

comment that the meaning of creating and using a human life —in embryonic form—has not been properly explored. Embryos share our "flesh and blood," and it would be callous or disrespectful to create a human life just in order to benefit another life. However, these embryos are created in IVF programs. So do the benefits granted by IVF treatment justify the expense, the creation of many embryos, and so on? Does IVF change the meaning of parenthood for the worse? If we allow that IVF is permissible, then to use embryos that would otherwise die in order to benefit other human beings seems an expression of compassion toward those who will benefit.

"THAT IN THE SOUL WHICH IS CALLED THE MIND IS, BEFORE IT THINKS, NOT ACTUALLY ANY REAL THING."

Aristotle, *On the Soul*

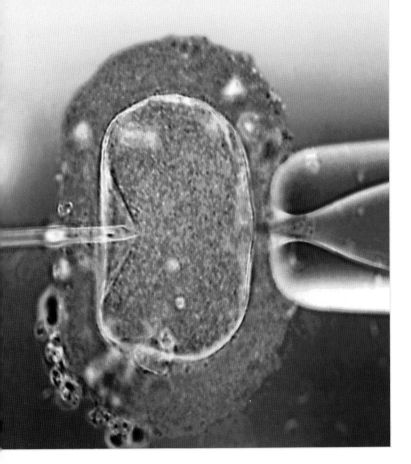

SO WHAT IS MORALITY?

The study of ethical concepts—right and wrong, good and bad—and of sentences that use these concepts is called metaethics. In metaethics, philosophers debate whether there are universal moral truths, or whether morality is simply an expression of emotions or cultural customs.

The reality of morality

"Moral realism" claims that good and bad are properties of situations and people, and right and wrong are properties of actions. Just as people can be tall or run fast, they can be morally good or bad. Just as actions can be done in 10 minutes or done from greed, they can be right or wrong. These moral properties are a real part of the world. Statements like "Murder is wrong" are expressions of beliefs, which can be true or false. Whether such statements are true or false depends on the way that the world is—on what properties an action, person, or situation actually has.

Moral realism is, for many, the "common sense" position on ethics. Many people believe that things really are right or wrong; it is not our views that make them so. Our experience of morality also suggests moral realism. First, we think we can make mistakes. Children frequently do; they have to be taught what

is right and wrong. If there were no facts about moral right and wrong, it wouldn't be possible to make mistakes. Second, morality feels like a demand from "outside" us. We feel answerable to a standard of behavior that is independent of what we want. Morality isn't determined by what we think about it. Third, many people believe in moral progress. But how is this possible, unless some views about morality are better than others? And how is that possible unless there are facts about morality?

MORE THAN A FEELING?

On the other hand, we are aware of cultural differences in moral beliefs (*see p.109*), a fact that can lead some to give up moral realism for relativism (*see p.120*). But tolerance of cultural differences tends to be quite limited. For example, very few people seem to think that because murder of members of other tribes or female

The fact that children need to be taught morality suggests that there are moral "truths" that can be learned in the same way as other facts can.

Nicolas Poussin's painting *The Judgment of Solomon* illustrates that moral decisions (in this case concerning the life of a child) can be difficult.

circumcision is morally permitted in some societies, that makes murder or female circumcision right, even in those societies. But we do know that, unlike other beliefs, morality arouses powerful emotions, and moral disputes are hard to settle. If we are inclined to think this is because there are no moral facts, we might be led to emotivism (*see p.115*).

FACTS AND VALUES

Here is the question: if there are facts about right and wrong, what sort of facts are they? How can a value (a moral "fact") be any type of fact? Values are related to evaluations. If no one valued anything, would there be any values? Facts are part of the world. The fact that dinosaurs roamed the Earth millions of years ago would be true whether anyone had found out about it or not. But it is more difficult to believe that values "exist" independently of us and our talk about values.

This comparison is unfair. There are lots of facts—for example, facts about being in love, or facts about music—that

Some facts are dependent on the human mind without being subjective. We know this piece of music by Bach is in the baroque style by its sound.

"depend" on human beings and their activities (there would be no love if no one loved anything). But they are still facts, because they are independent of our judgments, and made true by the way the world—in this case the human world—is. We can make mistakes about whether someone is in love, or whether a piece of music is baroque or classical in style.

Virtue theory provides one possible account of how moral facts relate to natural facts (*see p.108*). It claims that whether an act is right depends on whether it is what a virtuous person would do. A virtuous person is someone who has the virtues: traits of character that enable them to live a good life. What a good life is depends on human nature, and this is a matter of objective fact. So moral facts, about the good life and about right actions, are closely related to human nature, our universal desires, needs, and ability to reason.

Intuiting the truth

How do we know moral facts? If goodness just is happiness, then knowing what is good is just knowing what makes people happy. But if goodness were happiness, then asking "is it good to make people happy?" would be equivalent to asking "does making people happy make people happy?" Even if it is good to make people happy, it seems goodness is not the same as happiness. This argument applies to any account of goodness. So, intuitionists argue that goodness is a simple property that defies analysis.

Because goodness is not a natural property, we cannot know it from sense-experience. We must "intuit" it instead.

USING INTUITION

As a result, we may only be able to know about morality through intuition. But what on earth is intuition? We could argue that judgments about what is good are "self-evident." A self-evident judgment has no other evidence or proof but its own plausibility. But "self-evident" is not the same as "obvious:" our ability to make these judgments needs to develop first, and we need to consider the question very carefully. Recently, philosophers have argued that our emotions can (if virtuous) give us intuitive moral knowledge (*see pp.108–9*). For example, if I am compassionate and courageous, then I realize the importance of other people's pain, and I understand that my own fear about responding to it—while it shows me I may lose something for myself —doesn't stop me from helping them.

CAN WE AGREE?

The difficulty with "self-evident" judgments is that people can disagree about whether they are true or not. But suppose we could give reasons for thinking, for example, that pleasure is good because it forms part of a flourishing life for human beings. Is it self-evident that being part of a flourishing life makes something good? Either we say yes or we have to give another reason. Is this reason in turn self-evident? Can we escape relying on self-evident judgments? The answer is yes: when questioned, we can give reasons for believing any particular belief—but we must assume other beliefs in order to do so. We accept the set as a whole because it is coherent and makes sense of our experience.

Being orange is a simple property, but no one can explain what it is to someone who hasn't seen it. Goodness is the same.

EXPRESS YOURSELF

The English philosopher A. J. Ayer (see p.338) argued that a statement could be meaningful only if it met one of two conditions: it should be either analytic (see p.67) or empirically verifiable. This "principle of verification" implies that statements about right and wrong are meaningless. According to Ayer's principle, such statements are neither true nor false, because they do not actually state anything.

MEANING AND MORALS

If I say "murder is wrong," this is not analytic, nor can any empirical investigation show this. Instead, Ayer argued, ethical judgments express feelings. Philosophers have since rejected Ayer's principle of verification. By its own criterion, it is meaningless: the claim that "a statement only has meaning if it is analytic or can be verified empirically" is itself not analytic and cannot be verified empirically. But we can still argue that moral language is emotive: it is used to express our emotions of approval or disapproval. Moral judgments don't state facts; we use moral judgments to express our feelings and to influence the feelings

Public protests demonstrate that disagreements over moral issues are often highly emotive, and inspire people to action.

and actions of other people. But if this is all we are doing with moral language, it seems that there is no genuine discussion or reasoning in moral debate—we are just manipulating others. Emotivists respond that much moral discussion is about facts: whether a certain action or policy will have certain consequences. If we agree on all the facts, which is rare, what remains is a disagreement in attitude. This can still be discussed, because people do not have feelings or make choices in isolation. Moral disagreement, then, can be about the relations between different feelings that we have and policies we adopt.

What is going on when people disagree about a moral issue? Are they simply expressing their feelings, as A.J. Ayer (far left) argues?

"TWO THINGS FILL THE MIND WITH...
WONDER AND AWE...
THE STARRY HEAVEN
ABOVE ME AND THE
MORAL LAW WITHIN ME."

Immanuel Kant, *Critique of Practical Reason*

Are moral values facts?

That fact that moral disputes occur suggests that values are quite different from established facts. Here are three objections to moral realism, inspired by David Hume (*see pp.290–1*).

First, when two people disagree over a matter of fact, we normally know how to prove the matter one way or the other. But if two people agree over all the facts about abortion, for example, but still disagree on whether it is right or not, we cannot appeal to any "facts" in the same way.

Second, Hume notes that there always seems to be a leap in moral reasoning. We describe the facts of the case, and then we say "so he should not have done that." But how is it that we can go from talking about what is the case to talking about what should be the case? We cannot tell from what *is*, what *should* be. There is a logical gap between facts and values.

Third, moral judgments guide our behavior. If I think abortion is wrong, I will neither have nor perform an abortion nor encourage others to do so. But this is puzzling if the moral realist is correct: a fact, in and of itself, doesn't

Other people's suffering gives us a reason to help them. Moral realists argue that this claim states an objective fact, rather than an attitude.

silly. What we are doing is giving reasons that support our moral claims. For example: "eating meat is wrong, because of the suffering it causes to animals." Facts can be reasons that support moral

"HUMAN ACTIONS CAN NEVER... BE ACCOUNTED FOR BY REASON, BUT RECOMMEND THEMSELVES ENTIRELY TO THE SENTIMENTS."

David Hume, *An Enquiry Concerning the Principles of Morals*

lead to action. It seems that I need to care about the fact, and then the motivating force comes from the caring. But moral judgments are motivating in their own right. So perhaps they express not beliefs but, rather, what we care about.

MORAL FACTS ARE REASONS

In its own defense, moral realism claims that we appeal to the facts when we are trying to justify a moral judgment. If there were no connection, this would be

beliefs. It is either true or false that the practice of eating meat causes suffering to animals. The moral realist claims that whether this fact "is a reason to believe" that eating meat is wrong is also true or false. There are facts about the reasons we give for our moral judgments.

Compare reasoning in other contexts. If radiometric decay indicates that dinosaur bones are 65 million years old, this is a reason to believe that dinosaurs lived on Earth 65 million years ago. And it is a reason that supports this belief, quite independently of whether you think it is a reason or not. Facts about reasons are objective, just like facts about the natural world (natural facts). However, facts about reasons are a different type of fact: not the sort that scientific investigation can discover nor reducible to natural facts. They are normative (value-determining) facts about justification and reasoning.

We can now say that when two people agree on all the "facts" about abortion, but disagree on whether it is wrong, it is true that the dispute isn't settled by appealing to natural facts. Both parties can accept the natural fact that a fetus could become a human being without agreeing that this is a (strong) reason for thinking abortion is wrong. If we resolved the dispute over reasons as well, we would resolve the moral dispute. At least one person is making a mistake, because they are not seeing certain natural facts as the reasons they are.

Likewise, Hume is right to notice the logical gap between natural facts and moral judgments. However, the gap is bridged by facts about reasons, which determine whether a natural fact counts as a reason for believing a certain value judgment. It is still true that natural facts don't logically entail value judgments, but then it is rare for reasons to entail the judgments they support.

MORALS AND MOTIVATION

What about being motivated by moral judgments? There are two possible responses here. The first is to argue that because moral judgments are statements of fact, they are not motivating. There are some people, and perhaps all of us at certain times, for whom statements about morality are not motivating. They just don't care about morality. Moral judgments, then, are only motivating to people who care about morality.

The second response is to agree that moral judgments are motivating. But this is not puzzling, since they are not statements about natural facts, but judgments about what we have reason to do. And judgments about reasons are motivating on their own, because we are rational creatures.

Not everyone cares about morality. Certainly, the affectation of indifference to conventional morality is a part of youth counterculture in the West.

Is morality relative?

Morality can vary from culture to culture. How can we account for this? We could argue that different cultures, with their different ethical practices, are all trying to get at the truth about ethics, just as scientists are trying to find out the truth about the world. Or we can say that ethical practices are simply part of a culture's way of life. The relativist will say the latter. Relativism claims that two cultures that disagree over a moral practice are actually making claims that are, respectively, "true for them."

We don't tend to say this about scientific claims (for example, some cultures thought stars were pinpricks in the fabric of heaven—but they were just wrong, as stars have never been pinpricks). Why not? Because we have a different idea of how scientific disagreements can be resolved. With science, the best explanation is that the scientific theories we have agreed upon represent how the world is. In other words, the world guides our investigations, and we confirm or

Life in New York is very different from life in Fiji (*pictured, facing page*). Is it plausible to think that the different ethical practices of different cultures are all attempts to find the ethical "truth?"

RELATIVELY TOLERANT

Many people tend to think that relativism and tolerance go together, while moral realism implies moral imperialism. But this is a mistake. Tolerance is itself a moral value. "You should tolerate other cultures' values, because moral values are relative" is only true if your culture has the moral value of toleration. Suppose another culture is not tolerant. Relativism would suggest that we cannot object. But should we tolerate the intolerant? Few people think that tolerance is more important than preventing a racist murder, say; yet any number of cultures around the world have used racist ideas to justify murder. So if we believe that tolerance is a key moral value then perhaps we should not be relativists after all!

falsify hypotheses through experiment, until we arrive at certain understandings about what the world is like. Science investigates the physical world. If we look at the history of culture and how ethical practices develop, it is hard to see how different cultures might discover "the truth" about morality and ethical

F.D.R. Drive
Pearl St.

Centre St. NORTH
Chambers St. KEEP LEFT

Park Row SOUTH
KEEP RIGHT

F.D.R.
Pearl S

Welcome
anhattan

EXIT 10

EXIT 15

Island cultures in the South Pacific have different values from those found in urban Western environments. Life is different, and the customs and traditional prohibitions of the area reflect that.

conduct for a single ethical world. Relativism argues that ethical practices have developed to help people find their way around a social world. But there are many social worlds and many cultures, and they have, over time, developed different ways of doing things.

So, there is not just one social world that can guide ethical practices toward universal agreement. This doesn't mean that all social practices are acceptable—that no individual and no practice can be condemned morally. People do wrong all the time, and relativism does not pretend otherwise. But it claims that to condemn an action or practice as wrongful, one must use resources from within the culture to which that practice or individual belongs. You cannot judge a practice from outside its culture.

Slavery is no longer morally acceptable in most cultures. Is this simply change at work, or is real moral progress being made?

DOUBTS ABOUT RELATIVISM

Moral realists have three responses to cultural relativism. First, they can say that different ethical practices reflect the different environmental conditions in which cultures are situated, but not different ethical principles. For example, we try to keep our old people alive for as long as possible, whereas the Inuit used to abandon them on ice floes to die. But this doesn't mean killing old people is right for the Inuit and wrong for us. It is simply due to the conditions in which the Inuit lived. The demands of survival in a harsh environment meant that individuals who could no longer contribute to the welfare of the community had to be abandoned. It would be right for us to do the same thing if we lived in their conditions, and wrong for them if they lived in ours.

Second, most cultures around the world have prohibitions on killing, lying, and theft, and encourage care of the weak. Realists draw attention to just how many general ethical principles and virtues are shared by different cultures.

Third, realists draw attention to moral progress. We have become more humane than in the past, and we agree more widely about moral judgments, because we are discovering moral truths.

PHILOSOPHY OF MIND

What is the mind? This question lies at the very heart of the philosophy of mind and, despite the best efforts of some of the world's greatest thinkers, both philosophical and scientific, it remains profoundly puzzling. Philosophy of mind is one of the busiest branches of philosophy, and home to some of the most interesting recent developments.

The quest to understand the mind has led philosophers down many avenues of inquiry. They include such puzzles as the nature of consciousness, and the relationship between consciousness and the physical world. A related area of interest is aboutness, or "intentionality." How can our thoughts be about other things? What gives them their power to represent?

Philosophy of mind also concerns perception. What is perception? Is our awareness of the world direct, or is it mediated by mental phenomena? And to what extent does the mind contribute to what we experience?

The nature of personhood and personal identity are also addressed in the philosophy of mind, asking deceptively simple questions, such as: what is a person? When we look through photograph albums, we see photos of ourselves at different stages in life. What makes each of these individuals the same person? Memory, too, is a

focus of attention. What is memory, in essence? And how is it related to our continuing identity?

It is important to distinguish philosophy of mind from scientific disciplines such as psychology. While scientific inquiries into consciousness, perception, and memory can be relevant to the philosophy of mind, the philosophical approach involves not an empirical (observation-based) investigation into these phenomena, but a logical and conceptual one. In asking "What is the mind?", philosophers of mind are usually asking not for scientifically discoverable facts about the mind, but rather what the concept of mind involves. Their method includes exploring the logical and conceptual connections that exist between mind, behavior, and our various mental capacities.

The discoveries made within the philosophy of mind can have far-reaching consequences for other branches of philosophy. For example, answers to the question "What is a person?" might have serious ramifications for moral questions about euthanasia and abortion.

Despite advances in computing, human chess players can compete successfully against machines that can calculate millions of moves per second, illustrating the astonishing power of the mind.

THE CONSCIOUSNESS PUZZLE

Each of us is conscious of a rich inner mental life of emotions, thoughts, and sensations. But how does this conscious realm relate to the physical world? Is my conscious mind something over and above what is going on physically? Or is it itself physical?

A unique experience

Bite into an apple and you will enjoy a range of conscious experiences—the sight of its colorful peel, the waxy texture of its surface, its tangy smell, the distinctively sweet taste of its flesh. They form just a tiny part of the extraordinarily rich world of conscious experience to which you have access.

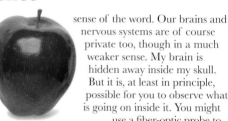

When you see an apple, it seems that your experience of its color, texture, and other qualities is uniquely your own. No one else can access it.

One interesting feature of these experiences is their privacy. When I look at a red apple, I have a "color-experience." I know what it is like for me to have that experience. No doubt you have a similar experience. But I can't know what it is like for you to have it. We cannot access each other's minds to check what sort of experiences the other is having. Our inner lives would appear to be private in a very strong

sense of the word. Our brains and nervous systems are of course private too, though in a much weaker sense. My brain is hidden away inside my skull. But it is, at least in principle, possible for you to observe what is going on inside it. You might use a fiber-optic probe to view the brain directly, or use a CAT (computed axial tomography) scanner to explore its inner workings. When it comes to my *mind*, on the other hand, it seems in principle impossible for anyone else to gain access. While you might have a conscious experience that is just like mine, you cannot have this very experience along with me.

You might ask: "What if my nervous system were wired up to yours, so that my brain received

NAGEL ON PERCEPTION

Thomas Nagel suggests that the subjective character of another being's experience is necessarily hidden from us. To illustrate this point he uses the example of bats. Bats "see" at night using echolocation. By emitting a piercing squeak inaudible to humans and then hearing the echo, a bat is able to perceive its environment in great detail. What sort of conscious experiences does a bat have when it "sees" using sound? Nagel points out that even if we knew all the physical facts concerning what goes on inside a bat when it uses echolocation, we still wouldn't know what the experience was like for the bat.

Bats hunt small insects in pitch darkness by using echolocation. What is it like to experience the world in this way? It seems we cannot know.

the exact same sorts of sensory stimulation as yours?" But even then, you would only have an experience exactly like mine. You would not have the very experience I have. My experience, it seems, remains inaccessible to you.

In 1974 the American philosopher Thomas Nagel explored the idea of the privacy of consciousness in his paper *What Is It Like to Be a Bat?* In it, he asks how we could know what it is like to experience the world from the point of view of another living being (*see box, facing page*). He concluded that however much we know about a bat's brain and body, we cannot know what it is like to *be* a bat.

MIND AND BODY DUALISMS

What is the relationship between our conscious minds and our physical bodies? According to the "substance dualist," mind and body are separate substances. But what is a substance? A substance, unlike a property, is

These ripples are simply complex movements of H_2O molecules. Some argue that conscious experiences are no more than complex brain processes.

something logically capable of existing on its own independently of other substances. This book is a substance; it can exist independently of other things. But its weight is not. The weight of the book cannot exist without the book. Weight is a mere property of those substances to which it belongs.

The substance dualist claims that the mind is a substance in its own right. René Descartes (*see pp.276–9*), perhaps the best-known of all substance dualists, believed that the mind is a "thinking" substance capable of existing independently of any physical body. A number of religions also adhere to a form of substance dualism, claiming that, after death, the mind leaves the physical body to dwell in some sort of non-physical domain.

Materialists, by contrast, believe that there is only one sort of substance— material substance. One obvious way of being a materialist is to insist that the mind is itself a material object. An obvious candidate for what this object might be is the brain. The scientist

Susan Greenfield of the University of Oxford has claimed: "You are your brain." We might also identify mental properties and processes with physical properties and processes. Scientists have discovered that the evening star is identical with the morning star, that water is identical with H_2O, and that heat is identical with molecular motion. In the same way, it has been suggested that science might establish that pain is identical with a certain brain state.

Other materialists, known as the logical behaviorists, believe that the mind is nothing over and above a set of complex physical dispositions possessed by a material substance—the body. To possess a mind is just to be disposed to behave in various complex ways. To be in pain, for example, is just to be disposed to writhe, cry out, and so on. As even a physical object can possess such physical dispositions, there is nothing problematic about a physical object possessing a mind. To suppose, along with the substance dualist, that my mind is a further "something" that exists over and above this material body and its

Substance dualism allows for the mind to exist independently of any physical body. The religious belief that we each have an immortal, immaterial soul is one version of this theory.

various behavioral dispositions is, for the logical behaviorist, to introduce an entirely mythical and superfluous "ghost in the machine."

DENYING THE MIND

A rather more radical form of materialism, eliminative materialism, denies minds exist at all. The existence of minds might seem obvious to us, but according to the eliminativist, as science progresses, it may turn out that minds are no more real than witches and demons. After all, a few hundred years ago the existence of witches and demons was also considered by many to be an obvious truth. Their evil influence was used to explain plagues and storms, for example. But of course, the proper explanation of plagues and storms turns out not to involve reference to anything remotely like witches and demons—they simply don't exist. According to the eliminativist, it is likely that the proper explanation of the behavior of human organisms will turn out not to involve reference to anything like minds or what supposedly goes on in them, such as thoughts and feelings. The correct explanation of our physical movements will involve reference to neural and other physical events that have no correlation

THE PINEAL GLAND

Descartes, faced with the problem of explaining how our immaterial minds might causally interact with our physical bodies, suggested that interaction takes place through the pineal gland, a tiny organ near the centre of the brain. Descartes believed this gland was filled with "animal spirits" which are able mechanically both to control the body and to convey perceptions from the body to the soul. Descartes thought that the pineal gland allowed communication between mind and body. We now know that the pineal gland controls melatonin levels, which govern certain metabolic functions.

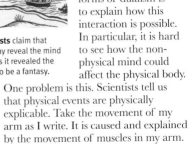

The pineal gland has been called the "third eye," an organ often represented in Buddhist art.

with anything supposedly taking place in the mind. Minds, and what goes on in them, may turn out to be a fiction.

DOUBLE IDENTITY

One of the more subtle positions on the relationship between the conscious mind and the material world is property dualism. Property dualists accept that materialists are correct in supposing there is only one sort of substance—physical substance.

But they suppose that material substances can have both physical and mental properties. And they suppose the mental properties are distinct from, and cannot be reduced to, physical properties. Some suppose, for example, that human brains possess two quite different sorts of properties: purely physical properties, such as weighing 4lbs (1.8kg), having two hemispheres, containing neurons; and mental properties, such as experiencing pain, thinking about cheese, remembering Vienna. The latter properties, says the property dualist, are extra properties that exist in addition to all the various physical properties possessed by that brain. Notice that while the property dualist

Eliminative materialists claim that science might one day reveal the mind to be a fiction, just as it revealed the notion of witchcraft to be a fantasy.

agrees with the materialist that there is only one sort of substance—material substance (so the property dualist is a materialist)—they nevertheless agree with the substance dualist that the facts about our conscious minds are facts over and above all the physical facts about us.

OBJECTIONS TO DUALISM

The best-known objection to dualism is the interaction problem. It seems obvious that our minds and bodies interact. If I consciously decide to raise my arm, I can raise it. And painkillers and psychoactive drugs illustrate that what happens in our bodies can affect what goes on in our minds. A difficulty facing all forms of dualism is to explain how this interaction is possible. In particular, it is hard to see how the non-physical mind could affect the physical body.

One problem is this. Scientists tell us that physical events are physically explicable. Take the movement of my arm as I write. It is caused and explained by the movement of muscles in my arm. These events are in turn caused by electrical stimulation passing down nerves from my brain. This brain activity itself has a physical explanation (even if

we don't know exactly what it is). But if either property or substance dualism is true, it is difficult to see how the facts about what is going on in my conscious mind could have any effect on what is going on physically. My conscious mind could be entirely removed and my body would continue on in exactly the same way, for the behavior of my body is wholly accounted for by what is going on physically. It seems, then, that my mind cannot have any effect on what is going on physically.

Some dualists accept this astonishing conclusion—that while the mind might appear to have an effect on what is happening physically, the truth is that minds are causally inert. They are like the shadow cast by a machine. Whenever the machine moves, the shadow moves, and vice versa. That might lead us to think that the shadow and the machine interact, but the truth is that the causation is in one direction only. The machine's movement causes that of the shadow, not vice versa.

Few philosophers accept that the mind is causally inert, however. Some argue that if dualism, in all its forms, has the consequence that our minds cannot affect what is going on physically, then dualism must be false. If the facts that account for my behavior are physical facts, then, if my mind is to have any causal effect on my body, the facts about my mind must also be physical facts.

ARGUMENTS FOR DUALISM

But there are also powerful-looking arguments favoring at least some form of dualism (either substance dualism or, at least, property dualism).

It is, at first glance, tempting to adopt a simple argument from appearances. It is true that pain doesn't seem like a brain state. But of course that does not establish that pain is not a brain state. After all, a glass of water does not seem like a huge collection of H_2O molecules, and yet that is precisely what it is.

Other, more sophisticated, arguments turn on conceivability. Here is an example. We are all familiar with the notion of "fool's gold": something that seems like gold, but isn't. Actually, the familiar sort of fool's gold, iron pyrites, doesn't even look or behave much like gold, though it fools the uninitiated. But we can at least conceive of a substance that is outwardly exactly like gold, only differing from it in terms of its atomic structure. If this substance were to lack the atomic number 79, which is the fundamental essence of gold, then it too would be mere "fool's gold," despite seeming exactly like the real thing. However, the philosopher Saul Kripke points out that while we can conceive

She learns something new—what it is actually like to experience the color red from the subject's point of view. She learns a new fact: the fact that the experience is *like this*. But Mary previously knew all the physical facts, so this new fact she learns is not a

"IT SEEMS... THAT MARY DOES NOT KNOW ALL THERE IS TO KNOW."

Frank Jackson, "What Mary Didn't Know"

of "fool's gold", we cannot conceive of "fool's pain." If it seems to someone that they are in pain, then they are in pain.

If pain were identical with some neurological state—brain state B, let's call it—then we would be able to conceive of fool's pain, for we could imagine that, though someone thought they were in agony, they weren't really in agony, because they were not actually in brain state B. But since fool's pain is inconceivable, pain cannot be identical with any such neurological state.

MARY'S WORLD

The philosopher Frank Jackson (*see box, right*) makes another, less technical argument supporting some form of dualism. Suppose Mary is born and raised by scientists within a wholly black-and-white environment. Her experiences are carefully controlled so that she never experiences color. She only ever experiences black, white, and various shades of gray.

Mary is clever, and when she develops into an adult, she becomes an amazingly good scientist. Mary discovers everything there is to know about what goes on inside a human being when they have an experience of "red," right down to the firing of the last neuron. When it comes to the physical facts about color perception, there is nothing Mary does not know. Then one of the scientists outside the room throws a ripe tomato into Mary's black-and-white world. Mary now has an experience she has never had before.

physical fact. Jackson concludes that there are more facts than just the physical facts alone.

So, we face a mystery. On the one hand, it seems that the mind must be physical if it is to have any causal effect on the physical world. On the other hand, Jackson's argument based on the black-and-white room, plus other impressive arguments, appear to show that the facts about our conscious experience are facts over and above the physical facts. This is a mystery with which scientists and philosophers continue to struggle.

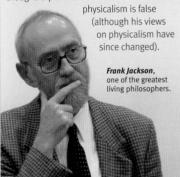

FRANK JACKSON

Distinguished Professor at the Australian National University, Frank Jackson's work covers philosophical logic, cognitive science, epistemology, metaphysics, and metaethics. Jackson is best known for his thought-experiment involving Mary and the black-and-white room. Jackson devised the thought-experiment in order to show that physicalism is false (although his views on physicalism have since changed).

Frank Jackson, one of the greatest living philosophers.

"DAVE, MY MIND IS GOING..."

Astronaut Dave Bowman shuts down the rogue computer HAL in Stanley Kubrick's 1968 film *2001: A Space Odyssey*. HAL's rebellion and acronymic name, alphabetically one letter away from the computer multinational IBM in each character, played on nascent fears of artificial intelligence.

COULD A MACHINE THINK?

Computers are developing rapidly. They can now be programmed to perform many of the tasks previously performed by human beings, and in many cases they perform better than humans. But does this mean that they might eventually think and understand?

Evolving technology

A great deal of our life is now computer-controlled, from in-car navigation and autopilots, railway systems and bank-managing, to email and word-processing. Musicians have even programmed computers to produce original, subtle, and beautiful musical compositions that other musicians have assumed must be of human origin. So it seems that computers can, in a sense, be "creative." But while computers become ever more sophisticated, could they ever reach the point where they might truly be said to think, understand, or even feel? Such

Could humans be described as "thinking machines," made of organic cells, not silicon?

a machine might at present be a technical impossibility. But as philosophers, we can still ask: is a thinking machine in principle possible? Or is there reason to suppose that, no matter how sophisticated computers might become, they will never achieve thought?

What if we were to program a computer to simulate human thought, understanding, and feeling? What if we then placed this computer inside a robot body, and covered its robot frame with fleshy material? If the computer/robot package were sophisticated enough, it might be able to convince people that it really did think and feel. But would this be a genuine thinking machine? Or would it merely simulate thinking?

In the classic film *Forbidden Planet*, from 1956, Robby the helpful robot can perform physical and mental tasks that far outstrip human capabilities, yet is programmed only to do his master's bidding.

"MY CONTENTION IS THAT MACHINES CAN BE CONSTRUCTED WHICH WILL SIMULATE THE BEHAVIOUR OF THE HUMAN MIND VERY CLOSELY."

Alan Turing, writing in 1947

It is obvious that in many cases a computer simulation will never be the real thing, no matter how closely it imitates reality. Take a computer simulation of a forest fire. You can make the simulation as perfect as you like, programming it to include every detail of the fire down to the movement of the very last atom, and it will still remain just a simulation, not a real fire. Put your hand inside the computer and it won't get burned. But in other cases, if the simulation is good enough, then it is not just a simulation. It is the real thing. Take mathematical calculation. A computer programmed to simulate mathematical calculation doesn't just simulate, it really does perform those calculations.

INTELLIGENT MACHINES

So would a computer programmed to simulate thought, understanding, and feeling really think, understand, and feel? Or would it only ever simulate? Many philosophers and scientists believe that if the computer were sophisticated enough, then there would be real thinking and feeling going on, not just simulation.

True, it is difficult to see how mere chips and wires could embody thoughts and feelings. But then it is equally mysterious that our brains are capable of doing it. We are biological machines. And we know from experience that biological machines can think and feel. So why can't man-made silicon-based

machines think and feel too? One popular reason for suspecting that no digital computer could ever think, understand, or feel is that a computer is merely a programmed device that does nothing more than mechanically respond to patterns of symbols fed into it. Does a computer flying a plane understand anything of what it is doing? Is it even aware that it is flying a plane?

The answer is no, of course. The computer is a box into which complex sequences of 1s and 0s are fed in from sensors around the plane, and out of which other sequences of 1s and 0s flow to control the ailerons, rudder, engines, and so on. The computer doesn't understand the significance of any of these complex patterns of symbols. It doesn't even know they are symbols. The computer understands nothing at all. It merely mindlessly and mechanically shuffles the symbols according to its program. But as all any digital computer does is mindlessly shuffle symbols in this way, then surely no conventional digital computer can ever understand anything.

ALAN TURING

Considered by many to be the father of computer science, Alan Turing devised a now-famous test of machine intelligence. In his 1950 article, *Computing Machinery and Intelligence*, Turing describes an "imitation game" in which a person, and a computer programmed to mimic human responses, are questioned separately by means of typed messages. The interrogator must decide which is answering. Turing claimed:

"I believe that in about fifty years' time it will be possible to programme computers... to make them play the imitation game so well that an average interrogator will not have more than a 70 per cent chance of making the right identification after five minutes of questioning."

Alan Turing was a brilliant logician who performed pioneering work in codebreaking during WWII.

THE CHINESE ROOM

In his 1980 paper *Minds, Brains and Programs* the philosopher John Searle presents one of the best-known thought-experiments in the philosophy of mind. A thought-experiment is an imaginary scenario designed to support or test a particular philosophical thesis. Searle's Chinese Room experiment is elegant and simple, and aims to show that no computer could ever achieve linguistic understanding.

MIMICKING THE MIND

Back in the late 1970s, John Searle examined some of the more dramatic claims being made by researchers working in the field of artificial intelligence (AI). One claim in particular struck Searle as unjustified. An AI researcher called Roger Shank had developed a computer program designed to mimic the responses of someone who understands a story. A story about a restaurant was fed in, followed by a series of questions, and the computer's program allowed it to provide appropriate

In Searle's experiment a person tries to match simple questions in Chinese with correct answers. This question asks "Where does the sun rise?".

answers in response. Some AI researchers claimed that Shank's computer did not just mimic understanding of the story, it genuinely understood. They also claimed that what the machine and its program did explains the ability of a human to understand the story and answer questions about it. Searle's thought-experiment is designed to demolish both these claims.

Searle imagines he is locked in a room with a list of instructions, written in English, for correlating cards with Chinese symbols on them. Outside the room are some native Chinese speakers. These

Searle's Chinese Room scenario aims to illustrate how the apparently intelligent behavior of computers does not, in fact, demonstrate real thinking and understanding.

Chinese speakers pass Searle a sequence of Chinese symbols, followed by a second sequence. Searle's instructions tell him how to follow the order and appearance of the two batches of symbols he has been given in order to select another batch to return in response.

The first batch of symbols are Chinese characters that tell a story. The second batch are questions about the story. And the English instructions are designed so that Searle can hand back appropriate answers in Chinese. The Chinese speakers outside the room would no doubt be impressed by the performance of the room's inhabitant, concluding, surely, that he or she understands Chinese. How else would this person be able to provide the correct answers?

But of course, Searle does not understand Chinese. Nor does he comprehend the story. In fact he need not even realize that the squiggles on the cards are Chinese symbols. All Searle is doing is shuffling cards with squiggles on them in accordance with the instructions. A digital computer, no matter how sophisticated, is also a symbol-shuffling device. Shank's

The answer, that the sun rises in the east, is identified by following a simple set of instructions.

computer might behave as if it understood the story and the questions fed into it. But that does not establish that the computer understands anything at all. Because it too does nothing more than shuffle symbols, it also understands nothing as far as the story and the questions are concerned. Just as Searle inside the "Chinese Room" followed his written instructions to provide answers, so the computer mechanically and mindlessly follows its program. The program allows the computer to simulate understanding, but in actual fact the computer does not understand anything at all.

SEARLE'S CONCLUSIONS

Searle does not deny that a machine might think. After all, we too are complex machines, albeit biological. But Searle thinks that in order to truly think and understand, you need to be made out of the "right kind of stuff," Searle believes that computers are not capable of thought, because they are not made of an organic brainlike substance.

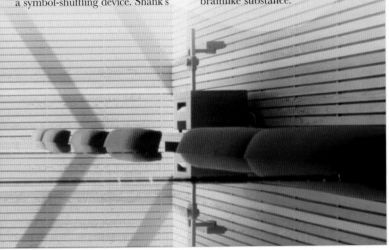

REPLICATING THE BRAIN

Perhaps those who believe computers will never be able to think and feel as we do have overlooked something. Does the machine inside the robot's head need to be a programmed, digital computer? Presumably not. What if, instead of placing a digital computer inside the robot's head, we furnish it with something much more brainlike?

Your brain is composed of billions of neurons and other cells woven together to form an immensely complex web. The neurons receive and pass on tiny electrical charges from neighboring neurons. This hub of electrical activity is connected up to your sense organs, from which complex patterns of electrical stimulation flow, allowing you to perceive the world around you. It is also connected to your muscles. By providing them with electrical stimulation, you are able to move your body around. Your brain functions, if you like, as a sort of central control room, receiving and transmitting

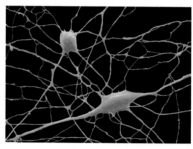

It is estimated there are about one hundred billion neurons networked together in an adult human brain. Some human neurons are several feet long.

fleshy brain does, and that controlled your muscles and body in exactly the same way too.

Such a "robot brain" is not a programmed digital computer, any more than your fleshy brain is. There is no symbol-shuffling going on inside it. So even if Searle's Chinese Room experiment (*see pp.134–5*) does establish that no programmed symbol-shuffling computer can understand, it does not establish that a robot equipped with a synthetic replica of the brain would not understand. Yet it seems Searle must deny that this robot-brained individual understands. For it is made out of the "wrong" materials.

There remains a temptation, of course, to say that, though this mechanical wonder might simulate thinking, understanding, and feeling, it is "just" a machine. But notice that this machine will itself deny that it is "just" a machine. After all, if its robot-brain architecture is exactly the same as your own, then so will be its output, with the result that its behavior will be exactly the

"YOU ARE YOUR BRAIN."

**Professor Susan Greenfield,
in the BBC TV series *Brain Story***

complex patterns of electrical energy. Now suppose that, instead of weaving together neurons to make an organic brain, we were to weave together tiny man-made inorganic electrical devices instead. If these tiny robot-neurons functioned in exactly the same way as normal neurons, interacting with their neighbors in exactly the same way as normal neurons, then we could use them in place of normal neurons. The result would be a "robot brain" that had the same causal architecture as your fleshy brain, that responded to electrical input from your senses in just the way your

same, as well. Like you, it will insist that it has thoughts and feelings. It will also be able to tell us all about what it is like to enjoy sensations or to experience love, hate, indifference, or a deep sense of longing (or at least it will be able to do so just as well as you).

If you are still convinced that there remains an essential quality to having a mind that this man-made robot must necessarily lack, then consider one last scenario. Suppose that, over the course of a year, we gradually replaced your own neurons with robot neurons one by one. If these robot neurons do exactly

Silicon-based computers can handle complex tasks, and can even be programmed to "learn" new approaches to problems.

the same physical job as your fleshy neurons (and let's just stipulate that they do), then this gradual replacement will not have any effect on your brain's functioning or on how it interacts with the rest of your body. So your outward behavior will remain entirely unaffected by the process.

If Searle is right and possessing a mind depends on what sort of material your brain is composed of, then the effect of gradually replacing your fleshy neurons with inorganic robot-equivalents should be the gradual removal of your mind.

But how plausible is this? Presumably, your mind is something you are aware of. Given your awareness of the mind you possess, you would notice if you began to lose it. And, were you aware of losing it, that is something you would mention. Yet as your organic neurons were replaced by robot neurons, there would be no change at all to your behavior. You would not report any "loss." How could you, for your behavior must remain exactly the same?

Could it be that this essential "something" that so many of us feel sure that we are inwardly aware of, and that we suppose any robot must necessarily lack, is ultimately an illusion?

THE FUTURE OF COMPUTING

In 1965, Intel founder Gordon Moore predicted that the computing power that can be fitted into a given space will double every two years. "Moore's law," as it has come to be known, has turned out to be roughly correct, although it is predicted that silicon-based computers will reach their limit in about 2015. This is largely due to overheating caused by packing circuitry onto ever-smaller pieces of silicon. To break through this "silicon barrier," new approaches to computing are being developed, including processors constructed on an atomic level that function in a completely different way to silicon chips and promise greater processing power.

Huge advances in computing have led to modern desktop computers that easily outperform the room-sized scientific machines of the 1960s.

PHILOSOPHY OF RELIGION

Philosophy of religion can perhaps be captured by the question: "What does it mean to say 'God exists?'" It asks what God is like; how we can know about God; and how religious language and belief should best be understood. In this chapter, we focus on whether God exists, and the place of reason in forming religious belief.

T he question of God's existence is central to debates in philosophy of religion. These debates usually revolve around a particular notion of God, one that arises from the Western philosophical tradition, although it has some links with ideas in other world religions. The "God of the philosophers" is defined by two closely related and fundamental concepts. First, God is the ultimate reality, the background against which everything else exists. Second, God is perfection. St. Augustine (*see pp.256–7*) wrote that to think of God is to "attempt to conceive something than which nothing more excellent or sublime exists"—or could exist, add other philosophers.

The concepts of God as perfection and as ultimate reality are linked by the idea, deriving from Plato (*see pp.244–7*), that perfection and reality are intimately connected. Simply put, what is perfect is more real than what is not. Perfection is typically thought to involve complete self-sufficiency—in other words, lacking nothing and not depending on anything. Again, this feeds back to the idea of God as the ultimate reality: that which is not the ultimate reality will depend on that which is, and so cannot be perfect.

THE NATURE OF GOD

In the Western philosophical tradition, then, perfection and ultimate reality define the nature of God. Thus a being that is not perfect and not the ultimate reality is simply not God. These twin concepts are taken to support the view of God as the omnipotent, omniscient, all-good creator of the universe, pure in mind or spirit (without a material body), and transcendent of space and (usually) time.

A great deal has been said about this notion of God—whether it is actually coherent, whether it matches the idea of God found in everyday religious faith, and even whether it is a projection of a peculiarly male fantasy of omnipotence and self-sufficiency. We will eschew these questions to ask whether such a God as this—or at least recognizably similar—exists.

The Prophet Zoroaster was the founder of the ancient Persian religion Zoroastrianism, claimed by some to be the first monotheistic faith. Zoroastrian theology concerning God, evil, souls, and other key concepts is thought to have greatly influenced later religions.

DOES GOD EXIST?

The attempt to show that it is rational to believe in God has a long history. The four arguments discussed here try to infer the existence of God from the idea of God, from the existence of the universe, from the evidence for the universe being designed, and from religious experience.

God must exist

St. Anselm (*see p.261*) argued that we can deduce the existence of God from the mere idea of God. Just by thinking about what God is, we can conclude that God must exist, like so:

By definition, God is that being greater than which none can be conceived.
God can be conceived of as just an idea, or as really existing.
It is greater to exist than not to exist.
Therefore, God must exist.

This argument is known as the ontological argument.

An 11th-century monk named Gaunilo replied that you could prove anything perfect must exist by this argument. For example, I can conceive of the perfect island, "greater than which cannot be conceived;" therefore, such an island must exist, because it would be less great if it did not. But this is ridiculous. There is clearly no such island. You cannot

Santa does not exist, but wouldn't it be better if he did? Nonexistent presents aren't as good as real ones!

infer the existence of something from the idea of its being perfect. St. Anselm was aware of this problem, and responded that the ontological argument works only for God, because the relationship between God and greatness or perfection is unique.

GOD THE GREATEST

Islands are not perfect by definition. Perfection is something an island can have or not have. An imperfect island is still an island, because perfection is an "accidental" property of an island, not an "essential" one. An essential property is one that something must have in order to be the thing that it is. By contrast, God must be the greatest conceivable being. By definition, God would not be God if there were some being even

We can think of a perfect island, but that does not mean such an island exists. Gaunilo objected that the same is true when thinking of God.

greater than God. Being the greatest conceivable being is an essential property of God. But to qualify as the greatest conceivable being, God must exist.

EXISTENCE AND PERFECTION

St. Thomas Aquinas (*see pp.264–7*) was unconvinced by Anselm's response. Existence, he said, is not a perfection, something that makes a being greater. So the argument does not show that God exists. According to Aquinas, it can, at most, show only that there is some link between the concept of God and the concept of existence, in that one requires existence while the other does not.

There is a further worry about the ontological argument. Suppose I define a "widget" as something that is round, red, and weighs five tons. I then define a "wodget" as something that is round, red, weighs five tons, *and exists*. The only difference between the two objects is that one exists and the other does not. I can easily conceive of a widget, but can I conceive of a wodget? Surely, if there are no widgets, then when I try to conceive of a wodget, I actually only manage to conceive of a widget. Because the thing I conceive of does not really exist, it

The Norse god Thor was known for his terrible temper. But God is not God unless perfect—which puts Thor out of the running.

obviously cannot be a wodget. A similar worry applies to Anselm's argument. The first premise asserts that I can conceive of "a being greater than which none can be conceived"— namely, God. But is the being I conceive of God? Not if God doesn't exist! So the argument appears to be question-begging: it presupposes God exists.

KANT'S OBJECTION

Immanuel Kant (*see pp.294–7*) is thought to have defeated the ontological argument, at least in this form, once and for all. According to Kant, the argument wrongly assumes that existence is a property. But things do not "have" existence in the same way that they "have" other properties. Consider whether the statement "God exists" is analytic or synthetic (*see p.67*). According to St. Anselm, it must be analytic—the concept "God" contains the idea of existence, so "God does not exist" is a contradiction in terms. But, Kant claims, existence does not add anything to, or define, a concept. To say something exists merely means that some object corresponds to the concept.

Existence, Kant concluded, is not part of any concept, even the concept of God. Therefore, it is not true that "God exists" must be true.

The beginning of everything

The question that lies at the heart of the "cosmological argument" for God's existence is "Why does anything exist—why *something* rather than *nothing*?" The argument is that unless God exists, this question is unanswerable.

A famous version of the argument, known as the Kalam argument, asks about causes. Of anything that exists and had a beginning, we can ask what caused it to exist. Of each of us, our parents are the immediate cause. But what caused them? Tracking back through time, we arrive at the beginning of the universe, around 13 billion years ago (scientists say). But what caused the universe? Something can't come out of nothing. What we need, it seems, is a cause which itself has no cause: only God fits the bill.

BEGINNINGS AND CAUSES

The Kalam argument assumes that every beginning has a cause, and that something cannot emerge out of nothing. David Hume *(see pp.290–1)* argued that we cannot know the truth of either of these claims: we can only establish them through experience. And although our experience is that everything so far has a cause, does this principle apply to the beginning of the universe? We cannot answer this question with any certainty, because we do not have enough experience of universes beginning!

Furthermore, the beginning of the universe was not an event like those that happen within the universe. It did not take place in space or time, since both came into existence along with the universe. So perhaps we cannot apply what we do know about beginnings to this case. As Bertrand Russell *(see pp.322–3)* put it: "the universe is just there, and that's all."

Could this universe have been caused by a previous (or another) universe, and so on, infinitely? In other words, rather than see the beginning of the universe as a creative act of God, we may conclude there is just an infinite regress *(see p.213)* of causes. Something has always existed.

The concept of infinite regress means, quite literally, that we cannot trace everything back to a single starting point —that there was no beginning, ever. Because the universe exists, claims this response, something that is in fact infinite (a series of causes) also exists.

While the idea of infinity makes sense, does it make sense to think that something infinite actually exists? There may be an infinity of causes (universe preceding universe), but this does not represent a particular (very large) number of previous universes, because infinity itself is not a number. Therefore, each new cause (universe) does not add one more cause to the series, since $\infty + 1 = \infty$. How, then, could this universe be one more universe coming into existence, if an infinity of universes preceded it?

Puzzles also abound about the notion of "preceding" universes. Since the start of this universe was also the beginning of time as we know it, it is not correct to say that another universe existed *before* this one. It may seem completely paradoxical, but if science is right, there is no such

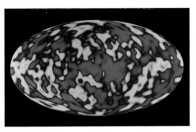

Radiation from the Big Bang detected by the Cosmic Background Explorer satellite seems to date it to some 13 billion years ago. To find the cause of the universe, we must look "outside" it. But there is no time before the beginning of time itself for anything else to exist.

time as 20 billion years ago; time itself began with the universe.

We noted that the question at the heart of the cosmological argument is "Why something rather than nothing?" If we say that something exists because something has always existed, we have still not answered the question of *why* anything exists at all. Although any event can be explained in terms of its cause, we may wonder what explains why the whole series of causes exists—finite or infinite.

The San people of the Kalahari believe that the universe was created out of nothing. While this is not a scientific explanation, it may nevertheless be a viable solution to the cosmological argument. What could precede the beginning of everything except nothing?

Must gods be perfect? Monotheistic belief systems tend to take the perfection of a single supreme God as read, but in faiths with many gods, human flaws may be tolerated: the Jain god Bahubali, whose statue this nun is tending, had to shed his pride to attain enlightenment.

AN ALTERNATIVE APPROACH

The philosopher of religion Richard Swinburne (b.1934) accepts that the objections to the cosmological argument (see p.142) show that God's existence is not logically proven. The argument, he says, should be understood as an inference that God is the best explanation for the existence of the universe, just as the best explanation for the existence of a painting is that an artist created it.

PERSONALIZED CREATION

Considered on its own, the claim "God exists" is very improbable. But in light of the cosmological argument, says Swinburne, it becomes more likely. When we also consider the arguments about design (see p.147–9) and religious experience (see p.150), it is more probable that God exists than that God does not.

Is God's existence the *best* explanation for the existence of the universe? The problem with scientific accounts is that science must assume scientific laws and the existence of something in order to provide an explanation. However, science itself cannot fully explain the fundamental scientific laws —*where* they come from or *why* they

Swinburne says that a creator God is the best and simplest explanation of the universe.

are the way they are—because all scientific explanations presuppose the existence of laws. And if we explain this universe in terms of another universe, we then have to explain the existence of that universe. Swinburne claims we need a different kind of explanation.

What he is referring to is a "personal" explanation based on what people do according to their beliefs, desires, and purposes. We explain the products of human activity, such as books and works of art, in terms of the intentions of the person who made them. The hypothesis that God exists and intended to create the universe (including its laws) provides a personal explanation for the existence of the universe.

Explaining design and order

What can explain the apparent order and design in the universe? According to the "teleological argument" for God's existence, only a mind, a designer, can properly explain the order we see around us. A traditional form of this argument, famously expressed and criticized by David Hume (*see pp.290–1*), uses the following analogy. Throughout nature, and particularly in living things, means seem very well adapted to ends. All parts of an eye, for example, are arranged so that they work together to provide vision, just as a human designer arranges the parts of a watch so that they work together to tell the time. But nature is far more impressive than a watch, so the designer must likewise far exceed our own power and intelligence. And as all parts of nature are so well adapted for their purpose, we suppose there to be a single designer.

EVOLUTION AS DESIGNER?

This analogy, Hume points out, is very weak. Human artefacts, such as watches, are not very much like natural things: watches are not alive and are not able to reproduce. Nature, or the universe as a whole, is even less like a watch.

The theory of evolution by natural selection, proposed by English naturalist Charles Darwin (1809–82) in 1859, shows how the *appearance* of design can occur naturally. Millions of random mutations take place in organisms. Some of these coincidentally help an organism to survive and reproduce, and are passed on to successive generations. Eventually they become an essential part of the organism. So organisms may appear to be designed, but they are the product of coincidence.

But what explains evolution? Perhaps God set up nature in such a way that life evolves by natural selection. Charles Darwin himself accepted this view.

A BOTCHED JOB?

Hume says that even if we can infer that the universe is designed, we cannot infer that the designer is God. It would seem that the designer needs more training—examples of poor design, such as natural evil (*see p.153*), suggest that the universe is the work of an apprentice. If we think evil is deliberate, rather than evidence of bad work, we should not think of the designer as good. Nor can we infer that God is infinite, since the universe is not. Finally, we cannot say that the designer of the universe also created it. To all this, Swinburne (*see facing page*) would reply that equating the designer to the traditional conception of God is the simplest solution.

If the universe is like a human artefact, being designed and created by an intelligence, should we infer that the designer is perfect, a real craftsman, or a bit of a bungler?

FINE TUNING AND INTELLIGENT DESIGN

While Darwinian ideas (*see p.147*) undermined arguments based on the analogy between living things and human artefacts, the science of cosmology has recently provided evidence of just how improbable a universe with life actually is. Cosmologists agree that at the moment of the Big Bang, matter-energy had to have a precise quantity, density, and initial velocity to create the conditions in which life could evolve.

AN INEVITABLE UNIVERSE?

Science, claims Richard Swinburne (*see p.146*), cannot explain such fine tuning. But if God made the universe and intended for life to evolve, then we would expect exactly the laws there are.

Do we really need an explanation for why the universe appears designed? Some things that seem coincidental are in fact inevitable (*see p.200; The gambler's fallacy*). Suppose that there are or have been millions of universes, each with different laws but few with life. With enough universes, a universe such as ours is bound to exist, and thus so would life. It doesn't need any special explanation: it simply has to happen.

For stars to form, the force of the Big Bang could not vary by more than 1 in 10 to the power of 60. That is as precise as hitting a 1 in (2.5 cm) target at the other side of the observable universe!

However, this argument only works if it is true—we have to assume the existence of huge numbers of other universes, which are inaccessible to us and for which we have no evidence. Swinburne claims that the existence of just one universe, designed by God, is a far simpler and better explanation.

INTELLIGENT DESIGN

The American biochemist Michael Behe (*b.1952*) has challenged the view that evolution can account for the "irreducible complexity" of living organisms. Behe defines irreducible complexity as "a single system which is composed of several interacting parts that contribute to the basic function, and where the removal of any one of the parts causes the system to effectively cease functioning." How can this be,

since whole systems do not evolve at once, but piecemeal? Yet without the whole system, each part would be useless and so would not evolve.

Many of the things we design are irreducibly complex. Consider a mousetrap: without all the parts present and in working order, you will never trap mice. Irreducible complexity, Behe argues, is evidence of design. The mechanism that propels bacteria consists of over 40 distinct parts. Without any one of these parts, the whole thing would be useless and bacteria would be unable to move.

This microbe's propelling "tail" has many working parts. Behe sees this as pointing to intelligent design.

Behe's argument understands each part in a system only as an element of that very system. But it often happens that something that evolved for one function is "coopted" into doing other tasks. Certain parts of the bacterial propulsion system, for example, work well as a kind of cellular pump in the absence of the rest of the system. They may have had nothing at all to do with movement when they first evolved.

Also, adaptations that are minor improvements initially can become essential components as an organism continues to evolve. Air bladders that functioned as lungs were advantageous, but not essential, for fish that made brief forays onto dry land. As they evolved into terrestrial creatures, lungs became essential for survival. However, that does not mean that lungs cannot be explained by natural selection. Natural selection can account for irreducible complexity.

"CELLS ARE SIMPLY TOO COMPLEX TO HAVE EVOLVED RANDOMLY; INTELLIGENCE WAS REQUIRED TO PRODUCE THEM."

Michael Behe, "Molecular Machines" (1998)

Knowing God via religious experience

Discussions of religious experience in philosophy generally focus on those experiences in which individuals feel that they are directly aware of God. To defend the view that these are genuine encounters with God, some philosophers compare such experiences to sensory perception—that is, an immediate awareness via our awareness that has no true sensory content. The person concerned feels they are immediately aware of God. This awareness tends temporarily to block out everything else, sometimes even to the degree that the distinction between the person and what they are aware of disappears ("mystical union").

"MY SOUL IS NOW SATISFIED BY NOTHING LESS THAN GOD."

St. Theresa of Avila (1515–82)

senses of something other than oneself. Unless we have good reason to doubt them, we usually treat perceptual experiences as *veridical*, meaning that they are truthful and based on reality. Furthermore, the fact that other people have similar perceptual experiences supports the claim that perceptual experiences show the world accurately.

Religious experiences likewise have striking similarities, despite occurring to very different people in very different circumstances. The best explanation of these experiences, and their common nature, is that they are veridical: in other words, they are genuine experiences of something divine. So it is reasonable to suppose God exists.

William James (*see p.315*) studied the similarities between religious experiences and noted that, like perception, they are experiential —quite different from *thinking* about God. However, they are not connected to any specific mode of sensory perception (such as sight or hearing). If there are visions, or words "heard," these form part of an

During intense religious experiences, mystics such as St. Theresa of Avila can feel so aware of God's presence that they lose all sense of their own separateness.

The heart of religious experience, James argues, is an immediate sense of the reality of the "unseen." This awareness may be inarticulate, beyond even an ability to think about it in any usual terms. Conceptualization—being able to express what was experienced—comes later.

Is the analogy with perception strong enough for us to infer that religious experiences are veridical? Sensory experience is universal among people, and is part of our every waking moment. It provides a high level of information and detail ("a picture is worth a thousand words"). By contrast, only some people have religious experiences, and only rarely.

Does this matter? If only a few people are able to recognize a Futurist painting, does that mean they are wrong or unreliable? We can't tell the truth of something from its frequency.

CULTURAL DIVERSITY

Different cultures use largely similar ways of understanding the world, in terms of objects with color, size, solidity, and so on. But religious experience in different cultures often produces very different ideas of divinity, from the Christian idea of God to Buddhist ideas of "nothingness." Given this diversity, why should we think any religious experiences are genuinely of God? Perhaps religious experience can never provide us with a whole theological system, just an intimation of the existence and nature of a spiritual reality. Just like witnesses in court, people may experience the same thing while disagreeing about what they have experienced.

Different cultures give very different accounts of the divine: this is the Hindu god Vishnu.

RARE AND FALSE

However, the objection is that because religious experiences are so rare, we cannot assume they are veridical. Part of the reason we trust perception is because it is widespread, common, and informative. We can also check one sense against another: I can see a book on the table before me, and I can feel it there too. Religious experience, on the other hand, is not confirmed by other senses.

It is worth noting that many religious experiences do involve visions or other apparently "sensory" experiences. Someone might see an angel appear before them, for example, or a burning bush. Interestingly, such experiences vary dramatically from one belief system to the next. Catholics tend to see the Virgin Mary, whereas the Ancient Romans saw Zeus and the Ancient Norse people experienced Odin. These differences suggest that a large part of what is experienced is conditioned by the expectations of the subject. And once we have accepted that these experiences are at least partly our own creation, that

surely significantly raises the probability that they are entirely our own creation.

True religious experiences can seem utterly compelling. But should not the wide variations in what is experienced, plus the fact that what is experienced is clearly heavily influenced by expectation, prompt us to approach them with caution?

Not many people can reliably identify this chair as being in the Louis XV style, but that does not mean we should doubt the knowledge of those who can.

FREUD ON RELIGIOUS EXPERIENCE

Sigmund Freud (1856–1939), the Austrian founder of psychoanalysis, argued that religious experiences may be dreamlike hallucinations triggered by deep-seated, unexpressed anxieties and wishes. We feel vulnerable and frustrated that there is so little we can do in the face of the uncontrollable forces of nature. Like insecure children, we crave protection, and religious belief provides us with the comfort we need.

DREAMS OR REALITY?

Freud argued that dreams are the product of powerful unconscious desires. He believed that religious experiences are similarly caused. They are hallucinations that occur when we are awake, and arise out of a longing for security and meaning. This would explain their characteristics. If they are hallucinations, we would expect them to be experiences rather than thoughts. Given the strength of the underlying desire, we can expect them to involve intense emotions. And because the wish is abstract, they will not be related to any particular mode of perception. They will feel as if there is something "beyond" that can offer reassurance and help us to make sense of life.

Some reply that even if religious experiences result from unconscious wishes, if we are made by God, then a relationship with God should be our deepest desire. So there may be more to the wish Freud thinks leads to belief than the fears he describes.

"RELIGIOUS IDEAS [FULFIL] THE OLDEST, STRONGEST, AND MOST URGENT WISHES OF MANKIND."

Sigmund Freud,
The Future of an Illusion

Our vulnerability in the face of uncaring nature, illustrated by Géricault's *The Raft of the Medusa*, makes us yearn for security.

THE PROBLEM OF EVIL

God is typically portrayed as being perfectly good, omnipotent, and omniscient. If this is true, we can assume that God not only wants to eliminate evil, but also that he can do so, and knows how to. But this poses the question: why then does evil exist? Because God does not?

Understanding the argument

What does "evil" refer to here? People normally use the term to mean morally wrong actions or motives, which we can describe as "moral evil." However, in this argument, evil also includes the suffering that results from non-moral events, such as that caused by earthquakes, illness, the predation of animals on each other, and so on. We can think of this as a kind of "natural evil." The concept of natural evil is very important in philosophical responses to the problem of evil.

The second issue to try to clarify is how the argument is supposed to work. One version, called the logical problem of evil, proposes that the mere existence of evil in the world is logically incompatible with the existence

of a good, omnipotent, omniscient God. This approach formulates the argument *deductively* (*see p.195*).

For the existence of evil to be logically incompatible with the existence of God, we have to suppose that, being good, God has the desire to eliminate all evil. But this supposition is not true if some evil is actually necessary for a greater good. For example, if we did not feel pain, we could never learn endurance; and perhaps losing what we love is the

The existence of a loving, all-powerful God is challenged by the terrible suffering—animal and human—that can be caused by natural disasters.

inevitable price we sometimes have to pay for having love at all. As Tennyson put it, "'Tis better to have loved and lost, than never to have loved at all."

Opponents of the logical problem of evil assert that some evil is necessary to make the world as good a place as it is. Furthermore, they may add, we would not be able to appreciate what is good, and thus would not desire it as we do, unless we had evil with which to contrast it. Consequently, God does not desire the elimination of all evil. However, even accepting this, it seems incontestable that

Natural disasters such as earthquakes, floods, and drought are often called "acts of God." However, it is hard to imagine how they serve a greater good.

God would desire to eliminate all *unnecessary* evil, which leads us on to a second version of the argument.

LOOKING AT THE EVIDENCE

The evidential problem of evil claims that the amount of evil and its distribution is incompatible with the existence of a good, omnipotent, omniscient God. It formulates the argument *inductively* (*see pp.196–7*). In other words, the way that evil exists in the world is good evidence for thinking that God does not exist.

It is clear that evil is not evenly spread among people and animals. Some are afflicted by evil more than others, and the innocent can suffer dreadfully. For example, children can die of terrible diseases, and animals can suffer in floods and drought. This seems exactly what an omnipotent, omniscient, good God would want to eradicate. So even if evil is necessary for a greater good, is *so much* evil necessary?

A theodicy is an argument that tries to justify evil, making it compatible with the existence of an omnipotent, omniscient, good God. The necessary evil approach is a theodicy, as is the proposition that evil is the result of our free will (*see opposite*) and the idea that evil is essential for our moral and spiritual growth (*see p.156*). Theodicies only work if they can show that this is, in a sense, the best of all possible worlds: that any less evil would lead to some important good being lost.

NO GOOD REASON FOR EVIL?

The evidential problem of evil appeals to an intuition: that there is no good reason that could justify the amount and distribution of evil in the world. Religious believers may respond that we cannot be sure of this. It may be that all evil serves a higher purpose, yet we simply do not, and perhaps cannot, know what that purpose is or how evil serves it. But what grounds do we have for thinking this? Is it probable that there is such a higher purpose? If it is not, then this response is rather like scepticism (*see p.50*), arguing its case on the basis that we cannot be certain. Such an appeal to ignorance needs a good reason behind it. An appeal to, for example, a revelation from God that everything is for the best will not be acceptable. If it is unlikely that God exists, it is unlikely that the revelation is genuine; and we will not know whether it is likely that God exists or not until we have solved the problem of evil.

DOES FREE WILL ACCOUNT FOR EVIL?

One theodicy (justification of evil) argues that evil is caused by the way in which we exercise our free will. God gave us free will, as something that is very good. Being morally imperfect, however, we do not always use our free will for good, and we sometimes bring about evil. But, runs the argument, it is still better to have free will and cause evil by its misuse than not to have free will at all.

EVIL AND "THE FALL"

The theodicy described above apparently only justifies moral evil. However, the Christian philosopher St. Augustine (*see pp.256–7*) argued that natural evil, too, is a result of moral evil—and of one Biblical event in particular. The choice of Adam and Eve to disobey God led to "the Fall," a metaphysical change altering both nature and human beings forever.

Augustine argued that the first abuse of free will by Adam and Eve led to humanity being "out of sorts" with nature.

The consequences of the Fall are enmity between human beings and animals, pain during childbirth, and the hardship we must endure to survive (see Genesis 3:15–19). All evil, both natural and moral, was thus caused by human free choice.

Relatively few people now believe that the Fall was a historical event. Through science we know that animals were suffering long before humans existed, so our free will cannot literally be the cause of natural evil. Even if the Fall were responsible, it would seem grossly unfair. Why should animals and children suffer as a result of a choice made by two people a long time ago? Free will may be a great good, but that does not mean we should never interfere with it. We do not appeal to the value of a murderer's free will to justify doing nothing to stop him. So why should God? Some reply that God would have to intervene so often to prevent all the evil we cause that it would undermine the very essence of our free will.

Because of the Fall we must sweat to eke out a living from the earth, to which we will one day return.

The vale of soul-making

Some people believe that evil is necessary for moral and spiritual growth, and that a world with moral and spiritual growth is better than a world without it. Virtues are impossible unless there is evil (natural and moral) to respond to and correct. We cannot be courageous, for example, unless there is real danger to face, and we cannot be benevolent unless people have needs. This is rather like the description of the world as the "Vale of Soul-making" by the poet John Keats (1795–1821). "Do you not see," he asked, "how necessary a World of Pains and troubles is to school an Intelligence and make it a soul!"

Does the need to become good really justify evil? Could God not simply create us virtuous? American philosopher John Hick (*b*.1922) replies that a person who has become good through confronting and dealing with evil "is good in a richer and more valuable sense" than someone who is created good. In short: no pain, no gain.

Most would agree that it is more than just obedience that motivates acts of courage by the military and emergency services in the face of real danger.

This theodicy only works if all evil leads to spiritual growth, which it does not seem to. Many people suffer terribly in a way that breaks their spirit, such as children who never recover from being abused. Others suffer at the end of their lives when there is little time to develop further, and some people grow spiritually but do not suffer much at all. Then there are those who die young, without having any opportunity for spiritual growth.

One response is that their suffering helps us, too. Richard Swinburne (*see p.146*) argues that if evil was predictable, being matched exactly to the need for growth, then two important virtues in particular could never flourish: faith and hope. These require a considerable level of unpredictability, since if the pattern of evil looked rational, we would have no need of them.

We may still wonder why goodness could not grow against more minor evils; and what purpose millions of years of animal suffering (assuming that animals do not grow spiritually) might serve.

FAITH AND REASON

It is often argued that faith and reason are fundamentally opposed to each other. However, fideism—the view that faith is beyond reason in questions of religious belief—has not always taken this form. Faith involves trust and commitment, but not (as is often implied) irrationality.

Genuine options

William Clifford (1845–79), an English mathematician and philosopher, argued that it is "wrong always, everywhere, and for everyone, to believe anything on insufficient evidence." Belief must be arrived at through patient investigation, not by stifling doubts. Forming beliefs on insufficient evidence makes us credulous and weakens our cognitive powers.

William James (*see p.150*) replied that it is occasionally right and even reasonable to believe something without sufficient evidence for its truth. We may face a "genuine option" that cannot be decided on the basis of evidence, where we feel we could believe either of two exclusive alternatives—such as "God exists" and "God does not exist." The decision must also be important, and the stakes must be high. In such cases, if our intellect cannot decide, then our emotions and will must.

FIDES ET RATIO

Some Christian fideists stress the inferiority of reason to faith, arguing that sin harms our ability to reason. What we think "rational" or "reasonable" to believe might be a reflection of our pride or self-centeredness. If we rely on reason, we will never know the truth about God and ourselves. Faith is the necessary corrective; only faith should be relied upon in coming to religious beliefs. The Catholic church, however, rejects this position.

In 1998, Pope John Paul II argued in his encyclical *Fides et Ratio* that rational knowledge and philosophical discourse are important for "the very possibility of belief in God."

"WE CANNOT ESCAPE THE ISSUE BY REMAINING SCEPTICAL AND WAITING FOR MORE LIGHT."

William James, *The Will to Believe*

In belief, we have two goals: not only to avoid error, but also to discover the truth. In daily life we often need to form beliefs while accepting some risk of error. For example, we trust a person when we begin a friendship with them. This requires us to have "faith" that they are trustworthy, before sufficient evidence is in to confirm this. It is not always wrong, then, for our will to influence our beliefs.

But while religious faith clearly deals with things that are important, the choice between belief and non-belief is hardly straightforward: which religion and which God, for example, does it concern? Nor is it obvious that the choice carries serious consequences: can we be sure that God only rewards believers with eternal life? So perhaps the question of religious faith is not a genuine option after all.

A leap in the dark

Søren Kierkegaard (*see p.310*) argued that religion is not a type of philosophical system, and so we should not weigh up religious faith in a philosophical way. True faith is characterized by passionate commitment; belief formed "objectively" is not, and thus may have no impact on one's life. Faith isn't only a matter of *what* we believe, but also of *how* we believe. The commitment that characterizes faith

we "cannot believe nonsense against the understanding, which one might fear, because the understanding will penetratingly perceive that it is nonsense and hinder [us] in believing it."

In other words, religious faith is incomprehensible in that it lies beyond the limits of reason. But reason is able to recognize that it has limits, and also that faith might legitimately lie outside these

> "IF I AM ABLE TO APPREHEND GOD OBJECTIVELY, I DO NOT HAVE FAITH; BUT BECAUSE I CANNOT DO THIS, I MUST HAVE FAITH."

Søren Kierkegaard, from *Philosophical Fragments*

requires a decision—a "leap" into the unknown. It is not something that can be established intellectually. This leap actually requires objective uncertainty. While Kierkegaard described faith as "incomprehensible," he also claimed that reason—if it recognizes its limitations—can help us to understand the commitment we make in faith. He remarked that

limits. To achieve faith, we must leap. If faith were wholly unreasonable, says Kierkegaard, that would inhibit our ability to make the leap. But it is not wholly unreasonable. There is a risk involved in making the leap, but it is not an entirely irrational risk to take.

Belief in God is not a run-of-the-mill belief; it is of a more profound nature. Kierkegaard argued that if we could reach belief in God by reason, it wouldn't bring with it the right sort of commitment.

The balance of evidence

Kierkegaard and William James (*see p.313*) maintain that reason is limited: there are some questions that reason cannot answer. Reason can recognize both its limitations and that faith may rightly act when reason is limited. Neither philosopher rejects reason *per se*, but they both reject the view that reason is capable of deciding on all matters of truth, and the idea that all beliefs should be formed just on the basis of the available evidence.

TO LEAP OR NOT TO LEAP?

But is it true that reason and evidence are unable to settle the matter of God's existence? Many philosophers believe that the problem of evil (*see pp.153–5*) provides an overwhelming rational case against the existence of God (even while admitting that reason has its limits). Not only do they believe the evidence against the existence of God is strong, they suppose the case for an all-powerful, all-good God is weak.

Kierkegaard and James believe that, because faith is not *unreasonable*, a leap of faith can be made. Certainly, they suppose that belief in God is not unreasonable in

the way that believing in fairies and goblins is, for example. But perhaps Kierkegaard and James are mistaken. Perhaps faith is *very* unreasonable. In the face of objections that might seem to show that belief in God is downright irrational, the onus is clearly on those who insist belief in God is not unreasonable to come up with arguments to support that modest position. Repeating that belief requires a leap of faith does not solve this problem.

THE LIMITS OF REASON

Is basing belief on reason and evidence really so simple? Consider these possibilities:

1. that believing in God is precisely as reasonable as not believing in God (the evidence is exactly balanced);

2. that we cannot tell what the balance of evidence is;

3. that, for some reason, our belief needs to be more certain than the evidence (either way) allows, so we should consider not just the evidence, but other issues as well.

Fideists (*see p.157*) have not tended to argue for (1), but some of their arguments support (2) and (3). They say that while reason cannot settle the question of whether we should believe in God, this does not mean we have no reason for such belief.

POLITICAL PHILOSOPHY

Political philosophy is the study of how we organize our societies—both the way we actually do this, and the way we might do it better. The key concepts of politics are familiar to all: freedom, equality, justice, rights, and so on. The challenge of political philosophy is to discover what these terms really mean, and how we can make them work together.

P hilosophers have concerned themselves with politics since at least the time of the ancient Greeks. Plato's *Republic*, which laid out the great thinker's vision of how an ideal political community might function, was the hugely influential and controversial opening to a debate that continues right up to the present day. From Plato and Aristotle to, in the 20th century, John Rawls and Charles Taylor, philosophers have tried to answer the fundamental question that underlies all political thought: how are we to live together?

The question is inescapable, since humans are social creatures, gregarious by nature. Our lives are inextricably entwined with those of countless other people. Some of these people we know well, others we know only vaguely, but the vast majority we shall never know at all. So we must pay attention to the business of living with those others, and this is the essence of politics.

Highly visual propaganda materials aim to extend the franchise in non-Western countries. Politics is about how we live together, and the struggle to get it right touches all our lives.

It is not difficult to argue that we need to bother with politics. It matters to us all, for example, that laws should be fair; that a class or a clique should not oppress us; that governments should be chosen in a democratic way (and thus be accountable); and that we should be clear not only about our rights, but also about the responsibilities we have towards one another. From tyrannical regimes to persecution and genocide, history is littered with examples of the terrible consequences of getting politics wrong— of not finding ways of living together.

UNDERSTANDING FREEDOM

To take up political philosophy is to try to develop this sort of thinking a stage further. It is to ask about the key ideas that frame and shape our political lives— concepts such as justice, equality, and freedom. Paramount among these in modern political philosophy is the notion of freedom. Understanding the role that the term plays is important in itself, but it also illuminates much else in the political arena. In particular, it takes us to the heart of one of the great debating points of political philosophy: why obey the state?

THE LIBERAL IDEAL

Individual freedom is the supreme value of liberalism, which defends the right of citizens to act and speak as they choose. The liberal ideal is of a citizen left at liberty to pursue his or her own idea of the good life, whatever it may involve, without interference from the state.

Negative freedom

Just about anyone, if asked, will tell you that freedom is a good thing. It is not hard to see why. Freedom is about being able to make choices for oneself, to have a life of one's own—to be autonomous. It is characteristic of the modern world that this freedom is highly valued.

Consider the simplest freedom we enjoy: the liberty to go where we like. Freedom of movement is what we take away from criminals when we punish them with imprisonment. Beyond that, there is common consensus that there should be the liberty to express one's views, practice any religion or none, marry or stay single. The denial of any of these freedoms would cause outrage.

Does freedom have any boundaries? Again, one does not have to ask a political philosopher for an answer to that question. Most people would surely agree that the limit to freedom must come when people use their liberty to harm others. Freedom to drive a car may be good—but not to drive it onto a crowded pavement. I may be free to own a gun to go hunting with—but not to fire it at random in a city center purely because I enjoy the noise it makes.

Liberalism strives for a world in which diversity and difference is tolerated, even celebrated, and in which state power is used to defend individual freedom, rather than restrict it.

We can express this idea of freedom, which is known as the harm principle, thus: a person should be free to do whatever they choose, provided that they do not cause harm to others. In other words, the essence of freedom is the absence of constraint. The role of the state, therefore, is to ensure the smooth running of a society of free individuals, and the laws that the state enforces should all have this as their purpose.

This view of liberty has been called "negative freedom." It is negative in that the freedom to do as one wants comes from the state stepping back to let people decide for themselves how to live their lives. It is as if the state leaves a blank piece of paper with the individual on which the citizen writes the script for his life. The state is effectively neutral: it does not insist that the citizen should make a particular set of choices. All the state requires is that the citizen pursues his choices without harming other individuals in the process.

Perhaps the most influential and eloquent statement of the concept of negative freedom is to be found in John Stuart Mill's *On Liberty*, written in 1859 (*see pp.308–9*). This work is also a classic

At the top of the liberal agenda is the creation of a society in which the sovereign individual is free, like the Romantic hero, to live life on his own terms.

statement of liberalism—the political philosophy that embraces this approach to freedom, the individual, and the state.

LIBERALISM AND INEQUALITY

The two key tenets of liberalism are the harm principle and the neutral state. To liberals, the free choice of the individual is more important than the nature of the thing chosen. So even if a choice seems mistaken or foolish, the individual, not the state, must be the judge of what is best.

One obvious consequence of this is that people will make different choices, adopt different values, and pursue different goals. To accept this is to adopt pluralism. In a pluralist society the state acts as a neutral umpire between different lifestyles and value systems, without favouring one over another. As a result, a clear divide is established between the *public* and the *private*, with the former comprising the state, and the latter, society (individuals and their associations, employment, etc.).

It follows that in the liberal, pluralist state the economy is going to be that of the free market—capitalism. This brings us to the third thing that liberals accept: inequality. When individuals compete with each other in the marketplace, there are always winners and losers. Although individuals are free to make their own choices, not all of those choices will be wise or lucky, and this inevitably produces inequality in the possession of goods.

LIBERTARIANISM

It is the attitude towards inequality that most clearly differentiates the two main strands of liberalism—libertarianism and social democracy (*see pp.170–1*). Libertarianism is the more relaxed about inequality, striving as it does for the unrestricted liberty of the individual acting in the "private" world of the free market. Libertarians want the state stripped back to its core function of providing security: protecting citizens from harm within (law enforcement) and without (armed forces). This has the added benefit of keeping taxes as low as possible, leaving people with the maximum freedom to spend their money as they wish.

The state's remit is merely to deter, detect, and apprehend those who would do harm. "Harm" here is interpreted as injury to persons, stealing, and damage to property—but little else. So if the citizen falls ill, loses her job, or needs to educate her children, the state is not obliged to help. If she is unable to pay for the goods and services she needs, she must rely on the charity of others, who may make the free choice to help her.

In this vision of society, the market is all-powerful. If nobody wants to buy what you are selling—your labor, for example —then you will find it difficult or even impossible to get what you want or need. With the market as the most powerful tool for expressing choices and allocating

resources, the result is likely to be wide disparities between rich and poor—a "liberalism for the rich." The idea of free individuals competing in the marketplace is something of a myth. In reality, what we get is not competing individuals but big corporations wielding massive power. And the freest are the biggest players in the market.

Before turning to the other main strand of liberalism, social democracy, it is worth looking at two further aspects of the liberal view – the social contract, and rights. Both have been relevant to non-liberal thinkers, but it is liberalism that has most emphasized their importance.

Libertarians accept that freedom necessarily results in inequality, but does a free market hand too much freedom to the winners?

THE HARM PRINCIPLE IN ACTION

According to the harm principle, the purpose of law is to prevent people from harming others. Where no such harm occurs, the law should not intervene. So if I, an adult, want to smoke knowing that I may be damaging my health, then no one has the right to stop me. If, on the other hand, it can be shown that my cigarette smoke is affecting the health of those around me, then there are grounds for restricting my right to smoke near others. This is the basis for much recent legislation banning smoking in enclosed public spaces.

The social contract

The idea of the social contract attempts to answer the question: why obey the state? After all, its laws, taxes, and police limit individual freedom. But consider the alternative. With no laws and no state, you could do whatever you liked. Of course, others could also do what they liked to you. This is the "state of nature" described by Thomas Hobbes (*see p.275*), who, living through Britain's civil wars (1640–60), had first-hand experience of how frightening such a scenario could be. Without a sovereign authority there can be no security, no peace.

Now we can see why people might want to organize a state. People agree to live under the rule of law because of the long-term benefits of such a move. They hand over powers to the state and lose some freedoms in order to be able to walk the streets safely. This is the contract: the state may command the citizen as long as he or

The idea of the social contract puts rulers on notice to govern for the benefit of the citizens – or risk, as England's Charles I was, being overthrown.

merely some external protector of negative freedom, but the actual expression of the rational will of the entire community—the "General Will."

CRITICISMS

It seems unlikely, say sceptics, that people emerged from the woods with the idea of the social contract already in their heads. Contracts imply the existence of a market, not a wilderness. Social contract theory has been criticized as a liberal fiction that enshrines the myth of the sovereign individual who freely consents to the state's authority. But to be the kind of person who could do such a thing one would have to be the product of a settled state, not its founder. Contracts and the people who make them are sophisticated creations. As Hegel (*pp.302–3*) argued, the state forms the individual, not vice versa.

The best response to this criticism may be not to think of the social contract as a supposed historical event, or as

> ## "...THE LIFE OF MAN IN A STATE OF NATURE... NASTY, BRUTISH, AND SHORT."

Thomas Hobbes, *Leviathan*

she is protected by its laws. John Locke (*see pp.282–3*) asserted that the state breaks its social contract with the people when it acts in a tyrannical way. A state that preys on its citizens is like a wild beast in the "state of nature" and has no right to rule. Citizens may then regard it as their duty to overthrow the state.

According to Rousseau (*see pp.292–3*), if the social contract is genuine and not based on lies and oppression, it is not

something we as individuals are supposed to have signed up to. Rather, as liberal philosophers such as John Rawls (*see p.340*) have stated, we should view it as a kind of thought-experiment—a tool to help us think about what the state is for, what it owes to its citizens, and what they owe to it. In other words, it is the kind of contract we would draft ourselves, if asked, to safeguard our (negative) freedom in a just society.

French suffragettes disrupt an election, tipping over the ballot box. Above, a bust of Marianne presides: during the Revolution, women's republican groups pleaded for the vote yet were denied it by the new civil laws, the *Code Napoléon*.

Rights

Another key element of the liberal view of politics is rights. Simply expressed, a right is a non-negotiable claim. If you have a right to something, then you must not be prevented from having or doing that thing; in addition, others are duty-bound to allow or even enable you to exercise that right. Rights can be seen as a way of defending certain freedoms against the power of the state, or against other citizens who may wish to deny us those freedoms.

Rights are thought of as being inviolable and somehow "pre-political." In other words, while the normal process of politics involves claims and counter-claims between citizens or between citizens and the state, a right is like a trump card—an absolute demand that a claim be recognized as valid, even if the exercising of that right goes against the welfare of the majority.

Of course, it is one thing to claim something as a right and quite another to get others to recognize it as such. In practice, most rights are only established after dedicated struggles by those who demand them. For example, in the West the right to vote had to be fought for by various groups excluded from the democratic process, including women, the "working classes," and black people.

THE BASIS OF RIGHTS

The idea of rights is an appealing one, since it balances that of the social contract (*p.167*). While the social contract justifies the powers that the state exerts over the citizen, rights impose limits on what the state can do to the citizen, and also specify which freedoms the state has a duty to defend. But upon what are rights based?

It has been argued that the possession of rights is grounded in our very nature as humans, conferred on us by God or by nature. This approach sees rights as part of the very essence of our humanity, placing them beyond the reach of politicians and the prevailing majority.

American and French revolutionaries of the 18th century used the language of rights—here in the US Constitution—to challenge the power of the state.

The drawback to this notion of "natural rights" is that it does not clarify how we *know* that we have these rights (do we intuit them?), or exactly how many rights we have (are there still more rights to be discovered?). Likewise, it does not explain why there is disagreement about what constitutes a right. An alternative way of looking at rights is to see them as things we have invented—as the product of political decisions, customs, or conventions. However, this approach is also problematic, as invented rights do not have the powerful pre-political force of natural rights. After all, if we invented rights, then we can surely change them – or even abolish them.

DEFINING RIGHTS

A further area of debate concerns what can and cannot be claimed as a right. Life, liberty of movement, free speech, and freedom of religion would all seem to be obvious contenders. Although these rights might not be respected everywhere at all times, they do at least have the merit of looking like important freedoms that are worth defending against the powerful. Naturally, such a list does not cover all the things people have claimed they have a right to—such a list would be vast, and would include the right to a vote, property, employment, and economic aid.

The difficulty here is that the more things that count as rights, the less room there is to move politically, since rights are supposed to be absolute claims, against which other considerations, however important, must give way. So should the right to free speech, for example, override all objections made on grounds of decency, respect for religion or race, and public interest? And what happens when two rights seem to clash? In some countries the debate over abortion has seen the right to life and a woman's right to choose placed firmly on different sides of the argument.

Despite such awkward questions, rights are here to stay. Revolutionaries have often used the language of rights to express their aspirations for a more just society. This is in part because rights bring a moral dimension to politics, beyond merely reining in the powerful: a demand for recognition and respect for all. Increasingly, this demand is being made in ways that transcend national boundaries. It is a view that has become enshrined in a number of documents, including the United Nations Declaration of Human Rights.

MARY WOLLSTONECRAFT (1759–97)

The British writer and feminist activist Mary Wollstonecraft was a tireless campaigner for a world grounded in reason, free from the oppression and intolerance that arise from prejudice and superstition. Her works include *A Vindication of the Rights of Men* (1790), a defense of the French Revolution in response to attacks by the conservative Anglo-Irish philosopher and politician Edmund Burke (*see p.299*). Her most notable work was *A Vindication of the Rights of Woman* (1792), in which she argued that the supposed inferiority of women had arisen not from nature, but because men had denied women proper education. Mary Wollstonecraft was the mother of Mary Shelley, the author of *Frankenstein* (1818).

In 1957, black students in Little Rock, Arkansas, had to be escorted by federal troops when they decided to assert their right to equal education with their white fellow students.

Social democracy

The twin concepts of the social contract and rights help to create the framework for a just society—a concept dear to the hearts of social democrats.

While social democracy values freedom highly, it differs with libertarianism on the role of the state in promoting that freedom. By pursuing the liberty of the individual in the free market to the extreme and shrinking the state to a minimum, libertarianism can exacerbate inequalities —with knock-on effects for the freedom of the poor. For example, if you have little money, then illness, joblessness, or lack of education will leave you less free than your richer neighbor.

In the race of life, social democrats aim to provide equal opportunities, not equal outcomes. The goal is to eliminate unfairness, not inequality.

To be free you must be able to exercise choice, but because choice is dependent on resources, this opportunity is often denied to the poor. Since poverty is usually a misfortune rather than a choice, why should the poor bear the sole responsibility for overcoming it?

A JUST, EQUAL SOCIETY

Social democracy takes this problem seriously. It rejects libertarianism as lacking in justice, and insists on equal freedom for all—and hence the elimination of unjust inequalities. The state thus has to intervene to ensure equal opportunities, as well as to soften some of the grosser inequalities of the free market. These interventions are usually aimed at making education, health-care, and welfare systems free or affordable, thus improving equality of life chances.

This is still a variety of liberalism, because social democrats accept that there will be inequalities. The state tries to ensure equality of opportunity, not of outcome, just as, at the start of a race on an athletics track, the runners in the outer lanes stand progressively further forward to ensure that all contestants have an equal chance—but not everyone will win.

The social democratic state is more expensive than libertarianism's minimalist state. The extra money must come from taxes, which are levied most heavily on the better-off. Even if taxing the wealthy like this is fair, it is still possible to criticize this model of "equal opportunities." Social democrats seem to be trying to support negative freedom, with all the differences of outcome that go with it, while at the same time attempting to intervene to minimize its worst effects.

The Fourth Estate by Giuseppe da Volpedo, an icon of the workers' movement in Italy, vividly portrayed the humanity of a unified underclass seeking justice from society.

POSITIVE ACTION

Unlike in a real race, social democrats must do more than just ensure everyone has a fair start. They must intervene repeatedly to correct a system that tends towards class divisions if left alone.

Imagine, for example, two families: in one the earners are highly paid lawyers, while those in the other family are in low-paid employment, such as street-cleaning. The lawyers' combined income is many times that of the cleaners. Although the state may provide an education for the children of the poorer family, the greater resources of lawyers will make a huge difference to their children's life chances, —a difference that the children will pass on, in turn, to their own offspring.

The state is required to both intervene to promote equal opportunities, and step back for the sake of individual liberty. The effect may be to encourage some upward social mobility, while simultaneously entrenching a class of people who derive their advantages from the wealth and contacts established by their parents.

DEFINING JUSTICE

Justice is something all endorse in theory, but few can agree about in practice. Justice is primarily concerned with fairness—with the morally correct distribution of good and bad things between people. One view has it that "each should be treated equally, unless there is a relevant difference between them." In other words, if there is one cake and two identical people, it would be fair and just to give each person an equal share of the cake. But in reality no two people are the same, so what is a *relevant* difference that might affect the way you distribute the cake? You might decide to give a larger helping to a malnourished individual (criterion: need), or to the person who helped you bake the cake (criterion: merit). And these are only two of the many differences you could pick out to use as your distribution criteria. Decisions about justice, and the relevant differences, are rarely easy, and are often furiously contested.

THE COMMON GOOD

Liberalism stresses the importance of individual choice, seeing the
state as an agency for safeguarding the right to choose while staying
neutral about what constitutes a good choice. A challenge to this view
comes from those philosophers broadly described as communitarian.

From rights to responsibilities

"Community" is a somewhat vague term
in political philosophy, but its use does
signal an important shift of emphasis
from the individual to the
citizen. Communitarians
emphasize the common
good, rather than the
rights and freedoms of
individuals. They argue
that always promoting
individual choice often
damages the public
interest. Take the issue of
urban traffic, for example.
People exercise their
freedom to drive into city
centres for work, shopping,
and leisure. The result is
congestion, accidents, and
pollution. The response
of communitarians might
be to limit or even ban
car use in cities, and encourage
alternative means of transportation. The
communitarian approach sees it as
justifiable to limit individual freedom for
the benefit of the community as a whole.

Critics of liberalism want to return
political debate and communal
decision-making to the heart of
civic life, as in previous centuries.

Communitarians accuse liberals of
encouraging a selfish concern with
individual rights and interests at the
expense of the common
good. Individualism can
be a one-sided demand to
have one's own way, while
neglecting the duties and
commitments essential for
a flourishing community.
But if people want fair
trials they must serve on
juries; if they want to be
parents they must shoulder
responsibilities; if they
want safe streets they must
act in their community.

SOCIAL ANIMALS

Communitarian ideas can
be traced all the way back
to Aristotle (*see pp.248–9*),
who claimed that "man is a political
animal"—a special animal, unlike the
god or the beast, that lives *socially*. The
political animal is moulded by society.
Looking to individual liberties alone

SOLIDARITY

Communitarians emphasize that the good
society needs more than rights and freedoms
for the individual—it needs a bond with one's
fellow citizens as well. Solidarity concerns
strengthening the bonds that unite groups and
communities. A trade union or a welfare state is
an institutional expression of solidarity. A trade
union promotes solidarity among workers, so
that together they may better their employment
conditions, while a welfare state symbolizes the
idea that all citizens are part of one community,
with a shared responsibility for each other.

In 1980s Poland, the trade union Solidarity united
opposition to the communist government, and
helped to bring about democratic elections.

ignores all the things that make us the people we are—few of which are the results of conscious choices. We are born into a family, learn a language, and are socialized into values, customs, and conventions. Immersed in a social whole, we are connected by a vast network of ties to others, with all the attendant affections, dependencies, duties, and so on.

Liberals tend to stress either the single individual and his or her rights, or abstract concepts such as universal "humanity." Yet this outlook fails to consider the specific communities that shape real people. "Woman" in general is an abstraction, but *this* Iraqi woman, in *this* village, with *this* family, history, language, religion, problems, and aspirations is someone who actually lives and breathes.

Communitarians expand the notion of the political beyond the state regulation of individuals into something we must all be concerned with in order to realize our humanity. They see the social contract (*see p.165*), in which individuals freely opt into the political state, as a myth, believing that people are only able to act politically because they are shaped by a complex social world. In other words, to make rational choices, I already need to have acquired the attitudes, capacities, and goals that make those choices both possible and meaningful. These things are slowly developed within me by my formation in a particular community.

Communitarians believe citizens should participate actively in the decision-making of their communities, and not leave it to others to make choices for them.

It thus does not make sense to wholly separate the individual good from the common good. Therefore, I must accept responsibilities as well as freedoms if I want the things that make me a free citizen to flourish. I must work for the good of something larger than myself.

THE QUESTION OF DISSENT

It is possible to accept communitarian ideas but still have serious reservations. What will be the fate of the dissenter or the unpopular minority in a state run along communitarian lines? What, for example, happens if our "real" Iraqi woman wants to reject aspects of the culture and community in which she is embedded? Communitarianism can have unpalatably conservative or repressive practical consequences. Communities have sometimes dealt harshly with those who differ from the majority, imposing a single view of how to live and what to believe and silencing the voices of dissent and opposition.

Communitarians answer that they are not somehow *against* rights or dissent. The common good, they say, is served by an active citizenry capable of vigorous debate, but which nevertheless shares a concern with the community, rather than the narrow politics of individual choice.

Positive freedom

It may be that the tension between the common good and individual freedom is more apparent than real. Some critics argue that liberals work with too limited an idea of freedom. Freedom is more than simply having opportunities to fulfil desires. Understanding the nature of those desires is equally important. Some desires may be unwelcome, such as a compulsive urge to shop or an addiction to gambling. Giving in to such desires, say critics, is quite the opposite of freedom. We need to reflect on our desires from a distance, in order to discern which ones we really *identify* with. If we do not identify with a desire, then we are enslaved by it and are not acting freely, no matter how unconstrained by others we may be.

The self that each of us has, with all its desires, is partly the product of social forces we did not choose as individuals. So just acting on whatever desires we happen to have is not freedom at all. According to this reasoning, true freedom

Advocates of positive freedom want society to express a kind of public freedom—a classical harmony between citizens and their institutions.

must involve a second level of evaluation: reasoning through what would be best to choose, or to become. This is the route to a more "positive" freedom.

Two things are important here. First, desires are heavily influenced by society. The context of our desires is political as

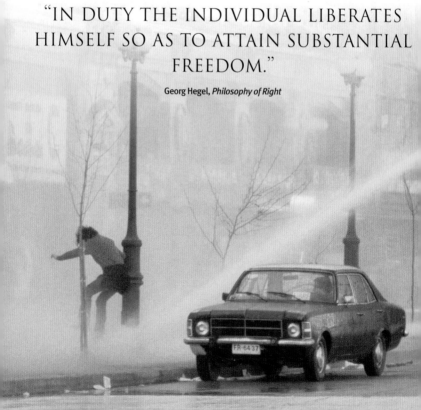

"IN DUTY THE INDIVIDUAL LIBERATES HIMSELF SO AS TO ATTAIN SUBSTANTIAL FREEDOM."

Georg Hegel, *Philosophy of Right*

well as psychological. The consumerist "shop till you drop" culture, for example, is manipulated by an industry that aims to make you buy things you do not necessarily want or need, or even afford.

Second, reason has a social dimension and is not neutral about what is good. The second, or "higher," level of evaluating one's desires is thus open to assessment by others. The individual does not always know best, which is why we often discuss problems and take advice. Furthermore, our reasoning is always *normative*—it necessarily involves evaluatively "loaded" terms such as fair, unjust, worthwhile, and hypocritical. These, too, are derived from the society in which we live.

SOCIAL FREEDOM

While negative freedom emphasizes the number of opportunities an individual has, advocates of positive freedom want to change the social phenomena that prevent people from *exercising* their freedom. These might include poverty, ignorance, consumerism, and the inequalities created by the free market.

Opponents of the positive freedom approach argue that there is really only one kind of freedom—individual choice —and that there is something troubling about the idea of what a person

---

CHARLES TAYLOR (b. 1931)

The Canadian Charles Taylor is a key voice in the liberal/communitarian debate. Although uneasy with the label "communitarian," Taylor criticizes the liberal conception of the self as being too shallow and abstract. He argues that we should understand the self in terms of "horizons of significance" —that is, the network of relations to others that gives the individual a stable context for making sense of their world. Without horizons of significance, choices become arbitrary and ultimately meaningless. His works include *Hegel* (1975), *The Sources of the Self* (1989), and *The Ethics of Authenticity* (1992).

---

reasoning properly *ought* to want. Would this lead to the coercion of the individual in the name of an oppressive collective "freedom?" Such critics have difficulty with the view that the individual may not be the best judge of what is good for her, and that some other agency—the state, the community, the party, or the leader— may claim it knows better and decide for her. If this is where the idea of positive freedom leads to, it looks like a dead end.

The proponents of positive freedom, such as Charles Taylor (*see box, above*), believe such fears are unsubstantiated. For them, true freedom involves fulfilling one's duties to a community. This includes the duty to transform that community if it denies freedom to all. A genuinely free society is thus one in which the citizens grasp the responsibility to protect and preserve whatever promotes social freedom. This view has had some powerful advocates, including Rousseau, Hegel, and Karl Marx.

Despite such heavyweight backing, liberal objectors maintain that positive freedom is a dangerous mystification, and that the only liberty that matters lies with the individual and their choices— whatever they may be.

Critics of positive freedom allege that the notion of a "higher" freedom than that of the individual can in practice lead to state tyranny.

The future of freedom

It may be that the idea of "freedom-as-choice" is incomplete or even misleading. Both our choices and our reflections on them are rooted in a social and historical situation, as are the goals and aspirations that inspire us to bring about change. Yet any society that wants its citizens to have the freedom to make their own choices must adopt something of a liberal stance toward opinion, lifestyle, and religious affiliation. Liberalism resonates with the growing desire by people to live their own lives, even if they should be thought wrong or strange by others. A free society is one in which it is safe to be unpopular. However, a liberalism that allows the free market the central role in shaping the social world may not serve the cause of freedom. That is why social democrats seek to limit the power of the market. It remains to be seen whether the difficult balancing act of encouraging an effective economy (to generate wealth) and redistributing some of that wealth to the less well-off (to limit inequalities) can be sustained in the face of the mighty transnational forces generated by globalization. As competition grows, the pressure may increase for politics to move in a more libertarian direction.

Liberalism has many critics, but do the alternatives offer anything better? Liberals point to the usually tragic outcomes of revolutions and of states dedicated to "higher" freedoms than those of liberal democracy.

Political freedom is never so prized as by those who have been denied it. Nelson Mandela (*below*) was imprisoned for 27 years by South Africa's apartheid regime.

HANNAH ARENDT (1906–75)

The German-born American philosopher Hannah Arendt argued that politics needs a public space in which people can act freely and reveal themselves to each other through what they do and say. In her own time she saw this political space threatened not only by the menace of Nazi and Stalinist totalitarianisms, but also, she believed, from processes at work in modern liberal democracies. Her books include *The Origins of Totalitarianism*, *The Human Condition*, and *Eichmann in Jerusalem: A Report on the Banality of Evil* (1963).

While the advocates of a more positive conception of freedom, such as Rousseau (*see pp.292–3*) and Marx (*see pp.311–2*), are not personally responsible for the excesses of Stalin's Soviet Union or Pol Pot's Cambodia, the question remains as to whether their approaches can lead anywhere else.

POLITICS IN PERIL?

Some modern philosophers have feared for the future of politics, and hence for freedom itself. Hannah Arendt believed that the greatest danger comes from the entirely managed society, in which there is no longer any public space left in which to argue and decide with one's fellow citizens what the public good demands. But as Charles Taylor (*see p.175*) has remarked, commentators often seem to divide too easily into "knockers" and "boosters" of modernity. The future, he argues, is likely to be more mixed and interesting than those simplistic attitudes suggest.

It is vital that political philosophers find ways of thinking beyond the nation state, since the real challenges of the 21st century will be global in nature. There are grounds for optimism, and they rest with something else recognized by Arendt: the freedom of the political animal to make things anew, to give birth to a future that does not repeat the past. The future of politics is the future of freedom.

PHILOSOPHY OF SCIENCE

The philosophy of science is one of the oldest subdivisions of philosophy, and can be traced back at least as far as Aristotle. It is now growing rapidly as the huge scientific advances of the last century have prompted philosophers to think more carefully about what science is. They may even help to shape its future.

The philosophy of science involves philosophical reflection on science. Philosophers of science do not address scientific questions – that is the job of scientists. Rather, philosophers of science tackle questions *about* science. For example: what is science? What distinguishes science from non-science? What is the role of observation in science? And how does science progress? Other questions focus on the concepts that science applies. What, for instance, is a law of nature? Another philosophical concern is the extent to which we are justified in supposing that unobserved entities are real. Should we suppose electrons really exist, for example, or are they just "useful fictions?"

THE BALANCE OF EVIDENCE

Some of the most central and important questions addressed by philosophers of science concern confirmation. Scientists construct theories they believe are

The discovery of DNA, a momentous breakthrough by Watson, Wilkins (*pictured*), and Crick, signalled a "paradigm shift" in scientific thought. Philosophers consider the implications of new ways of thinking.

confirmed by what they observe. Such confirmation, however, comes in degrees. A theory might be very slightly confirmed by a piece of evidence, or it might be very strongly confirmed. We suppose that the more strongly a scientific theory is confirmed by the available evidence, the more rational it is to believe it. One question we might ask about confirmation is: what makes one theory more strongly confirmed than the next? Another, more fundamental, question is whether our scientific theories are ever confirmed at all. The 18th-century philosopher David Hume argued that while we suppose what we have observed up to now can confirm our scientific theories, such observations do not in fact provide any confirmation at all (*see pp.90–3*). If Hume is correct, all theories, from the theory that the Earth goes around the sun to the theory that the center of the Earth consists of hot molten cheese, are equally rational. The problem Hume raises is known as the "problem of induction," and it is one of the most central in the philosophy of science.

THE PROBLEM OF INDUCTION

We all rely heavily on inductive reasoning. We suppose that because the sun has risen every day in the past, we have good grounds for supposing it will rise tomorrow. But if the philosopher David Hume (*see pp.290–1*) is correct, the past provides no clue at all as to what will happen next.

Great expectations

The most reliable form of argument is deduction. In a valid deductive argument (*see p.195*), the premises logically entail the conclusion. To take a simple example:

Socrates is a man.
All men are mortal.
Therefore Socrates is mortal.

If you were to claim the premises are true and the conclusion false, you would be involved in a logical contradiction.

In an inductive argument (*see pp.196–7*), by contrast, the premises are not supposed to provide a logical guarantee that the conclusion is

Past experience makes us feel certain that some events will happen. Who could possibly doubt that the sun will rise tomorrow?

true. Rather, the premises are supposed only to provide *evidence* that the conclusion is true. Here is an example:

Swan 1 is white.
Swan 2 is white.
Swan 3 is white...
Swan 1,000 is white.
Therefore: all swans are white.

If we observe one thousand swans, and they are all white, we conclude that all swans are white. We suppose that the premises of our argument make it reasonable to draw that conclusion. But of course there is no logical contradiction in supposing that even though the first thousand swans we have observed have been white, the next one will not.

The fact that every swan we have observed up to now has been white is no guarantee that all swans are white.

We rely on inductive reasoning all the time. Whenever we make a prediction about what will happen in the future or about what is happening, or has happened, in those parts of the universe we have not observed, we rely on inductive reasoning to justify our claims.

For example, I suppose that the chair on which I am about to sit will support my weight. What is my justification for believing that? Well, the chair has always supported my weight in the past. So I conclude that it will do so on this occasion too. Of course, the fact that the chair has supported my weight in the past does not provide me with any logical guarantee that it will do so now. It is possible that the chair will collapse. Still, we suppose that the fact that the chair has always supported me before gives grounds for supposing it will continue to do so.

Scientists also rely heavily on inductive reasoning. They construct theories that are supposed to hold for all places and times, including the future. They justify theories by pointing to what they have observed. But claims about what has been observed up to now do not logically entail claims about the future. So, if scientists are to justify these theories, they cannot do so using deductive argument. They must rely on inductive reasoning instead.

IS NATURE UNIFORM?

The philosopher David Hume questions whether we are ever justified in drawing such conclusions about the unobserved. Hume claims that whenever we reason inductively, we make an assumption. We assume that nature is uniform. We assume that the same general patterns exist throughout nature. For what if we

"'TIS NOT, THEREFORE, REASON WHICH IS THE GUIDE OF LIFE, BUT CUSTOM THAT ALONE DETERMINES THE MIND, IN ALL INSTANCES, TO SUPPOSE THE FUTURE CONFORMABLE TO THE PAST."

David Hume, *A Treatise of Human Nature*

didn't assume that? Then we would not draw the conclusions we do. I would not conclude that because the chair on which I am about to sit has always supported me before, it will support me now. It is only because I believe that the same general regularities extend throughout nature, including the future, that I suppose that the chair will support me next time. But it is here that Hume detects a problem. Whenever we reason inductively, we assume that nature is uniform. But if we are to justify our belief that induction is a reliable method of arriving at true beliefs, we need to justify this assumption.

JUSTIFYING OUR BELIEFS

Hume points out that there are two possibilities. We might try to justify the claim that nature is uniform using experience. Or, we might try to justify it independently of experience, perhaps by showing that the claim is some sort of logical truth. The trouble with this second suggestion is obvious enough. The claim that nature is uniform is clearly not a logical truth. There is no logical contradiction involved in supposing that, although nature has been uniform around here up to now, it won't suddenly become a chaotic, jumbled-up mess with things behaving in a random, unpredictable way.

Which leaves but one possibility for justifying the assumption that nature is uniform. We will have to justify it by appeal to experience. One way in which we could do this would be if we could directly observe all of nature. Then we could just observe that it is uniform throughout. But of course we can't do

How can we know that the laws of physics that we observe locally extend to the whole universe? It may in fact be a patchwork.

this. We can directly observe only a tiny portion of the universe. Certainly, we can't directly observe the future.

In which case, our justification will have to be by means of an inference based on what can be directly observed. So why can't we observe that nature is uniform around here at the present time, and then conclude that nature is likely to be uniform throughout?

The problem, of course, is that this bit of reasoning is itself inductive reasoning. We would be relying on inductive reasoning in our attempt to show that inductive reasoning is reliable. But this, surely, is an unacceptably circular way of justifying something. It would be like trusting in the claims of a psychic by pointing out that he himself claims to be reliable. That is no justification at all.

Hume concludes that though we do reason inductively, we really have no justification at all for supposing that inductive reasoning is likely to lead us to true conclusions. We possess no grounds at all for supposing that things will continue to behave in the same way as they have in the past. Yes, I believe this chair will support me when I next sit on it, that this pen will fall when I release it, and that the sun will rise tomorrow just as it always has. But the astonishing truth is that I have just as much reason to suppose that the chair will collapse, that the pen will slowly rise into the air, and that tomorrow morning a million-mile-wide luminous inflatable panda will emerge over the horizon.

Of course, Hume's conclusion sounds insane. We would ordinarily consider someone who believes that a million-mile-wide panda will replace the sun to be mad. But if Hume is correct, this "insane" belief is no less reasonable than our own belief that the sun will rise instead. The predictions of a madman are no more or less reasonable than those of our greatest scientists.

On Hume's view, using induction to justify induction won't do. That would be like trusting a fortune-teller because she herself claims to be trustworthy.

"BUT IT WORKS"

It can be tempting to respond to Hume's problem of induction by pointing out that inductive reasoning has been highly successful. By relying on inductive reasoning, scientists have achieved extraordinary things, from electric light

> "THE SUPPOSITION THAT THE FUTURE RESEMBLES THE PAST IS NOT FOUNDED ON ARGUMENTS OF ANY KIND, BUT IS DERIVED ENTIRELY FROM HABIT."
>
> David Hume, *A Treatise of Human Nature*

bulbs and computers to space travel and genetic modification. These towering achievements in science and engineering all depended upon inductive reasoning. Doesn't this provide us with excellent grounds for supposing that inductive reasoning is a reliable method of arriving at true beliefs?

The trouble with this justification of induction is, again, that it is itself a piece of inductive reasoning. It points out that induction has been extremely successful up to now, and concludes that it is likely to continue to be successful in the future. But we run into the circularity problem again: using induction to justify induction is like trusting in the claims of an advertisement because the advertisement itself says it is trustworthy.

If Hume is correct, it is as rational to expect the next horse's body to sport the torso of a man as it is otherwise.

APPEALING TO RATIONALITY

While we believe we are justified in drawing conclusions about the future, and while we believe the predictions of our greatest scientists are more likely to be true than those of a madman, Hume, astonishingly, appears to have shown these beliefs are entirely irrational. Philosophers continue to grapple with this thorny problem. Some have

By relying on inductive reasoning scientists have achieved stupendous results. Man has walked on the moon. Doesn't this show induction is reliable?

suggested that the meaning of the word "rational" is: to reason deductively or inductively. So we don't need to justify the claim that "induction is rational," any more than we have to justify our belief that all bachelors are unmarried or that all mothers are female. These claims are, if you like, analytic (*see pp.66–7*), or "true by definition."

One difficulty with this move is that even if we accept that the claim that "induction is rational" is "true by definition," the problem is only postponed. Hume asks us how we can know that induction will reliably lead us to true beliefs about the future. Insisting that induction is rational is "true by definition" merely raises the question: what grounds do we have for supposing that "being rational" will reliably lead us to true beliefs about the future? Why suppose "rationality" will be any more a reliable guide to the future than relying on the guesses of madmen?

The problem of induction has led some thinkers to seek alternative ways of establishing scientific truths (*see overleaf*).

JUST HOW RADICAL IS HUME'S THEORY?

It is easy for those who are new to philosophy to underestimate just how radical Hume's position on induction really is. His conclusion is not, as it might at first glance appear, that we cannot be completely certain what will happen in the future. We can all agree that there is at least some room for error when it comes to predicting the future. Rather, Hume's conclusion is that we have no grounds at all for supposing things will continue on in the same way as they have up to now. If Hume is correct, science is a wholly irrational activity, and the predictions made by scientists are no more rational than those of the insane.

"Mad scientists" only appear in fiction. But according to Hume, the inductive reasoning used by all scientists is more or less mad, insofar as it has no rational basis.

FALSIFICATIONISM

The philosopher Karl Popper (*see p.332*) offers a radical solution to Hume's "problem of induction" (*see pp.180–5*) and the doubt it casts upon scientific theories. According to Popper, science does not rely on induction but progresses instead through the "falsification" of theories.

Ruling out error

Suppose I believe that all swans are white. Then, on a visit to New Zealand, I see a black swan. My observation that there exists a black swan falsifies – that is, renders untrue – my original theory that all swans are white.

Notice that the reasoning used here is *deductive*, not *inductive* (*see also pp.194–7*):

I observe that the following is true: there exists a non-white swan.
The truth of this claim entails that my theory "all swans are white" is false.

Karl Popper's view is that, rather than progressing through theories being *inductively* confirmed, science actually progresses through theories being falsified via *deductive* reasoning. Scientists construct theories from which they can then deduce certain testable consequences. Those theories that fail to be falsified by the tests are retained. Those that are falsified are discarded, and new theories that account for this falsification are constructed. They too are then tested; those that are found to be false are discarded, and so on. Note that, as falsification does not involve inductive reasoning, Hume's problem of induction is side-stepped. Rather than solving the problem of induction, Popper's account of how science progresses attempts to avoid it altogether.

FINDING GOOD THEORIES

Popper's theory does not say that all theories that have yet to be falsified are equally good. Some theories remain better than others. What makes one unfalsified theory preferable to another is the fact that it could be more easily falsified. But what makes one theory more easily falsified than another?

One way in which a theory might be more easily falsified is if it is wider-ranging. Consider these two theories about gravity:

All objects fall toward the center of the Earth.
All objects in London fall toward the center of the Earth.

The first theory is more wide-ranging. It predicts everything that the second theory predicts, but it

By observing the mountains of the moon with a telescope, Galileo falsified Aristotle's theory that all heavenly bodies are perfectly spherical.

KARL POPPER ON GENUINE SCIENCE

According to Popper, any genuinely scientific theory will be falsifiable. That is to say, there will be some possible observation that would falsify it. On Popper's view, a properly scientific statement makes a positive claim about how the world might be. It runs the risk of being false – the world may turn out not to be as the theory claims. Unfalsifiable statements fail to make any such claim. They are consistent with however the world might be, but then they lack genuine empirical content. For example, saying that "Emeralds are green, or emeralds are not green" is an unfalsifiable claim – whatever we might observe is consistent with its truth. So it is not genuinely scientific. Popper suggests that this is a way of distinguishing between those theories that are genuinely scientific and those that are mere pseudo-science. Genuinely scientific theories are falsifiable. Theories that claim to be scientific but are unfalsifiable are fake science. According to Popper, both Marx's theory of history and Freud's theory of the unconscious fail this test of falsifiability. Popper argues that whatever counter-evidence one might try to bring against Marx's or Freud's theories, there always turns out to be a way in which the theory can accommodate it. According to Popper, their theories are not "bad" scientific theories. Rather, they are not scientific theories at all.

Sigmund Freud's couch is an icon of modern psychology. But Popper argues that Freud's theory is unscientific.

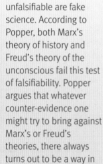

also predicts a great deal more. Because it predicts more, it is more easily falsified than the second theory.

Another reason why one theory may be more easily falsified than another is if it makes more precise predictions. Consider this claim:

All happy people wear bright colors.

This is a rather vague assertion. What is happiness, exactly, and how are we to measure it? Where precisely is the boundary between being happy and not being happy? What is to count as bright? These and other questions immediately spring up as soon as we consider testing the claim. And, of course, because of this vagueness, someone determined to defend the claim can always explain away an apparent falsification by saying "Ah, but that's not what I meant by 'bright'," or "But this person is not what I would call 'happy'." That makes the claim much harder to falsify.

A theory that makes precise, unambiguous predictions about quantifiable, measurable phenomena is far more easily falsified. For example, the theory that every rock weighs precisely 17.6oz (500g) can very easily be falsified with the aid of a simple set of scales. Instruments of measurement, such as gauges and thermometers, provide scientists with an effective tool when it comes to testing their theories.

AVOIDING THE "AD HOC"

Suppose I believe that "all wood burns". I then get a delivery of logs, none of which will burn. This observation falsifies my theory that all wood burns. How might I respond? One possibility would be to amend my original theory to:

All wood burns except the wood delivered last Sunday.

Unlike my original theory, this new theory avoids being falsified by the batch delivered on Sunday. But falsificationists

The more falsifiable a theory is, the better. An unfalsified theory that makes precise, measurable predictions is better than one that is vague and woolly. Calibrated tools help us falsify some theories.

do not consider this sort of modification desirable. The reason is that this modification is entirely ad hoc (a term derived from Latin that means "for this purpose"). It is unacceptable because it adds nothing to the original theory in terms of further testable consequences – I cannot, after all, arrange to have another batch of logs delivered last Sunday to test it.

But not all modifications need be ad hoc. Suppose I observe that the wood that did not burn was wet. Then I might amend my theory like so:

All wood burns except wood that is wet.

This modification is not ad hoc because it leads to new tests. I can now begin testing samples of wet and dry wood to check whether my new hypothesis is correct.

A real example of such an ad hoc move involves Aristotle's theory that all heavenly bodies are perfectly spherical. Galileo developed a telescope that revealed mountains and valleys on the moon. This observation appeared to falsify Aristotle's theory insofar as it seemed to prove that the moon, at least,

is not perfectly spherical. But some tried to defend Aristotle's theory by modifying it slightly. They claimed there must be an invisible substance filling the valleys of the moon right up to the tops of its mountains. So the moon is perfectly spherical after all. This development of Aristotle's original theory was ad hoc because it added nothing to that theory in terms of further testable consequences. There was nothing anyone could do at the time to test whether any such invisible substance was actually present. Somewhat sarcastically, Galileo then claimed that there was indeed such an invisible substance, only it was piled up over the mountains too, making the moon even more lumpy than it appears.

WHERE FALSIFICATION FAILS

One obvious worry that might be raised about falsificationism is its acceptance of the claim that we have not the slightest grounds for supposing any scientific theory is true. This claim is, at the very least, highly counterintuitive. Would it not be preferable if we could come up with some other solution to the problem of induction, a solution that would allow us to avoid this bizarre conclusion? Of course, in reply, the falsificationist may insist that there is no better solution.

A different worry is that falsificationism does not provide an accurate account of how science does, or should, progress. Take, for example, the Copernican

Copernicus predicted the phenomenon of parallax accurately, but could not verify it. Modern astronomical instruments confirm that stars are so distant that parallax, while it exists, is hard to detect.

"IN SO FAR AS A SCIENTIFIC STATEMENT SPEAKS ABOUT REALITY, IT MUST BE FALSIFIABLE: AND IN SO FAR AS IT IS NOT FALSIFIABLE, IT DOES NOT SPEAK ABOUT REALITY."

Karl Popper, *The Logic of Scientific Discovery*

theory that the Earth revolves around the sun. When first proposed, critics pointed out two observations that seemed to falsify Copernicus's theory. First, if the Earth moves, then an object dropped from a high tower should appear to fall at an angle, rather than straight down. For if the Earth moves some distance during the period the object is falling, the object should land that distance away from the spot directly below where it was released. But of course, when objects are released from towers, they always fall vertically. This observation appears to falsify the Copernican theory immediately.

Second, if the Earth travels around the sun, then the fixed stars should appear to move back and forth across our field of vision over the course of a year (in the same way that, were you to look due north while walking around a lamppost, the houses across the street would move back and forth across your field of vision). But no such apparent movement, or "parallax," was observed.

The absence of observable parallax also seemed to falsify the Copernican theory. Some attempted to defend Copernicus by insisting that the stars must be too far away for parallax to be detectable by the instruments of the time (which, it turns out, is true). But, of course, this was an ad hoc move. There was, at that time, no way in which this new claim about the distance of the fixed stars could have been falsified.

Yet despite these and other objections, Copernicus's theory was not rejected, and rightly so. Scientists in later years confirmed that Copernicus was correct and that both the objections above were mistaken. Since falsificationism says his theory should have been rejected, it seems that falsificationism is itself mistaken, because it fails to describe accurately how science does, and should, proceed.

When Copernicus made his claims about the Earth orbiting the sun, critics claimed that the behavior of falling objects disproved them. But as science advanced, his claims were ultimately vindicated.

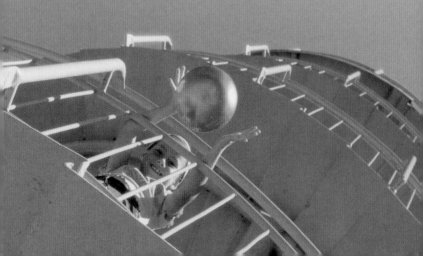

PHILOSOPHY TOOLKIT

PHILOSOPHERS COME UP WITH THEORIES THAT ARE BIZARRE, EXCITING, AND SOMETIMES DOWNRIGHT DISTURBING. THAT IS NOT THE MAIN AIM OF THEIR WORK, OF COURSE. WHAT THEY WANT TO KNOW, ABOVE ALL ELSE, IS WHAT IS TRUE. REASON IS THE TOOL THAT THEY APPLY TO HELP THEM REACH THAT GOAL.

Philosophers want their theories and solutions to stand at least a fairly good chance of being correct. They try to achieve this by applying reason. They subject theories to close critical scrutiny, and attempt to make the best possible case for supposing them to be correct.

It's easy enough to get your hair in shape, but what about what's inside your head? Unfortunately, there is no labor-saving appliance that makes you a better thinker—you have to practice.

It is tempting to think of our "powers of reason" as our ability to string together logically rigorous chains of reasoning, and also to spot where a chain contains a faulty link, much as a computer can be programmed to do. There is no doubt that an ability to construct, and detect flaws in, complex chains of reasoning is a core skill for any philosopher to have. But the term "powers of reason" really refers to a much wider and varied set of mental abilities than this. Becoming a good philosopher involves developing a whole range of thinking skills and virtues, including, for example, the ability to make points that are clear, precise, and relevant.

Philosophers also need the ability to stick with a problem and show patience and determination. As well as being tenacious, they should be able to take a step back and think imaginatively and creatively—to notice, for example, where a solution that works in one area might be useful in another.

Other mental skills that are valuable in philosophy include the ability to weigh up probabilities and evidence reliably, the ability to recognize (and counter) your own biases, and the ability to spot fallaciousness in your own and others' reasoning.

By becoming familiar with some of the thinking skills that any good philosopher is likely to possess, skills that go to make up his or her intellectual "toolkit," you will be able to tackle all kinds of issues and arguments more effectively.

Philosophical dueling requires mental agility. A little training in key thinking skills will enable you to fend off fallacious arguments and sharpen your own reasoning.

REASONING

In philosophy, we often want to make a reasoned case for believing something, or we want to spot where someone has made an unreasonable move. One way in which we might justify a conclusion is by using deductive or inductive argument.

One of the ways in which we can apply reason is as a filter. You might think of your mind as a basket into which all sorts of beliefs might tumble—from sensible ones such as that the Earth is round to ridiculous ones such as that the Earth's core is made of cheese. By applying your powers of reason to these various beliefs—by subjecting them to critical scrutiny—you can sift them, allowing through only those that have at least a good chance of being true. How demanding should this filter be? Descartes famously decided to subject all his beliefs to critical scrutiny, allowing through the filter only those that could not be doubted. A less stringent but still very robust requirement would be to allow through only those beliefs that have a high probability of being true.

Deductive reasoning

Perhaps the most obvious way of showing that a claim is reasonable is by producing a sound *argument (see box, below)* in its support. Such an argument is an *inference* involving one or more *premises* and a *conclusion*, where the premises are supposed rationally to support the conclusion.

A SIMPLE ARGUMENT

Here is a straightforward example of a deductive argument:

Premise 1: **Tom is a human.**
Premise 2: **All humans have brains.**
Conclusion: **Tom has a brain.**

In any deductive argument, if the premises logically entail the conclusion, we say that the argument is *valid*. The argument above, for example, is valid. If the premises of the argument are true, then the conclusion must be true too. Anyone asserting the premises but denying the conclusion is involved in a logical contradiction.

> "WATSON, YOU CAN SEE EVERYTHING. YOU FAIL, HOWEVER, TO REASON FROM WHAT YOU SEE."
>
> Sherlock Holmes,
> **"The Adventure of the Blue Carbuncle"**

Reason, we suppose, has great truth-detecting powers. However, you can produce a deductive argument that is perfectly valid—that is, logically sound—but that has a false conclusion, because one or more of the premises used to construct it is not true. For example:

Premise 1: **Elvis Presley is alive.**
Premise 2: **All living things reside in Brazil.**
Conclusion: **Elvis Presley resides in Brazil.**

Like the first example, this argument is valid. Given the two premises, the conclusion must follow. But its conclusion is false—because the premises are false. So, in order to ensure that we have a conclusion that is true, we need to ensure two things—both that the argument is valid, and that all of its premises are true.

WHAT IS AN ARGUMENT?

When philosophers talk about an argument, they are usually referring not to a disagreement, but to a sequence of one or more premises and a conclusion. The premises are supposed rationally to support the conclusion. These arguments can be simple—or highly complex. Often, a philosophical book or treatise consists of one big argument made up of a series of smaller ones. Each needs checking to ensure that the conclusion is true.

Inductive reasoning

Deductive argument (*see p.195*) is not the only legitimate form of inference. In an inductive argument, one also draws a conclusion from certain premises. But the premises do not, and are not intended to, logically entail the conclusion; they are merely supposed to provide the conclusion with rational support.

MAKING GENERALIZATIONS

Suppose that I wanted to confirm whether all peaches have pits. How might I do this, given that I don't have access to all the peaches there are? I might try to confirm it by cutting through 1,000 peaches, and then laying out my reasoning like so (*see right*):

> **Peach number 1 contains a pit.**
> **Peach number 2 contains a pit.**
> **Peach number 3 contains a pit...**
> and so on until...
> **Peach number 1,000 contains a pit.**
> **Conclusion: All peaches contain pits.**

The more peaches I cut to reveal pits, the more reasonable it is for me to conclude that the next one I cut will also contain a pit.

This argument contains no fewer than one thousand premises and a conclusion, but the premises do not *logically* entail the conclusion—it remains possible that the 1,001st peach will not contain a pit. Still, despite not being deductively valid, we suppose that such inductive arguments can provide us with good grounds for supposing their conclusions are true. Surely, the more peaches I observe that contain pits, the more reasonable it is for me to believe they all do. This type of argument is called enumerative induction: we observe a number of cases of X being Y, and then generalize to the conclusion that all Xs are Ys (or that the next X will be Y).

INDUCTION AND EMPIRICAL SCIENCE

Scientists construct theories that are supposed to hold for all places and all times, including the distant future and past. But the scientists cannot themselves directly observe all times and places. So they must rely on what they can observe in order to justify their claims. It is inductive reasoning that allows them to do this. For example, scientists may note that every action they have observed has been accompanied by an equal and opposite reaction, and then use enumerative induction to conclude that *all* actions are accompanied by equal and opposite reactions. Or they may observe certain experimental results, note that the existence of a theoretical entity such as a black hole provides the best available explanation of those results, and so conclude that black holes exist. That would be a scientific application of inference to the best explanation.

SOLVING PUZZLES

Enumerative induction is not the only form of inductive reasoning: another type is known as "inference to the best explanation." Here, the existence of something may be posited as the best available explanation of something else:

X is observed.
The existence of Y provides the best available explanation of X.
Conclusion: **Y exists.**

For example, suppose I am investigating the scene of a murder that took place only moments ago. I notice a pair of shoes poking out from under a twitching curtain. There is no logical guarantee there is anyone there, of course— perhaps the shoes are empty and the curtain is being blown by the wind. Still, that there is someone behind the curtain may provide the best available explanation of what I can observe. In which case, it is reasonable for me to conclude that there is someone hiding there. This is "inference to the best explanation" in action.

Theoretical particles such as electrons cannot be seen, but scientists conclude that they exist because this conclusion is the best available explanation of their observations.

Stranded on a desert island, I see footprints that are not my own. I conclude that there is someone else on the island, because it is the best way to explain why the footprints are there.

"I STOOD LIKE ONE THUNDERSTRUCK."

Robinson Crusoe, thrown into a fever of speculation on seeing a footprint in the sand.

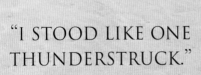

FALLACIES

A fallacy is an error in reasoning. Often, the error is not obvious, with the result that people are easily duped by the argument. Some of the best-known philosophical arguments involve classic fallacies. Learning to spot such faulty reasoning is an important philosophical skill.

Cogent inductive and deductive arguments (*see pp.195–7*) have a truth-preserving quality. If you feed true premises into a valid deductive argument, you are guaranteed to arrive at a true conclusion. If you feed true premises into a sound inductive argument, you are likely to arrive at a true conclusion. But

in an argument that is fallacious, the premises do not rationally support the conclusion. The form of such an argument is not truth-preserving, although it may of course appear to be truth-preserving. We need to be careful that we are not seduced into believing falsehoods by such fallacies.

The relativist fallacy

"It's true for me" is a comment commonly made by those who see they are losing an argument. It provides them with a handy last-ditch "wild card" to play. Of course, what is believed varies from one person to the next. But can truth vary in the same way?

DO YOU BELIEVE IN FAIRIES?

What is "It's true for me" supposed to mean, exactly? Suppose you are trying to convince your goblin-fixated friend that there are unlikely to be goblins living in his closet. But then he says "Well, that there are goblins in there is true for me." Perhaps what your friend is suggesting is that the truth of the matter of goblins' existence is relative? That there is no independent, objective truth about them—it is simply whatever each of you believes it to be. Why might he think that?

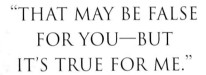

"THAT MAY BE FALSE FOR YOU—BUT IT'S TRUE FOR ME."

Jenny: **Belief in fairies is patently false. There's no evidence to suggest that fairies exist, and plenty of evidence that they don't. So it's ridiculous for you to believe in them.**
John: **Well, that fairies exist may not be true for you. But it's true for me!**

One common confusion is to slide from what is true about a person's belief to the truth of what they believe. It may be true that I believe Paris is the capital of Germany. It doesn't follow that "Paris is the capital of Germany" is true. If it did, I could make any claim true by believing it: "I can fly," for example. Clearly, most truths are not relative in this way.

It seems some truths are relative. That witchetty grubs can be a delicious meal, for example, is true for some Australians, but is false for people from many other cultures.

RELATIVE TRUTHS

Someone commits this fallacy when they do not provide grounds for supposing that the "truth" in question is indeed relative. When someone tries this tactic on you, a useful first step is to ask whether they are suggesting the truth is always whatever they believe it to be. If they say "yes," you may be able to explain why they are wrong. If they say "no," then presumably they are just pointing out that they disagree with you, which is obviously true and does not undermine your case.

The gambler's fallacy

Stand next to a lottery outlet for a while, and it won't be long before you hear someone say that they won't make the mistake of picking the numbers that came up the previous week, as those numbers are less likely to come up now. This is an example of a type of faulty reasoning known as the "gambler's fallacy."

WEIGHING UP THE ODDS

In the classic version of this fallacy (*right*), someone first considers the probability of event A happening over a period of time. They notice that, over the first part of that period, the actual incidence of A is much lower than what is probable, and conclude that A is therefore much more probable over the rest of the period. They predict a short-term increase in the probability of A to "even things up" over the longer term. The fallacy works in reverse too—people regularly avoid picking the numbers in the

> *Jenny:* **Still buying those scratch cards?**
> *John:* Yes. I've been playing regularly for three years and I haven't won a thing.
> *Jenny:* **So why do you bother?**
> *John:* Well, as I haven't won anything yet, I must be due a win soon!

"MY HOUSE GOT HIT BY LIGHTNING, SO THERE'S LESS CHANCE IT WILL HAPPEN AGAIN."

lottery that came up the week before. Of course, the fact that a particular number keeps coming up, or rarely comes up, in the lottery might make you suspect that its occurrence is not random after all. Or perhaps something is making the dice you are playing with come up a six every time—maybe your dice is loaded. But the one thing you shouldn't think is that, if you rolled a six five times in a row, you are *less* likely to roll a six the next time.

ONE PLAY AT A TIME

If you understand how probability actually works, you won't fall for the gambler's fallacy. Each time a game of chance is played, its result *cannot be affected* by the result of previous games. The good news is that if you win the lottery one week, it won't make you any less likely to win again—even with exactly the same numbers.

The appeal to authority

We are often justified in believing something because an authority on the subject tells us that it is true. If a car mechanic advises me to put water and not oil in the radiator of my car, I would follow their advice. But sometimes such "appeals to authority" are suspect.

IS TRUST IN "AUTHORITY" JUSTIFIED?

At the simplest level, someone who believes they are likely to find their perfect partner because a fortune cookie told them so is assuming that the cookie is a reliable source of information. You may think this is a ridiculous example. But think of how often advertisers expect us to trust in a "celebrity" endorsement. Why should a TV personality be better informed about car insurance or face packs than you or I? Even when someone has gained professional qualifications, they may not be relevant—someone who has gained expertise in one field is often trusted to be an authority on all sorts of subjects that they are not expert in.

Advertising often makes appeals to authority. In this illustration, the presence of a policeman adds gravitas to the brand's slogan.

"I believe that homeopathy works." "Why so?" **"Because Dr. Smedley told me so."** "Is Dr. Smedley some kind of medical expert, then?" **"No, he's a professor of mathematics."**

In the example on the left, Dr. Smedley's area of expertise is math, not medicine. There is no reason to suppose that Dr. Smedley's views about homeopathy are any better informed than are yours or mine. We should also be wary of hidden agendas. Suppose scientists at the Supawhite labs tell us that Supawhite toothpaste cleans brighter than any other brand. To what extent can scientists working for a particular company be trusted to give unbiased advice about its products? Or, when "government experts" tell us that the present government is doing better than any other, can they really be trusted?

ASK YOURSELF WHY

When faced with an appeal to authority, always ask yourself: is the person in question really an authority? Are they an authority on the relevant subject? Can I be confident that this authority is not biased? Is the view of this authority consistent with that of the majority of competent authorities in this area?

If the answer to any of these questions is "no," you would be wise not to place your trust in the authority in question.

Orson Welles's famous radio performance of *War of the Worlds* in 1938 panicked some listeners into thinking aliens really were invading. Many of us tend to place great faith in the media's authority.

The post-hoc fallacy

"Post hoc" is Latin for "after this," from the phrase *"after* this, therefore *because of* this." In the post-hoc fallacy, someone mistakenly concludes that, simply because one event happened after another, the first event is, or is likely to be, the cause of the second. Superstitious people are often particularly prone to the post-hoc fallacy.

NO REASON TO BELIEVE

Obviously, the mere fact that one thing happens after another does not normally give us much reason to suppose that the two events are causally connected. Suppose I turn on my toaster. Shortly afterward a volcano erupts on Mars. Did my turning the toaster on cause the Martian eruption? Of course not. There is no reason at all to suppose that these two events are causally connected.

I had been worrying about my driving test. So John bought me a rabbit's foot for luck. I took the foot and passed with flying colors. So you see, the rabbit's foot worked! I am going to take it to all my other exams to help me pass them too.

BEWARE COINCIDENCE

Here is another example: "John's psychic healer gave him a twig to chew on. And he got better! So you see, following the psychic's advice really did make him well." Again, the fact that one thing happened after another is taken to be good evidence of a causal connection. Of course, there may be one. Perhaps John's twig-chewing really did make him better. The point is that a single "one-off" observation does not remotely justify such claims.

Tiger Woods wears a red shirt in the final round of every golf tournament. "Good luck" rituals may boost confidence, but do they really have "magical" powers?

FAULTY CONNECTIONS

To avoid the post-hoc fallacy, don't leap to conclusions. Noticing that one event occurs immediately after another might give us grounds for investigating whether the events are causally related. But it does not, by itself, make it rational to believe there is such a connection.

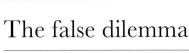

The false dilemma

It is common to argue like this: Either A or B. Not A. Therefore B. But sometimes we are presented with arguments that insist we have just two mutually exclusive choices—A or B—when in fact there is a wider range of options. These are "false dilemmas."

MORE THAN EITHER/OR

Here is a perfectly acceptable argument. Either one has a pilot's license or else one is not permitted to pilot a plane. John doesn't have a pilot's license. Therefore John may not pilot a plane. The following argument, however, is not acceptable. People either have blond or black hair. I do not have black hair. Therefore I am blond. The flaw here is obvious: the first premise of the argument is false, because people can have hair of many different colors, not just black or blond. Or consider the statement "Either we give to charity or we go on vacation." This is a false dilemma if the two options are not mutually exclusive—that is, if we could actually do both.

Salespeople often use false dilemmas when persuading customers to buy: "Your choice is to buy A, or inferior product B." You could buy neither.

Politicians sometimes use false dilemmas to try to force us into making a decision we do not in fact have to make. In the example below, it may not be true that Zenda is planning to take over the world. If so, the choice with which we are presented is a false one. But notice that, even if Zenda is intent on world domination, the option of any kind of diplomatic solution to the problem is not there.

> **Either we invade Zenda or we allow Zenda to take over the world.**
> We don't want Zenda to take over the world, do we?
> So we should invade Zenda.

The nuclear deterrent argument might involve a form of the false dilemma fallacy: either we have nuclear weapons, or we put ourselves at serious risk of attack.

OUR CHOICE IS SIMPLE

When you seem forced to choose between two alternatives, check whether they really are the only available options. Are you being railroaded by false dilemma? A phrase that should always ring alarm bells is "Our choice is simple." For example: our choice is simple—we can either send our children to after-school programs that will teach them good values and skills, or entrust them to the after-school teachings of Jerry Springer and violent video games.

Affirming the consequent

This seductive fallacy is committed whenever someone reasons: If A is true, then B must follow. B is true, therefore A. Such faulty arguments are remarkably common. A recent study indicates that over two-thirds of people without any training in informal logic regularly commit this fallacy.

DANGEROUS ASSUMPTIONS

Joe is busy rewiring his house. He is about to touch a wire when he suddenly wonders whether he remembered to turn off the power. He looks up and sees that, although the light is switched on, it remains off. So Joe reasons that the power must be off (*see right*). Confident he'll be safe, Joe touches the wire and gets an electric shock. Why? The power was on after all. Joe has been electrocuted by reason of a faulty bulb—and a bit of faulty reasoning.

> If the power is off, then the light won't come on.
> The light won't come on.
> Therefore the power is off.

Joe's argument—if A, then B. B, therefore A—wasn't valid. When you reason: if A, then B; A, therefore B, your argument is valid. It is a form of argument that philosophers call *modus ponens*. In it, A is called the *antecedent* (going before), and B the *consequent* (following on). It doesn't work if you affirm B—the consequent—and then conclude A.

If Craig doesn't want to see me again, he'll say he's busy tonight, reasons Kate. Craig texts her to say he has to work late, and Kate immediately concludes, without further reason, that he is not interested in her.

GO THE RIGHT WAY

In all probability, you sometimes make the same sort of mistake as Joe. To avoid this type of faulty reasoning, keep an eye out for "If... then...." claims and make sure the logic of the argument runs in the right direction. That way you won't end up being fried like Joe.

The genetic fallacy

In the genetic fallacy, it is assumed that if one thing, B, has its origin in another thing, A, any properties possessed by A are also likely to be possessed by B. In the acorn-and-oak-tree example below, we can see clearly that this is not the case. But why is this fallacy so troublesome in arenas such as religion and politics?

Oak trees come from acorns. Acorns are small and shiny. Therefore oak trees are small and shiny.

DOES EVIL BEGET EVIL?

Eggs have hard shells. Chickens come from eggs. So chickens have hard shells too. How can anyone sensible commit the genetic fallacy? Yet the philosopher Friedrich Nietzsche has been accused of doing just that. Nietzsche's argument against modern Christian morality is that it has its roots in the "slave morality" of ancient Rome, born of the resentment slaves felt toward their masters. The slaves effectively reversed what their masters believed was of value, making weakness "good," their masters' warrior ethos "bad," and so on. But even if Nietzsche is right, does that necessarily discredit Christian morality? Nietzsche seems to assume that pointing out a defect in the origin of a thing discredits the thing itself. But that is usually fallacious reasoning.

"FRED'S FATHER WAS A NAZI, SO FRED MUST BE A NAZI TOO."

Watch out for this fallacy in political debate, as in: "democracy in Freedonia was born of a violent and bloody struggle, so Freedonia's democracy must be a bad thing." Here's a particularly seductive example: "the Klingons' terrorist activity is the result of a legitimate grievance. Therefore the terrorist activity must itself be legitimate."

LIKE FATHER, LIKE SON?

If someone encourages you to believe that if something originated in something bad (or good) that thing must itself be bad (or good), it is always worth taking a closer look at their argument. They may have committed the genetic fallacy.

We may commit the genetic fallacy when we are shocked that Luke Skywalker's father is not brave and good like his son, but is Darth Vader.

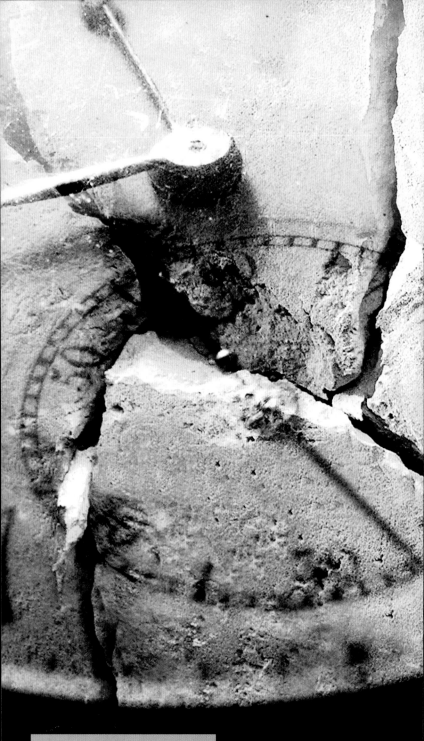

Fallacious reasoning can produce conclusions, just as, even though it is not a reliable timepiece, a broken clock tells the right time twice a day.

The masked man fallacy

The German philosopher Gottfried Leibniz's law—
"Identical objects must share all the same properties"—
is commonly relied on both inside and outside philosophy. However,
there are a number of important exceptions to this law. The "masked
man" is one of the classic fallacies concerning identity.

LEIBNIZ'S LAW

Philosophers and scientists often consider identity claims. For example, an ancient astronomical discovery was that Hesperus, the evening star, is identical with Phosphorus, the morning star. What appeared to be two distinct objects turned out to be one and the same—the planet we now call Venus. Scientists also claim that certain properties are identical—for example, that heat and molecular motion are one and the same.

> Mountain A is 16,000 feet high.
> Mountain B is not 16,000 feet high.
> **Therefore: mountain A is not identical with mountain B.**

Nepalis to the south of this mountain —what we know as Mount Everest— call it Sagramatha; Tibetans seeing it from the north (*below*) know it as Chomolungma. In fact, "Sagramatha is Chomolungma" is a true identity claim.

How are such claims put to the test? Leibniz noted that if two objects are identical, then any property possessed by one object will also be possessed by the other. Leibniz's law provides us with a useful tool. Suppose an explorer discovers what he believes to be two separate mountains. The explorer might decide to apply Leibniz's law systematically to its features and properties, as in the example above, to see whether this is true. If identical objects share all the same properties, then as soon as the explorer discovers a property possessed by one mountain that is not possessed by the other, it shows that the number of mountains he has discovered is two, not one.

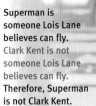

Superman is someone Lois Lane believes can fly. Clark Kent is not someone Lois Lane believes can fly. Therefore, Superman is not Clark Kent.

ENTER THE MASKED MAN

Suppose I witness a masked man rob a bank. Later, detectives tell me their chief suspect is my father. Horrified, I attempt to prove my father's innocence by pointing out that the masked man has a property my father lacks. The masked man is someone I believe robbed the bank, but my father is not

"I DON'T BELIEVE MY DAD DID IT. SO IT CAN'T BE HIM."

someone I believe robbed the bank. By Leibniz's law, the masked man cannot be my father. Both premises of this argument are true. Yet clearly, my father could still turn out to be the masked man. There is something wrong with this argument. But what? The answer is that Leibniz's law does not apply to all properties. It works for properties such as being 16,000 feet high. It does not work for properties such as "being someone I believe robbed a bank"—or, more generally, whenever the property in question involves someone's psychological attitude toward something.

A MATTER OF ATTITUDE

Whenever you come across an application of Leibniz's law, check whether the property involves someone's psychological attitude toward something—for example, what they believe, fear, hope, know, and so on about one thing and not another. If so, as in the example of what Lois Lane believes about Superman and Clark Kent (*above*), the argument is faulty.

The slippery slope fallacy

We are often warned against stepping onto "slippery slopes"—greasy slides that lead down to where the really bad stuff lies. But beware of overestimating risk: unless the proponent of a slippery slope argument can provide good grounds for supposing such a slide is inevitable, or even just likely, their argument is fallacious.

RINGING WARNING BELLS

We've all heard the saying: "Give them an inch, and they'll take a mile." It and others like it are used as warnings against even one small move, on the grounds that it will lead to an unstoppable chain of events. Suppose, for example, I ask you to lend me a dollar. Your friend advises you against lending me the money, warning that it might only be a dollar today, but I'll be back tomorrow asking

> If you lend Stephen one dollar today, tomorrow it will be two dollars, then ten dollars. Pretty soon he will owe you thousands!

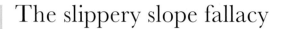

"IT'S JUST THE THIN END OF THE WEDGE."

Could animal cloning be the first step on a "slide" to human cloning? Decision makers must evaluate how slippery any particular slope could be before changing legislation.

for a bigger loan, and so on, until I bankrupt you. But obviously, if you lend me one dollar today, you can still easily refuse to lend me two dollars tomorrow or ten next week. The slide from owing one dollar to owing thousands is not inevitable. In fact it is not even likely. As it stands, this is a fallacious use of the slippery slope.

It is possible this argument might be salvaged. Perhaps your friend can show both that I am an inveterate borrower and that you find it hard to say "no" once you have said "yes." In that case, their warning begins to look more credible. But your friend does need to be able to provide these additional grounds. Without them, the warning is hollow.

Slippery slope arguments often crop up in connection with the legalizing of things, such as recreational drugs, euthanasia, genetic engineering, and so on. For example, it is very commonly suggested that if we allow couples to select the sex of their baby today, tomorrow we will allow selection for eye and hair color, and pretty soon we will have to permit "designer babies."

When rock and roll was born, many warned that this was the first step for society on a slippery slope to total moral degeneracy.

CREATING A MONSTER

Does the "designer baby" argument commit the slippery slope fallacy? Yes, it does, if no justification is provided for supposing that we cannot or will not simply stop at some point along the "slide" from selection of sex to, say, the full-blown Frankenstein-type experiments that some people fear. Perhaps such a slide is likely. But simply to say "well, it *could* happen" isn't to say it *will* happen. It *could* be that we all go out tomorrow and start murdering each other. I'm sure you don't believe that for a moment. The onus is on the proponent of any such argument to show more than that it could or might be so. If they cannot, they too have committed the slippery slope fallacy.

Legalizing marijuana would be just the start. Before we know it, the government will be legalizing heroin and crack cocaine too.

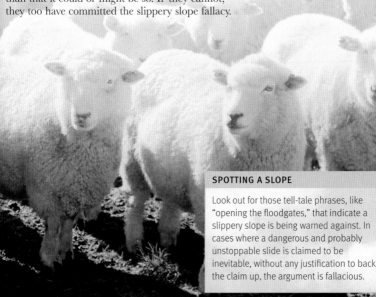

SPOTTING A SLOPE

Look out for those tell-tale phrases, like "opening the floodgates," that indicate a slippery slope is being warned against. In cases where a dangerous and probably unstoppable slide is claimed to be inevitable, without any justification to back the claim up, the argument is fallacious.

THINKING TOOLS

Thinking philosophically is a skill and, like most skills, the more you practice, the better you get. This section introduces a few of the philosopher's "tricks of the trade"—tools which, once mastered, can be applied in many different areas of philosophy.

There are many such tools to aid thinking—what follows is merely a small sample. Most of the thinking tools detailed in this section warn against making a common sort of mistake or error. These include category mistakes— wrongly assuming that the sort of thing that can be said of one category of thing can also sensibly be said of another; offering explanations that, on closer examination, are circular and so generate a regress; and falling for the all-too-seductive charms of pseudoprofundity.

Also included is an outline of a particular approach to answering a certain type of philosophical question, known as the "method of counter-examples." This vigorous form of back-and-forth debate has been popular with thinkers since the Ancient Greeks, although in more recent times the Austrian philosopher Ludwig Wittgenstein (*see pp.326–7*), with his theory of "family resemblance," has suggested that this approach may be not so much a philosophical tennis match as a wild-goose chase.

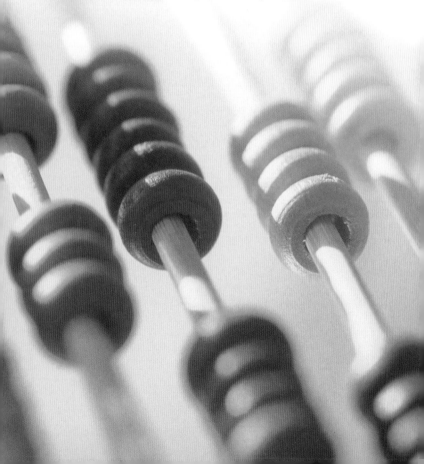

Spotting a regress

In philosophy we often want to explain things. On closer examination, however, our explanations sometimes turn out to take for granted what they are supposed to explain. Where that is the case, a regress looms. Spotting where an explanation or argument generates a regress is an important philosophical skill.

KNOWING WHERE TO STOP

Things fall when not supported. My glass does not fall because it is supported by a table. The table does not fall because it is supported by the Earth. So why doesn't the Earth fall? Ancient Hindu thinkers supposed that the Earth sits on the back of an enormous elephant. What holds up the elephant? Why, a giant turtle. You can see that a regress looms here. However many gargantuan creatures we introduce, we will never really succeed in explaining why everything doesn't fall. At each step we merely postpone that mystery.

The Hindus avoided this regress by making the turtle the exception to the "things fall" rule. It is the one thing that requires no further support. But if we are going to introduce an exception to the rule, why go so far as the turtle? Why not just make the Earth the exception to the rule instead? We do not, as yet, have any justification for introducing any of these cosmic beasts.

Is our behavior explained by the actions of little people running around inside us? If it is, do these little people have even smaller people inside them, and so on?

Similar regress problems crop up in philosophy. If everything has a cause, then God must exist as the cause of the universe. But if everything has a cause, so does God. It seems we will need to introduce a second God as the cause of the first, a third God as the cause of the second, and so on. Of course, just as the ancient Hindus made the turtle the exception to the rule, we might insist that God is the exception to the rule that everything has a cause. But then why not make the universe the exception to the rule, instead? We have not, as yet, been given any more reason to suppose God exists than we have to suppose there exists a giant turtle.

Hindu mythology makes the turtle the exception to the rule—the only thing not requiring support. But why not further cosmic beasts holding it up? And if so, what is holding them up?

Pseudoprofundity

Around the globe, audiences sit at the feet of marketing experts, lifestyle consultants, mystics, cult leaders, and other self-styled gurus waiting for the next deep and profound insight. How do these elevated individuals come by their wisdom? Unfortunately, in some cases the audience is duped by pseudoprofundity.

WEIGHTY WORDS

The art of sounding profound is fairly easily mastered. You too can make deep- and meaningful-sounding pronouncements if you are prepared to follow a few simple rules. First, try stating the incredibly obvious. Only do it v-e-r-y s-l-o-w-l-y, with a knowing nod. This works particularly well if your remark has something to do with one of the big themes of life: love, death, and money. Here are some examples: "Death comes to us all;" "We all want to be loved;" "Money is used to buy things." Try it for yourself. If you state the obvious with sufficient gravitas, following up with a pregnant pause, you may soon find others

A guru is, properly, a religious or spiritual guide. Today, we see the term applied to any number of "experts," from "diet doctors" to "personal growth facilitators."

start to nod in agreement, perhaps muttering "How true that is." Now that you have warmed up, let's move on to a different technique—the use of jargon. A few big, not-easily-understood words can enhance the illusion of profundity. All that is required is a little imagination. To begin with, try making up some terms that have similar meanings to certain familiar words, but that differ from them in some subtle and never-fully-explained way. For example, don't talk about people being happy or sad, but about people having "positive or negative attitudinal orientations," which sounds far more impressive.

Now try translating some dull truisms into your newly invented language. For, example, the obvious fact that happy people tend to make other people

The carefully crafted jargon used by modern business and lifestyle "gurus" can be as mesmerizing as the words of evangelical preachers.

"LIFE IS OFTEN A FORM OF DEATH..."

The slogans of the Party in George Orwell's *Nineteen Eighty-Four* cryptically pair words with opposing meanings, such as "War is peace"—another easy way of generating the illusion of profundity.

happier can be expressed as "positive attitudinal orientations have high transferability." Also, whether you are a business guru, a cult leader, or a mystic, it always helps to talk of "energies" and "balances." This makes it sound as if you have discovered some deep mechanism or power that could potentially be harnessed and used by others. That will make it much easier to convince people that if they don't buy into your advice, they will be missing out.

Unfortunately, some cult leaders, business gurus, and mystics make cynical use of these and similar techniques to generate the illusion that they possess deep insights. Now you see how easy it is to generate pseudoprofundities of your own, I'm sure you will be less impressed next time you encounter them.

Method of counterexamples

Philosophers often ask questions of the form "What is X?," but outside philosophy, they are rarely asked. We usually assume we can answer them quite easily—until we try. In fact, they are notoriously difficult to answer. One of the oldest approaches to answering them is known as the method of counterexamples.

NO EASY ANSWERS

In the dialogs of Plato, there are many examples of questions of the type "What is X?" Plato has Socrates ask the citizens of Athens questions such as "What is courage?," "What is beauty?," and so on. The Athenians usually think they know the answers, and offer definitions that, at first sight, look very plausible. Socrates, however, is quickly able to reveal the inadequacy of their definitions: one way in which he does this is by employing the method of counterexamples.

> **Mike:** What is a dog?
> *Stephen:* A mammal that barks.
> **Mike:** But seals are mammals and they bark, but they aren't dogs. And Rover here is a dog, but he can't bark!

To explain the method, here is a more mundane example. Suppose we ask "What is a chair?" This appears to be a simple question, easily answered. We might begin with: "A chair is an object built to be sat on." This sounds perfectly plausible. Except that, with a little ingenuity, it is possible to think of counterexamples: a park bench, for example, is built

"WHAT IS JUSTICE?"

Socrates

to be sat on, but it is not, strictly speaking, a chair. Or suppose you find a large chair-shaped boulder, and you install it in your yard as a piece of garden furniture. The boulder is now a chair, yet it certainly was not built to be sat on.

Faced with these counterexamples to our definition, we might attempt to refine it. Perhaps we might try "A chair is an object

Socrates asked "What is courage?" of the Athenian general Laches, then countered his answer with an example that did not fit his definition.

used for just one person to sit on." This definition gets around our two counterexamples: a bench no longer qualifies as a chair, because a bench is used to seat more than one person. And by switching from "built to be sat on" to "used for sitting on," our boulder-chair does now qualify as a chair. However, there are counterexamples to this new definition: a bicycle seat, for example, is used for just one person to sit on, but a bicycle seat is not a chair. We might then refine our definition still further, like so: "A chair is an object with legs that is used for just one person to sit on." This definition rules out bicycle seats, since they don't have legs. Unfortunately it also rules out our boulder-chair, which also does not have legs. In order to deal with these new

What is a chair? We all know the answer—or do we? It can be remarkably difficult to come up with a definition that does justice to all the possible shapes and styles of chair.

NECESSARY OR SUFFICIENT?

In asking the question "What is X?," philosophers are typically looking for a special sort of definition. For example, a triangle might be defined in this way: "Something is a triangle if and only if it is a three-straight-sided closed figure."

Being a three-straight-sided closed figure is a *necessary* condition of being a triangle—necessarily, anything that isn't straight-sided is not a triangle. Being a three-straight-sided closed figure is also *sufficient* to qualify something as a triangle—necessarily, if something is a three-straight-sided closed figure, then it is a triangle.

When philosophers ask "What is X?" they typically look for a definition that gives the necessary and sufficient conditions for *being an X*. Counterexamples to such a definition will show either that the definition does not specify a necessary condition, or that it does not specify a sufficient condition.

Paul's mother: **If you don't do well at school, you'll never make anything of yourself.**
Paul: That's not always true, Mom. What about Marlon Brando? He was expelled from school, but went on to be a really successful actor.

counterexamples, we have to try to refine our definition still further. Using this method—by continuing to refine the definition, finding more counterexamples, then refining again—we may hope to get closer and closer to a satisfactory definition.

WE DON'T KNOW, AND YET WE DO

Socrates often asked "What is X?" of those who we might assume are best-placed to know what "X" is, before using counterexamples to reveal the limitations of their answers. For example, in the dialog the *Laches*, he asks the Athenian general Laches: "What is courage?" The general defines courage as standing firm in battle. But Socrates quickly comes up with a counterexample to this definition: someone might stand firm in battle, but simply out of foolish endurance, putting both themselves and others in danger. That would not be courage. A genuinely courageous person knows both when to stand firm and when to retreat.

After several more attempts by Laches to define courage, Socrates concludes that, though there must be some essential feature common and peculiar to all acts of courage in virtue of which they are courageous, we remain ignorant about what this essential feature is. Even though Laches is courageous himself, he is unable to define what "courage" actually is. It seems that even to him, the "essence" of courage is hidden.

Yet the method Socrates employs in order to try to show this—the method of counterexamples—suggests that, at some level, we do possess this knowledge. After all, Laches is able to recognize that someone who foolishly holds fast in battle is

not truly courageous. He recognizes that such a person is a counterexample to his definition, so he must, at some level, already know what courage is. If Laches did not know what courage was, how would he be able to recognize that he has been confronted with a counterexample?

When we ask "What is X?," it seems that the knowledge we seek is, in a sense, something that we already possess. It is, if you like, buried within us (in fact, Socrates believed it is innate). We are just unable to bring this knowledge to the surface and make it clear and explicit. The method of counterexamples is designed to help us do this.

In the eye of the beholder? Many things can be thought of as being beautiful, be it works of art or music, the curves of a classic car, or the simplicity and complexity of nature—but what is beauty itself? In Plato's dialogs, Socrates concludes that answers to such questions are somehow hidden from us.

"WHAT IS BEAUTY?"

Socrates

Family resemblance

When we ask the question "What is art?" we may assume that there must be one quality that all works of art have in common—something that "makes them" art. Yet it is very difficult to identify what this quality is. Perhaps we should question the assumption that there must be such a common feature.

SEARCHING FOR A LINK

The history of Western philosophy is in large part constituted by unsuccessful attempts to identify elusive common denominators. In the dialogs of Plato (*see pp.244–7*), Socrates (*see pp.242–3*) supposes there must be something that all beautiful things have in common in virtue of which they are beautiful; something all works of art possess in virtue of which they are works of art, and so on. Socrates then demolishes various suggestions as to what this one feature might be by applying the method of counterexamples (*see pp.216–9*). The Austrian philosopher Wittgenstein (*see pp.326–7*) makes the radical suggestion that the hunt for the common quality may, in many cases, be a wild-goose chase. He suggests it may be more helpful to think in terms of "family resemblances." If you look at a photo of a large family gathering, you will see similarities. Some members of the family will have the same eyes, others the same nose, and so on. Yet, despite these overlapping similarities, there need be no one feature shared by all the faces.

"WHAT IS ART?..."

Although squashes come in all shapes, sizes, and colors, they form a recognizable family. Nonetheless, there may be no single visual characteristic that all members of the family share.

KEEPING IT IN THE FAMILY

Wittgenstein calls this kind of similarity "family resemblance." It is easy to construct our own family resemblance concept. Let's define the term "widget" as follows: something is a widget if, and only if, it possesses three or more of a set of six characteristics (*right*). The illustrations below show a variety of objects that, by applying our criterion, can be seen to belong, or not, to the widget family.

Widget characteristics:
1. It is portable
2. It costs over $100
3. It can be blown through
4. It makes a noise
5. It is longer than it is wide
6. It has holes

Widgets
This clarinet, telephoto camera, and python are all widgets. Note that there is no one characteristic that all widgets must possess.

Non-widgets
This kite, diamond, and armchair are all non-widgets, because they possess fewer than three of the widget characteristics.

"...THERE MUST BE SOME ONE QUALITY WITHOUT WHICH A WORK OF ART CANNOT EXIST..."

Clive Bell

Wittgenstein suggests that many concepts—perhaps he would include art—are best understood in terms of such resemblances. He illustrates this with the example of games. "Consider for example the proceedings that we call 'games,'" he writes. "I mean board games, card games, ball games, Olympic games, and so on. What is common to them all?... If you look at them, you will not see something that is common to all, but similarities, relationships, and a whole series of them at that." If Wittgenstein is right, then the search for a quality that is common to all works of art, for example—a question that preoccupied the philosopher of art Clive Bell—could be misconceived. Whenever you are confronted by a "What is X?" question, it is always worth considering whether X might be a family resemblance concept.

Degrees of reasonableness

It is sometimes assumed that if neither a belief nor its denial are conclusively "proved," then the two beliefs must be more or less equally reasonable or unreasonable. This, however, is false. The beliefs may still differ dramatically in their reasonableness. There is, if you like, a scale of reasonableness on which beliefs may be located.

JUSTIFYING OUR BELIEFS

Some beliefs are very reasonable indeed. It is reasonable for me to believe that there is an orange on the table in front of me, because I can see it there. It is also reasonable for me to believe that the tree outside my house still exists, because it was there when I last looked, and I have no reason to suppose anyone has removed it in the meantime. And it is reasonable for me to believe that Japan exists, despite the fact that I have never actually been there. I possess an enormous amount of evidence that Japan exists, and hardly any evidence to suggest that it doesn't.

It is very reasonable for the character Truman Burbank, in the 1998 film *The Truman Show*, to believe that the world he lives in is real, when in fact almost every aspect of it is fake. This does not make his belief less reasonable.

Of course, despite being highly reasonable, these beliefs could conceivably turn out to be false. The orange I seem to see might be a hallucination, and the tree in my yard could have been removed by pranksters. In the film *The Truman Show*, the main character is duped into thinking he is living his life in the real world, when in fact everything around him is a carefully managed set created for a television program. I could be the unwitting victim of a similar complex conspiracy to make me believe Japan exists when in fact it does not.

So let's acknowledge that I might be mistaken in my beliefs. But this is not to say that they aren't very reasonable: most of them clearly are, and lie toward the top of the "scale of reasonableness." At the bottom end of the scale lies the belief, say, that fairies and goblins exist. This is a very unreasonable thing to believe: there is no good evidence that these tiny folk exist and plenty of

Highly reasonable The oranges in front of you are real.

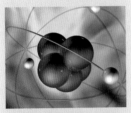

Very reasonable Electrons exist, even though we can't see them.

Quite reasonable Aliens exist—given the size of the universe.

Quite unreasonable Elvis lives: his "death" was a conspiracy.

Highly unreasonable
Leprechauns and fairies are real.

"WHO ARE YOU GOING TO BELIEVE, ME OR YOUR EYES?"

Groucho Marx

evidence that they are fictions. Around the middle of the scale of reasonableness lie beliefs which are neither highly reasonable nor highly unreasonable. Take the belief that there are intelligent life forms living somewhere out there in the universe. True, we have no direct evidence of any such extraterrestrial intelligence. On the other hand, we know that intelligent life has evolved on this planet, and we also know that there must be countless other similar planets out there. So it is not especially improbable that there is intelligent life out there somewhere.

Beliefs can change their position on the scale of reasonableness over time. A few decades ago, belief in electrons was considered fairly reasonable. Given the additional scientific evidence that has since accrued, it is now very reasonable. The belief that the world is flat, which was once not particularly unreasonable, is now very

We may not have conclusive proof that highly reasonable beliefs are true, nor that outlandish ones are false—we can't prove beyond all doubt that fairies don't exist, for example. Still, belief in fairies is low on the scale of reasonableness.

unreasonable indeed. The scale may also vary from one person to the next, if one has access to evidence the other lacks.

Some consider that belief in God is no more reasonable than belief in fairies. Others believe it is fairly reasonable—at least as reasonable as, say, belief in extraterrestrial intelligence. Those who claim to have had direct experience of God, or who think miracles and so on constitute fairly good evidence that God exists, may place belief fairly high up on the scale, even while acknowledging that their belief is not "proved" (*see box, below*).

"ANGELS EXIST." "NO THEY DON'T." "PROVE IT."

Sometimes, when someone has been given very good grounds for supposing a belief is false, they respond by saying: "But you can't prove *B* is false, can you? *B* might be true!" They think this shows belief *B* is still pretty reasonable—perhaps even as reasonable as the belief that *B* is false. Here is a philosophical example. Even if we cannot conclusively prove either that God does exist or that he doesn't, it doesn't follow that the belief that God exists is just as reasonable or unreasonable as the belief that he doesn't. If there are very good grounds for supposing God exists and little reason to suppose he doesn't, it is far more reasonable to believe in God than it is to deny God's existence. Conversely, there might be powerful evidence that God doesn't exist, and little reason to suppose he does, in which case atheism may be by far the more

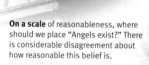

On a scale of reasonableness, where should we place "Angels exist?" There is considerable disagreement about how reasonable this belief is.

reasonable position to adopt. We should not allow the fact that neither belief can be conclusively proved to obscure the fact that one belief might be much more reasonable than the other. Unfortunately, theists (believers in God) sometimes respond to atheist arguments by pointing out that as the atheist has not conclusively *proved* there is no God, belief in God must be reasonable after all. Actually, even if the atheists can't conclusively prove there is no God, they might still succeed in showing that belief in God is very unreasonable indeed—perhaps even as unreasonable as belief in fairies or leprechauns. Pointing out the absence of "proof" against a belief does not push it much up the scale of reasonableness.

Category mistakes

The expression "category mistake" was introduced by
the English philosopher Gilbert Ryle (*see p.331*) in his
book *The Concept of Mind*. Someone commits a category mistake when
they mistakenly assume that things in one category can have the
characteristics proper only to things in another category.

MIND AND BODY

Suppose you invite someone to see your home,
and give them a tour of the rooms. But at the end
of the tour, your guest then asks to see your home.
They have assumed that your home is in the same
category as the various rooms they have visited.
The truth, of course, is that those rooms together
constitute your home, and your visitor has made
a "category mistake." Gilbert Ryle believes
Descartes (*see pp.276–9*) makes just this type of
mistake in supposing the mind is a substance in
the same category as a physical substance.

> The forwards, midfielders,
> defenders, and goalkeeper
> have all run out onto the
> field. But where is the soccer
> team?

The tourist who says "Yes, I know
where all the different colleges are,
but where is Oxford University?"
has made a basic category mistake: the
University is composed of the colleges.

For Descartes the mind, not being a physical object,
must be an immaterial object. The truth, claims
Ryle, is that to possess a mind is to possess a whole
series of behavioral dispositions. As they are
dispositions physical organisms can possess, no
further immaterial "something" is required. To
suppose otherwise is to commit a category mistake.

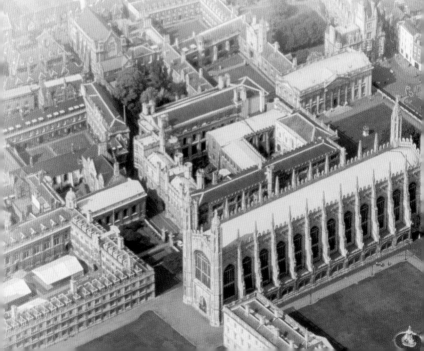

WHO'S WHO
IN PHILOSOPHY

IN THIS FINAL CHAPTER WE HAVE GATHERED TOGETHER MORE THAN A HUNDRED OF THE MOST SIGNIFICANT PHILOSOPHERS TO HAVE LEFT THEIR THOUGHTS AND THEORIES TO POSTERITY, FROM THE THINKERS OF MILETUS IN ANCIENT GREECE, SOME 2,500 YEARS AGO, RIGHT UP TO THE PRESENT DAY.

Philosophy comprises a cumulative and evolving body of ideas, and the speculations of individual thinkers do not stand alone, but, rather, develop in dialog with tradition. For this reason, while an isolated description of an individual's life and works can provide a useful impression of a particular thinker, a more rounded portrait is to be gained by exploring the references to related thinkers and topics in this book, and, of course, their own essential works.

Are philosophers born or made? An infant Jean-Paul Sartre begins a lifetime's pondering on what it is to exist in the world.

Included in this chapter are those thinkers whose ideas have made the most notable impact on the course of philosophy. Presenting them in chronological order by year of birth, particularly when compared with the timelines of key events in Chapter Two, reveals links with social, cultural, and political history, while tracing the development of ideas across the centuries. Where dates are uncertain, *ca.* (*circa*) indicates an estimate, and where evidence exists only of when a thinker was known to be active or "flourishing," *fl.* (*floreat*) indicates so.

A striking feature of any history of philosophy is the remarkable diversity of interests, aims, and approaches, and how different thinkers have very different notions of what it is that they are doing as philosophers. Philosophy's own conception of its proper domain is continually changing. Each generation sees the emergence of new issues of concern, and fields of inquiry considered in the past to be the province of philosophers have developed into independent sciences such as physics, biology, and psychology. Moreover, questions that appeared of the utmost importance to one generation may well be ignored by the next, only to be revived again centuries later. Despite all this, these thinkers form part of a common enterprise: their work represents an ongoing critical engagement with questions that are both novel and perennial.

Busts of the great Classical thinkers line the walls of the Hall of Philosophers in the Capitoline Museum in Rome. Their intellectual influence is still felt today.

Siddhartha Gautama

● *c.* 563–483 BCE 　⚑ Terai, northern India

In the 6th century BCE, a wandering ascetic sat beneath the Bodhi Tree and resolved to meditate until he had grasped the ultimate truth of things. He found enlightenment there, and his discoveries inaugurated one of the world's great religions, as well as a complex philosophical system.

LIFE AND WORKS

Legends about Siddhartha's life grew in the century after his death, and his biography has become an elaborate narrative used for the purpose of instruction. He was born at Lumbini, in the Terai lowlands near the foothills of the Himalayas in modern-day Nepal. Legend has it that his family were the leaders of the clan of the Shalyas, and, anxious that he should not be diverted from his duty, his father shielded him from ugliness and suffering by keeping him within the grounds of his palaces. Siddhartha was married at 16 and had a son named Rahula, which means "fetter." However, the story goes that he left the palaces four times, encountering in turn an old man, a sick man, a corpse, and finally an ascetic—a holy man. These shock encounters with human suffering and mortality prompted him to seek a remedy to the human condition by following the example of the ascetic.

Shortly thereafter, aged 29, he secretly left his wife and child in search of spiritual understanding. He studied meditation techniques and austerities, and finally reached enlightenment at 35. He then made his important First Sermon, *Setting in Motion the Wheel of the Dharma*. He set up an order to spread his teachings and spent the rest of his life as an itinerant teacher, wandering from village to town in the Ganges basin. Shortly after his death, at a gathering of his disciples, senior monks recited his teachings for the assembly to memorize. Transmitted orally, they were not recorded in writing for centuries.

A prayer wheel represents the Wheel of the Dharma. Its hub stands for discipline, the essential core of meditation practice.

KEY IDEAS

In his First Sermon the enlightened Siddhartha—the Buddha—outlined his main teachings in four "noble truths." The first of these and the starting point for Buddhism demands that we wake up to the reality of human suffering. We must all endure pain, sickness, and death. Each of us will at some time suffer emotional distress and grief. This is not to say that life is unrelentingly painful, but, since all pleasures are fleeting, it remains intrinsically dissatisfying. Moreover, suffering will characterize our existence for innumerable more lives, since we have all lived before and will be reborn in an endless cycle.

This apparently bleak—Buddhists would say realistic—view of life is backed up by reference to the thesis of the radical impermanence of all things. According to the Buddha everything is in a state of continual flux. However, our reluctance to accept the insubstantiality of things produces a sense of frustration and unease and is the cause of desire. We crave permanence, both in things

ACHIEVING NIRVANA

In Buddhism, there are two nirvanas. One can be attained in this life and is the transformed psychological state attained by Siddhartha, in which the enlightened one experiences deep spiritual joy without anxiety. Final nirvana is reached when an enlightened one dies, and represents the final end to the cycle of rebirth and suffering. So what exactly happens to us at death? The Buddha likened the cycle of rebirth to a flame being passed from one candle-wick to another. There is no substantial continuity, just a continuity of the process of consumption. Final nirvana is like the flame being blown out: it is not the end of the self as such, since there is no substantial soul. Rather it is an end to the illusion of self, as all false distinctions between self and world break down. The processes of craving and consumption which are premised on the obsession with self and which fuel the rebirth process are extinguished.

and in the self, and in this way we become slaves to cravings that can never be satisfied. And this gives us the second noble truth, namely that all suffering is the product of insatiable desire.

PATHS TO ENLIGHTENMENT

In his own analogy, the first two truths constitute the Buddha's identification and diagnosis of the sickness that characterizes the human condition. But the proper reaction to the recognition of our disease is not despair. The third noble truth tells us that there is a cure to our suffering, and the fourth details how it is effected, in other words, the course of treatment. Contrary to what we might expect, however, the treatment is not to find the object of our desires. As we have seen, the satisfaction of desire is always merely temporary and leads inevitably to further desires, so repeating the cycle and fuelling the flame of our suffering.

Instead, the third noble truth teaches that an end to suffering is only to be found by reaching "nirvana." Nirvana means "blowing out" or "quenching" desire, and is to be achieved by overcoming our attachment to the ego and its needs. Looking inward reveals that we have no essential nature, no self or soul, and are no more than the sum of the various mental and physical processes that make us up. Once it is recognized that the substantial self is an illusion, the striving associated with our efforts to satisfy its desires will dissipate, and we can escape from the cycle of rebirth. The way to achieve nirvana involves following the "eightfold path": a series of guidelines to follow for the virtuous life which make one desireless, but also compassionate and clear-minded. It is estimated that there are now 350 million practicing Buddhists worldwide.

SEE ALSO ▶ Ancient Eastern thought (pp.26–7) • Religious experience (pp.150–2)

Buddhist monks walk along a dusty path, bearing alms bowls. There are strict rules governing the conduct of such monks, who must rely on charitable donations for sustenance and material needs.

Thales of Miletus

● *fl. ca.* 585 BCE   ⚑ Greece

Thales is generally considered the first philosopher of the West and the father of science. He and the Milesian thinkers who followed him were the first to search for naturalistic explanations of phenomena rather than to appeal to myths and the actions of anthropomorphic gods.

LIFE AND WORKS

Very little is known for certain of Thales's life and, as no writings survive, we have to rely on legend and accounts of his teachings by other writers. Aristotle's *Metaphysics* is one important source, but this was written 200 years after Thales's death. Another is Diogenes Laertius, who lived in the third century CE. We know that Thales was from the Greek colony of Miletus, and some sources say that he traveled widely during his lifetime, gathering ideas from various cultures such as Babylon and Egypt. Legend has it that he introduced geometry to Greece, having learned it from the Egyptians. His cosmology certainly owes much to the Egyptians, who believed the Earth floated on water. It is stated that to prove the value of his

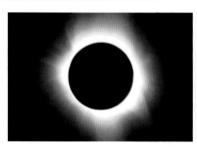

A noted astronomer, Thales successfully predicted an eclipse of the sun, reported by Herodotus, which we now know to have taken place in 585 BCE.

learning, Thales applied his knowledge of the stars to predict a good olive harvest, bought up all the local olive presses, then profited by renting them back to the growers to meet the demand.

KEY IDEAS

Thales is best remembered for the claim that the ultimate substance from which all things are composed is water, so all the apparently different things we observe around us, including earth and air, plants and animals, are ultimately reducible to one substance. This is often seen as the first in a long line of scientific hypotheses examining the nature of everything that leads directly to modern physics. The water theory is closely linked in Thales's philosophy to the cosmological claim that the Earth is a disc floating in a vast sea, and that it originated from water by a process of solidification. He appears to have arrived at this view by observing the behavior of moist substances as they turn either solid or liquid, while he

also noted that water is absorbed by all plants and animals, suggesting that they must be composed of it.

But it was Thales's skills in astronomy, geometry, and engineering that seem to have secured his reputation as a great sage. Diogenes Laertius describes how Thales determined the height of the pyramids by measuring their shadows at the moment when his own shadow was equal to his height. Thales is also said to have been able to measure the distance of ships out at sea from the shore, and to have diverted the Halys River so that the Lydian army could ford it and march against the Persians.

SEE ALSO ▸ Ancient Greece *(pp.24–5)* • Democritus and atomism *(p.241)*

Pythagoras

⏺ *ca.* 570–495 BCE   🏛 Greece

In the figure of Pythagoras are combined two very different strands of thought, both hugely influential. He was mystical and may even have claimed to be divine, while at the same time he invented the deductive method in mathematics and made various key scientific discoveries.

LIFE AND WORKS

The many legends that surround Pythagoras's life make separating the history from the fiction a difficult task. Born on the Greek island of Samos, he fled the tyrant Polycrates, and possibly traveled in Egypt, but certainly he ended up in Croton in southern Italy. There he founded a community of disciples with a bizarre set of rules, including not eating beans or allowing swallows to share one's roof. His disciples were committed to the pursuit of esoteric knowledge as well as to a quasi-religious reverence for their leader and founder.

Pythagoras's teachings are known only through his followers and so it is not easy to discern which are really due to him, but doubtless his most important contribution was his application of mathematics within philosophy and science. The idea that the universe can be explained mathematically has been enormously fruitful in the development of scientific knowledge. He is also seen as the forefather of the tradition in Western philosophy, which extends into the era of 18th-century rationalism, that regards mathematics as the paradigm of genuine knowledge, and deductive reasoning as the key to metaphysical truth. His notion that the intellect is the route to genuine knowledge and his distinction between the sensible and intelligible realms have long been enduring themes within Western thought.

Pythagoreans' Hymn *to the Rising Sun*: the committed followers of Pythagoras greeted the sunrise to celebrate the start of each new day.

KEY IDEAS

Pythagoras's religious views appear to have involved belief in the immortality of the soul and the idea that all things in existence have been and will be born again in an endless cycle. He taught that actions in this life will be rewarded or punished in the next, and that since all living things are reincarnated we should treat all animals as our kin. Escape from the endless cycle of rebirth is possible through living the philosophical life of disinterested contemplation.

the other two sides) had been known for centuries, Pythagoras's proof established it as an eternal and necessary truth.

Unlike all truths about the physical world, no matter how enduring, mathematical truths are for ever. Moreover Pythagoras regarded the mind's apprehension of mathematical objects as superior to the imperfect versions of them perceived in the physical world. All circles perceived by the senses are approximate, yet we are

"ALL THINGS ARE NUMBERS."

Attributed to Pythagoras

While the mystical elements in his thinking can appear rather at odds with Pythagoras's mathematical and scientific discoveries, in fact they are closely allied. He valued the speculation of the sage as the route to wisdom, and mathematics as the means to uncovering otherwise impenetrable truths about the world.

Pythagoras originated the idea of treating numbers as shapes, as, for example, they appear on dice; and today we still speak of the square and cube of numbers. His fascination with mathematics was based on the timeless and universal nature of its discoveries. So while the fact about right-angled triangles (namely that the square of the hypotenuse is the sum of the squares of

able to understand the idea of a perfect circle with the mind. This led to the idea that precise reasoning deals with a superior world of supersensible objects.

But mathematics also has its empirical applications. Pythagoras is credited with the astronomical discovery that the morning and evening stars are the same planet, Venus. He also discovered that the intervals on a musical scale are exact arithmetical ratios, and he believed that similar mathematical reductions could be found in other areas of scientific inquiry. This set in motion the Pythagorean project to discover the mathematical principles that underlie the shifting appearances of the sensible world: that at root, reality is expressible in numbers.

Pythagoras was the first to see that musical intervals could be expressed as mathematical ratios.

SEE ALSO ▶ Reason and experience (*pp.66–73*)

Lao Tzu

◒ *fl.* 6th century BCE   ⚑ China

Lao Tzu means "old master" in Chinese, but who the man was who bears this title, and whether he really lived at all, is uncertain. In any case, he is credited with authorship of one of the most important works in Chinese philosophy, and is regarded as the father of Daoism.

LIFE AND WORKS

Legend has it that Lao Tzu was keeper of the archives of the Imperial Library of the Zhou Dynasty. According to accounts dating back at least to the 4th century BCE, Lao Tzu met Confucius when he visited his library in search of wisdom. Lao Tzu is said to have felt sorry for Confucius and his obsession with man-made distinctions, such as between right and wrong. He told him to give up his airs and graces and that his respect for ritual and custom was misplaced. Confucius is said to have been overawed by Lao Tzu's wisdom, likening him to a dragon. Lao Tzu eventually became exasperated with the ways of men and, aged 80, turned his back on society and disappeared into the desert.

ESSENTIAL TEXTS *Dao De Jing*

KEY IDEAS

The *Dao De Jing* stands in contrast to the ideas of Confucius as one of the two dominant influences on the development of Chinese thought. Its concerns are broad, dealing with personal spirituality, ethics, politics, and metaphysics. But while the Confucian *Analects* focus on social relations, the *Dao De Jing* is far more concerned with how the individual should approach life. Moreover its style is often elliptical and the approach is far more mystical in flavor. It is written in two parts, the Book of Virtue (*De Jing*), dealing with politics and ethics, and the Book of the Way (*Dao Jing*), dealing with metaphysics. "Dao" is usually translated as "way" and refers to the governing principle of life and the universe. It is the natural working of things. The *Dao De Jing* says that we cannot grasp the Dao in language and the ineffability of the subject matter may account for some of the difficulty in interpretation. If we attempt to grasp the Dao by exercising our intellect, we are bound to fail. Indeed, thinking is the cause of all problems and all striving is counter-productive. Rather, we should avoid the pursuit of goals and allow the Dao to flow through us. This approach to life, known as *wu-wei*, or "nonstriving," is the key to living in tune with the Dao.

SEE ALSO ▸ Confucius *(pp.236–7)*

The burning of incense plays a key role in Daoist prayer and ceremonies.

Confucius

⊖ 551–479 BCE   🏳 China

Confucianism first flourished in China's classical age (550–200 BCE), becoming the official philosophy of the Han Dynasty in 140 BCE. It has remained a guiding force in Chinese thought to this day, and stresses personal integrity as the means to promote social cohesion and harmony.

LIFE AND WORKS

Confucius was of aristocratic descent, but his father was already 70 at the time of his birth and died when he was three, leaving his mother, aged 18, to bring up the family in comparative poverty. By the age of 15 Confucius had elected to devote his life to learning, and in 527 BCE, when his mother died, he turned the family home into a school.

Confucius lived in the province of Lu during a time when the degenerating feudal system in China was fuelling a period of some considerable political unrest. He deplored the moral degeneracy that characterized political life, and reckoned the only way to address it was to return to the values of the past. For this reason he taught ancient classic texts, and it is said that he would sing verses from them, accompanying himself on the zither. He would teach any committed student,

Seeking "the Way," Confucius traveled around China for many years, searching for a place to practice his social ideals.

regardless of social standing. While teaching, his interest in politics led him to join the local government and he rose to the position of Minister of Justice. The reforms he introduced are said to have been so successful that crime was virtually eliminated.

However, the ongoing political instability led Confucius, at the age of 50, to leave Lu and embark on 13 years of travel in an unsuccessful search for a ruler who would help him put his political ideas into practice.

He returned to Lu in 484 BCE and spent his remaining days teaching while his disciples recorded his ideas for posterity in the *Analects* (*Lun-Yü*). Confucius's school was first continued by his disciples, and Mencius and Xunzi are the best known of his later followers.

ESSENTIAL TEXTS The *Analects*

CONFUCIUS ON SOCIETY

All citizens should have an allotted role in the well-run state and Confucius emphasized the responsibilities of individuals to discharge the social duties afforded them by their position. Confucius laid great store by social conventions and practices—what he called "rites and music"—as a means to promote social harmony. Rites help to cement social roles and hierarchies while music is able to bring people together in mutual respect and shared enjoyment. Moreover they underpin the basic social roles and relationships that are the fabric of a well-ordered society. For these reasons, Confucius believed rulers should encourage the observance of traditional customs and rites, such as marriage.

KEY IDEAS

In the *Analects*, Confucius is portrayed not as an original thinker, but as a communicator of traditional ideas concerning the proper manner in which to conduct political life. He advocated a return to traditional values and methods of government in order to deal with the social unrest and feudal infighting that characterized the times. By careful attention to the time-honored customs of ordinary people and, through the study of various ancient scriptures, to key political events in the past he claimed to have discovered those traditional social structures that reflect the natural order. Adherence to the principles of this order would enable a common government for the whole of China to be restored, and with it, lasting peace and prosperity.

Insofar as Confucius's teaching reflects the traditional values of a feudal society, it perhaps inevitably stresses the central importance of conventional familial and social roles. He identified archetypal relationships, such as between husband and wife, parent and child, and ruler and subject—and the reciprocal duties they carry with them. So, for example, a subject has a duty to obey the ruler, but the ruler also has a duty to listen to criticism from their subjects.

ENCOURAGING PROGRESS

While he is usually portrayed as a conservative thinker, Confucius's use of the scriptures belies a reformist agenda. For example, he argued that rulers should be selected on their merits, rather than by lineage; that they should show genuine devotion for their subjects; and that they needed to develop a virtuous character in order that they might earn respect and compliance from the citizenship. Like the great leaders of the past, rulers need to promote the moral education of the people and ensure they have all their material needs. Government should operate by appealing to the natural morality of the people—which at core means treating others as you would be treated. Forcing people to conform is not the purpose of government, and force is not necessary when those in power discharge their duties properly. Confucius argued that good government must foster an internalized respect for appropriate moral conduct, rather than the fear of punishment. Only then can society be expected to run smoothly.

SEE ALSO ▸ Political philosophy (*pp.160–77*)

Traditional music and ceremonial rites, said Confucius, help bind societies together and promote harmony.

Heraclitus

🌑 *fl. ca.* 500 BCE   🏛 Greece

Heraclitus's idea that an eternal order exists beneath the shifting world of appearances had a profound influence on Plato, and since the rediscovery of Heraclitus in the 18th century his influence has grown. Nietzsche saw in Heraclitus a thinker who valued becoming over being.

LIFE AND WORKS

Heraclitus was born in Ephesus, on the coast of modern Turkey. His writings, now lost, were renowned in antiquity for their obscurity. However, fragments of his thoughts do survive in the work of other authors, and these suggest a disagreeable character who was dismissive of his fellow citizens. He had few kind words to say about the philosophers of Miletus or even the great poets, suggesting, for example, that Homer should be whipped. Diogenes Laertius states that Heraclitus grew increasingly misanthropic and went to live in the mountains, viewing society as too corrupt. Upon becoming ill, he returned to Ephesus but succumbed to his sickness.

ESSENTIAL TEXTS *On Nature* (lost). Fragments of his work survive, mostly in Diogenes Laertius's *Lives of the Eminent Philosophers*.

The grand ruins of the ancient town of Ephesus, home of Heraclitus, can still be visited today.

KEY IDEAS

A reasonably coherent picture of Heraclitus's ideas can be reconstructed from the fragments of writings that have survived in the works of others. He likened the world to fire, by which he seems to have meant that all things are in a continual process of flux. Plato quotes him as saying that you cannot step into the same river twice, meaning that no things or states in the universe remain eternally the same, and that what we think of as enduring entities are always in a process of becoming something else.

Heraclitus stressed conflict as the force that drives the process of becoming, but at the same time, underlying this constant strife, there is unity in the *logos*. "Logos" is the Greek word for "law" or

"rationale," and Heraclitus's idea seems to be that the strife which characterizes reality is unified within a rational cosmic harmony, one which may be grasped by human reason and logical debate.

This cosmic order or law unifies opposites, for harmony underlies discord. Heraclitus deploys many paradoxical examples of the unity of opposites – such as "the path up and down is one and the same"—in making this point. The message is that nothing remains the same, for the law of the universe is one of constant conflict, change, and renewal, just as the sun is born anew each morning.

SEE ALSO ▶ Plato (*pp.246–7*) • Nietzsche (*pp.316–7*) • Hegel (*pp.302–3*)

Parmenides

◗ *ca.* 515–*ca.* 445 BCE ⚑ Greece

Parmenides was the first philosopher to produce rigorous arguments in support of his conclusions. His ideas appear in the form of an epic poem in which he encounters a goddess who advances by bold arguments the surprising view that, despite appearances, reality is an unchanging whole.

LIFE AND WORKS

Little is known of Parmenides's life other than that he was born in Elea around 515 BCE. According to Plato, he visited Athens aged about 65 and met the young Socrates. It is likely that he was familiar with the works of Heraclitus, Pythagoras, and the Milesians, as his writings seem to present his views in opposition to his predecessors' thoughts. His arguments are found in his epic poem, *On Nature*, probably written when he was still a young man. Presented in three parts, it produces rational arguments for his metaphysical conclusions concerning the true nature of reality, contrasting this with the way the world appears to the senses of ordinary mortals. Parmenides was the founder of the Eleatic school.

ESSENTIAL TEXTS *On Nature*

KEY IDEAS

In the first section of *On Nature*, the Way of Truth, Parmenides begins the argument by presenting us with an opposition between "what is" and "what is not," and argues that since what is not does not exist, it cannot be an object of thought. He then explores the nature of what is, and argues that it cannot be created or destroyed, since something cannot come from nothing. Being, therefore, must be eternal.

He argues that all change within being is impossible since this would require a move from what is to what is not (that which does not exist). Moreover, change is not just confined to the temporal realm, for what is must be equally everywhere, and so there can be no differentiation between objects.

With these arguments Parmenides concludes that the universe is one—unchanging, imperishable, unbounded, and indivisible. So why do we perceive a world of multiplicity and change? Parmenides's answer is that the world as it appears to the senses is an illusion, and he later presents a cosmology with which to contrast the reality discovered by reason. In this way, he is the first to advance a systematic dualism of appearance and reality.

SEE ALSO ▶ Reason and Experience: two ways of knowing (*p.66*).

The Way of Truth is the more desirable of Parmenides's two paths of inquiry.

Zeno of Elea

⬤ *fl. ca.* 450 BCE   ⚑ Greece

Zeno was a member of the Eleatic school, founded by Parmenides, and was called the "father of the dialectic" by Aristotle. He is best known for his paradoxes, which try to show that all movement is impossible, and which had an important impact on the development of Greek thought.

LIFE AND WORKS

Although it was written nearly a century after Zeno's death, Plato's dialog, the *Parmenides*, is still the best source of information about his life. Plato says that Zeno, when aged around 40, accompanied Parmenides to Athens, where he met with Socrates, then a very young man. According to Plato, Zeno collected his arguments into a book, but sadly it has been lost. We know of his paradoxes of motion from Aristotle, who described him as the father of the dialectic because of his method of argumentation. The mathematical problems that Zeno's paradoxes raise about the idea of a continuum were not adequately dealt with until the modern era. His arguments against infinite divisibility spurred Democritus's development of Atomism (*see facing page*).

KEY IDEAS

Zeno was a defender of his teacher Parmenides's bold claim that reality is very unlike the variegated and changing world that we see around us, and is in fact motionless, uniform, and simple (*see p.239*). According to this view, movement and plurality are illusions of the senses, and in demonstrating this, Zeno was probably the first to deploy the method of argument known as *reductio ad absurdum*. Zeno began from the position of his opponents—that movement, change, and so on were real —and, by showing that contradictory consequences followed from it, was able to reject it. According to Proclus, Zeno produced over 40 such paradoxes, although only a few survive. They include the "Dichotomy," which says that one can never reach the finishing line in a race since first one must reach the halfway point; and then the point halfway though the second half of the course; and then the point halfway through the final quarter; and so on, ad infinitum. Zeno also imagined Achilles and a tortoise, pitted against each other in a race. According to Zeno, Achilles cannot overtake the tortoise since he must first reach its current position, but by then the tortoise will have moved on, and so will always hold a lead.

Achilles and the tortoise is perhaps the best known of Zeno's arguments against the possiblility of motion.

Democritus

ca. 460–371 BCE Greece

Democritus, along with the more shadowy figure of Leucippus (known to have been active in 440 BCE), was the co-founder of Atomism, but determining precisely which of its doctrines originated with whom is probably not possible.

Democritus was a contemporary of Socrates, although Plato never mentions him, perhaps because of a dislike for his mechanistic metaphysics. According to Aristotle, the Atomist theory developed as a response to Parmenides's arguments against the possibility of change and movement. Their way around his arguments was to embrace the possibility of empty space, the "void," into which matter can move. The essentials of the theory are that the universe is composed of an infinite number of microscopic corpuscles. The corpuscles themselves contain no void, so they cannot be divided: hence *atomon*, which means un-cuttable. The different shapes and arrangements of atoms account for the physical attributes of material things, and their various movements and collisions account for the changes we observe in things. The soul, too, is composed of very fine atoms, and is thus material, ruling out the possibility of an afterlife.

Mozi

479–438 BCE China

An engineer by trade, Mozi came from a humble background. His expertise was in fortifications: he designed, among other things, ladders for storming city walls. Despite his understanding of military matters, he was a pacifist and traveled around his war-torn region trying to dissuade rulers from fighting.

Mozi opposed the Confucian concern with ritual, seeing it as merely an empty show of conformity. Instead, he emphasized the importance of self-knowledge and authenticity in moral behavior. He also rejected the idea that society should look to the ancients for examples, arguing that the correct way to organize society is to be determined by rational and practical attention to contemporary realities. Moral actions are those that can be demonstrated to be useful in promoting genuine human good. Rituals, which serve no purpose, and warfare, which promotes only suffering, are to be

Both Sun Yat-sen and Mao ZeDong (*pictured left*) regarded the humbly born Mozi as a true philosopher of the people.

rejected. Where Confucians emphasized one's social role, in particular familial duties, Mozi argued for an impartial love for all humanity, or *bo-ai*. Love of one's own family leads to conflict with others and, ultimately, to wars between states. Mozi saw heaven as a moral force that ensured people's actions were rewarded and punished. His thought is preserved in the *Mozi*, and interest in his outlook has been reawakened latterly by the Republicans and Communists in China.

Socrates

◉ 469–399 BCE   🏛 Greece

As Socrates wrote nothing himself, we can only glean his thoughts via his student Plato's writings. How faithful these are is a matter of debate, but certainly Socrates believed that no one sins knowingly, and that critical reflection on the true nature of moral virtues is essential to the good life.

LIFE AND WORKS

We know little of the details of Socrates's life. He was born in Athens; his father was a sculptor and his mother a midwife. As a young man he served in the army against Sparta in the Peloponnesian War but otherwise remained in Athens, where he married and had several children. We do know more about the man himself: in battle he showed remarkable physical fortitude and endurance, and by all accounts displayed great bravery. He is described as having an ugly, pug-like face and as being a shabby dresser. He would stand motionless for hours, apparently lost in thought, and claimed to hear a divine inner voice that would deter him from courses of action. But despite these oddities, Socrates had great humor, and his wit and charisma attracted devotion of many. His critical questioning, however, irritated some Athenians, and although Socrates survived the era of the Thirty Tyrants after Athens' defeat by Sparta, just four years after democracy was reinstated he was brought to trial and condemned to death for impiety and corrupting the young. Although he could have escaped, Socrates elected to accept his sentence and willingly drank the hemlock that killed him. Plato attended the trial and was prompted to preserve his mentor's memory in dialogs.

KEY IDEAS

Socrates was predominantly interested in the moral questions that affect our lives, such as what is just, courageous, and good. He saw it as his mission to expose others' ignorance of the true nature of such virtues and was renowned for embarrassing the wise men of the day by revealing the confusions implicit in their moral thinking. His approach began by posing his interlocutors a question such as "what is courage?" or "what is love?" and proceeded by examining the limitations of their responses. He was searching not for a dictionary definition, but for the essential natures of such

The death of Socrates has become an iconic event in the consciousness of the West. It is the ultimate expression of the individual putting his moral integrity above his physical wellbeing, and his own conscience before the demands of authority.

concepts: in other words, what it is that all courageous acts share that makes them courageous. The difficulty that we have in discovering the essence of such concepts revealed, he claimed, the deep ignorance in which we all live about what really matters.

For Socrates, the critical spirit was the important thing, as recognition of one's own ignorance was the crucial first step toward knowledge. It is only once we realize that we don't know what we thought we knew, that we will begin the search to discover it. Socrates did not claim to teach such knowledge himself but rather, like a midwife, his talent lay in helping others to give birth to the innate knowledge lying within their minds.

The method for bringing forth ideas through question and answer is known as the *elenchus*, or dialectic. While he rarely offered definitive answers himself, it is clear from the manner of his questioning that Socrates did hold certain substantive views about ethics. Principal among these is the thesis that moral integrity is its own reward. He maintained that doing evil damages the perpetrator far more than those to whom evil is done, for while external misfortunes may befall one, the true good life consists in purity of the soul. He believed that no one would willingly do what they knew to be bad and therefore that bad actions must be the result of ignorance. It follows that knowledge of moral virtue is in our best interests and should be our key objective, and thus exposing others' ignorance is doing them a favour. Sadly the Athenian democratic regime did not see it this way, hence Socrates was tried and executed.

SEE ALSO ▸ Plato (*pp.244–7*) • Method of counterexamples (*pp.214–7*)

"*If we are ever to have pure knowledge of anything, we must get rid of the body and contemplate things by themselves with the soul by itself.*"

Phaedo 66a

Plato

○ *ca.* 427–347 BCE ⚐ Greece

Plato was the first philosopher to produce a substantial body of work that has survived and, with Aristotle, has been the most important influence on Western philosophy; so much so that the philosopher and mathematician Alfred North Whitehead famously remarked that its entire history since has been no more than "a series of footnotes to Plato."

Plato was a pupil of Socrates, and by his own account, attended the trial of his teacher, although not his execution. He was deeply affected by these events.

LIFE AND WORKS

Born into a noble Athenian family, Plato was related to those involved in the aristocratic rule of the Thirty Tyrants (404–403 BCE), but if his background did not predispose him to a dislike of Athenian democracy, the trial and execution of his teacher, Socrates, in 399 BCE certainly did. Plato, then aged 30, left Athens and traveled, possibly in Egypt, and later in Sicily, where it is likely that he encountered Pythagorean philosophy (*see p.247*). Returning to Athens in 387 BCE, he founded the Academy. Based on the principle that students should learn to criticize and think for themselves, rather than simply accept the views of their teachers, it is generally regarded as the first university. Many of the finest intellects in the classical world were schooled at the Academy, including Aristotle. Plato twice visited Sicily again to tutor Prince Dionysius in the hope of producing a philosopher-ruler, but with no great success.

THE DIALOGUES

The majority of Plato's works are in dialog form and are traditionally divided into early, middle, and late dialogs. The early dialogs feature Socrates as the main protagonist and are generally thought to be reasonably accurate portrayals of the thought of Plato's mentor. Socrates is typically seen questioning the opinions of his interlocutors on one of the moral qualities, for example courage or piety, and then exposing their ignorance to its true nature. However, in these dialogs, the inquiry is rarely taken forward to explore the positive nature of the object under discussion. In the middle dialogs, we find Plato beginning to develop the positive doctrines for which he is known. The later dialogs are fascinating for their detailed critiques of Plato's own earlier theories.

ESSENTIAL TEXTS
Apology, Phaedo, Republic, Laws.

KEY IDEAS

Plato observed that claims about physical things can never be made without qualification. For example, it cannot be said of any object that it is fully beautiful, or of a person that they are completely courageous. They will always be only

existence of the "Idea" or "Form" of beauty, courage, and other general terms. The Form is the universal to which such terms refer. What makes an oak tree, for example, a member of a particular class of thing—oaks—is that it resembles or

"THE TRUE LOVER OF KNOWLEDGE NATURALLY STRIVES FOR TRUTH... AND SOARS WITH UNDIMMED AND UNWEARIED PASSION TILL HE GRASPS THE ESSENTIAL NATURE OF THINGS."

Republic 490a

beautiful or courageous in some respect and to some degree, and so must fall short of the ideal of beauty or courage. But if no thing in the world can truly be said to be beautiful, how do we arrive at the idea of beauty? And what is it that all courageous acts have in common? Plato answers both questions by positing the real

"partakes of" the eternal Form of the oak. The particulars in the physical world that partake of the Form, such as the many beautiful things, are imitations of or approximations to the ideal. This Form cannot be observed with the senses; rather, it is our capacity to grasp this paradigm through

Plato's school, the Academy, survived for over 800 years, until the Romans decided it was a threat to their new-found Christianity.

a kind of intellectual vision that enables us to recognize the particulars of sense for what they are. This in essence is the Theory of Forms, for which Plato is best remembered (*see also pp.76–81*).

KNOWLEDGE

Plato agreed with Heraclitus (*see p.238*) that all things in the world perceived by the senses are forever becoming something else. No matter how enduring, all facts about physical reality will one day cease to be. But knowledge, Plato reasoned, has to be of what fully is, and he took this to mean that we cannot truly have knowledge of the world of the senses. So knowledge must concern the Forms, or those objects that do not change and decay: which fully are what they are. In this way Plato divides reality into two realms, the physical world of *becoming*, and a world of *being* full of eternal and perfect Forms. It is the task of the philosopher to come to a full awareness of the Forms that underlie the shifting world of the senses. Following Socrates's lead, the method to achieve this is "dialectic:" a cooperative union of minds which, by critical questioning, would gradually analyze concepts and draw closer to the truth. However, to grasp the Forms requires apprehending the ultimate reality, which is the Form of the Good. Plato saw this as the goal of all inquiry because it is in terms of the good that all explanations should be made. In other words, before we can explain anything we need to recognize in what way it is good for its purpose.

IMMORTALITY OF THE SOUL

The dialectic is essentially a method for analyzing the concepts we already possess, albeit largely implicitly. For Plato, we ordinarily have only implicit knowledge of Forms and the task of philosophy is to bring the knowledge latent within us to consciousness. Thus learning is not really discovering anything new, but recollection. Plato draws parallels between this method and

Plato regarded the arts, including Greek theater (*above*) with great suspicion. He believed them to be a false representation of reality.

a priori reasoning (*see p.66*) in mathematics. Recognizing the truth of a geometric proof, for example, is possible because we are not really learning anything new, but simply recognizing something we were acquainted with prior to birth. If all knowledge is recollection, as Plato claims, this shows that the soul exists before birth and leaves room for the possibility that it might survive bodily death.

PLATO'S UTOPIA

The *Republic* represents the first of many attempts to outline an ideal society. Plato rejects democracy as a system of government on the grounds that the people are not well qualified to rule. Those who are likely to rise to the top in a democracy are not going to be the types of people we would want to have governing. His model is a state in which internal conflict has been abolished and each citizen fulfils their allotted role. This means instituting a rigorous regime of training and selection to produce an elite group of rulers who are wise and incorruptible. These, the guardians of his state, will truly deserve the name "philosophers" because they are genuine lovers of wisdom. And they must acquire knowledge of the Good, so that they can govern effectively for the good of the state as a whole.

INFLUENCES ON PLATO

The influence of Pythagoras and Socrates is key to Plato's philosophy, but it is hard for the historian of ideas to extricate Plato's ideas from those of his teachers. From Pythagoras, Plato learned that the world appearing to the senses is too unstable to be an object of true knowledge, as well as the more mystical elements of his thinking, the importance of mathematics, and the idea of philosophical speculation as a means of purifying the soul. From Socrates, Plato gained his interest in ethical issues and the importance of acquiring knowledge of the good through dialectic.

Aristotle

◔ 384–322 BCE   ⚑ Greece

The sheer range of Aristotle's work is staggering, and the subject divisions and names he deployed have endured to this day: ethics, logic, metaphysics, meteorology, physics, economics, and psychology. For more than 2,000 years, his influence on European thought has been profound.

LIFE AND WORKS

Aristotle was born in Stageira, northern Greece. He had connections with the royal family of Macedonia, his father acting as physician to King Philip. His parents died when he was young and at the age of 17 Aristotle was sent to Athens to study at Plato's Academy. There he remained for 20 years as student and teacher until Plato's death. But he was passed over as the next head of the Academy, possibly because of his opposition to certain Platonic doctrines, and left Athens. In 343 BCE he accepted an invitation to become tutor to the King's son, Alexander. After Philip's death, Aristotle returned to Athens, now aged 49, and set up his own school—the Lyceum (also known as the Peripatetic School, because of Aristotle's preference for pacing up and down when discussing philosophical problems). However, like Socrates before him he was charged with impiety, in 323 BCE, and rather than allow the Athenians to "sin twice against philosophy" he escaped, only to die a year later of a stomach complaint. The story that he died by throwing himself into the sea because he could not explain the tides is probably apocryphal.

The extent of Aristotle's influence on Alexander has caused much conjecture, but his former pupil's many conquests and the library in Alexandria ensured the enduring legacy of Aristotle's ideas.

Aristotle tutored Alexander the Great as a boy, and in time his ideas spread and endured across an empire that stretched to the Indian Ocean.

ESSENTIAL TEXTS *Metaphysics*; *Nicomachean Ethics*; *Politics*; *On the Soul*.

KEY IDEAS

Aristotle was deeply influenced by Plato but was suspicious of the otherworldly elements in his teacher's thinking, and in particular the view that knowledge of the world cannot be accessed via the senses. The trajectory he pursued on leaving Plato's Academy is far more empirically minded and values the piecemeal investigations of the scientist. Knowledge, for Aristotle, is not a simple matter of disinterested speculation, but involves getting one's hands dirty. Where Plato saw mathematics as the paradigm for knowledge, Aristotle saw the importance of observation of the bewildering variety of phenomena in this world. His critique of Platonism

this is organized. Different oak trees are the same not because they are made of the same substance, or (contrary to Plato) because they resemble the "Form" of the oak, but because they share a common structure. Inanimate objects similarly take a form that determines their characteristic activity or usage. For example, the organization of the parts of an axe determines what it is in terms of its function: to chop wood. Defining things in terms of their purpose makes Aristotle's theory of substances "teleological." He saw everything in the universe as definable in this way. Aristotle's notion of form also led him to disagree with Plato on the nature of human beings. He did

"EVERY REALM OF NATURE IS MARVELOUS."

Parts of Animals 645a

also points out that knowledge must be grounded on what it is possible to experience, and thus the starting point for philosophy must be the senses. If we start to speculate on what lies beyond our experience we stray into mysticism.

WHAT IS EXISTENCE?

Aristotle was interested in the question of "being:" of what kinds of things there are, and what it is for something to exist. His concern with this world inevitably drove him to take issue with Plato's Theory of Forms (*see pp.76–81*)—the view that a world of universals exists independently of particular things. Aristotle reckoned that universals have no existence beyond the many exemplars we see around us. So, there is no such thing as the ideal oak tree, distinct from those growing around us. Things or "substances" are comprised not just of brute physical matter, but also of the form that it takes. What makes a plant or animal what it is not the material stuff from which it is composed, but the way

not see our essence as a substance distinct from our physical bodies. So the idea of the self persisting after the body has gone is nonsensical.

ETHICS AND POLITICS

Aristotle views us as primarily social beings and government as there to help us achieve a good life within society. As its role is to facilitate rather than dictate, he rejects the idea of Plato's state run by philosophers, believing that a democracy is more likely to achieve this goal. Humans strive for wellbeing and the means to achieve this is to live virtuously and engage in intellectual contemplation. Aristotle offers practical guidance in how to live the good life, identifying the virtues we should pursue for human wellbeing as lying between two extremes of vice – generosity, for example, being the "golden mean" between the two extremes of meanness and extravagance, and so on.

SEE ALSO ▶ Plato (*pp.244–7*) • Plato and the Forms (*pp.76–81*) • Dualism of mind and body (*pp.124–7*)

Diogenes of Sinope

● *ca.* 400–*ca.* 325 BCE   ⚑ Greece

Diogenes taught for most of his life in Athens and was the founder of the philosophical school known as the Cynics. He turned his back on the trappings of convention and civilized life, regarding reason and nature as better guides to conduct.

Diogenes followed the example of Antisthenes, a contemporary of Plato who, after Socrates's death, abandoned his aristocratic life and worked among the poor. Diogenes was, however, far more radical. He taught that virtue lies in overcoming artificial desires and so he lived a simple existence, carrying all his possessions with him and sleeping in a barrel. His contemporaries found his lifestyle rather unseemly and for this reason he was called "cynic," from "*kynikos*" meaning "like a dog." There are innumerable stories about his life, but possibly the best known is that he was once visited by Alexander the Great, who asked whether there was anything he could do for him. Diogenes replied that he could stand out of his sunlight.

Diogenes Searching *for an Honest Man*, by Jan Victors: the founder of the Cynics used shock tactics to promote his radical ideas in Athenian society.

Pyrrho of Elis

● *c.*360–272 BCE   ⚑ Greece

Pyrrho is commonly described as "the Sceptic," and indeed philosophical scepticism is often referred to as "Pyrrhonism." Although he left no writings, his ideas inspired a school of belief that has played a vital—if sometimes destructive—role at the heart of the philosophical enterprise.

Pyrrho was the first philosopher to embrace scepticism systematically as the central principle of his own philosophy. Suspending judgment about beliefs was not just a means to determine what we should and should not believe, but was treated by Pyrrho as the only reasonable reaction to the fallibility of our faculties, and the apparent fact that powerful arguments can be given equally on both sides of a question. One tradition has it that Pyrrho's scepticism about the senses was taken to such an extreme that he had to be accompanied by his acolytes to prevent him from walking over cliffs,

which he could not know for sure were there. Another, however, has him reckon that in the absence of firm knowledge we have to be content with appearances, so that he recommended living according to conventional beliefs and practices as the least disruptive course of action.

Pyrrho may have been led to his position by observing the huge diversity of cultural beliefs and customs while serving on Alexander the Great's campaigns. His example inspired the Sceptical school in ancient philosophy, which developed the idea that suspension of belief leads to tranquility of mind.

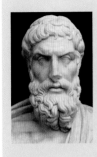

Epicurus

● 341–270 BCE   ♙ Greece

Epicurus followed Democritus in arguing that everything is composed of tiny indivisible particles of matter. The shapes and movements of these atoms are sufficient to explain all phenomena in the cosmos. It follows that humans, and their "souls," are simply matter in motion.

LIFE AND WORKS

Epicurus's father was a schoolteacher in the colony of Samos. Epicurus himself taught on Lesbos and later set up his own school in Athens, known as the "Garden" because the teaching went on in the garden of his house. It was non-authoritarian in approach and accepted women and slaves. It became the center for propagating Epicurus's philosophy, which advocated a temperate life, eschewing all religious beliefs and practices. His most important disciple was the poet Lucretius, whose work *On the Nature of Things* introduced Epicureanism to the Roman world.

ESSENTIAL TEXTS Although a prolific writer, few fragments survive, mostly in Diogenes Laertius's *Lives of the Eminent Philosophers*, such as "Letter to Herodotus" and "Letter to Menoeceus."

KEY IDEAS

As a materialist, Epicurus argued that the gods had no involvement in human affairs and that humans are composed of atoms, like everything else. So when we die, our souls will dissipate with our bodies and therefore physical death is the end of us. Contrary to what one might suppose, Epicurus took the implication of this to be that it is irrational to fear death, since, as the end of all possible experience, it can mean nothing to us. Moreover, since in death we experience neither pleasure nor pain, the only punishments or rewards that we can expect must be in this life. Therefore it is our duty to maximize our happiness before we die. This hedonistic doctrine was caricatured by his detractors as recommending the unbridled pursuit of base pleasures, whereas in fact Epicurus believed the highest pleasures to be intellectual, and the greatest of all to be philosophizing with one's friends. He argued that to pursue pleasure without concern for the morrow will not allow one to maximize one's wellbeing in the long term. Far more rewarding is a careful approach where physical desires are reined in so that simple pleasures can be enjoyed more fully. The aim is for an equilibrium, rather than extremes of pleasure, which inevitably lead to pain.

SEE ALSO ▶ Does God exist? (*pp.140–9*) • Mill (*pp.308–9*) • Hobbes (*p.275*) • Bentham (*p.300*)

Epicurus believed he gained as much pleasure from a diet of bread and water as did a rich person from fancy foods.

Zeno of Citium

● *ca.* 332–*ca.* 265 BCE   ⚑ Greece

As founder of Stoicism—a philosophy that influenced the
Hellenistic world and, later, the Roman Empire, counting
the emperor Marcus Aurelius among its adherents—Zeno
saw the world as rationally ordered and argued that mental
tranquillity is achieved through control of the passions.

LIFE AND WORKS

Zeno, a merchant from the Greek colony
of Citium on Cyprus, moved to Athens
and studied under the Cynic philosopher
Crates. To help his pupil overcome his
attachment to social convention, Crates
publicly embarrassed him by smashing
a pot he was carrying, so covering him
with lentils. Whether or not this had the
desired effect, Zeno inherited the Cynics'
distrust of social niceties, which he
regarded as irrational, and founded the
Stoic school of philosophy, named after
the portico—*stoa* in Greek—where he
lectured. He lived an ascetic life, as
befitting his philosophy. Although he
wrote of a utopia in the *Republic*, none
of his works has survived. It is said that,
having fallen and broken a toe, Zeno
took this as a sign that he was being
called to death, and strangled himself.

KEY IDEAS

What we know of Zeno's teachings we
must reconstruct from the later Stoics
whom he influenced. He was a materialist
and followed Heraclitus in regarding the
soul as made of fire. He also argued that
the course of nature was rigidly
determined, with all the elements
emerging from fire and ultimately
returning to fire in an endless cycle. The
Stoics were pantheists who held that the
supreme creative force of the universe
permeates all things and that the natural
world is rationally ordered by the divine
law-giver. The virtuous life is one that is
in harmony with this natural order, so we
should accept what we cannot change
and not rail against fate: ideas that
characterize "stoicism" in the
popular imagination.

Zeno admired Socrates for his
equanimity in the face of death, his
renowned ability to endure physical
hardship, and his lack of interest in
mundane pleasures. He is sometimes
called Zeno Apathea, since he taught
that *apathea*—that is, passionlessness—
is the way to happiness.

Zeno argues that we should resist enslavement to
our emotions and passions and, like logical
Mr. Spock in *Star Trek*, follow the path of reason.

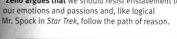

SEE ALSO ▶ Heraclitus (*p.238*) • Socrates
(*pp.242–3*) • Diogenes (*p.250*)

Han Feizi

◓ *ca.* 280–233 BCE ⚑ China

With Li Si, Han Feizi founded the School of Legalism, which emphasized the imposition of law to ensure public order. With its emphasis on the interests of the state rather than individual freedoms, it became the philosophical justification for Chinese imperial government.

LIFE AND WORKS

From the ruling family of the state of Han, Han Feizi studied with Li Si under the Confucian master Xunzi. Hoping to influence the King of Han, he offered him his political ideas and advice, apparently without much success. However, his writings came to the attention of the nearby ruler of Qin, Shi Huangdi, later to become first Emperor of China. In 234 BCE Qin attacked Han and, sent as an emissary, Han Feizi met Shi Huangdi. However Han Feizi's former fellow student Li Si, now chancellor of Qin, turned Shi

Huangdi against Han Feizi and he was imprisoned. From prison he wrote to Shi Huangdi with advice on how to gain hegemony over China's warring states, but Li Si, continuing to work against his old colleague, sent him poison in prison so that he could commit suicide, which he did. Despite this, Legalism had a profound influence on Shi Huangdi, and, more recently, on Mao ZeDong.

China's first emperor, builder of the unifying Great Wall, was influenced by the Legalism of Han Feizi.

ESSENTIAL TEXTS *Han Feizi*

KEY IDEAS

Han Feizi lived toward the end of a period of war and unrest at a time when the need for civil order was uppermost in many thinkers' minds. During this period the big debate between his own teacher, Xunzi, and the other great Confucian of the day, Mengzi (Mencius), had been over whether human beings are naturally evil or good. Mengzi argued that feelings of sympathy are inborn and need only to be nurtured, whereas his opponent argued that socialization is required to instil moral behavior. Han Feizi sided with Xunzi, arguing that people are motivated by personal gain and the desire to avoid punishment and,

therefore, that education and a strict system of laws and punishments are key to ensuring moral behavior. Han Feizi also rejected the Confucian emphasis on tradition, favoring the introduction of a new codified legal system. For Han Feizi the ruler was also bound by the law, but other Legalists, including Li Si, saw the ruler as exempt from the strictures binding ordinary citizens so long as order was maintained. This has led to comparisons with Machiavelli and been seen as justifying totalitarianism.

SEE ALSO ▸ Lao Tzu *(p.235)* • Machiavelli *(pp.270–1)* • Marx *(pp.311–2)* • Political philosophy *(pp.160–77)*

Plotinus

⬤ 204–270   🏳 Egypt

Living during a period of great unrest within the Roman Empire, Plotinus devoted himself to pursuing knowledge of the ideal world that lay behind the illusory world of appearances. His version of Platonism determined the development of Christian metaphysics in the Middle Ages.

LIFE AND WORKS

We know of Plotinus's life through the biography written by his student Porphyry to preface the *Enneads*. He studied in Alexandria, capital of the intellectual world at that time, for 11 years, and here he would have had extensive training in the Greek philosophy of antiquity, including, of course, Plato. He joined the Roman Emperor Gordian III's military expedition to Persia and India, it is said, to learn about Eastern philosophy. Unfortunately the expedition was abandoned after the Emperor Gordian was assassinated by his army in Mesopotamia in 244, and Plotinus seems to have abandoned his plans to explore the ideas of the East. Instead, at the age of

40, he went to Rome and set up a school where he taught his brand of Platonism, which became known as Neo-Platonism. There he sought permission to found a community based on Plato's *Republic*, to be called Platonopolis, but Emperor Gallienus withdrew his support for the project. After 20 years' teaching in Rome, he was encouraged by his student Porphyry to collect his ideas into some systematic form for posterity. After Plotinus's death Porphyry edited his writings into six books, with nine treatises in each, which are known as the *Enneads*.

The Library at Alexandria was where Plotinus studied Greek philosophy and, possibly, Buddhism, which was known of in Egypt at this time and may have influenced Plotinus's ideas.

KEY IDEAS

Plotinus revered the work of Plato and his own philosophy grew out of his efforts to systematize and defend the main metaphysical claims of the Platonic system. In Plotinus, the Form of the Good becomes the "One," the highest of his three "hypostases," or levels of reality. The One is the absolutely simple first principle of his system. It cannot be captured in language since to predicate anything on it would be to set limits to it. As with Plato's Form of the Good, the One transcends being but is at the same

time that from which all being derives and which makes knowledge possible. It is self-causing and self-sustaining, and all being is said to "emanate" from it, thereby producing the other two hypostases, namely Intellect (Nous) and Soul. The doctrine of emanation does not involve a conscious act of creation, as with the Christian God, but rather of ontological dependence (*see pp.140–1*). Intellect is the realm of the Platonic Forms and so is where the being of differentiated existence derives;

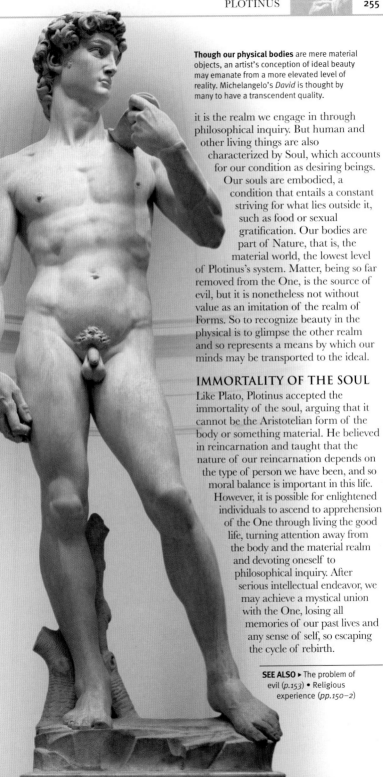

Though our physical bodies are mere material objects, an artist's conception of ideal beauty may emanate from a more elevated level of reality. Michelangelo's *David* is thought by many to have a transcendent quality.

it is the realm we engage in through philosophical inquiry. But human and other living things are also characterized by Soul, which accounts for our condition as desiring beings. Our souls are embodied, a condition that entails a constant striving for what lies outside it, such as food or sexual gratification. Our bodies are part of Nature, that is, the material world, the lowest level of Plotinus's system. Matter, being so far removed from the One, is the source of evil, but it is nonetheless not without value as an imitation of the realm of Forms. So to recognize beauty in the physical is to glimpse the other realm and so represents a means by which our minds may be transported to the ideal.

IMMORTALITY OF THE SOUL

Like Plato, Plotinus accepted the immortality of the soul, arguing that it cannot be the Aristotelian form of the body or something material. He believed in reincarnation and taught that the nature of our reincarnation depends on the type of person we have been, and so moral balance is important in this life. However, it is possible for enlightened individuals to ascend to apprehension of the One through living the good life, turning attention away from the body and the material realm and devoting oneself to philosophical inquiry. After serious intellectual endeavor, we may achieve a mystical union with the One, losing all memories of our past lives and any sense of self, so escaping the cycle of rebirth.

SEE ALSO ▶ The problem of evil (p.153) • Religious experience (pp.150–2)

Augustine of Hippo

◔ 354–430   **⚐** North Africa (modern Algeria)

One of the great saints of the Catholic faith, Augustine produced, by his own account, an incredible 230 works. The best known are his autobiography, the *Confessions*, in which he recounts his sinful life and discovery of God, and the *City of God*, his description of the divine kingdom.

LIFE AND WORKS

Augustine had been raised as a Christian by his mother in North Africa, but in his youth, while studying at Carthage, he became dissatisfied with the apparent simple-mindedness of the Christian scriptures. In search of a religion worthy of a philosopher, he became a junior member of the Manicheans, a sect founded by the prophet Mani who had been crucified in Persia in 277.

Although, according to his *Confessions*, Augustine's days in and around Carthage studying and then teaching were rather licentious, by the age of 18 he had settled down with the unnamed mother of his son. Why they never married is

After years of internal struggle and turmoil, Augustine embraced the faith of his childhood once more and converted to Christianity.

unclear: it may be that she was an ex-slave, in which case marriage would have been forbidden under Roman law. In 384 the family moved to Italy where Augustine fell under the influence of Neo-Platonism which, not without some struggle, helped to persuade him to resume the religion of his mother and convert to Christianity in 386. He returned to North Africa in 391 and, now ready for a life of celibacy, became presbyter and, later, Bishop of Hippo. From there he set up a community of disciples at his birthplace, Thagaste in Numidea. He died in Hippo at the age of 75 as the town was being besieged, and subsequently sacked, by Vandals.

ESSENTIAL TEXTS *The Confessions*; *City of God*.

KEY IDEAS

Augustine famously abandoned his early Christian faith principally because he could make no sense of the idea of an immaterial creator of the material universe, and because of its inability to deal with the problems of evil and suffering. The latter difficulty arises from the Christian commitment to its creator-God being all-knowing, all-loving, and all-powerful. Such a being would have to know about the evil in his creation while also

Augustine identified free will as the source of human evils such as the Holocaust, thus absolving God.

However Manicheanism did not provide a lasting resolution to Augustine's inquiring mind, and his encounters with the works of Plato (*see pp.244–7*) and Plotinus (*see pp.254–5*) offered him a way out of these difficulties. The Neo-Platonic idea of an immaterial world of Forms and of the Good or One as the first principle of all being allowed for a spiritual creator who is the cause of all things. Only God is fully real; the created world is less

> ## "GOD IS NOT THE PARENT OF EVILS... EVILS EXIST BY THE VOLUNTARY SIN OF THE SOUL TO WHICH GOD GAVE FREE CHOICE."
>
> *Contra Fortunatum Manichaeum, Acta seu Disputatio* Ch. 20

being both willing and able to eliminate it. The fact that he has failed to do so strongly militates against his existence. It is perhaps unsurprising, then, that Augustine initially found Manicheanism more satisfactory, since it characterizes the universe from the outset in terms of the struggle between evil and good.

PREDESTINATION AND SIN

Despite Augustine's thirst for spiritual communion with God, he found his physical desire for the company of women hard to overcome. And yet he did not claim that it was by an act of will alone that he was finally able to embrace the faith. Augustine's doctrine of predestination means that it is a matter of God's choice whether we will be saved or burn eternally in hell. Augustine's view of original sin—the Fall—as the source of suffering chimed well with the account in Genesis and became the official view of the Church. Adam's guilt is passed down the generations, making us all justly punishable.

real as it is distanced from him. At the same time, God illuminates objects of intellectual contemplation. So, while the senses are an unreliable source of knowledge, genuine understanding begins with the inner contemplation of one's own mind, and gradually works upward toward contemplation of God. Finally, true spiritual enlightenment is achieved through union with God.

A JUSTIFICATION OF EVIL

Augustine's theodicy remains one of the most ingenious ways of dealing with the problem of evil. He begins by arguing that evil is not a substantive thing in its own right, but rather a privation or lack of good. Everything that God has created is good, and evil only occurs when his creation is corrupted. So God cannot be held responsible for the creation of evil, which occurs through the free actions of angels and humans.

SEE ALSO ▶ The problem of evil (*pp.153–4*) • Does free will account for evil? (*p.155*)

Boethius

ca. 480–524/6   Italy

Sometimes considered the last of the Roman philosophers and the first of the Scholastics, Boethius is important for transmitting Greek thought into the Latin tradition of medieval philosophy. His influence on the philosophy of the Middle Ages was immense.

Anicius Manlius Severinus Boethius was born into a patrician Roman family and studied Greek in Athens and Alexandria. He served the Ostrogoth king of Italy, Theodoric, and rose to the position of head of all government and court offices. However, he was accused of treachery and imprisoned in 523, tortured, and eventually executed. His dramatic fall from a position of wealth, prestige, and power forms the backdrop to his most famous work, the *Consolation of Philosophy*, in which he describes how Lady Philosophy consoles him on his perceived misfortunes, thereby disclosing a Christian outlook deeply influenced by Neo-Platonism. His other works include Latin translations of some of Aristotle's work; commentaries on Aristotle; and also works on logic.

Boethius is consoled by Philosophy personified in his prison cell as he awaits execution. He recounts their dialogs in his *Consolation of Philosophy*.

Al-Farabi

870–950   Persia

Al-Farabi was a Neo-Platonist, identifying Allah with the "One" of Plotinus. He was also influenced by Aristotle and wrote commentaries on his work, as well as on many other subjects, including logic, medicine, music, and natural sciences.

Historians dispute whether al-Farabi's birthplace was Faryab, in modern Iran, or Farab, in modern Kazakhstan. But it is certain that he arrived in 901 in Baghdad, where he spent much of his life teaching and writing, while still traveling widely. His reputation spread and he came to be known as the "second teacher" after Aristotle. The details of his death are hazy; some say he died of natural causes, others that he was murdered by bandits.

Al-Farabi regarded philosophy as a calling conferred by Allah and as the unique route to true knowledge. So although the Koran is indeed revealed by Allah, its claims must be treated as symbolic and culturally relative. For example, al-Farabi argued that the soul does not generally survive bodily death, and thus discussion of immortality in the Koran should not be taken as literally true. Despite this, he did allow that a philosophical life devoted to the intellect could lead to immortality. In this life, he opined, philosophers have a duty to guide people in matters of statecraft and his *Virtuous City* describes a Platonic utopia ruled by philosopher prophets.

Avicenna (Ibn Sina)

🌑 980–1037 🏴 Persia

Avicenna's philosophical system is a synthesis of Neo-Platonic and Aristotelian traditions with Muslim theology. A key philosopher of the Middle Ages, he was equally significant in the sciences. His *Canon of Medicine* was the main medical textbook used throughout medieval Europe.

LIFE AND WORKS

We know of the first 30 years of Avicenna's life via his autobiography, with the remainder supplied by his disciple al-Juzajani. Born near Bukhara, capital of modern-day Uzbekistan, his remarkable intellect was in evidence from an early age: at 10 years of age he was treating people, curing the King of Bukhara of a mystery illness. As reward he was given access to the royal library, where he pursued his research for some years. By 21 he was a court physician and political administrator, but when the region became politically unstable, he

"IN MEDICINE WE OUGHT TO KNOW THE CAUSES OF SICKNESS AND HEALTH."

On Medicine

had memorized the Koran and at 14 he became interested in metaphysical problems, reading Aristotle's *Metaphysics* 40 times to memorize the words, although he confessed he did not understand them until he had read al-Farabi's commentaries. He taught himself medicine and by the age of 16 moved on to aid other rulers, ending his years in the service of the Prefect of Isfahan. Some 150 of his works on philosophy survive and 40 on medicine, by far the most important being *The Book of Healing*, which is an encyclopedia of philosophy, and the *Canon of Medicine*.

Avicenna the physician attempts to correct spinal curvature in a patient.

ESSENTIAL TEXTS *The Book of Healing* (*Kitab al-shifa*); *Canon of Medicine* (*Al-qanun fil-tibb*).

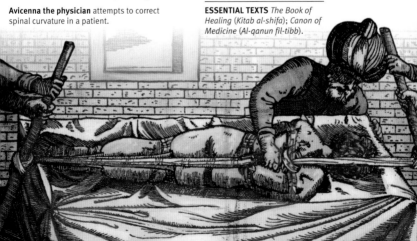

KEY IDEAS

Avicenna's philosophy is a refinement of that of al-Farabi (*see p.258*), although his approach tends to downplay the Neo-Platonic elements in favor of Aristotle. Developing Plotinus's idea of a hierarchy of being from the One, or Allah, down to the world of matter, he argued that all human souls are immortal and that the intellectual pursuit of the intelligible world was the route to ultimate union with Allah and a better afterlife.

THE KALAM ARGUMENT

Along with other Muslim philosophers of the period, Avicenna propounded a version of the cosmological argument for God's existence (*see p.142*) known as the "Kalam argument," which derives ultimately from Aristotle. It begins from the observation, gained from al-Farabi, that all things in the universe are possible beings, meaning that they might not have existed and have no inherent reason for existing. The "essence" of such beings is said to be distinct from their "existence," so the fact that they exist is not determined by what they are. Therefore they must depend on something else for their existence, and must be caused to exist by something else. However, this cannot be true of everything that exists, otherwise there would be an infinite regress and no ultimate ground for the existence of anything. It follows that there must be a being whose existence is necessary, which is its own cause and sustains everything else in existence: namely Allah.

Theological tensions exist between Avicenna's ideas and the teachings of the Koran.

AVICENNA THE SCIENTIST

A crater on the Moon has been named after Avicenna (the Latinized name of Ibn Sina) in recognition of his remarkable achievements as an astronomer and scientist.

Among his scientific claims that have proved correct is that sight is not a power of the eye to grasp an object, but that a source of light emits luminous particles that travel at a finite speed and that the eye picks up. He also observed the silhouette of the planet Venus against the Sun and thereby correctly inferred that Venus must be closer to the Sun than is the Earth.

As a necessary and perfect being, Allah cannot change, and so is eternal. Allah cannot have acted to create the universe as this would involve change, and therefore, for Avicenna, the universe "emanates" of necessity from the nature of Allah. In this he follows the Neo-Platonist idea that all being emanates from God as its sustaining cause. But this view raises certain theological difficulties for both Islamic and Christian thinkers, as it is in tension with the Koranic and Biblical accounts of the Creation. Also, if the universe emanates from God, then everything is necessary. This implies that events and actions are predetermined, thus problematizing ideas of moral responsibility and divine justice.

SEE ALSO ▶ Does God exist? (*pp.140–9*)

Anselm of Canterbury

● 1033–1109 ◪ Italy

A gifted scholar, Anselm produced his masterpiece, the *Proslogion*, in 1078. He became Archbishop of Canterbury, and held the position until his death, despite long power struggles with the Crown which forced him into exile several times.

Anselm left his family home in Aosta in Piedmont at the age of 23, with the intention of becoming a monk, and after some years of traveling, he joined the Benedictine Abbey at Bec in Normandy, France. He rose swiftly through the ranks and was made Abbot in 1078. Bec was a powerful monastery and a major seat of learning. As Abbot, Anselm traveled frequently to England and, in 1093, was appointed Archbishop of Canterbury, head of the Church of England.

Anselm summed up his philosophical enterprise as "faith seeking under-standing," meaning that reason deepens one's grasp of truths established by revelation. He devised various arguments in support of the main articles of the Christian faith, such as the Trinity and the Atonement. But Anselm is best known as the inventor of the "ontological argument" *(see pp.140–1)*, which appears in the *Proslogion*. This argument does not just try to establish the existence of the greatest conceivable being, but also the various attributes that God must have in virtue of being the greatest: that he is omnipotent, omniscient, self-existent, and so on. Despite having powerful detractors, including Aquinas and Kant, debate over Anselm's argument has resurfaced in recent years.

Al-Ghazali

● 1058–1111 ◪ Persia

Al-Ghazali was head of the prestigious Nizamiyyah school in Baghdad from 1092 to 1096, when he wrote *The Opinions of the Philosophers*, expounding the Neo-Platonist and Aristotelian views of Islamic scholars, including al-Farabi and Avicenna.

Born in Tus in modern-day Iran, al-Ghazali rose to become one of the most celebrated scholars of the golden era of Islamic philosophy. His lectures at the Nizamiyyah school drew in hundreds of scholars and brought al-Ghazali great wealth and respect.

Eventually he began to regard the views in *The Opinions* as un-Islamic, and produced a sceptical companion work, *The Incoherence of the Philosophers*, which set about refuting them by using philosophical argument rather than appealing to faith. This attack on philosophical reason was sufficiently powerful for Averroes *(see p.263)* to feel the need to produce an extended defense in the *Incoherence of the Incoherence*.

After some years al-Ghazali resigned his post at the Nizamiyyah school, gave away his wealth, and took up a spiritual journey as a wandering Sufi in the holy lands. His autobiography, *The Delivery from Error*, suggests that this decision followed his recognition that revealed truth cannot be discovered by philosophical argument, but only through devoting oneself to mystical practices. He later returned to teaching and to his home of Tus, where he spent his final years.

Interest today in the work of al-Ghazali often focuses on his analysis of causality, in which he denies direct material causes between events, arguing that causal regularities are made possible by the will of God.

Pierre Abelard

● 1079–1142　 France

Remembered less for his philosophy than for his tragic love affair with his pupil Héloïse, Pierre Abelard was nevertheless a remarkable scholar and teacher. A proponent of the Scholastic method of philosophy, he opposed the dominant realist position on universals inherited from Plato (*see pp.244–7*).

Abelard attended the Cathedral School of Nôtre Dame, Paris. He was a brilliant student, and became a charismatic teacher. By the age of 22 he had set up his own school in Paris, and went on to acquire the Chair at Nôtre Dame aged just 34.

Renowned for his skills in dialectic, Abelard stood against the popular realist approach, stating that universal terms, such as "oak tree," are just words that do not denote anything real over the many particular oaks that exist.

Abelard met Héloïse in 1117, when she was just 16. She became pregnant and gave birth to a son named Astrolabe.

The lovestruck Héloïse of romantic legend was also herself a brilliant scholar; she was to become abbess of her convent.

They married in secret, but when the marriage became public, Abelard sent Héloïse off to become a nun. Her family castrated him in revenge and Abelard became a monk. Some of the letters that the two exchanged have survived, and the affair has become one of the great romance stories of European literature.

Abelard continued to court controversy and make enemies—his work was condemned as heretical in 1121, and in 1132 he survived an attempt on his life. He summed up his life in his *History of My Misfortunes* of 1132. Eventually he left the monastery and became a hermit.

Moses Maimonides

● 1135–1204　 Spain

Maimonides wrote on Jewish law as well as medicine, but philosophers remember him for his *Guide for the Perplexed*. The *Guide* exerted considerable influence on medieval Scholasticism, in particular on Aquinas and Duns Scotus.

Maimonides came from a line of Jewish scholars and studied the Torah under his father. Although they lived under a liberal Islamic regime in Andalusia, its fall to the conquering Almohades in 1148 forced the family into exile, first in Spain and then, from 1158 on, in Morocco. They eventually settled in Egypt, where Maimonides became physician to the Wazir of the Sultan Saladin.

The *Guide for the Perplexed* is an attempt to ground Jewish theology in Aristotelianism, while at the same time departing from Aristotle where he is in conflict with scripture. The *Guide* offers various proofs for the existence of God and determines some of his attributes—for example, that he is not corporeal. With these proofs, Maimonides defended a form of "negative theology:" that is, the idea that we cannot do justice to God by describing him in anthropomorphic terms, and since no predicate is adequate, we can only approach a description of him obliquely, via what he is not.

Averroes (Ibn Rushd)

● 1126–1198 ⚑ Spain

Averroes, the last of the great philosophers of Islam's golden era, was the greatest commentator on Aristotle. His work led to the rediscovery of Aristotle by medieval Christian thinkers, and it is here that it had most influence, as Islamic religious study turned away from philosophy.

LIFE AND WORKS

Averroes lived in Andalusia at the time of Islamic rule when intellectuals enjoyed comparative freedom from political interference. Descended from a family of judges, he was educated in law and medicine as well as theology and philosophy. He became a judge in Seville and Córdoba in 1169 and was subsequently court physician to the Caliph of Córdoba. During this latter period he produced his extensive commentaries—38 in all—on Aristotle. *The Incoherence of the Incoherence* was a refutation of al-Ghazali's defense of orthodox Islamic teaching against the Aristotelian and Platonic elements in much scholarship. Averroes's defense of philosophical reason brought him into conflict with the clerics and in 1195 he was accused of heresy and banished.

KEY IDEAS

Averroes's philosophy is essentially Aristotelian with Neo-Platonic elements. In common with other Islamic thinkers of the era, he held that the universe is organized as a hierarchy, with Allah, who is pure form, at one end and formless matter at the other. Allah is the supreme good and that to which the human soul aspires to acquire knowledge. However, contrary to al-Ghazali, he claimed that there are distinct routes to the acquisition of such knowledge: revelation *and* reason. Thus, in *The Incoherence of the Incoherence*, Averroes attacked al-Ghazali's attempt to show that reason is incapable of demonstrating key metaphysical truths, and thereby reinstated the claims of philosophy to adjudicate on theological issues. This is not to say that revelation has no place: simply that there are different paths to the truth. Averroes held the view that what is immortal in human beings is a universal soul—that is, one shared by all. So there is a collective immortality, but no personal survival: an idea reminiscent of Buddhism and anathema to later Christian thinkers.

SEE ALSO ▸ Reason and faith (*p.157*) • Al-Ghazali (*p.261*) • Avicenna (*p.259*) • Plotinus (*pp.254–5*) • Plato (*pp.244–7*) • Aquinas (*pp.264–5*)

Averroes (*left*), imagined in conversation with Porphyry, the great third-century Neo-Platonist teacher and author.

"*Some truths about God exceed all the ability of human reason... But there are some truths which natural reason also is able to reach. Such as that God exists.*"

Summa Contra Gentiles Book 1

Thomas Aquinas

● 1225–1274 🏴 Italy

The rediscovery of Aristotle's works after the Dark Ages (500–1000) ushered in a new era of intellectual endeavor in Europe. Aquinas was the most important figure in this reawakening, and his work has remained the intellectual underpinning for the metaphysical, cosmological, and ethical commitments of the Catholic Church to this day.

LIFE AND WORKS

Born in the kingdom of Naples to a noble family, Thomas Aquinas began his education at the monastery of Monte Cassino at the age of five. He subsequently studied at Naples, where he discovered Aristotle, and in around 1243 he resolved to join the Dominican order. In an effort to dissuade him from this route, Aquinas's brothers kidnapped and imprisoned him for two years. Among other methods, they tried to tempt him with a prostitute, but Thomas drove her away with a firebrand and burned a crucifix on his door. When his brothers finally relented, Aquinas joined the order and was sent to study under the Aristotelian teacher Albertus Magnus in Cologne and Paris. He remained under Albertus's tutelage for many years until, in 1257, he attained his master's degree and license to teach.

Thomas Aquinas is considered by many to be the greatest theologian of the Catholic Church. His brand of philosophy, called "Thomism," still informs Catholicism today.

AQUINAS THE TEACHER

Aquinas traveled and taught in various European centers of learning, engaged actively in the theological controversies of the day, and wrote prolifically. However, on December 6, 1273, he had a mystical experience and stopped writing (leaving his great work the *Summa Theologiae* unfinished), saying that all he had written seemed like straw compared to what had been revealed to him. Four months later, the Pope ordered him to attend the Council of Lyons, but during the journey, he was taken ill and died.

Although Aquinas was sometimes dubbed "the dumb ox" because of his slowness of speech and his stocky build, his intellect and character impressed all around him. His teacher Albertus Magnus was prophetic in saying that "one day the bellowing of this ox will resound throughout the world," and in 1323, Thomas Aquinas was pronounced a saint by Pope John XXII. His Scholastic philosophy has received a resurgence of attention in recent years.

ESSENTIAL TEXTS
Summa contra Gentiles;
Summa Theologiae;
commentaries on
Aristotle.

KEY IDEAS

Aquinas believed the mind at birth to be a "tabula rasa" or blank slate, and so all our knowledge must come to us from our sense-experience. He distinguished two distinct avenues by which we can acquire knowledge. One is to reason on the basis of evidence gleaned from the world around us. The other is revelation. But while Aquinas drew a clear division between what he termed "natural" and "revealed" theology, he believed that their discoveries ought to be compatible, for both represent God-given routes to the discovery of the same reality. So it is unsurprising that he should regard the work of the great pagan philosopher Aristotle, properly interpreted, as ultimately consonant with Christian teaching; and this is why he devoted much of his intellectual energies to the construction of a resolution between these two systems of thought.

ESSENCE AND EXISTENCE

Aquinas inherited from Aristotle an interest in being, and he adheres to the notion that each thing has an "essence" or defining characteristic that makes it the thing that it is. But the question of *what* something is, the question of its essence,

"THREE THINGS ARE NECESSARY FOR THE SALVATION OF MAN: TO KNOW WHAT HE OUGHT TO BELIEVE; TO KNOW WHAT HE OUGHT TO DESIRE; AND TO KNOW WHAT HE OUGHT TO DO."

Two Precepts of Charity

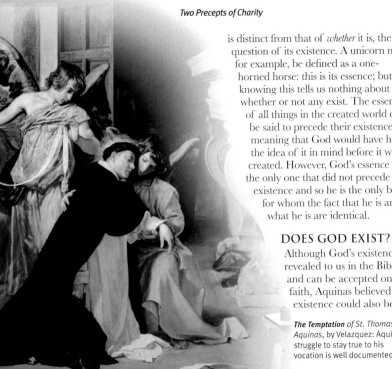

is distinct from that of *whether* it is, the question of its existence. A unicorn may, for example, be defined as a one-horned horse: this is its essence; but knowing this tells us nothing about whether or not any exist. The essences of all things in the created world can be said to precede their existence, meaning that God would have had the idea of it in mind before it was created. However, God's essence is the only one that did not precede his existence and so he is the only being for whom the fact that he is and what he is are identical.

DOES GOD EXIST?

Although God's existence is revealed to us in the Bible, and can be accepted on faith, Aquinas believed his existence could also be

The Temptation of St. Thomas Aquinas, by Velazquez: Aquinas's struggle to stay true to his vocation is well documented.

demonstrated. However, he rejected Anselm's ontological argument (*see also pp.140–1*), claiming that the expression "God exists" is not self-evident to us. God's existence cannot be established by the use of reason alone, but only with arguments based on evidence from the nature of the world. Aquinas famously offered five such demonstrations, the first three of which are versions of the cosmological argument, the fourth of the moral argument, and the fifth of the teleological argument (*see also pp.147–9*).

HOW WE PERCEIVE GOD

While we may prove his existence through reason, the true nature of God cannot be grasped by our finite minds. Our language refers to the world of experience, and so cannot accurately describe a transcendent being. Thus when we speak of God as being wise or compassionate, our descriptions inevitably fall short of the reality. But this does not mean that our descriptions of God are false or meaningless. Rather, such terms are being used analogically: we are saying that these qualities exist in him in a more perfect way than we can understand from our experience.

THE SOUL

Like Aristotle, Aquinas believed that each living thing has a soul, which is the form of the body and its principle of unity, and that the human person is a psychophysical unit. What distinguishes us from other animals as spiritual beings is the possession of our rational element. The intellect, being concerned with matters spiritual, is immortal, and so, contrary to Aristotle, Aquinas claimed that physical death was not the end of us. However, for us to enjoy eternal life, the soul, which is naturally suited to union with the body, must be reunited with it at the General Resurrection.

NATURAL LAW ETHICS

Aquinas's ethics also take their starting point from Aristotle and the idea that all created things have an end, or purpose, and the fulfillment of that purpose is their good. For a Christian this makes perfect sense since it is in the nature of the universe that each thing is part of the divine plan, and thus whatever is

DANTE AND AQUINAS

Dante's cosmology reflects that of Aquinas, with its series of concentric spheres sustained by the first principle—the prime mover, or God. In his *Divine Comedy*, Dante encounters the pagan philosophers Socrates and Plato in Hell, but when he enters Paradise he meets the glorified spirit of Aquinas. Dante's admiration for Aquinas was such that it is often said that the *Divine Comedy* is the *Summa Theologiae* in verse. Like Aquinas, Dante regarded the pursuit of wisdom as integral to the virtuous life.

Dante and Virgil peer into a circular Hell that has claimed the souls of the Greek philosophers of antiquity, while Aquinas dwells in Paradise.

the natural purpose inherent in something's design will constitute what is best for it. Human beings are no exception, but what distinguishes us from other things is that we can, as rational beings, become aware of our purpose and so freely direct ourselves toward it. Aquinas argues that reason tells us that our wellbeing or happiness is our good and this includes the satisfaction of our basic desires for, for example, nourishment and procreation. But this is not to say that wellbeing is to be equated with health, riches, pleasure, or any other mundane goods, but, rather, consists in living a virtuous life within the community, the pursuit of intellectual endeavor, and the contemplation of the essence of God.

SEE ALSO ▸ Does God exist? (*pp.140–9*)

Ramon Llull

● 1232–1316 ⚑ Spain

Educated at the court in Mallorca, Llull developed a mystical version of Neo-Platonism. After a vision of Christ, he joined the Franciscan order and worked as a missionary in North Africa. Convinced that rational argument could persuade Muslims and Jews to convert to Christianity, Llull wrote his great work, *Ars Magna*. This attempted to demonstrate the truths of Christianity from the basic concepts accepted by all monotheists. He devised complex techniques to generate different combinations of the set of basic concepts, hoping to convert all and so combine human knowledge into a single system.

Meister Eckhart

● *ca.* 1260–1327 ⚑ Germany

Little is known of Eckhart's early life. He joined the Dominican order at Erfurt and held various administrative posts and lectureships around Europe. A follower of Aquinas (*see pp.264–5*), his thinking deviated from mainstream Scholasticism, as did the mystical imagery of his prose. He is best known for his sermons (in the vernacular), which dwelt on the presence of God within man's soul. Condemned for heresy, he defended himself saying that the florid language he used to inspire his listeners to good deeds might have led him to stray from the path of orthodoxy. He recanted to avoid being burned to death.

John Duns Scotus

● *ca.* 1266–1308 ⚑ Scotland

Duns Scotus became a Franciscan in 1281 and was ordained 10 years later. Among the most influential of the medieval metaphysicians and logicians, he produced a complex version of the cosmological argument for God's existence (*see pp.142–3*).

Duns Scotus studied and taught at Oxford and then in Paris, from where he was expelled briefly for siding with the Pope against the king.

He argued, against Aquinas (*see pp.264–5*), that predicates, when applied to God, retain the same meaning as when used of ordinary objects. On the issue of universals, he was a realist while at the same time maintaining that we can apprehend particulars directly through perception without the mediation of general concepts; he coined the term *haecceity*, meaning "thisness," for the quality a particular has that makes it the individual it is. He also

Duns Scotus speaking to his students, some of whom heavily edited his works after his death.

defended our natural faculties against sceptics, claiming that knowledge can be acquired by their proper use and without the need for divine "illumination."

Duns Scotus's treatment of these and many other issues is characterized by the rigor and intricacy of his arguments, which earned him the sobriquet "The Subtle Doctor." Later philosophers were not so complimentary, and the difficulty of much of his argumentation led detractors to condemn his followers, who were known as "Dunses"—hence the derogatory term "dunce."

William of Ockham

● *ca.* 1285–1347 ⚑ England

Ockham was a Franciscan who studied and later taught at Oxford and, possibly, in Avignon. It was while in Avignon that he became involved in a controversy with the papacy which led to him being excommunicated, although his philosophy was never officially condemned.

In the great medieval debate on universals (*see* Plato, *pp.244–7*), Ockham argued against the "realist" view that general terms refer to entities existing independently of particular things. In his support for the "nominalist" claim that universals are abstractions from our experience of particulars, he is often regarded as a forerunner of modern British empiricism. Students of philosophy are familiar with the methodological principle that bears his name, Ockham's Razor, by which "entities should not be multiplied beyond the necessary:" in other words, one should always appeal to the smallest possible number of factors in explaining anything.

Most parents believe, like Ockham, that the simplest explanation for events is usually the correct one.

Nicholas of Cusa

● 1401–1464 ⚑ Germany

Nicholas of Cusa received his doctorate in canon law at Padua University in 1423 and worked as an emissary for the papacy. He became a Cardinal and was appointed to the diocese of Brixen in 1450. However, a dispute with Duke Sigismund of Austria, who briefly imprisoned him, prevented him from fulfilling his duties after 1460. *On Learned Ignorance* (1440) argues that the limitations of our intellect mean we can have no positive knowledge of God. Reason is bound by the law of non-contradiction, but in God, opposites are united in a way we cannot grasp, and since the universe mirrors God, it too is infinite and unfathomable. In astronomy, Nicholas of Cusa predated Copernicus in suggesting that the Earth is spherical and that it orbits the Sun.

Erasmus

● *ca.* 1466–1536 ⚑ Holland

Erasmus was a key figure in the new humanism of northern Europe's Renaissance. Ordained in 1492, he studied in Paris, and devoted his life to scholarship at various universities around Europe. Erasmus was a critic of orthodox Catholicism, seeing it as his mission to reform organized religion. His *In Praise of Folly* (1509) satirized religious practices and argued for a faith freed from Scholastic theology. Though his project had much in common with Luther's, Erasmus disagreed with his views on free will. He produced new Latin translations of the Bible and a Greek edition of the New Testament.

Niccolò Machiavelli

● 1469–1527 ▣ Italy

Machiavelli's account of how monarchs must wield political power to achieve their ends made his name synonymous with unscrupulous dealings, and *The Prince* was condemned as the work of the Devil. He argued that whether an action is justified depends on the ends it is intended to achieve.

LIFE AND WORKS

Machiavelli spent his life in Florence. He worked as a diplomat for the Florentine Republic (established after the fall of the Medici in 1494), engaging in missions around Italy, France, and Germany. In the process he met many important political figures, such as King Louis XII of France, the Pope, and, significantly, Cesare Borgia (upon whom it is thought *The Prince* was modeled). When the Medici returned to power in 1512, he was accused of conspiring to oppose their return, imprisoned, and tortured. Maintaining his innocence, he was eventually freed by the new Pope in 1513 and went into a forced retirement from political life on his estate. He continued

his political theorizing and, hoping for a return to political life, dedicated *The Prince* (1513) to the Medici. His *Discourses On Livy* (1517) is an analysis of Livy's history of the Roman Republic, and its support for republicanism is probably closer to his true views. Machiavelli's notoriety spread quickly during his own lifetime to the point where the term "Machiavellian" became synonymous with the scheming and ruthless deployment of political power.

ESSENTIAL TEXTS *The Prince; The Art of War; Discourses On the First Ten Books of Livy.*

KEY IDEAS

Before Machiavelli's time it was commonplace for political theorists to describe the organization of the perfect state and outline the virtues required of the ideal ruler. Through such discussion, it was felt that practitioners of the art of government would be provided with a model to which they might aspire. What these thinkers tended to ignore is how states are actually organized and how, as a matter of fact, political order is maintained. In *The Prince*, the work for which he is best known, Machiavelli set out to inject a dose of realism into political philosophy. Presented as a handbook for princes in the exercise of political authority, and written in a deliberately provocative manner, it discusses how to win and retain power, grounding its claims in historical evidence. While it might be nice to

The webs of intrigue spun by the noble families of Renaissance Florence were fashioned into political theory by Machiavelli in his infamous work, *The Prince*.

have a virtuous monarch, in practice, he argued, it is unrealistic. Moreover, adherence to our common notions of moral decency is not conducive to effective government, since apparently advising rulers to ignore moral concerns in the exercise of political power, it can also be argued that Machiavelli's real intentions were to argue that, regrettably, it is often necessary, in the pursuit of

> # "IT IS A SOUND MAXIM THAT REPREHENSIBLE ACTIONS MAY BE JUSTIFIED BY THEIR EFFECTS, AND THAT WHEN THE EFFECT IS GOOD... IT ALWAYS JUSTIFIES THE ACTION."
>
> *Discourses* 1.9

immoral actions are often necessary in order to realize political objectives. A successful prince must be adept at making an appearance of moral integrity, while being prepared to act ruthlessly to achieve his goals.

Machiavelli's analyses of the role of force, dissimulation, promise-breaking, and so on, as means to one's political ends, earned him his enduring reputation for scheming ruthlessness. While *The Prince* has been interpreted as

worthy ends, to perform actions that can appear morally evil. The worthy ends Machiavelli had in mind were the avoidance of civil disorder or external aggression, evils of which he was acutely aware after his experiences of political instability in Florence. His other great work, the *Discourses*, discusses effective republican rule and the need for tolerance of internal dissent and public support for the government.

SEE ALSO ▶ Political philosophy (pp.160–77); Are moral values facts? (p.118–9)

Francisco de Vitoria

◔ 1480–1546 🏳 Spain

A highly regarded theologian, de Vitoria was a Thomist (*see* Aquinas, *p.264–7*) and founder of a Scholastic movement known as the School of Salamanca. His name is associated primarily with the theory of Just War and the project to develop a code for international relations grounded in natural law.

Francisco de Vitoria grew up at the time of Spain's political unification and its discovery and subsequent conquest of the Americas. He joined the Dominicans in 1504 and taught in Paris from 1515 to 1523, when he returned to Spain and took the Chair in Theology at the University of Salamanca. A key figure during Spain's cultural Renaissance, he argued that the Christian faith should not be imposed on the indigenous peoples of South America and that they should be afforded rights to property and self-government, although he did believe in Spain's right to build an empire.

Francisco de Vitoria lived in an era of Spanish conquests and colonization, but had severe misgivings about aspects of his nation's conduct.

Michel de Montaigne

◔ 1533–1592 🏳 France

One of the most influential writers of the French Renaissance, Montaigne is perhaps best known for his invention of the "essay" as a modern literary form. His most important work, first published in 1580, was simply entitled *Essais* (*essais* is French for "attempts"), and contained a series of short discussions on a variety of topics. In his essays, he argued that belief is fallible, and he revived and modernized ancient scepticism—his "motto" was *que sais-je?* (what do I know?)—and his works influenced the scepticism of both Descartes (*see pp.276–9*) and Hume (*see pp.290–1*). Montaigne believed in God, and did not see conclusive reasons for breaking with traditional religious belief, nor for the kind of religious fervor that led to persecution in his own time.

Giordano Bruno

◔ 1548–1600 🏳 Italy

An unorthodox thinker, Bruno was influenced by Nicholas of Cusa (*see p.269*) and the *Corpus Hermeticum*—a set of occult treatises believed, at the time, to predate Ancient Greek philosophy. From Nicholas he took the idea of a universe infinite in space, in which our solar system is just one of many supporting intelligent life, as well as the notion of the concordance of opposites. His system is pantheistic and animistic: God is immanent in a universe composed of "monads," or animate atoms—ideas that anticipate Spinoza and Leibniz (*see pp.284–5*). These views, and his interest in magic and astrology, were deemed heretical by the Church so he was condemned and burned at the stake. His refusal to recant his views led him to be embraced as a martyr to free thought.

Francisco Suárez

◒ 1548–1617 🏴 Spain

The last great proponent of Scholasticism and a leading exponent of Jesuit theology, Suárez is hailed as the greatest Scholastic philosopher after Thomas Aquinas. He argued against the divine right of kings, and is regarded as one of the spiritual founders of international law.

LIFE AND WORKS

Born in Granada, Suárez joined the Jesuits in 1564. He studied philosophy and theology in Salamanca, graduating in 1570. During his career he filled various distinguished teaching posts in Iberia and in Rome. He was a productive writer, and his reputation grew rapidly. He was soon regarded as the greatest living philosopher, known as the Distinguished Doctor, and it is believed that Pope Gregory XIII attended his lectures in Rome. He wrote on many topics but is best known for his writings on law—*De legibus ac Deo legislatore* (1612)—and metaphysics—*Disputationes Metaphysicae* (1597). In his 1613 work *De Defensione Fidei*, he argued that the people have the right to dispose of a tyrannical king. His last words were "I never would have thought it so sweet to die."

KEY IDEAS

Suárez's metaphysical outlook is basically Aristotelian but his *Metaphysical Disputations* represent a systematic attempt to deal with the "science of being." Although a Thomist, he disagreed with Aquinas on several key issues. In the controversy over universals that so dominated much of Scholastic thought, Suárez maintained that only particulars exist. He also argued that between Aquinas's two kinds of divine knowledge—knowledge of what is actual and knowledge of what is possible—there exists "middle knowledge," knowledge of what would have been the case had things been different. He believed that God has middle knowledge of all our actions, without this meaning that God caused them or that they are necessary.

SEE ALSO ▶ Plato (pp.244–7) • Aquinas (pp.264–7) • De Vitoria (*facing page*) • Aristotle (pp.248–9)

Suárez's works were publicly burned by royal command in London for their criticism of the absolute power of kings.

Francis Bacon

◔ 1561–1626   ⚑ England

Although he held the position of Lord Chancellor in the English court, Bacon is more famous for his philosophy of science. He recognized that scientific knowledge could procure power over nature for mankind and saw it as a route to prosperity, social progress, and human well-being.

LIFE AND WORKS

The youngest son of the Lord Keeper of the Great Seal, Francis Bacon studied law, then entered the English parliament. He rose to become Lord Chancellor in 1618, before being jailed for accepting bribes. Bacon was stripped of his titles and position, and held in the Tower of London. Banned from public office, he devoted his remaining years to writing, and his vision for a college dedicated to scientific research has been seen as the inspiration for the founding of the Royal Society in 1660. His *Novum Organum* (1620) argued that experiment should be the basis for all science and, true to his principles to the end, he died of pneumonia after testing the theory that snow could be used to preserve a chicken.

ESSENTIAL TEXTS *Novum Organum.*

KEY IDEAS

Bacon was acutely aware of the fancies to which we are in thrall and which must be eliminated to pursue scientific knowledge effectively. He described four classes: first, the "idols of the tribe:" delusions that our nature subjects us to, such as our tendency to accept sensory evidence uncritically. Second, the "idols of the marketplace"— chimeras produced in our dealings with others, especially confusions caused by words. The third "idols of the cave" are misconceptions peculiar to an individual by upbringing. Finally, the "idols of the theater" are the delusions of grand philosophical systems such as fabricated by the Scholastic followers of Aristotle.

He likened Scholastic metaphysicians to spiders spinning fine theories from materials originating exclusively within their own minds. What was needed was careful attention to the facts. But Bacon also rejected the approach of unthinking "empirics" who, like ants, mindlessly gather information but fail to use it to forge hypotheses. Instead, scientists should be like bees: they should collect data through experimentation and observation, then search for regularities so as to frame hypotheses concerning the laws of nature. These hypotheses should be subjected to test and experiment so that they may be confirmed or refuted. This system of "induction," often called the Baconian method, helped to inspire and guide the new science emerging in the 17th century.

SEE ALSO ▸ The problem of induction (*pp.180–1*) • Falsificationism (*pp.186–7*) • Popper (*p.332*)

Bacon argued that the intricate problems that metaphysicians construct have no relation to reality.

Thomas Hobbes

● 1588–1679 🏴 England

The first modern materialist, Hobbes boldly maintained in a deeply religious age that there is no such thing as a spiritual substance. He is best known for his political philosophy: that it is rational for individuals to submit to a strong sovereign to ensure order and peace.

LIFE AND WORKS

After graduating from Oxford, Hobbes tutored the Earl of Devonshire's son and traveled extensively around Europe, making acquaintance with the intellectuals of the day, such as Descartes, Galileo, and Gassendi. He returned to England only to flee for France in 1640 before the outbreak of the English Civil War, in which he sided with the Royalists. During this time he tutored the exiled future king, Charles II, produced the third set of objections to Descartes's

A frontispiece to Hobbes's *Leviathan*, with its sovereign ensuring order and stability.

Meditations, and began his philosophical trilogy with *The Citizen* (1642). His great work, *Leviathan*, was published in 1651, but it attracted unfavorable attention from the French authorities, prompting his return to England just as Oliver Cromwell's Commonwealth came to an end. Hobbes continued to write and live an active intellectual life until his death, aged 91.

ESSENTIAL TEXTS *The Citizen*; *On Matter*; *On Man*; *Leviathan*.

KEY IDEAS

Like the ancient Atomists, Hobbes held that the world consists exclusively of material particles in motion, arguing that the very idea of a non-material substance, key to the traditional concepts of God and the human soul, is self-contradictory. Thus the behavior of the whole universe, including human action, is explicable on purely mechanical principles. This implies that the mind can be explained in terms of motion in the body and, in particular, within the brain. Sensation, imagination, even abstract thought, are reducible to material processes: all motivation, our aversions and appetites, are ultimately just the push and pull of particles in motion.

Out of this materialist account of human nature grows Hobbes's political philosophy. Because humans have similar

desires, they will come into conflict in a world of limited resources. In *Leviathan*, Hobbes imagines a "state of nature" that is the situation prior to the formation of society, in which each person pursues their own self-interest: a state in which each of us is at war with everyone else. Everyone would be far better off if they were to cooperate, so it must be rational for each of us to curtail our freedom and follow laws, so long as everyone else does the same. This can be achieved, Hobbes argues, by a social contract that gives power to a sovereign with the might to enforce universal compliance to laws.

SEE ALSO ▶ Humanism and the rise of science *(pp.34–6)* • Machiavelli *(pp.270–1)* • The social contract *(p.165)*

> *"I am not only lodged in my body, like a pilot in his ship, but… joined to it very closely and indeed so compounded and intermingled with my body, that I form a single whole with it."*
>
> Meditations

René Descartes

● 1596–1650 🏴 France

The eloquence and accessibility of Descartes's prose inaugurated "modern" philosophy. In undermining the traditional Scholastic philosophy of the medieval period he laid the foundations for a systematic approach to the acquisition of knowledge, based upon measurement and mathematical reasoning, which is still the basis of science today.

LIFE AND WORKS

Born in a village near Tours in France, Descartes was educated at a Jesuit college where he displayed great aptitude for mathematics. In 1617 he began a military career, and traveled widely around Europe during the Thirty Years' War until resigning his commission in 1621. He continued to travel until 1629 when he settled in Holland. Here, he began work on his *Treatise on the World* – an account of the nature and workings of the physical universe.

When Descartes heard of the Roman Inquisition's condemnation of Galileo for his defence of the Copernican system in 1633, he withdrew the *Treatise on the World* from publication. His first published work, the *Discourse on Method*, introduced his metaphysical views to the world as well as giving an autobiographical account of his own intellectual development and an outline of his views on the proper approach to the acquisition of knowledge.

Descartes argued that we must rely on the intellect to reveal the essence of matter beneath what appears to the senses.

GROWING FAME

Unsatisfied by the reception his *Discourse on Method* received, in 1641 Descartes wrote the *Meditations on First Philosophy* as an attempt to bring his philosophical ideas to a much wider audience. In 1644 he published his *Principles of Philosophy*, in which he restated his philosophical views, alongside discussions of physics and cosmology from his earlier and still unpublished work *Treatise on the World*.

With his fame gathering apace across Europe, he took up an invitation in 1649 to tutor Queen Christina of Sweden in philosophy. A demanding pupil, Queen Christina expected lessons to begin at 5 a.m., three days per week, and last for five hours each. Unused to this new regime, as well as the severe cold of winter in Sweden, Descartes contracted pneumonia and died within a few months of the appointment.

ESSENTIAL TEXTS
Discourse on Method; *Meditations on First Philosophy*; *Principles of Philosophy*; *Treatise on the World*.

KEY IDEAS

Descartes was not just a philosopher of the first rank but also a brilliant mathematician. He invented the branch of mathematics known as coordinate geometry, and the graph: the x and y axes are known as Cartesian coordinates after him. Indeed it is Descartes's fascination with mathematics that is the key to understanding the method and ambitions of his philosophy. He was impressed by the fact that conclusions reached in mathematics have the character of certainty and universality. And although these conclusions are often complex and far from obvious at the outset, they can be reached by incremental steps from initial principles that are simple and self-evident, such as that a sphere is bounded by a single surface, or that twice two is four.

At a young age Descartes realized that the traditional philosophy he was being taught contained much that was doubtful and disputed. If only, he thought, the mathematical model could be applied to philosophy and science, we could hope to establish indisputable and enduring knowledge of the world. Thus Descartes

discovered his ambition: to establish the foundations and framework for the whole of human knowledge to come, so unifying science within a single system.

THE METHOD OF DOUBT

In order to discover something "firm and constant in the sciences," Descartes believed, following the mathematical model, that he needed first to establish basic principles that were beyond doubt. And in order to discover such principles, he elected to subject all his previous opinions to the most radical scepticism he could muster. If any beliefs could survive this baptism of fire, he reasoned, they would be worthy foundations for his new body of knowledge. To this end, Descartes raised doubts about the reliability of his senses on the grounds that they can be deceptive. He wondered whether he might not be dreaming and raised the possibility that he might be being deceived in all his perceptions by some powerful and malicious spirit. Such a spirit would be

Descartes spent four years writing his *Treatise of the World*; with his other works, this would have a lasting impact on the intellectual development of Europe.

able to trick him about even the simplest and most compelling beliefs, such as that squares have four sides, and that he possessed a physical body. The fruit of his radical scepticism was the first certainty of his new system of knowledge and his most famous discovery: whether or not he was being deceived, he could not doubt that he existed. His own consciousness and what he was directly aware of were certainties that not even the evil spirit could dispel: "I am thinking, therefore I am."

Descartes's diagrams in which he outlined the possible "routes" taken by impulses to and from the brain were ahead of their time.

GOD'S EXISTENCE

Despite this initial success, to make confident progress beyond this point Descartes still had to dispel the specter of scepticism. Only if a non-deceiving God existed could the possibility of the evil spirit be eliminated and progress made in rebuilding a body of knowledge. So, to guarantee the reliability of human cognition, Descartes offered two arguments for the existence of God. One is a version of the ontological argument

carefully, never making any rash judgments, he could build a system of knowledge free from error. The system Descartes developed was one that argued that although the senses can be misleading, by careful use of the corrective of reason, science can be set on the right footing. Length, depth, and breadth are the essence of matter and thus the physical sciences should rest solidly on geometry and mathematics.

DUALISM

From the fact that he was directly aware of his own conscious mind even while he might doubt the existence of anything physical, including his own body, Descartes was led to suppose that his essence lay in being a purely thinking thing.

Although a distinct substance, this immaterial self is for Descartes intimately conjoined with the physical body, at least while it is alive. And while the physical world, including the body, is describable mathematically and follows precise

"WHETHER I AM AWAKE OR ASLEEP, TWO AND THREE ADDED TOGETHER ARE FIVE..."

Meditations

first articulated by Anselm (*see pp.261*); the other, the "trademark argument" (*see also pp.68–9*), argued that our idea of a perfect being cannot have been produced by anything less perfect than God himself, and therefore that God must have planted it within our minds to enable us to know our maker and come to recognize that we can attain the truth through the proper use of reason. With this divine guarantee, Descartes could advance from his first principles, and so long as he proceeded

physical laws, the world of the mind is free to pursue its own thoughts. That minds are not determined is evidenced by our ability to use language and respond to circumstances in unpredictable ways. This ability cannot be reduced to mechanical principles, and thus while the material world is to be reduced to mathematical science, the human soul requires a science of its own.

SEE ALSO ▶ Reason and experience (*pp.66–73*)

Benedictus Spinoza

● 1632–1677   ⚑ The Netherlands

Spinoza was the most radical of the early modern thinkers. He applied the methods of mathematics to philosophy and constructed an elaborate metaphysical system according to rational principles. His criticism of organized religion, and his liberal political views, won him many enemies.

LIFE AND WORKS

Driven from Portugal by the Inquisition, Spinoza's family settled in Amsterdam where Baruch (later Benedictus) was born. He had an Orthodox Jewish upbringing and was a gifted student, but he quit his formal studies aged 17 to join the family business.

In 1656 Spinoza was shunned by the Jewish community as the inevitable consequence of giving voice to ideas that were to appear in his later writings, such as his denial that the Jews were the chosen people; his rejection of the idea of a personal God, or that the Bible is revealed truth; and the denial of the immortality of the soul. He changed his name to its Latin form, Benedictus, and left

Spinoza made his living crafting lenses for the optical instruments, like this microscope, of the new age of scientific investigation.

Amsterdam, finding employment as a lens crafter, grinding and polishing lenses for telescopes, microscopes, and the other new optical instruments of the day.

Spinoza completed the only work he would publish in his life-time under his own name, a critical exposition, *Descartes's Principles of Philosophy*, in 1663. At this time he was also working on the *Theological-Political Treatise* which, published anonymously in 1670, secured his infamy, and his masterpiece, the *Ethics*, published posthumously. Spinoza died young of tuberculosis, probably precipitated by inhaling glass dust while grinding lenses.

ESSENTIAL TEXTS *Descartes's Principles of Philosophy (Principia philosophiae cartesianae); Theological-Political Treatise (Tractatus Theologico-Politicus); Ethics.*

KEY IDEAS

Spinoza's masterwork, the *Ethics*, is presented in the manner of a geometry textbook. Beginning with axioms and definitions of, for example, "substance" and "attribute," it deduces a series of theorems, and ultimately constructs a complex system embracing metaphysics, ethics, and psychology, all established in the same dispassionate manner as if studying lines, planes, and solids.

In the first section, Spinoza establishes that there can be only one substance, so there can be nothing outside the natural

world. Since this one substance is everything that there is, it answers to what we normally mean by the words "Nature" and "God," meaning that these are one and the same. Although Spinoza deployed several arguments to prove God's existence, the apparent identification of God with material substance seemed to many to be tantamount to atheism, and was the principal reason for his denunciation as an apostate and his notoriety as a challenging and dangerous radical.

TWO WAYS OF KNOWING

While there is only one substance, it has different modes, and there are two of which we are cognizant, namely mind and matter. In other words, the mental and physical constitute the two ways in which we are aware of the one substance. This development of Descartes's dualism of mind and body appears to imply that all physical things, not just human bodies, are to some degree sentient. Another implication is that the disintegration of the body must involve the death of the person, hence there is no room for otherworldly rewards or punishments.

THEOLOGY AND POLITICS

In the *Theological-Political Treatise*, Spinoza was the first to examine the Bible and scriptures as historical documents rather than revealed truth, and he concluded that they were written by many human authors over many years. He rejected the theology of the Old Testament as anthropomorphic and argued that its myths and stories should not be taken literally. The importance of the Bible lies in its moral message. Close textual analysis, Spinoza argued, reveals its support for the tolerance of different religious views.

Like Hobbes before him (*see p.275*), Spinoza used the idea of an original state of nature in his political thinking, but he used it to argue that the right of government to exert powers extends only so far as it can expect cooperation from its citizens, and that government should allow for freedom of expression and religious practice as the best means to ensure good public order.

Spinoza defended democracy as the most stable form of government and the system that best promotes individual wellbeing—something that can only be achieved by escaping enslavement to our passions for ephemeral goods and religious superstitions, and living in the pursuit of knowledge.

Seventeenth-century Holland was a liberal and progressive environment in which scientific and philosophical enquiry thrived—as seen in Rembrandt's *The Anatomy Lesson of Dr. Nicolaes Tulp.*

SEE ALSO ▸ The consciousness puzzle (*pp.124–7*) • Philosophy of religion (*pp.138–59*) • Grounding morality in reason (*p.105*) • The liberal ideal (*pp.162–71*) • Descartes (*p.276–9*)

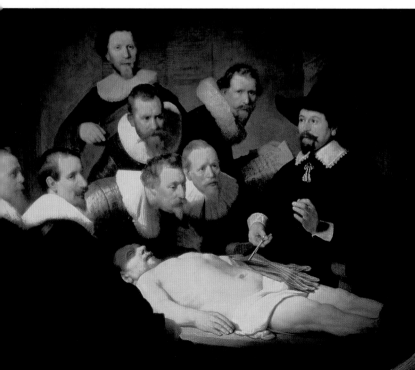

John Locke

◗ 1632–1704 ⚑ England

As the first of the great British empiricist philosophers, Locke's project was to determine the limits of human knowledge. Since this comes via the senses, its acquisition must be piecemeal, limited by the finite nature of our experience and so leaving some concerns beyond our ken.

LIFE AND WORKS

Locke's father fought on the side of the Parliamentarians in the English Civil War, and Locke remained committed to the view that the people, not the monarch, are ultimately sovereign. He studied at Westminster School and Oxford, where he went on to teach, gaining a degree in medicine. During this time, his encounter with Aristotelian scholasticism did not endear him to philosophy. However, in 1675 he spent some years in France, where his studies of Descartes's philosophy made a lasting impact. In 1681 his patron, the Earl of Shaftesbury, was tried for treason, and soon after Locke left England for Holland, where he worked on his *Essay Concerning Human Understanding*. He was

active in support of the accession of William of Orange and after the Glorious Revolution of 1688, Locke returned to England. In 1690 he published the *Essay* and the *Two Treatises of Government*, the works which secured his reputation. He subsequently became more engaged in the business of government.

ESSENTIAL TEXTS *Essay Concerning Human Understanding*; *Two Treatises of Government.*

KEY IDEAS

Locke was deeply influenced by Robert Boyle's "corpuscular" theory of matter, a revival of the ancient Atomists' idea that the universe is composed of particles too small to be seen, and that the behavior and appearance of all material things can be explained in terms of these particles. These solid corpuscles are describable in geometric terms—they possess position, size, and shape and they move around in space—but our perception of qualities such as colors, smells, and sounds is produced in us by the insensible arrangements of these particles. So Locke's picture of reality is firmly mechanistic.

Locke adheres to a "representative" theory of perception, meaning that perception is a consequence of the impact of physical objects upon our sense organs and that the sensations produced are like a picture of reality. We have direct access only to our own sensations and must infer from these the nature of the world beyond. He argued that knowledge is possible only of the observable characteristics of objects, not of what they are in themselves. In this way he gives the sceptic room to question our knowledge of reality.

POLITICS

Locke's political philosophy was as influential as his work in epistemology. Following Hobbes (*see p.275*), Locke used the device of the state of nature to justify political authority. Before politicization, humans would have banded together to defend themselves, and needed to find an impartial judge to adjudicate in internal conflicts. The judge would need the support of the community as a whole. Each individual would need to recognize the supreme authority of the law. There is, therefore, an implied contract between subjects and rulers: the ruler's authority is not absolute; rather, ultimately the ruler is answerable to the majority. If the ruler breaks the terms of the contract, the governed have the right to rebel.

Locke opposed the divine right of kings, in which God's representatives acknowledge at the coronation the monarch's direct descent from Adam.

SEE ALSO ▸ Mind-dependence (*pp.82–99*) • The liberal ideal (*pp.162–71*)

Gottfried Wilhelm Leibniz

● 1646–1716   ⚑ Germany

Leibniz stands alongside Spinoza as one of the foremost rationalist philosophers of the modern era. He developed an intriguing philosophy of mutually interlocking theses, with the consequence that an exposition of it can begin almost at random since each idea leads on to the others.

LIFE AND WORKS

In his early career, Leibniz worked for the Baron Boineburg, and then for the Duke of Hanover in many capacities, including secretary, counselor, diplomat, and librarian, conducting his academic studies in his spare time. He was known for his work in law, geology, physics, and engineering, as well as for his philosophy. On one diplomatic mission to England, he was received by the Royal Society, to which he presented his invention: a calculating machine, the first that could execute all four arithmetical operations.

On his way back from England in 1676, he visited Spinoza in Holland and read some of his unpublished writings. He wrote a page-by-page commentary on Locke's *Essay Concerning Human Understanding*, although on hearing of Locke's death, he decided not to publish. He was best known in his lifetime as a mathematician, and although he discovered calculus independently of Newton, in 1711 the Royal Society accused him, apparently with Newton's blessing, of plagiarism, an accusation not finally put to rest until after his death. However, Leibniz's reputation in Britain and France was already in decline. In his novel *Candide*, Voltaire famously caricatured him in the naively optimistic figure of Pangloss; and the fashionable empiricist spirit of the 18th century saw Leibniz's standing fall still further. German philosophers, however, maintained interest in him, and since the late 18th century, respect for this complex and ingenious thinker has gradually deepened; he is now recognized as one of the great European minds.

ESSENTIAL TEXTS *Discourse on Metaphysics*; *The New Essays on Human Understanding*; *Theodicy*; *Monadology*.

LEIBNIZ ON MIND AND BODY

Leibniz denied that any two substances, mind and body included, can interact. And yet experience appears to teach that damage to my foot causes pain in my mind. Leibniz argues that this appearance is produced by each substance unfurling its own programed development. The damage to my body coincides with the occurrence of a pain in my mind because both substances follow a preordained set of instructions.

Leibniz compares the synchronicity of mind and body to two clocks working independently of each other but programed to run in tandem.

KEY IDEAS

Leibniz's presentation of his system in the *Monadology* begins with an analysis of the nature of substance. A true substance, he reasons, must be totally independent of anything else, since to be causally affected by any other substance would compromise its status as an individual, distinct thing. It follows that any change occurring within a substance must simply be the consequence of its preceding state, and so its whole development must unfold according to its own internal dynamic. The universe, Leibniz argues, is composed of an infinite number of such substances—what he termed "monads." And since each monad is an individual thing, it must be "simple," that is to say, without parts—meaning that Leibnizian monads are living immaterial minds rather than physical atoms. Thus, Leibniz's vision of reality is pan-psychic and pan-organic, and the recent discovery of the microscope appeared to confirm his view that each perceived parcel of matter is a living body within which there live further organisms, ad infinitum.

THE DIVINE PLAN

Leibniz was aware that his metaphysical conclusions sat uneasily with the common-sense view that the universe is composed of extended, material objects in causal interaction with each other. His response was that space and causality are merely apparent, existing only in the perception of each mind or monad. God underpins the whole system, for he preprogramed the monads at the Creation so that they each unfurl their nature according to their own internal dynamic and experience the perceptions they would have were there causal interaction among them. Thus each monad reflects what occurs in all the other monads in the universe, meaning there exists a pre-established harmony between all created substances. Given God's nature as all-good and all-powerful, it follows that this world must be the very best possible: everything that happens occurs according to the divine plan and nothing can occur otherwise than as it does.

> "EVERY BIT OF MATTER CAN BE CONCEIVED AS A... POND FULL OF FISH. BUT EACH MEMBER OF THE ANIMAL, EACH DROP OF ITS BODILY FLUIDS, IS ALSO SUCH A POND."
>
> *Monadology 67*

Plato and Aristotle take the center ground in Raphael's *The School of Athens* (*see also pp.22–3*). Their influence reverberated down the centuries into the Renaissance, when pagan antiquity was "rediscovered" and this painting completed, through to the philosophers of the Enlightenment.

George Berkeley

◗ 1685–1753 🏴 Ireland

Berkeley claimed that "to be is to be perceived," and thus the universe is essentially mental rather than material. But this does not mean, according to Berkeley, that nothing exists beyond our perceptions, for God perceives all things. God thereby sustains everything in existence.

LIFE AND WORKS

Berkeley was educated at Trinity College, Dublin, where he became familiar with the works of Descartes and Locke. In 1709 he was ordained as a minister in the Anglican church and began to publish the works for which he became famous while still in his 20s, starting with *A New Theory of Vision* and the *Principles of Human Knowledge*. The *Principles* dealt with the existence of matter; a second part, dealing with the existence of minds, or souls, was lost on a voyage to Italy and never rewritten. Berkeley traveled to England, where he published the *Three Dialogues*, and went on to Paris, where he is known to have discussed his ideas with the Cartesian philosopher Malebranche. Subsequently based in London, he worked on the institution of a missionary college in Bermuda, traveling to Rhode Island in 1728 to publicize the idea. There he wrote *Alciphron or the Minute Philosopher* (1732). Unsuccessful in raising funding for the college, he returned to Ireland and, in 1734, became Bishop of Cloyne. His final work, *Siris* (1744), is remembered only for promoting the medicinal benefits of tarwater.

ESSENTIAL TEXTS *Essay Towards a New Theory of Vision*; *A Treatise Concerning the Principles of Human Knowledge*; *Three Dialogues between Hylas and Philonous.*

A statue of Berkeley honors his career at Trinity College, Dublin.

KEY IDEAS

Berkeley's philosophy starts out by embracing the empiricist principle, only just revived by Locke (*see pp.282–3*), that there is nothing in the mind that does not first come to it through the senses. Like Locke, Berkeley believes that all our concepts are akin to copies of sense-experiences, and it is these copies that allow us to think about what is not currently in our experience. So, I can think about dogs because I have first experienced a dog, and my mind has retained the concept of it. Conversely, we cannot form a concept of something if we have not first had some sense-

Berkeley argued for God's existence on the basis that the coherence and predictability of our perceptions meant that they must have been put there.

> "IN SHORT, IF THERE WERE EXTERNAL BODIES, IT IS IMPOSSIBLE WE SHOULD EVER COME TO KNOW IT; AND IF THERE WERE NOT, WE MIGHT HAVE THE VERY SAME REASONS TO THINK THERE WERE THAT WE HAVE NOW."

Principles I, 58

experience of it. For example, I can have no idea of the color red unless I have first experienced red.

MIND AND MATTER

With this in mind, Berkeley turns to Locke's concept of matter. As a representative realist, Locke claims that matter is the stuff that underlies our perception, causing us to have sensations, but which we cannot directly apprehend. In a commonly used analogy, there hangs a veil between us and the world so we are never able to perceive what reality is like in itself. But this leads to a contradiction, claims Berkeley. For if all concepts come from experience, we cannot possibly have a coherent concept of something we cannot experience. Therefore the representative realist's idea of matter is a philosophical confusion.

Berkeley draws the striking conclusion that matter does not exist and that all we can know is the contents of our own conscious experiences. In asserting that we could have knowledge of material substance, Locke broke the fundamental tenet of empiricism—that human knowledge is limited to what we can experience. If we cannot penetrate the veil of perception, then we are not warranted in supposing that anything exists beyond it. Indeed, according to Berkeley, we cannot make sense of the idea that our experiences are resemblances of a reality we cannot access. We can understand how one sense-experience can be like another, since both are mental. But we cannot claim that an experience can resemble something wholly non-sensory and non-mental. With these arguments, Berkeley held a position which Boswell in his *Life of Samuel Johnson* called an "ingenious sophistry." Yet the idealist tendency has endured in various guises to the present day.

SEE ALSO ▸ The peculiarity of philosophical doubt (*pp.50–1*) • Mind-dependence (*pp.82–9*)

David Hume

● 1711–1776 ⚑ Scotland

Probably the greatest philosopher to have written in the English language, Hume was best known in his day as a historian. However, it is his revolutionary approach to epistemological issues that made him a key figure in the Enlightenment and for which he is remembered today.

LIFE AND WORKS

Hume was born to a minor landowning family in the Scottish borders and studied law at Edinburgh University. He turned away from the Presbyterian views of his upbringing and, after graduating, moved to La Flèche in northern France, where Descartes had been educated. There he concentrated on his writing and in 1739 published his *Treatise on*

"I dine, I play a game of backgammon, and am merry with friends:" Hume's prescription for dispersing the clouds of "philosophic melancholy."

Human Nature. He returned to Edinburgh and in 1742 wrote his *Essays Moral and Political*. Disappointed with the reception of these works, which he decided he had published too early, he produced his two *Enquiries*, which presented the same ideas as the *Treatise* but in a more accessible manner. His six-volume *History of England* made Hume's name and secured him a good income for the rest of his life. He applied unsuccessfully for the Chairs in Philosophy at Edinburgh and Glasgow universities, doubtless because of his reputation for scepticism, in particular concerning religion. His *Dialogues*, which make some of the most devastating attacks on religious belief in the philosophical canon, were not published until after his death.

ESSENTIAL TEXTS *A Treatise of Human Nature; Enquiry Concerning Human Understanding; Enquiry Concerning the Principles of Morals; History of England; Dialogues Concerning Natural Religion.*

KEY IDEAS

Hume tried to describe the human mind in the same manner as other natural phenomena, by finding the general laws accounting for all mental processes. Following in the empiricist footsteps of Locke (*see pp.282–3*) and Berkeley (*see pp.288–9*), Hume regarded the senses as our key source of knowledge. He divided the mind's contents into two categories: "impressions," the perceptions we enjoy when the world impacts upon the senses; and "ideas," which are less vivid copies of impressions. Ideas are the concepts and thoughts that we are able

to conjure in our minds of things we are no longer experiencing. The philosophical point of this distinction is to insist that there is nothing in the mind —even the most abstract thought—that is not simply sensation transformed.

SIMPLE AND COMPLEX IDEAS

Simple ideas must come from simple impressions, but complex ones may be created in the mind by rearranging the simple ideas. In this way we are able to form concepts, such as that of a unicorn, of things we have not experienced.

Importantly, however, if we cannot entirely trace an idea back to simple original impressions, then it cannot be a genuine idea. Hume uses this as a means to conduct important critiques of key philosophical concepts such as those of the self, God, material objects, and causation. For if we cannot discover the origin of these concepts, then we will need to rethink what we mean by them and the uses to which we put them.

Dorothy is surprised by a talking scarecrow in *The Wizard of Oz*. If Hume is correct, it is as reasonable for us to expect our world to start behaving in an Oz-like fashion as it is to expect it to carry on as before.

MORAL PHILOSOPHY

Hume argues that moral judgments are not based on objectively observable facts. When we say that an act is morally wrong, we communicate the way we feel about it. But this does not mean that morals are a totally

> "REASON IS, AND OUGHT ONLY TO BE THE SLAVE OF THE PASSIONS, AND CAN NEVER PRETEND TO ANY OTHER OFFICE THAN TO SERVE AND OBEY THEM."

A Treatise of Human Nature

THE SELF

To give one example, Hume argues that when he looks into his mind he finds a stream of impressions and ideas, but no impression corresponding to a self that endures through time. He concludes that the self is nothing over and above the stream of perceptions we enjoy. An "enduring self" is just a fiction produced by our imaginations.

subjective matter. All human beings share in a common nature that makes us experience feelings of sympathy for our fellows, and because sympathy is programed into us, moral judgments reflect universally agreed truths.

SEE ALSO ▶ Cause and effect (*pp.90–3*) • Explaining design and order (*p.147*) • The problem of induction (*pp.180–5*)

Jean-Jacques Rousseau

◉ 1712–1778   🏴 Switzerland

Rousseau is known as the first philosopher of Romanticism and for his *Social Contract*, in which he argues that human beings are innately good but have their behavior corrupted by society. He also produced plays, poetry, and music as well as one of the great autobiographies of European literature.

LIFE AND WORKS

Rousseau ran away from home at 16 and escaped to France, where he came under the protection of Madame de Warens. She persuaded him to convert to Catholicism and became his lover. He made his living as a tutor, musician, and writer, firstly in Lyon and, after 1742, in Paris. There he lived with a woman and fathered five illegitimate children, all of whom were handed over to an orphanage. He met the *philosophes* (*see box, below*) and contributed to Diderot's *Encyclopédie*. In 1750 his *Discourse on the Sciences and Arts* won the Academy of Dijon prize. His subsequent *Discourse on the Origin of Inequality* developed his ideas on the corrupting influence of society. In 1762 he published *Emile*, in which his

educational theory is expounded, and outlined his political theory in *The Social Contract*. These works invited persecution and his books were burned in his native Geneva. This seems to have precipitated some kind of paranoid breakdown in the late 1760s from which Rousseau never fully recovered. He entered an unsettled period, staying at one point with David Hume (*see pp.290–1*) in England. But his paranoid accusations against Hume led to his return to Paris. There he wrote a searingly frank autobiography, the *Confessions*.

ESSENTIAL TEXTS *Discourse on the Origin and Foundation of the Inequality among Mankind; Emile or Education; The Social Contract.*

KEY IDEAS

Like Hobbes (*see p.275*) before him, Rousseau's political philosophy in *The Social Contract* begins by imagining human beings in a "state of nature," in order to describe the origins of social organization. Unlike Hobbes's, his image of human nature is a romantic one. He paints man's mythical original state as one in which humans are in unity with nature and exhibit natural sympathy for one another. It is society that represents the origin of oppression and inequality as the development of reason corrupts and stifles our natural sentiments of pity.

Rousseau envisages a different manner in which society might be organized, believing that as people

begin to see the benefits of cooperation, they might willingly give up their natural rights in order to submit to the "general will" of society. The general will is not

THE *PHILOSOPHES* OF PARIS

Rousseau was among a number of France's most outstanding writers and thinkers, including Voltaire and Montesquieu, to contribute to the great *Encyclopédie* edited by Denis Diderot (*pictured*). This 20-year project, a landmark of the Enlightenment, resulted in an extraordinary compendium of knowledge and learning, and the group of French intellectuals who compiled it became known as the *philosophes*.

It is only once the "noble savage," idealized in Paul Gauguin's painting *Eiaha Ohipa* (*Not Working*), falls from the original, innocent state of nature that their problems begin.

simply an aggregate of each individual's will, but, rather, the will for the common good of society as a whole. Freedom within such a society, for Rousseau, is not a matter of being permitted to do whatever one pleases, for satisfying one's desires is no kind of freedom but a kind of slavery to the passions. Rather, genuine freedom involves living according to social rules expressive of the general will, of

EDUCATIONAL THEORY

Rousseau's conviction that society is a corrupting influence on the natural state of man is of a piece with his educational theory. While admitting himself to be a

"MAN IS BORN FREE, YET EVERYWHERE HE IS IN CHAINS."

The Social Contract 1, ch. 1

which one is an active, contributory participant. For this reason, if we are not prepared to bend to the general will, we may have to be "forced to be free," since the general will represents what we really want, even if we don't realize this. Rousseau argued for direct rather than representative democracy: that is, a system in which each citizen has a direct say in the running of the affairs of state, since direct participation is necessary for one to identify one's own will with the general will.

poor father, he had strong views on child-rearing, believing that there is a natural way in which human beings develop and learn, and education ought to operate by facilitating this natural process rather than working aggressively against it, as with traditional educational approaches. He also emphasized the importance of physical health, which to him was just as significant as intellectual development.

SEE ALSO ▸ The social contract (p.165) • Rights (pp.168–9) • The communitarian challenge (pp.172–3)

"*Metaphysics is a dark ocean without shores or lighthouse, strewn with many a philosophic wreck.*"

Attributed to Immanuel Kant

Immanuel Kant

● 1724–1804 ⚑ Germany

Kant characterized his work as a bridge between the rationalist and empiricist traditions of the 18th century, and his revolution in epistemology and metaphysics is perhaps the most important philosophical development of modern times. But his influence in the areas of philosophy of religion, ethics, and aesthetics has been equally profound.

LIFE AND WORKS

Kant spent his entire life in the town of his birth, Königsberg, the then capital of East Prussia (now Kaliningrad in Russia), never traveling more than a day's journey from home. He enrolled at Königsberg University in 1740, where his principal philosophical studies concerned Leibniz (*see pp.284–5*). After graduating, Kant became a private tutor before obtaining a lectureship at the university in 1755, teaching a range of subjects including physics, anthropology, and geography, as well as philosophy. At age 45, he was appointed Professor of Logic and Metaphysics.

Immanuel Kant was one of the most influential European philosophers since the Ancient Greeks.

WEIGHTY WORDS

Kant published his inaugural dissertation in defense of his appointment, but then nothing followed for 11 years. However, by his own account, his encounter with the philosophy of Hume (*see pp.290–1*) had awakened him from a "dogmatic slumber," and during these years he was working on his revolutionary *Critique of Pure Reason*, finally published in 1781. The book is long and difficult, which may explain the fact that it did not receive much attention at the time. Kant's disappointment at its reception led him, in 1783, to summarize its ideas in the *Prolegomena to any Future Metaphysics*. His first work of moral philosophy, the *Groundwork*, was published in 1785.

Meanwhile, his reputation was growing, and it gradually reached the point where he became concerned by the direction being taken by those who claimed to be influenced by his philosophy, namely early proponents of what would come to be known as German Idealism.

Although Kant never traveled far and was said to lead such a regimented routine that people could set their clocks by him, he was not a solemn figure. In reality he enjoyed a rich social life and was known for his brilliant lectures.

ESSENTIAL TEXTS
Critique of Pure Reason; Prolegomena to any Future Metaphysics; Groundwork to the Metaphysics of Morals; Critique of Practical Reason; Critique of Judgment.

KEY IDEAS

The problem that Kant first set himself was to find out how to make positive discoveries about what lies beyond human experience. He was spurred into action by Hume's sceptical insistence that substantive knowledge about the world requires sensory experience—that it is impossible to extend our knowledge by the use of reason alone. If correct, this theory restricts the bounds of human knowledge. In particular, it makes knowledge of the existence of material substances, cause and effect, and the self impossible.

To overcome this difficulty, Kant attempts to show that we can discover significant truths about reality "a priori" (or through pure reason; *see p.66*), by examining the conditions of possibility for our experience. Rather than ask the traditional question of whether our knowledge accurately reflects reality, Kant asks how reality reflects our cognition. He had come to recognize that what we know is determined by the nature of our sensory and cognitive apparatus. In other words, while human knowledge starts with experience, it requires ordering by the human mind. And it is possible, using reason, to describe the structure that experience must take and so discover universal truths about our world.

So what is this structure? Kant noted that all our experience of the world is *spatio-temporal*: space and time are the a priori conditions of sense-experience, and are the necessary structure imposed on experience by us. Kant also attempts to isolate general categories of thought that enable us to organize the material of sense. These categories include substance —that things are made of material *stuff*— and cause and effect—that events are related in lawlike ways—and are necessary conditions for the possibility of knowledge. Like space and time, these are features of the world as it appears to minds, not as it is in itself. In this way Kant overcomes Hume's scepticism by showing that we can

Reason tells the sighted that oxygen is there despite it being invisible. How does this apply to those who have been blind since birth? Kant argues that our sensory apparatus determines how we know about the world.

acquire knowledge of the world *as it appears to us*. However, this means we cannot have knowledge of the world beyond appearances. The real world—what Kant calls "noumena"—may not be spatio-temporal, contain substances, or obey laws of cause and effect; indeed, we can say nothing definite about it. And since we can only apply reason to the universe as it appears—to "phenomena"—we cannot use it to discuss the universe as a whole or what lies beyond it. This led Kant to outlaw much traditional metaphysical speculation—the existence of God, the cause of the universe and whether it has limits in space and time, the immortality of the soul—since such issues cannot be resolved by appeal to real experience.

ETHICS

If science is about the apparent world that obeys causal laws, then what of human beings? Are our actions determined by physical laws? Kant believed it was evident from experience that we are free, so we must be more than phenomenal beings. It

A PARADIGM SHIFT

The astronomer and mathematician Copernicus (1473–1543) recognized that the movement of the stars and planets cannot be explained by them revolving around the observer; rather, the observer must be revolving. In the same way, Kant argued that we cannot discover what it is possible for us to know by focusing on the world. Rather, we must place the structure of our cognitive capacities and the way in which they shape the world we experience at the center of our inquiries.

Copernicus rationalized the galaxy with a new model in which the sun, like Kant's self, became the center around which all revolved.

A moral duty is an unconditional or "categorical" demand on our behavior. It does not require us to do something because of what we may gain; it says we should do it simply because we have a duty to do it. Kant contrasts such categorical imperatives, which are genuinely moral, with hypothetical imperatives, which are not. Hypothetical imperatives require us to do something

> ## "THUS THE ORDER AND REGULARITY IN THE APPEARANCES, WHICH WE ENTITLE NATURE, WE OURSELVES INTRODUCE."
>
> *Critique of Pure Reason*, A 125

must be our noumenal self that is the source of free will and allows for moral agency. For Kant, only agents who can deliberate rationally about their choices can be said to be free. We cannot expect our duties to be delivered by any higher authority, or imposed by our emotions: we must discover them for ourselves through the autonomous use of our reason. Only reason is universal and can make universal demands on our behavior. Thus what makes an action truly moral is that it is motivated by a rational acceptance of duty, not any other motive such as self-interest, guilt, or even compassion.

in order to reach some other goal. For Kant, only an imperative that truly has universal application (that is right in all equivalent circumstances) can be moral. Our duty must be always to act in such a way as we would will all others to act too. For Kant this is equivalent to saying that we should always treat others as ends in themselves and never as means to our ends—that is, we should respect others' goals rather than ever use them as a way of obtaining our own ends.

SEE ALSO ▸ Mind-dependence *(pp.82–99)* • Does God exist? *(pp.140–9)* • What should I do? *(pp.102–3)*

Adam Smith

⬤ 1723–1790   🏴 Scotland

Best known as an economist, Smith was also a notable moral philosopher. His *Wealth of Nations* defends free-trade capitalism and was the first systematic study of the workings of commerce. His belief in the free market makes him, for many, the father of modern libertarianism.

LIFE AND WORKS

Smith was baptized in July 1723 in Kirkcaldy. He studied at the University of Glasgow and then at Oxford, before returning to Scotland in 1748. For a time he lectured in Edinburgh, where he became close friends with Hume (*see pp.290–1*) and began to develop the ideas that would form the *Wealth of Nations*. In 1751 Smith obtained the Chair in Logic at Glasgow, and published the

Theory of the Moral Sentiments in 1759. He left the university in 1763 to tutor a Scottish nobleman, with whom he toured France and met many of the *philosophes*. He returned to Kirkcaldy and, in 1776, published his most famous work.

ESSENTIAL TEXTS *Theory of the Moral Sentiments; Inquiry into the Nature and Causes of the Wealth of Nations.*

KEY IDEAS

Smith's *Wealth of Nations* is important principally for establishing economics as an independent discipline. From it developed both classical and modern economic theory. Smith's main argument

An "invisible hand" controls the market, according to Smith; demand dictates the price of goods and governments can adopt a "laissez-faire" approach.

is that free trade is the route to economic success on the grounds that a free market, of its own accord, will tend to produce a healthy range of goods while securing the correct levels of production. Any shortage will boost demand, leading to an increase in prices. This will, in turn, increase production as producers take advantage of lucrative profit margins. On the other hand, any surplus will naturally lead to a decrease in price, thereby reducing the producers' interest in marketing the product. So, although the players involved are self-interested, a capitalist system will tend to keep prices low and ensure that there is an incentive for meeting a range of human needs, and so it should serve the interests of all without the need for state interference.

Although he was embraced by libertarian thinkers, Smith himself recognized the limitations of the market and allowed for public services and education of the poor to be paid for out of general taxation.

SEE ALSO ▸ Negative freedom (*pp.162*) • The social contract (*p.165*) • Marx (*pp.311–2*)

Edmund Burke

🖳 1729–1797 ◫ Ireland

Burke is remembered for supporting the American colonies' fight for independence from Britain, and for his opposition to the French Revolution: an apparent inconsistency that has bedeviled his reputation. A conservative thinker, he defended reforms grounded in existing traditions.

LIFE AND WORKS

Born when Ireland was part of the British Empire, Burke was raised an Anglican. After graduating from Trinity College, Dublin, he traveled to London in 1750 to study law, but gave up to tour Europe. *A Vindication of Natural Society*, in which Burke defends an anarchistic political position, appeared anonymously in 1756, but he disavowed the work after becoming a politician, claiming it was a satire. His *Philosophical Enquiry into the Origin of Our Ideas of the Sublime and Beautiful* influenced Kant's thinking.

ESSENTIAL TEXTS *Philosophical Enquiry into the Origin of Our Ideas of the Sublime and Beautiful*; *Reflections on the Revolution in France*.

Burke joined Parliament in 1765 as a member of the governing Whig party, who lost power in 1783. He remained in Opposition until he retired in 1794.

KEY IDEAS

Burke's writings are characterized by the floridity of their rhetoric, rather than the careful reasoning of their arguments. In the political arena, he was primarily a practical thinker, concerned to influence policy rather than to lay down an abstract political philosophy. On joining the House of Commons, Burke became involved in efforts to dilute the power of the monarch, George III, and to defend the claims of the American colonies against British Imperial authority.

However, his *Reflections on the Revolution in France* in 1790 reveals another side to his political character. Here he discusses the connections between the Revolution and Rousseau's philosophy and predicts that, by tearing up the fabric of society, revolution opens the door to terror and tyranny. Burke was suspicious of the rise of atheism in France and viewed the

Revolution as an illegitimate usurpation of power, rather than an assertion of democratic rights. He attacked Rousseau and other French intellectuals—the *philosophes*—for believing that through theoretical speculation, divorced from tradition and political practicalities, a perfect design for society might be discovered. He argued that feelings of instinctive kinship are far more significant in maintaining social cohesion than abstract reason, emphasizing the importance of established social structures and inherited rights in securing political order. Burke's theory was vindicated as France's revolutionary ideals gave way to the Reign of Terror and the autocracy of Napoleon's regime.

SEE ALSO ▶ Political Philosophy (*pp.160–77*)
• Rousseau (*pp.292–3*)

Jeremy Bentham

◖ 1748–1832   🏳 England

Bentham wrote on ethics, politics, economics, and the law, and is best known as the founder of utilitarianism, the view that what is morally good is whatever maximizes happiness for most people. He argued for political and legal reforms that would benefit the population as a whole.

LIFE AND WORKS

Bentham studied law at Oxford and qualified at Lincoln's Inn. However, he became so disillusioned with the state of English law that he never practiced, working instead for its reform. He came to fame as a critic of the conservative political theorist Blackstone with his *Fragment on Government* and founded the *Westminster Review*, a radical quarterly later edited by John Stuart Mill, through which he pursued his lifelong campaign for political and social reform. He was made an honorary citizen of the French

Bentham's embalmed corpse (with wax head) on display at University College London, which he founded.

Republic in 1792 in recognition of his powerful critiques of traditional arguments adduced in support of established injustices, despite his rejection of the *Déclaration des droits de l'homme* as metaphysical nonsense. Before he died, Bentham arranged to have his body preserved as an "auto-icon," which may be viewed in London's University College to this day.

ESSENTIAL TEXTS *Fragment on Government*; *An Introduction to the Principles of Morals and Legislation*.

KEY IDEAS

Bentham believed that "Nature has [given us] two sovereign masters, pleasure and pain"—in other words, that the search for pleasure and avoidance of pain are the sole motivating forces for humans. On this basis, he argued that the morality of an action is a function of its tendency to promote pleasure or pain. This he termed the principle of utility. Thus the morally right thing to do, and, significantly, the morally proper social or legal policy to adopt, is always whatever offers the greatest balance of pleasure over pain for the population as a whole.

Bentham's ambition was to establish the perfect legal system and so make human beings virtuous. To this end, his reform agenda required that legislation

be framed exclusively in terms of the utility principle. To give legislators a yardstick for measuring the aggregate of pleasure produced by policies, he devised a "hedonic" calculus. This took into account the duration, intensity, and so on of pleasures or pains, providing a scientific basis for making social policy.

The utilitarians had great influence over reforms in Britain with a supposedly rational basis for determining legislation as contrasted with fictions such as natural rights, or appeals to religious authority. Bentham's influence is still evident in any cost-benefit analysis for policy decisions.

SEE ALSO ▶ Normative ethics (*pp.102–11*) • Mill (*pp.308–9*)

Johann Gottlieb Fichte

● 1762–1814 ⚑ Germany

The first philosopher to pick up on the Kantian revolution and the first of a group of thinkers known as the German Idealists, Fichte called for a moral reawakening in Germany after the defeats by Napoleon. His lectures are cited among the foundations of German nationalistic totalitarianism.

LIFE AND WORKS

Fichte's first work, *Attempt at a Critique of All Revelation*, was published anonymously and, given its Kantian flavor, mistaken for a work of the great man. This earned Fichte his reputation and a professorship at the University of Jena in 1793. Fichte was forthright in his unorthodox views on the nature of God, which were taken as tantamount to atheism; this, and his support for the French Revolution, forced him from his post in 1799. Kant disowned his disciple but Fichte moved to a post at Berlin University, associated with the Romantic circle, where he gave his celebrated *Addresses to the German Nation*.

ESSENTIAL TEXTS *Attempt at a Critique of All Revelation*; *Science of Knowledge*; *Science of Rights*; *The Way to the Blessed Life of the Doctrine of Religion*.

KEY IDEAS

At root a Kantian thinker, Fichte continued Kant's project but with certain key adjustments. Kant argued that we can only have knowledge of a world of appearances: that things in themselves lie beyond human understanding. In arguing that the knowing subject must posit the existence of such a world, Kant should, according to Fichte, have recognized that the thing in itself exists *for* consciousness. The process by which the ego becomes aware of itself necessarily involves contrasting itself with what it is not, the non-self. And insofar as it is a condition of self-knowledge that we project the existence of a thing-in-itself, its existence is posited in order to be contrasted with the self. This effectively means the self constitutes the whole of reality, and so the ego is identified with the ultimate reality. In order to avoid collapsing into a form of idealism in which objectivity becomes impossible, Fichte looks to the idea of self-legislating rules, and picks up on Kant's idea of the self as the legislator of moral law. The ego's recognition of its activity as producing objectivity is characterized as the "absolute," making Fichte the first absolute idealist.

SEE ALSO ▶ God and the mind (*pp.86–89*) • Kant (*pp.294–7*)

Fichte claimed that knowledge of the self becomes possible only by contrasting it with that which it is not—the world of the non-self.

Georg Hegel

● 1770–1831 ⚑ Germany

Hegel became the foremost German philosopher in his own lifetime, his project encompassing the whole of history, reality, and thought in one philosophical system. Reality is constituted by *Geist* ("mind" or "spirit"), a dynamic force that directs the process of history toward its ultimate goal.

LIFE AND WORKS

Born into a Protestant family, the young Hegel had ambitions to be a clergyman and enrolled at a seminary in Tübingen, where he met Schelling (*see p.306*) and the poet Hölderlin. After receiving his doctorate, he pursued an academic career in philosophy, taking up a lecturing post at Jena University where Schelling also taught, and they collaborated on the *Critical Journal of Philosophy*. In 1805, as Napoleon prepared for the battle of Jena, Hegel finished his first major work, *The Phenomenology of Spirit*. Hegel's sympathies lay with Napoleon as the harbinger of the principles of a new world order and he later edited a Napoleonic newspaper. In 1816, after the appearance of *Science of Logic*, he obtained the Chair of Philosophy at Heidelberg and, later, Berlin. In 1831 he was decorated by Friedrich Wilhelm III but died four months later of cholera.

ESSENTIAL TEXTS *The Phenomenology of Spirit*; *The Science of Logic*; *The Philosophy of Right*.

An artist imagines Hegel, an admirer of Napoleon, greeting the victorious Emperor as he tours the streets of Jena during the French occupation.

KEY IDEAS

Hegel took a holistic and organic view of reality as a spiritual process, aimed at an ultimate goal or purpose. The nature of this process is fully amenable to rational investigation, its meaning and purpose discernible through an investigation of history, which will reveal to us our nature and place in the world. Hegel uses the term *Geist* to refer to this world process within which individual minds are unimportant, mere pawns in a dynamic driven by its own inexorable logic.

THE DIALECTIC

The logic of the march of history is what Hegel terms the "dialectic." Any given situation contains tensions that make it inherently unstable, so fueling historical change. Hegel shows how the same dialectical logic, a movement from "thesis" to its "antithesis" and on to "synthesis," applies to the development of social, economic, and political history; and also to the development of religious and philosophical ideas. Since conflict is

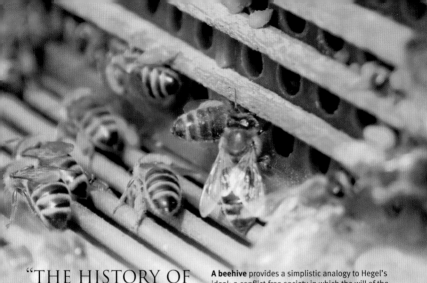

> # "THE HISTORY OF THE WORLD IS NONE OTHER THAN THE PROGRESS OF THE CONSCIOUSNESS OF FREEDOM."
>
> *The Philosophy of History*

A beehive provides a simplistic analogy to Hegel's ideal: a conflict-free society in which the will of the individual is subsumed to the collective good.

the engine of change, overcoming conflicts and achieving harmony will mean an end to history. In social terms, this means the realization of a state that has overcome internal strife. In terms of ideas, tensions cease when *Geist* reaches self-realization, that is to say when it comes to know itself, recognizing that it is the ultimate reality. In other words, Mind has become self-aware and recognizes the truth of Hegel's absolute idealism in which there is nothing—no thing in itself—that is opposed to consciousness. Since this final transformation is achieved in Hegel's own philosophy, it represents the culmination of the historical process.

HEGEL AND FREEDOM

In the political arena, the end of history means human liberation. But Hegel's notion of freedom is very different from the liberal account as found in Mill, which defines it in terms of the absence of constraints, since this ignores the forces that determine the choices we make and which lie outside our control. Hegel is alive to how history determines our nature and the choices of which we are capable, and so for him true freedom can only occur once we take control of these forces. This cannot happen so long as society is treated as an atomized collection of individuals, each pursuing his or her own objectives, but only once the individual's will is absorbed into that of the collective and recognized by reason to be shared by all. Then it will no longer be something from which we feel alienated, and we will recognize our social duty as being in our own interest. Rid of conflict in a rational, harmonious community, we will become self-legislating and, thereby, finally free.

SEE ALSO ▶ The liberal ideal (*p.162*) • John Stuart Mill (*pp.308–9*) • Marx (*pp.311–2*)

A DIVIDED LEGACY

Hegel seemed to believe that the constitutional monarchy of the Prussia of his own day represented the culmination of history, a position for which he was accused by Schopenhauer (*see overleaf*) of selling out to his patron, the King, and which served as a basis for the Prussian nationalism of the Right Hegelians. However, the Left Hegelians, among whom the young Karl Marx was counted, recognized the flaws in contemporary Prussia as the fuel for a new dialectical movement, this time of a revolutionary nature.

Arthur Schopenhauer

⬤ 1788–1860   🏴 Prussia

Schopenhauer's prose is among the most magnificent in the German language, but his philosophy is known for its pessimism, which he placed in opposition to the optimism of his contemporary Hegel. Life is a process of continual suffering from which art may give some temporary respite.

LIFE AND WORKS

In his childhood Schopenhauer spent periods in Hamburg, Paris, and in an English boarding school. On his father's death, possibly by suicide, he moved with his mother to Weimar in 1806. She was a successful novelist and held literary soirées at the family home. The young Schopenhauer had a broad education. He received his doctorate from the nearby University of Jena and initially pursued an academic career, taking a position at the University of Berlin. He taught there at the same time as Hegel (*see pp.302–3*), whom he despised as a charlatan. In a combative move, he timetabled his lectures to coincide with those of his adversary. Unsurprisingly, given the dominance of Hegel's philosophy at the time, hardly anyone attended Schopenhauer's lectures and

eventually he left the university. He lived the remainder of his days on his inheritance, a solitary, irascible figure who achieved a measure of fame late in life.

Schopenhauer arrived at his own philosophical system relatively early in his career, as set out in the *Fourfold Root* and *The World as Will and Representation*, and his later works are essentially refinements and defenses of it. He also produced two important essays, *On the Freedom of the Will* and *On the Basis of Morality*, both submitted as prize essays and published together as *The Two Fundamental Problems of Ethics*.

ESSENTIAL TEXTS *On the Fourfold Root of the Principle of Sufficient Reason*; *The World as Will and Representation*; *The Two Fundamental Problems of Ethics*; *Pararga and Paralipomena*.

A SIMPLE LIFE

Schopenhauer's pessimism is perhaps best summarized in his acronym for *WELT* (meaning World): *Weh* (woe), *Elend* (misery), *Leid* (suffering), *Tod* (death). He believed that through ascetic living and a life of self-denial, the endless cycle of striving can be avoided. By abolishing striving, the phenomenal world becomes nothing: time and space, subject and object, and the self are all extinguished.

Schopenhauer himself did not practice what he preached. He continued throughout to live comfortably, enjoying fine foods and various romantic liaisons—a fact that has caused some to question his sincerity.

Through living a life of chastity, poverty, self-chastisement, and fasting, the ascetic is able to escape the cycle of human misery.

KEY IDEAS

Schopenhauer follows Kant (*see pp.294–7*) in treating the phenomenal world as subject to causal determinacy, or, as he referred to it in his thesis, the "principle of sufficient reason." But whereas Kant thought the noumenal world (the world as it is in itself) to be beyond our knowledge, Schopenhauer argued that we can access it "from within" via the "Will." He identifies the Will as an impersonal force controlling all things, including us. As the concept of plurality is applicable only to the realm of appearances, this Will is the single underlying force operating below the whole of the phenomenal world. Thus the universe is a great cosmic drive for existence manifested in particular conscious beings.

Influenced by Hindu thought, Schopenhauer calls the phenomenal realm "the veil of Maya," characterized as an endless cycle of striving and suffering. Will produces desires that are never ultimately satiable, and since we are subject to its control, we have no control over our own lives—hence Schopenhauer's infamous pessimism.

Schopenhauer was also influenced by Plato's Theory of Forms: he thought that we recognize universal archetypes, or Forms, that manifest themselves in the things we observe in the phenomenal world. Because the arts deal with the universal in the particular, they give us a route by which to escape from the phenomenal world. The aesthetic experience is a transforming one as it enables us to penetrate beyond the world of individuality and so, if only briefly, to find release from suffering.

Another route out of suffering may be found by overcoming the striving produced by Will, which can be achieved by following an ascetic lifestyle (*see box, facing page*). Schopenhauer here follows Buddha's teaching, which states that as suffering is the product of desire, we must overcome desire.

SEE ALSO ▸ Plato and the Forms (*pp.76–81*) • Kant (*pp.294–7*) • Buddha (*pp.230–1*)

> "MUSIC IS THE UNCONSCIOUS EXERCISE IN METAPHYSICS IN WHICH THE MIND DOES NOT KNOW THAT IT IS PHILOSOPHIZING."

Attributed to Schopenhauer

Friedrich Wilhelm Joseph von Schelling

● 1775–1854 ▶ Germany

Like Fichte and Hegel, Schelling started out as a theologian but, imbued by
the spirit of Kantianism, he turned to an academic career in philosophy. He
studied with Hegel at Tübingen University and took a position under Fichte
at Jena before taking Chairs at Würzburg, Erlangen, Munich, and Berlin.

Schelling coined the term "absolute
idealism" for the post-Kantian insight
that the thing-in-itself could be
dispensed with, and the self and world
identified. This idealism was injected
with a Romantic view of nature as a
complex of physical processes
constituted by spirit, or "*Geist.*" Thus he
developed the pan-psychic view that all
of nature, not just the organic, is mental,
and that mechanistic accounts of reality
are inadequate. Human consciousness is
nature become conscious, and the
process of human history is one aimed
at self-knowledge, to the point at which
the Absolute reveals itself and false
oppositions between self and world,
mind and matter, are undone. Art is key
to his system, for through art, humanity
taps into the essence of reality, since
reality is itself a work of art created by
God. Schelling had a great impact on
Hegel (*see pp.302–3*), in particular in
his recognition of the importance of
history and his organic-cum-spiritual
conception of reality.

Auguste Comte

● 1798–1857 ▶ France

Comte's importance lies in his recognition of the historically
conditioned nature of human intellectual endeavor. He
regarded each science as having its own methodology
and being bound to evolve through three key stages.

An atheist, Auguste Comte developed
a theory of human intellectual and
sociological development according
to which both progress through three
stages: the theological, the metaphysical,
and the positive. The most primitive
stage, represented by the
medieval period in
European history, is
characterized by belief
in the supernatural.
This gives way to the
metaphysical attitude, in
which belief in unseen
forces is retained, but
speculation on the nature of
reality develops. From here
there emerges the "positivist"
scientific age, of which Comte
was the herald. The genuinely
scientific attitude confines itself
to description and prediction based
on observable regularities; it does not
try to *explain* phenomena.

The study of human society and its
evolution, or "sociology," a term coined
by Comte, was itself about to come of
age as a recognized science,
with laws constructed on the
basis of observable data.

Comte's zeal for his new
positivist ideology was such
that he proposed an atheistic
religion with its own
ceremonies and festivals,
even devising a calendar of
"secular saints" such as the
economist and philosopher
Adam Smith (*see p.298*).

For Comte, superstition governs the first
stages of development in any society.

Ralph Waldo Emerson

● 1803–1882 US

A poet and essayist, Emerson was also the major American philosopher of the 19th century. The leading figure of the New England Transcendentalists, his ideas were inspired by the European Romantic movement and absolute idealism.

Although not a systematic thinker himself, Emerson's vast output of essays, speeches, and sermons caused his ideas to generate considerable interest. His major themes are the unity of nature, with each particle of matter and each mind being a microcosm reflecting the whole, stressing the fundamental continuity between self, world, and the divine. He rejected social conformity and traditional authority, advocating self-reliance and personal integrity as the sole moral imperatives. The compelling aphoristic style of his essays has ensured Emerson's enduring appeal, influencing, among others, his godson William James and Nietzsche, some of whose aphorisms read as virtual translations of Emerson.

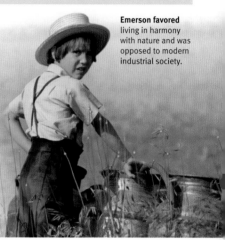

Emerson favored living in harmony with nature and was opposed to modern industrial society.

Ludwig Andreas Feuerbach

● 1804–1872 Germany

Feuerbach studied theology and philosophy at Berlin under Georg Hegel (*see pp.302–3*), later developing his own naturalistic brand of Hegelianism. His most important work, *The Essence of Christianity* (1841), developed his anthropological interpretation of religious belief.

Feuerbach noted that human beings are the only animals who are conscious of themselves as members of a particular species, and that we recognize the essence of humanity to contain various virtues, such as our capacities for reason, love, and benevolence. However, we are alienated from our essence and project our feelings onto a transcendent being, supposing him to be all-knowing, loving, and so forth. Thus God is an illusion, a projection of our own idealized inner nature, and what is true in religious feeling is in reality the love of humanity. Once we recognize the fact of our alienation, it can be overcome, and our love of God can be properly directed to our fellow human beings. Thus the essence of man can be realized on Earth in a democratic republic.

Feuerbach's importance to the history of philosophy lies primarily in his influence on Marx, and in particular his use of the concept of alienation, in both his critique of religion and his view that material needs are the foundation of political and social structures. His *Thoughts on Death and Immortality* (1830) argued against the transcendence of God and personal immortality, positions considered too radical for Feuerbach ever to secure an academic post.

John Stuart Mill

◒ 1806–1873   🏴 England

Mill's philosophical view was empiricist in that he based judgments on what could be observed rather than forming them by the use of reason alone. His ethical position, utilitarianism, is consequentialist, evaluating the observable results of an action in order to determine its moral worth.

LIFE AND WORKS

John Stuart Mill's father, the philosopher and economist James Mill, educated his son himself, ensuring he was well versed in the classics as well as in utilitarian ethics and liberal politics. According to his autobiography, Mill had read the histories of Hume and Gibbon by the age of six, mastered Greek and Latin by seven, become a proficient logician by 12, and an expert economist by 16. This intensive regime took its toll and he suffered a nervous collapse aged 20, after which he developed a more pragmatic approach. During the 1830s he edited the *Westminster Review*, which was founded by Jeremy Bentham (*see p.300*), and worked for the East India Company until 1858. He had a romantic liaison with a woman and married her after she had been widowed, renouncing his right to her property. He was elected to the House of Commons to represent Westminster in 1865, but later lost the seat.

ESSENTIAL TEXTS *System of Logic*; *Utilitarianism*; *On Liberty*; *Examination of Sir William Hamilton's Philosophy*; *The Subjection of Women.*

KEY IDEAS

Mill inherited the utilitarian outlook of his father and Jeremy Bentham, which holds that actions are morally praiseworthy to the extent that they promote human happiness. However, he perceived various inadequacies in Bentham's account. One was Bentham's insistence that all pleasures are equally valuable, whether they be base physical pleasures, the pleasures of friendship, or aesthetic pleasures that require effort and education to be enjoyed. Mill reckoned that the last of these had greater value, and argued that education for all would improve general happiness by opening up new avenues to fulfilment.

Mill was an early defender of women's liberation, as satirized in this 1860s *Punch* cartoon.

A second development away from Bentham's utilitarianism was Mill's recognition of the importance of rules in our moral thinking. Certain apparently immoral actions, such as to lie, steal, or even commit murder, may be justified, according to Bentham, if they bring about good consequences. The ends, in other words, may justify the means. But this does not sit well with people's moral intuitions that some actions are intrinsically wrong. Moreover, ideals such as justice appear to be valued independently of any happiness they may bring, and Bentham ignores the fairness of happiness's distribution. Mill argues that general acceptance of moral principles can often be justified on utilitarian grounds alone.

FREEDOM

Mill reckoned that human fulfillment requires individual liberty and argued for freedom of thought and expression. He believed that one's freedom should only be constrained by its impact on the freedom of others, and therefore there should be a private arena in which the state should not interfere, in which the individual's freedom to experiment with his or her lifestyle is absolute. In other words, coercion is only permitted to prevent harm to others. This rules out the right of the state to enact laws that protect citizens from themselves.

MILL AND SCIENCE

In the *System of Logic*, Mill discusses laws of induction as the basis for discovering causal laws, and explores the nature of scientific discovery and explanation. He hoped to be able to apply scientific principles to social phenomena and so find out the causes of events. The book also draws an influential distinction between denotation—what a term refers to—and connotation—the sense of a term.

SEE ALSO ▶ Political philosophy (*pp.160–77*) • Utilitarianism: be happy (*pp.102–3*) • Cause and effect (*pp.90–3*) • Frege (*p.318*) • Hegel (*pp.302–3*)

Pleasure derived from cultural appreciation, said Mill, elevates the masses: here, workers enjoy Chinese opera. Mill advocated education for all as a way of improving everyone's quality of life.

Søren Kierkegaard

● 1813–1855　🏴 Denmark

The philosopher who laid the foundations for existentialism, Kierkegaard accused Hegelian thinkers of ignoring individual experience, the personal relationship with God, and the significance of individual choice—the areas where ethical and religious questions are most pressing.

LIFE AND WORKS

Kierkegaard developed his lifelong distrust of Hegelianism while studying theology at Copenhagen University. In 1843 he wrote *Either/Or*, dramatizing a choice between the "aesthetic" and "ethical" ways of living, after deciding not to marry his fiancé. Later that year he published *Fear and Trembling* and *Philosophical Fragments*, and in 1845 *Stages in Life's Way*, which outlined his own "religious" way of life. His best-known work is an analysis of despair, *The Sickness unto Death* (1849). A recluse in later life, Kierkegaard became a local figure of fun after a dispute with a publication, yet he continued to rail against the established church until his death.

ESSENTIAL TEXTS *Either/Or: A Fragment of Life*; *The Sickness unto Death*.

KEY IDEAS

Kierkegaard's philosophy begins in his reaction against the abstract system-building of Hegelianism, which ignores both the uniqueness that exists in things and the concrete reality of individual consciousness. Kierkegaard reaffirms individual choice as the original locus of responsibility and authenticity. His use of pseudonymous authorship allows him to explore the experiences of a variety of subjective perspectives as the individual confronts different affective dimensions of the human condition.

Kierkegaard was also vehemently opposed to the state church of Denmark, which, he believed, was structured to distance the individual from any authentic relationship with God. He saw religious commitment as a leap of faith in the face of the uncertainty of the existence of God. His influence is also humanist, emphasizing the need to recognize one's freedom to choose how to live within a godless universe.

SEE ALSO ▶ Hegel (pp.302–3) • Because God says so (p.107) • God must exist (pp.140–1) • A leap in the dark (p.158)

Our relationship with God is a private matter for the individual; we must make our own decisions and moral choices, however difficult.

Karl Marx

● 1818–1883   ﰡ Germany

Marx's ideas had a profound effect on world history: within 66 years of his death, about a third of the world's population was living under regimes claiming allegiance to his philosophy. He thought that reality was historically constituted, containing internal conflicts that drive change.

LIFE AND WORKS

Although Marx's ancestors were rabbis, his parents converted to Lutheranism and he was vehemently anti-religious from a young age. He studied law at university but turned to philosophy, showing his early interest in materialism by writing his doctoral thesis on the ancient Atomists, Democritus and Epicurus. He was involved with the Young Hegelians, being particularly influenced by Feuerbach's materialist version of Hegelianism (*see p.307*), but his atheism excluded him from an academic career. In 1843 Marx went to Paris and met his lifelong collaborator, Friedrich Engels. Engels's family ran a successful business in Manchester and from him Marx learned of the conditions in industrial England and about British economic theory. The pair were exiled in 1845 and moved to Brussels, where they wrote the *Communist Manifesto* in 1848. They returned to Germany to take part in the revolutions of that year but Marx had to seek refuge in London, where he spent the rest of his life with his family in poverty, supported by Engels's business. The first volume of his great *Das Kapital* (*Capital*) was published in 1867; the second and third appeared posthumously.

ESSENTIAL TEXTS *Capital I*; *Capital II*; *Capital III*.

KEY IDEAS

Like Hegel, Marx believed that the process of history was open to rational investigation and that the law governing its transformations was *dialectical*—in other words, historical situations contain internal conflicts that make them inherently unstable, so leading to their demise and the rise of a new state of affairs. Unlike Hegel, however, Marx saw the inexorable logic driving the course of history as firmly material, not spiritual. Because it was material forces as they affect human action that were the engine of social change, Marx turned to focus on economics. According to Marx, it is the means of production and distribution, and the dialectical conflict between distinct socio-economic classes that these produce, which determine the course of history. They drive the social changes observable between, say, feudal and industrial societies and determine the nature of distinct social classes and class conflicts. Economic forces determine "superstructural" social phenomena such as political institutions, religions, ideologies, philosophies, and the arts, and this means that we need to read these as

Film poster for *Battleship Potemkin*, set at the start of the Marxism-inspired Russian Revolution.

expressions of their social situation and time. For example, religion serves the purpose of sustaining the status quo in which the workers are oppressed—hence Marx's claim that it is the opium of the people. Similarly, the arts merely serve the ideology of the ruling class.

Marx analyzed capitalism in terms of the opposition between those who own the means of production, the capitalists, and the industrial workers. Labor is the ultimate source of value, and profit is the result of exploitation of the workers by extracting more value from their labor than is paid in wages. The workers are alienated from the products of their labor because they do not own them, and they are dehumanized and isolated by mass-production. According to Marx, capitalism inevitably leads to increased polarization between capitalists and workers as ever-greater profits are squeezed from an ever-larger and more impoverished labor force. Eventually this must lead to revolution. Once the workers take control of the means of production, the profits will be used to benefit all, bringing an end to class

> ## "WHAT THE BOURGEOISIE PRODUCES ABOVE ALL IS ITS OWN GRAVEDIGGERS. ITS FALL AND THE VICTORY OF THE PROLETARIAT ARE EQUALLY INEVITABLE."
>
> *Manifesto of the Communist Party* 6: 496

conflict and the processes of dialectical change. Marx regarded this analysis as a scientific demonstration of the inevitability of the end of history and the institution of communism.

Marx did not live to see the workers' uprisings in Russia and China. He believed that a revolution in which workers seized control of the means of production would be the end of dialectical change.

SEE ALSO ▸ Hegel (*pp.302–3*) • Political philosophy (*pp.160–77*)

Charles Sanders Peirce

● 1839–1914 ⚑ US

Best known as one of the founders of the distinctively
American philosophical approach called "pragmatism,"
C. S. Peirce was influenced by Kant and acted as a key
influence on his close friend William James (*below*).

Peirce was primarily a professional
scientist rather than a philosopher, and
his laboratory experience remained a key
influence on his thought. Against the
modern tradition in philosophy, he held
that the way to acquire knowledge was
not as a lone investigator in search of
certainty, but via the experimental
approach of a community of scientific
inquirers examining uncertainties within
a system of accepted beliefs.

Peirce's reading of Kant (*see pp.294–7*)
was his principal philosophical influence,
and he saw himself as continuing Kant's

project in the light of modern advances
in logic, many his own. According to
Peirce's pragmatism, the meaning of
a term is exhausted by the practical
effects it has on our actions and the way
we conduct inquiry, and so is definable
in terms of its rational usefulness.

Peirce remained relatively unknown
during his lifetime and failed to hold
any academic post in philosophy for
more than a few years. Nonetheless
he produced a vast corpus of papers
(*Philosophical Papers*, 1931–5) that helped
to establish his importance.

William James

● 1842–1910 ⚑ US

William James spent his entire career at Harvard, starting out in medicine
before moving on to psychology and then to philosophy. An early paper,
"The Will to Believe" (1897), reveals his lifelong attraction to religious belief,
arguing that belief in God can be justified by something other than evidence.

James's first major work, the *Principles of
Psychology* (1890), is best known for the
idea of the "stream of consciousness,"
which opposed the traditional empiricist
notion of discrete items of experience in
favor of a continuous flow, where both
the immediate past and immediate future
color the quality of the present moment.
In 1902 James explored mysticism and
religious experiences in *Varieties of Religious
Experience* (*see also pp.150–1*) before taking
up Peirce's "pragmatism" (*above*). This
developed from a theory of meaning to a
theory of truth, proposing (in *Pragmatism*,
1907), that the truth of a statement is
defined not by the fact that it agrees with
reality, but rather in terms of the practical
use to which it can be put—it can be
"true," for example, if it accurately
predicts experience.

William James came from a wealthy cosmopolitan
New York family, which included his brother, the
novelist Henry James, on the left in this picture.

Toward the end of the 19th century, as migrants flocked to the United States, the country's first philosophical movement—pragmatism—emerged. Harvard's department of philosophy, home to the pragmatists C. S. Peirce and William James, was considered by many to be the finest in the world.

Friedrich Nietzsche

● 1844–1900   ⚑ Germany

Largely overlooked during his own lifetime, Nietzsche correctly predicted that the time for his philosophy was yet to come. Indeed his influence has burgeoned since the second half of the 20th century through movements such as existentialism, post-structuralism, and postmodernism.

LIFE AND WORKS

The son of a Lutheran pastor, the young Nietzsche was a brilliant scholar and his early academic career in philology advanced meteorically, culminating in his appointment to the Chair of Classics at the University of Basel aged just 24.

The defining moment in Nietzsche's intellectual development came in 1865 when he accidentally discovered Schopenhauer's *The World as Will and Representation* (1818). The influence of the composer Wagner, whom Nietzsche befriended as a student, is also evidenced in his early works. However, he fell out with Wagner over his opera *Parsifal*, which Nietzsche considered to be too Christian. In 1879, due to deteriorating

health, Nietzsche abandoned his academic career and embarked on several years of traveling around Alpine towns. During this period he published various collections of aphorisms and produced the literary-philosophical masterpiece *Thus Spoke Zarathustra*. He continued to write and publish at a phenomenal rate despite deteriorating health until he suffered a collapse on a street in Turin in 1889, having witnessed a man beat a horse. Nietzsche never recovered his sanity but his renown gathered pace around Europe.

ESSENTIAL TEXTS *The Birth of Tragedy; Human, All Too Human; Beyond Good and Evil; On the Genealogy of Morals; Thus Spoke Zarathustra.*

KEY IDEAS

Nietzsche's earliest philosophical concerns were the fruit of his engagement with Schopenhauer's atheistic vision of a world governed by irrational forces and characterized by striving and suffering (*see pp.304–5*). But while Nietzsche applauded the elimination of any spiritual dimension to the human condition, he rejected Schopenhauer's pessimistic reaction to it. In a Europe that had lost faith in the divine order that underpinned its traditional value system, the proper response was not to sink into nihilism, but to rise to the challenge to forge new values for a new age.

Nietzsche's whole philosophical project may be seen as his attempt to blaze a trail out of the malaise brought on by the death of God. It is in *Beyond Good and Evil* and *On the Genealogy of Morals* that Nietzsche develops his best-known critiques of the Judeo-Christian values that he hoped to overcome. According to his analyses, what we normally consider as "good" is really a valorization of the condition of the weak. The Christian denial of the differences between human

Christian morality is the morality of the herd, condemning as "evil" those noble types who stand out from the crowd, asserted Nietzsche.

beings, its pretended humility, its universal love, its rejection of bodily passions and of a sinful world, all issue from a resentful rejection of the life-affirming values of a noble, higher type of human being. The attempt of this slave morality to tame the beast within us is to be resisted so that noble values, with their bold expression of strength and power, might be revitalized. From this appears Nietzsche's great challenge to humanity, and the great remedy to nihilism: his vision of the "Superman" – a new breed of human who would transform established values.

PERSPECTIVISM

Nietzsche's critical fire is also directed against the philosopher's will to truth. Knowledge, he suggests, can never be grasped, since it is impossible to arrive at an objective conception of the world independent of some interpretation. This is not to say that Nietzsche rejects the idea of truth *per se*, for he allows that from within interpretations, views can be true. But it does mean that different interpretations must be judged in terms of the values that they express. One implication of his "perspectivism" is that conflict must be integral to philosophical discourse, and Nietzsche's aphoristic style can be seen as an attempt to multiply perspectives in order to open up new avenues of thought and fashion the armory for the philosophy of the future.

> **SEE ALSO ▸** Is morality relative? (*pp.120–1*) • The genetic fallacy (*p.205*)

"IF TRUTH IS A WOMAN... WHAT THEN?"

Preface to *Beyond Good and Evil*

The direct approach taken by dogmatic philosophers has inevitably failed to discover the truth. Nietzsche suggests that truth might instead have to be beguiled or seduced.

Gottlob Frege

◔ 1848–1925   ⚑ Germany

A founder of the analytic tradition in philosophy, and among the first to develop logic beyond Aristotle—clearing the way for the explosive development of modern logic in the 20th century—Frege worked to find secure foundations for number theory, and greatly influenced the philosophy of language.

LIFE AND WORKS

Frege attended Jena University, completed his doctorate at Göttingen, then returned to Jena as Professor of Mathematics. His first major work was *Begriffsschrift* (1879), meaning "conceptual notation," and his attempt to ground arithmetic in logic, *The Foundations of Arithmetic*, appeared in 1884. His philosophy of language is principally contained in three key essays: *Function and Concept* (1891), *On Concept and Object* (1891), and, most importantly, *On Sense and Reference* (1892), in which he investigated the nature of semantic concepts such as the distinction between sense and reference, which has been key within the philosophy of language.

ESSENTIAL TEXTS *Begriffsschrift*; *The Foundations of Arithmetic*; *Function and Concept*; *On Concept and Object* (1891); *On Sense and Reference*.

KEY IDEAS

Frege's approach to philosophical logic from the perspective of a mathematician succeeded in effecting a revolution in the discipline. *Begriffsschrift* introduced developments such as propositional calculus, truth functions, and formal notation—which remains current today —to express quantifiers and variables. These breakthroughs enabled modern

logic to develop rapidly. In *The Foundations of Arithmetic* Frege defended a version of Platonic realism with numbers as abstract objects existing independently of the mind, and number theory as concerned with the relations between them. He tried to reduce arithmetical operations to logical truths via set theory, although the work of Bertrand Russell (*see pp.322–3*) in this area led to this project's demise. Despite this, Frege's work has had an enormous impact on philosophy.

The names **"Everest"** and "Chomolungma" refer to the same mountain, but the words don't mean exactly the same thing—ask a confused explorer. The meaning of a term depends not just on what it refers to but the way it refers, its sense—or so Frege maintained.

Edmund Husserl

◕ 1859–1938 ⚑ Germany

As founder of the phenomenological movement, Husserl had a profound influence on 20th-century philosophy in Europe. Phenomenology, or theory of appearances, focuses on describing the way the world appears to consciousness without any presuppositions about the world beyond.

LIFE AND WORKS

Born in Moravia in the modern Czech Republic, Husserl completed his doctorate at Vienna in 1883. While there he attended the lectures of Franz Brentano (an influential figure in philosophy and psychology) and then obtained a teaching post at Halle, where he began work on the *Philosophy of Arithmetic* and his massive *Logical Investigations*. He obtained the philosophy professorship at Freiburg,

where Heidegger was teaching, in 1916 and remained there until he retired in 1928. With the rise of the Nazis, Husserl was subject to anti-Semitic attacks and his works were banned.

ESSENTIAL TEXTS *Philosophy of Arithmetic*; *Logical Investigations*; *Ideas Pertaining to a Pure Phenomenology and to a Phenomenological Philosophy*; *Cartesian Meditations*.

KEY IDEAS

In his early work, Husserl attempted to give an empiricist account of our grasp of mathematical concepts through an analysis of the psychological processes by which we acquire them. Frege (*see facing page*) famously criticized these attempts as insufficiently alive to the objectivity of mathematics, the truths of which are logically independent of how an individual might arrive at them. Husserl appears to have taken these criticisms on board and rejected the "psychologism" of his early work, coming to see objectivity in terms of "essences" intuited by the mind, and in *Logical Investigations* he argued that the laws of arithmetic are not psychological, but ideal and necessary.

PHENOMENOLOGY

Husserl noted, after Brentano, that mental states are always directed beyond themselves. Consciousness is always consciousness *of* something, and this "intentionality" became the centerpiece of his new philosophical methodology,

Fear when we see a spider is a fear *about* or *of* spiders: what Husserl called "intentionality."

"phenomenology." This involves a pure description of the contents of conscious experience. One must suspend belief in the natural world and all the assumptions that this brings to experience. Thus we can examine the essential content of experience and its intentional structure, and so describe the mind's intuition of the essences of the objects of experience.

SEE ALSO ▶ Phenomenalism (*p.88*) • Heidegger (*pp.328–9*)

Henri Bergson

◯ 1859–1941   🏴 France

Bergson was influential in the world of literature as well as philosophy. He drew a sharp distinction between knowledge gained through the intellect that requires concepts and deals with the external world, and knowledge of the mind through intuition—the true method for philosophy.

LIFE AND WORKS

Schooled principally in Paris, Bergson graduated from the Ecole Normale Supérieure in 1881. He became Professor at the Collège de France in 1900 where he remained until retiring in 1920. In 1901 he published *Laughter*, an essay on the meaning of comedy, and in 1907 *Creative Evolution*, which contained his critique of Darwin. In 1908 he met William James (*see p.313*), who introduced Bergson to the

English-speaking philosophical community. Awarded the Nobel Prize for Literature in 1927, he published his last major work, the *Two Sources of Morality and Religion*, in 1932. He died of bronchitis brought on by waiting in line in the rain to register as a Jew for the Vichy government.

ESSENTIAL TEXTS *Time and Free Will; Matter and Memory; Two Sources of Morality and Religion.*

KEY IDEAS

At the heart of Bergson's philosophy lies the notion of "duration," time as it is immediately experienced, contrasted with objective time as measured by clocks. We conceive the latter on the model of space as a homogenous medium, quantifiable and divisible into equal intervals. This, the time of the scientist, is radically unlike the lived experience of duration as a unified

and continuous flow, each moment of which is qualitatively unique. According to Bergson, we are aware of duration through an immediate and non-conceptual mode of cognition he termed "intuition." Unlike the intellect, intuition does not separate the knower from the thing known or divide experience into quantities, but coincides with its object.

ELAN VITAL

By intuition we are aware of the freedom of the will. It also reveals that the movement of duration is driven by a vital force or "*élan vital*," which Bergson regarded as integral to life and deployed in his critique of Darwinian natural selection. For Bergson, a mechanistic account of the development of life overlooks the need for a creative force which propels inert matter into novel forms or organization.

A Madeleine dipped in tea conjures vivid memories in *Swann's Way*, by Proust, who was influenced by Bergson's idea that our implicit memory of our whole past can be awakened by a chance taste or odor.

Nishida Kitaro

● 1870–1945 🏴 Japan

Nishida grew up at the time Japan was opening up to European influences after centuries of cultural isolation. He studied Daoism and Confucianism at school and Western philosophy at Tokyo University, graduating in 1894. He practiced Zen meditation techniques in Kyoto, where he also taught at the University.

Nishida was the first to attempt to deploy Western philosophical methods to explore Eastern ideas, in particular those of Zen Buddhism. In so doing he established philosophy as practiced in the West as an object of serious study in Japan, ultimately founding the Kyoto School. Key to his philosophy is the "logic of place," designed to overcome traditional Western oppositions between subject and object through a return to the state of "pure experience" that the Zen meditator aspires to, in which distinctions between knower and thing known, self and world, are lost.

Two of Nishida's key works are *An Inquiry into the Good* (1905) and *The Logic of Place and the Religious Worldview* (1945).

The tranquil "Philosopher's Walk" in Kyoto was so named because Nishida used to meditate there.

George Santayana

● 1863–1952 🏴 Spain

Spanish by birth, Santayana lived in the United States from the age of nine and wrote all his works in English. He taught at Harvard between 1888 and 1912, where he wrote the *Sense of Beauty* and *Life of Reason*. After retiring to Rome, he wrote *Scepticism and Animal Faith* and *Realms of Being*, which give the full statement of his mature philosophy.

Santayana was influenced by the pragmatism of Peirce and James (*see p.313*), with whom he studied and worked at Harvard, and argued that human cognition needs to be understood in terms of its evolutionary purpose. He urged the cultivation of the human imagination as the route to human flourishing.

Miguel de Unamuno

● 1864–1936 🏴 Spain

Poet, playwright, philosopher, Professor of Greek, and essayist, Unamuno opposed the dictatorship of Primo de Rivera and was exiled from Spain from 1924 to 1930. Returning during the second Republic, he sided with Franco's rebels before repudiating them, leading to his arrest and death. Unamuno embraced a version of what Ortega y Gasset called vitalism (*see p.324*): in *The Life of Don Quixote and Sancho* he sided with the knight in his crusade against reason. *The Tragic Sense of Life* argues that the desire for immortality may be quixotic but is an inevitable reaction to the human condition. Out of this absurd hope arises the need for faith in God.

Bertrand Russell

◉ 1872–1970   🏴 England

Russell's most widely read work is probably his masterly *History of Western Philosophy*; however, of greater philosophical importance were his efforts to reduce arithmetic to logic, his logical atomism, and his theory of descriptions, all achievements of his early career.

LIFE AND WORKS

From an aristocratic family, Russell was educated at home, like his godfather, John Stuart Mill. He read mathematics at Cambridge and stayed on to study philosophy after his degree. His interest in mathematics was rekindled by meeting the mathematician Peano in 1900; and in 1901 he discovered Russell's Paradox and produced his theory of definite descriptions and theory of types to deal with it. Between 1907 and 1913 he collaborated with his teacher on *Principia Mathematica*, an attempt to reduce math to logic.

After war broke out, Russell lost his position at Cambridge for his pacifist activities and, in 1919, was imprisoned

Trinity College, Cambridge, where Russell studied and taught. He was something of a mentor to the young Ludwig Wittgenstein.

for five months, when he wrote an *Introduction to Mathematical Philosophy*. He subsequently visited the Soviet Union, taught in China, and worked in the United States; but again he lost positions because of his views. He supported the war effort against the Nazis and, in 1944, he returned to Cambridge after writing his *History of Western Philosophy*. He was awarded the Nobel Prize in 1950.

ESSENTIAL TEXTS *The Principles of Mathematics*; *Principia Mathematica* in 3 volumes; *History of Western Philosophy*.

KEY IDEAS

Russell's important early work relates to the foundations of mathematics. He wanted to demonstrate that arithmetic is ultimately derived from logic, a claim known as logicism. The *Principia Mathematica*, a collaboration with A. N. Whitehead, has this as its goal. He made important contributions to philosophical logic in trying to overcome the difficulties for set theory and for the logicist project that arose out of Russell's Paradox.

LOGICAL ATOMISM

Russell believed that ordinary language embodied all manner of confusions, and that recasting philosophical problems in

a logically precise way would enable one to solve them. This led him to develop a theory of what makes a language meaningful, known as logical atomism. The theory states that the meaning of terms is what they stand for, and that meaningful sentences must reflect states of affairs in the world; hence their meaning must ultimately be grounded in our experience. Philosophical analysis of sentences cast in ordinary language should be able to break them down into simple "atomic" sentences. These atomic

Russell (center, with hat), a committed civil-rights activist and pacifist all his life, campaigned until his death for nuclear disarmament.

sentences are, Russell held, knowable by direct acquaintance, and might, for example, state the content of a simple perception. The critical point of this view is that sentences that cannot be analyzed into simples (*see also p.326*) grounded in experience are not about anything, and so are meaningless.

EMPTY NAMES

However, Russell's theory of meaning meets with the problem of how to analyze sentences that include references to non-existent entities. If we take, for example, the sentence "Pegasus does not exist," it seems to say something true about a certain entity: Pegasus. The difficulty is that there is no such entity for the name "Pegasus" to refer to. In which case, how can the sentence succeed in saying something meaningful, let alone true? Russell argues that we need to analyze such sentences to reveal their true form. "Pegasus does not exist" perhaps says that the winged horse does not exist, which is in turn analyzed by Russell as asserting that nothing is uniquely a winged horse. The apparent reference to a non-existent individual has now disappeared.

SEE ALSO ▸ Frege (*p.318*) • Wittgenstein (*pp.326–7*) • Mathematical knowledge (*p.73*)

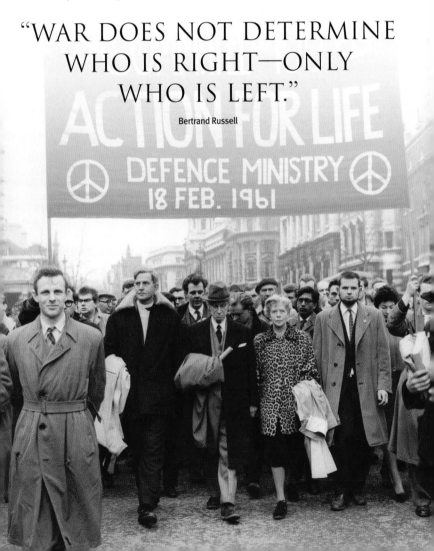

"WAR DOES NOT DETERMINE WHO IS RIGHT—ONLY WHO IS LEFT."

Bertrand Russell

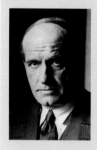

José Ortega y Gasset

🔵 1883–1955 🏴 Spain

Ortega has been said to have stood Descartes's *cogito ergo sum* on its head, thus: "I live, therefore I think." He argued that what he called "vitalism" or "vital reason" is the third way between idealism and realism, so what is real is neither the self, nor the mind, nor the material world, but life.

LIFE AND WORKS

Ortega held the post of Professor of Metaphysics at Madrid between 1910 and 1936. In 1917 he also became a contributor to the newspaper *El Sol*, where he published, in essay form, his two principal works: *Invertebrate Spain* and *The Revolt of the Masses*. The latter made him internationally famous. A supporter of the Republic, he went into voluntary exile during the Civil War, returning only in 1945. Among those strongly influenced by Ortega y Gasset were Xavier Zubiri, Pedro Laín Entralgo, José Luis López-Aranguren, and Julián Marías. His influence can also be seen in existentialism and the work of Heidegger, which Gasset himself apparently often pointed out.

ESSENTIAL TEXTS *Invertebrate Spain*; *Meditations on Don Quixote*; *The Revolt of the Masses*.

KEY IDEAS

Life, claimed Ortega, is a dialectic between the self and the situation in which it finds itself—"I am myself and my circumstances"—and "my life is a task," a project in which the individual creates him or herself. For Ortega, reason is a tool in the service of life, and he replaces the idea of objective truth with the perspective of the individual. His denial of a fixed human nature and

In his *Meditations on Don Quixote*, Ortega's perspectivism celebrates the individual's creative vision to forge his or her life.

focus on individual freedom to transform reality are reminiscent of existentialism (*see* Jean-Paul Sartre, *p.336*). However, unlike Sartre, and despite his support for the Spanish Republic, politically Ortega favored aristocratic rule in which an elite would maintain and lead culture. *The Revolt of the Masses* (1929) opposed the celebration of mediocrity without vision or forward-looking values that characterizes mass culture.

SEE ALSO ▶ Heidegger (*pp.328–9*)

Max Scheler

● 1874–1928 🇩🇪 Germany

Scheler began his academic career at the University of Jena in 1901, where he came under the sway of Husserlian phenomenology (*see p.319*). Moving to Munich, in *Formalism in Ethics* (1907) he used the phenomenological method in a critique of Kant, defending the idea that there are objective moral values apprehended not by the intellect, but through "feeling." In our relations with others, we are directly aware of their emotions, love being the force behind ethical action. After World War I, Scheler took the Chair in Philosophy and Sociology at Cologne, publishing *On the Eternal in Man*, an exploration of the phenomenology of the religious attitude. In *Man's Place in Nature* he reveals how God, man, and the world form one process, of "becoming."

Titus Brandsma

● 1881–1942 🇳🇱 Holland

Brandsma, a Carmelite monk, became a priest in 1905, obtaining his doctorate in philosophy from the Pontifical Gregorian University in Rome, and taught at the Catholic University of Nijmegen. He saw the Carmelite order as treading a third way between Dominican intellectualism and the Franciscan emphasis on the emotions as the route to God. However, he is principally remembered not for his many theological lectures but for his vocal opposition to Nazism. He was arrested in 1942 and deported to the Dachau concentration camp where he was executed. In 1985 he was beatified by Pope John Paul II.

Karl Jaspers

● 1883–1969 🇩🇪 Germany

Originally a psychiatrist, Jaspers became one of the seminal thinkers of existentialism. He was Professor at Heidelberg, first of psychiatry and, from 1921, of philosophy, until he was removed by the Nazis in 1937. After the war he became Professor at Basel.

Jaspers extolled Kierkegaard and Nietzsche as philosophers concerned to explore the human condition from the perspective of the individual's struggle with it. Philosophy should be about bringing the individual along the road to self-discovery and an authentic way of living, rather than pursuing a vain effort at objectivity and systematization. He argued that this involves confronting our finitude and embracing the "transcendent."

Ernst Bloch

● 1885–1977 🇩🇪 Germany

A Marxist philosopher, Bloch emphasized the possibility of a world free of exploitation and oppression. He spent his early career in Germany and Switzerland, where he took refuge during World War I, writing *The Spirit of Utopia* (1918). In 1933 he fled the Nazis, ending up in the United States, where he began work on his magnum opus, *The Principle of Hope* (1954–59). After World War II Bloch taught in Leipzig, but with the building of the Berlin Wall, he took asylum in 1961 in West Germany. His unorthodox Marxism regards reality as driven by a dynamic and teleological process. On the political level this aims at a socialist transformation of the world. Religion may be the opium of the people, but its mystified vision of heaven on earth is attainable. Although an atheist, Bloch's principal influence has been on Christian liberation theology.

Ludwig Wittgenstein

● 1889–1951   ⚑ Austria

Wittgenstein's philosophical career divides into two distinct periods. His early ideas are summarized in the *Tractatus* and his later ones in *Philosophical Investigations*. Both periods are linked by his conviction that philosophical problems result from confusions in language.

LIFE AND WORKS

The youngest of a wealthy Austrian industrialist's eight children, Wittgenstein considered becoming a monk but instead studied mechanical engineering in Berlin and, in 1908, traveled to Manchester to pursue a doctorate in aeronautical engineering. There he came across Russell's *Principia Mathematica* (*see pp.322–3*). His interest in the fundamentals of mathematics and logic led him to show Frege (*see p.318*) an essay he had written while the latter taught at Jena. Frege advised him to pursue his studies under Russell at Cambridge. With the outbreak of war in 1914, Wittgenstein enlisted in the Austro-Hungarian army, ending up in a POW camp near Monte Cassino in Italy. He continued his philosophical work during the war, eventually

publishing the *Tractatus* in English in 1922. After the war he changed his lavish habits, and gave all his money to his siblings, who were already rich and would not be corrupted by it.

Believing that the *Tractatus* had solved all the problems of philosophy, Wittgenstein became a primary school teacher, but his ferocious temper and exacting demands made him unsuitable. Eventually it became clear to him that his approach in the *Tractatus* had been simplistic, so in 1929 he resumed his philosophical research at Cambridge and became a professor in 1939.

ESSENTIAL TEXTS *Tractatus Logico-Philosophicus*; *The Blue and Brown Books*; *Philosophical Investigations*; *On Certainty*.

KEY IDEAS

The *Tractatus* attempts to clarify how language functions by offering a version of logical atomism (*see p.322*)—the view that all meaningful discourse can be analyzed into simple claims that picture atomic facts. Wittgenstein's picture theory of representation says that a proposition makes a claim about the world by containing elements—names that stand for elements of reality. By combining these names in different ways, we are then able to picture corresponding states of affairs. For example, by naming the cat *a* and the mat *b*, and by then placing *a* over *b*, the proposition "the cat sat on the mat" can be pictured. A proposition will be true only when objects in the world are combined as it pictures them.

On Wittgenstein's view, the basic names stand for "simples"—logically unanalyzable and indestructible components of empirical reality. All meaningful discourse must, on analysis, reduce to the way these simples are combined: to scientific discourse, in other words. In this way, Wittgenstein dismisses much metaphysical speculation as nonsense.

However, the *Tractatus* is notable for its cryptic gestures toward what must be "passed over in silence," including religious and ethical discourse, and metaphysical speculation concerning the structure of experience and the nature of the self. Indeed in his

WITTGENSTEIN'S HOUSE

Having solved all the outstanding problems of philosophy, Wittgenstein turned his hand to architecture and designed and built a house for his sister. His exacting standards made him extremely difficult to work with—he required the heaters, for example, to be exactly positioned so as not to spoil the symmetry, and even if they were only fractionally wrongly placed it would send him into fits of rage.

Wittgenstein's approach to architecture was as meticulous as his approach to philosophy, and he won praise for his Modernist style.

later period, Wittgenstein came to recognize that his picture theory could not account for all the uses to which language is put. The abstract and clinical character of the early work gave way to a thinker alive to the variety and nuances of real discourse. Yet the notion that philosophical problems flow from a lack of clarity about language remained.

The *Investigations* suggest that rather than having one function, language is used in a wide variety of ways. Rather than assuming that the fundamental linguistic unit is a name standing for a thing, he now

emphasizes the extraordinary range of ways that expressions are used. It is not just scientific language that is meaningful. There exist many different forms of discourse, each with their own rules and "grammar." Philosophical confusions arise when we are seduced by superficial similarities between expressions into overlooking differences in use. They can be resolved by refocusing our attention back on actual linguistic practice.

SEE ALSO ▸ Family resemblance (*pp.220–1*) • The incoherence of scepticism (*pp.56–7*)

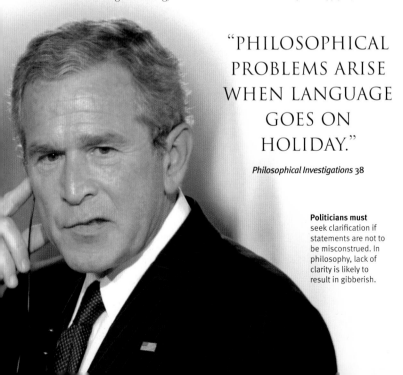

> "PHILOSOPHICAL PROBLEMS ARISE WHEN LANGUAGE GOES ON HOLIDAY."
>
> *Philosophical Investigations* 38

Politicians must seek clarification if statements are not to be misconstrued. In philosophy, lack of clarity is likely to result in gibberish.

Martin Heidegger

● 1889–1976   🏳 Germany

Heidegger's influence is seen in the existentialist movement and Derrida's deconstructionist project. His preoccupation was with the "science" of being, and his "fundamental ontology" emphasized what it is *to be* in the world rather than philosophy's concern with *knowing* it.

LIFE AND WORKS

Heidegger had been groomed by his family for the priesthood, receiving an education funded by the Catholic church first in Konstanz, and then at Freiburg, where he studied Catholic theology. However, he switched to philosophy, receiving his doctorate and becoming a lecturer there in 1915. In 1916 Husserl joined the department as professor and his thought had a significant impact on Heidegger's development. In 1923 he obtained the

Chair at Marburg on the strength of his publication of *Being and Time*. He then returned to Freiburg to take Husserl's place on the latter's retirement in 1928.

Attracted by Nazism, Heidegger joined the Party in 1933; he became Rector of Freiburg University that same year and gave a notorious acceptance speech. After the war, he was banned from teaching until 1951 because of his association with the Nazi Party. He spent the rest of his life writing and lecturing.

Heidegger's involvement with the Nazi movement and exactly how it should figure our reading of his philosophy remains a matter of controversy.

ESSENTIAL TEXTS *Being and Time*; *What is Metaphysics?*

KEY IDEAS

Heidegger's major work, *Being and Time*, declares that the Western philosophical tradition since the Greeks has forgotten the "question of being," and has been interested only in the present, thereby ignoring the temporal dimensions of past and future.

EXISTENTIALISM

The goal of *Being and Time* was to reopen the question of what being is, by exploring how we confront the fact of our own existence and the manner in which the world appears to us. Heidegger returned to Descartes's "I think, therefore I am" (*see pp.276–9*) to produce his own version of the Cartesian *cogito*: "*Dasein*"—literally, "being there"—is the term he used for this original mode of human consciousness. *Dasein* differs from the Cartesian *cogito* in that it is "always already" in the world, rather than separated from it. Where Descartes treats his knowing mind as the source of certainty and contrasts the world of material things with it, Heidegger emphasizes the lived reality of our being in a world not of our own choosing. Thus *Dasein* involves a material

"I SAW IN [THE NAZI PARTY] THE POSSIBILITY OF AN INNER RECOLLECTION AND RENEWAL OF THE PEOPLE AND A PATH THAT WOULD ALLOW IT TO DISCOVER ITS HISTORICAL VOCATION IN THE WESTERN WORLD."

"The Rectorate," 1933/34, *Review of Metaphysics* (1985), p.483

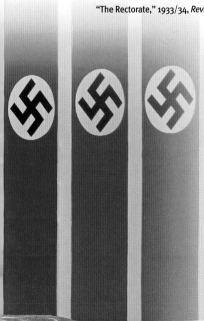

embodied existence located in time and in a socio-historical setting with other people, all dimensions ignored by the Cartesian "I." The being of *Dasein* is an open-ended project of "becoming:" we create ourselves through our actions and choices. Heidegger describes the affective dimensions of being: the experiences of boredom, anxiety, guilt, and dread. In dealing with the most general problems of the human condition, he is often regarded as the father of existentialism.

Heidegger was a critic of mass culture and modern technological society for distancing man from nature, leading to a loss of the original oneness with being possessed by primitive humanity. This may explain his attraction to those elements in Nazism that appeared to signal a return to the old culture and the land, contrasted with the technocratic modernism he perceived in the US and USSR.

SEE ALSO ▸ Husserl (*p.319*) • Sartre (*p.336*) • Derrida (*p.344*) • Gadamer (*p.330*)

Rudolf Carnap

● 1891–1970   ⚑ Germany

A key defender of "logical positivism," a philosophical position that owes much to Wittgenstein (*see pp.326–7*), Carnap held that claims that cannot be verified by experience are empirically empty and so lack meaning. Into this category falls all traditional metaphysics, which is the product of linguistic confusions.

During his early career, Carnap taught at Jena and Prague universities, then, during the Nazi era, in the US. His papers "Pseudo-problems in philosophy" (1928) and "Elimination of metaphysics through logical analysis of language" (1932) elucidated his version of the verificationist theory of meaning, according to which a statement is only meaningful if it can be established by experience.

One of the first to recognize the importance of the advances in logic made by Gottlob Frege (*see p.318*) and Bertrand Russell (*see pp.322–3*), Carnap linked these to empiricism in developing his account of how knowledge of the world is constructed out of the elemental data of experience. *The Logical Structure of the World* (1928) elaborates this view, but Carnap later came to regard individual experience as too subjective a basis for scientific knowledge. He later wrote that many apparent metaphysical questions do not hinge on any substantive issue, but boil down to a practical choice over how we describe the matter. Thus the choice between phenomenalism and realism is really one between linguistic frameworks. His later works include *The Logical Syntax of Language* (1934), *Meaning and Necessity* (1947), and *Logical Foundations of Probability* (1950).

Hans-Georg Gadamer

● 1900–2002   ⚑ Germany

Known for his theory of interpretation or "philosophical hermeneutics," Gadamer opposed the idea that the interpretation of texts requires an objective understanding of the authors' intentions.

Gadamer studied under Heidegger (*see pp.328–9*), held positions at Marburg and Leipzig, and became Professor at Heidelberg. In his major work *Truth and Method* (1960) he argues that we cannot escape the conditioning of our own historical situation, and thus the process of understanding a text necessarily involves two perspectives: those of the author and the interpreter. This means that interpretation is a two-way process in which these perspectives merge in a "fusion of horizons." Furthermore, because any text remains open to the possibility of new interpretations, continually revealing new aspects of itself, this process cannot be pinned down to a set method.

Gadamer's commitment to the idea of dialog was reflected in his engagement in public debates with fellow-philosophers Habermas and Derrida.

Gilbert Ryle

⬤ 1900–1976   🏴 England

Influenced by Wittgenstein, Ryle believed that many of the
problems of philosophy were simply confusions arising
from the abuse of language, and that its purpose should be
to dissolve these confusions through linguistic analysis. His
work paved the way for late-20th-century theories of mind.

LIFE AND WORKS

Ryle studied and taught at Oxford
University. He was first influenced by
phenomenology during the 1920s and
later espoused a form of the "ordinary
language" philosophy that dominated
Oxford in the '40s and '50s. His paper
"Systematically Misleading Expressions"
introduced the idea that philosophy was
about clarifying the logic of expressions:
an approach developed in his 1938 paper
"Categories." He was recruited to do
intelligence work during the war, and
became Professor of Metaphysical
Philosophy at Oxford while also editing
the prestigious journal *Mind* from 1948 to
1971. Aside from *The Concept of Mind*
(1949), he published *Collected Papers* (1971),
Dilemmas (1954), and *Plato's Progress* (1966).

ESSENTIAL TEXTS *The Concept of Mind*; *Categories*.

KEY IDEAS

Ryle noted philosophers' tendency to
suppose that expressions that function in
a superficially similar way grammatically
are members of the same logical category.
Such "category mistakes" cause much
philosophical confusion, so careful
attention to the underlying function of
ordinary discourse becomes the means
to overcome philosophical problems.

In the *Concept of Mind* Ryle set out to
map the "logical geography" of our
ordinary concepts of mind

and body in order to end the difficulties
that had plagued this branch of
philosophy. The principal source of
confusion has been, he claims, the
Cartesian tendency to treat the mind as
a non-physical machine within the body,
from where it produces human behavior.
Ryle coined the phrase "the ghost in the
machine" in caricature of this category
mistake, and his analysis attempts to
show that talk of the mind
is simply talk about behavior.

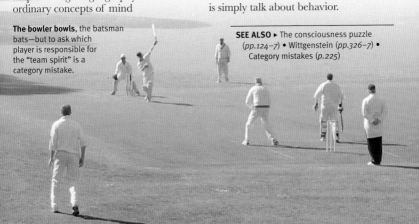

The bowler bowls, the batsman
bats—but to ask which
player is responsible for
the "team spirit" is a
category mistake.

SEE ALSO ▸ The consciousness puzzle
(pp.124–7) • Wittgenstein *(pp.326–7)* •
Category mistakes *(p.225)*

Karl Raimund Popper

● 1902–1994   ⚑ Austria

Popper is best known as a philosopher of science and for his critiques of utopian political philosophies. He argues that science does not progress by generalizing from observations, but through making bold conjectures which must then be tested. A scientific theory gains power from its testability.

LIFE AND WORKS

Popper completed his PhD in Vienna in 1929. His first work, *The Logic of Scientific Discovery*, outlined his views on scientific method, later developed in *Conjectures and Refutations*. In 1937, as a Jew facing the imminent annexing of Austria by Nazi Germany, Popper emigrated to New Zealand. During the war years, he wrote *Open Society and Its Enemies*, a defense of liberal democracy through a critique of

the political philosophy of Plato, Hegel, and Marx. After the war he taught at the London School of Economics, becoming Professor in 1949. In *The Self and Its Brain*, written with John Eccles, he defends a form of mind-body interactionism.

ESSENTIAL TEXTS *The Logic of Scientific Discovery*; *Open Society and Its Enemies*; *The Poverty of Historicism*; *Conjectures and Refutations*; *Objective Knowledge*; *The Self and Its Brain*.

KEY IDEAS

Like Carnap and the logical positivists, Popper saw science as the paradigm of rational inquiry. But he was concerned by Hume's "problem of induction." Hume argues that no matter how many instances of a generalization we might happen to observe, they fail to confirm a hypothesis —it remains as rational to reject the hypothesis as to accept it. Rejecting

Popper argued that science progresses by eliminating theories that prove to be untrue: for example, when the sight of a black swan disproves the theory that all swans are white.

Bacon's "inductivist" view of scientific method, Popper argues that theories are refuted, not confirmed, by empirical evidence, therefore scientific advance becomes a matter of putting forward hypotheses in order to try to falsify them. To be genuinely scientific, a theory must lay itself open to being refuted, since a theory that cannot be refuted does not make a claim about the world.

SEE ALSO ▶ The problem of induction (*pp.180–5*) • Bacon (*p.274*) • Carnap (*p.330*) • Quine (*p.337*)

Theodor Adorno

⬤ 1903–1969 ⚑ Germany

Musicologist, literary critic, sociologist, and philosopher, Adorno was a key figure in the Frankfurt School, which aimed to give a new direction for Marxist thought in the wake of Communism's failure in Western Europe and its degeneration into Stalinism in the east.

LIFE AND WORKS

A brilliant scholar with an intense interest in music, Adorno studied musicology, sociology, and philosophy at Frankfurt University. In 1925 he moved to Vienna to study under the composer Alban Berg. He returned to Frankfurt to teach and became involved in the Frankfurt Institute of

Adorno admired the atonal music of Schoenberg and detested jazz, seeing it as a sop to the masses.

Social Research under his friend Max Horkheimer. In 1933 the Nazis revoked his teaching license and he emigrated to England, then to the US. After the war he returned to Frankfurt and became head of the Institute and prominent in the Frankfurt School with Horkheimer and Marcuse.

ESSENTIAL TEXTS *Dialectic of Enlightenment*; *Philosophy of Modern Music*; *The Authoritarian Personality*; *Minima Moralia*; *Negative Dialectics*.

KEY IDEAS

By the 1930s the age of mass-production and mass culture had arrived and it became clear to leftist thinkers such as Adorno that the point at which capitalism would succumb to the proletarian revolution predicted by Marx had passed. Capitalism had discovered the means to perpetuate itself and Adorno's interdisciplinary approach—with investigations into popular culture and aesthetics, often deploying the tools of psychoanalysis—was concerned to explore the mechanisms with which contemporary society defused the forces of revolutionary change. *The Dialectic of Enlightenment*, written in collaboration with Horkheimer, examines the problems with modernity and, in

particular, the uncritical embrace of "reason" which, rather than being a force for liberation, has today become another mechanism of social control through technology. Meanwhile the culture industry and mass media, particularly in the US, producing artificial needs for readily digestible products and entertainments designed to pacify the new consumer, involve a similar process of domination. In *The Authoritarian Personality*, Adorno describes the personality of those attracted to fascism as one which submits readily to authority yet exults in exerting power over others.

In the 1960s Adorno engaged in a famous dispute over positivism, opposing Popper's "critical rationalism."

SEE ALSO ▸ Marx (*pp.311–2*) • Popper (*facing page*) • Habermas (*p.343*)

"HELL IS OTHER PEOPLE."

Jean-Paul Sartre, *Huis Clos* (*No Exit*)

Jean-Paul Sartre

◐ 1905–1980   ⚑ France

The foremost exponent of existentialism in the post-war years, Sartre taught that human freedom is total, demanding that we face up to the responsibility of what we do and who we become. He explored his themes in plays, novels, and criticism as well as through academic philosophy.

LIFE AND WORKS

Sartre studied philosophy at the Ecole Normale Supérieure in Paris, where he met his lifelong companion, Simone de Beauvoir. His 1945 lecture *Existentialism is a Humanism* made his name, along with various works for the theater. Marxist sympathies led him into political activism, for example in supporting the Algerian struggle against French colonial rule. He turned down the Nobel Prize for Literature in 1964 and, with his eyesight failing, produced his study of Flaubert, *The Idiot of the Family*, in 1972.

Les Deux Magots café in Paris is where Sartre met with Simone de Beauvoir. At his funeral, 50,000 people turned out on the capital's streets.

ESSENTIAL TEXTS *Nausea; Being and Nothingness; Critique of Dialectical Reason; The Idiot of the Family.*

KEY IDEAS

At a young age, Sartre rejected the "bourgeois" values of his upbringing, and the search for a freely chosen and authentic way of living—one not determined by authority, religion, or tradition—became one of his dominant themes. His philosophical approach is rooted in Husserlian phenomenology and the attempt to describe the universal structures of human experience from the subjective perspective of the Cartesian *ego*. What is "existentialist" in Sartre's thought is this emphasis on the actual experience of being human, and he charts this experience as much through his novels and plays as in more traditional philosophical works.

Sartre drew a radical distinction between physical matter and conscious-ness, the latter characterized by its freedom. No matter what our situation, we are free to "negate" it—to imagine things

differently or strive to change them. It is through our choices and actions, therefore, that we freely create ourselves, yet confronting the responsibility this entails has its psychological price. The "nausea" of his first novel's title refers to the pathological reaction of the hero, Roquentin, to the reality of his own freedom and his search for meaning in a world of things radically indifferent to him. In *Being and Nothingness* Sartre further explored our being-in-the-world, exposing the bad faith—our tendency to self-deception—by which people try to evade responsibility for their actions. In *Critique of Dialectical Reason* he attempted to resolve the tension he saw between the subjective starting point of his philosophy and the "scientific" Marxist view of history.

SEE ALSO ▸ Kierkegaard (*p.310*) • Husserl (*p.319*)
• Heidegger (*pp.328–9*) • de Beauvoir (*p.338*)

Willard Van Orman Quine

● 1908–2000 ⚐ United States

Regarded by many as the most important philosopher of
the English-speaking world in the second half of the 20th
century, Quine produced highly original work in logic,
ontology, epistemology, and the philosophy of language.
He saw philosophy as continuous with the natural sciences.

LIFE AND WORKS

Born in Akron, Ohio, Quine studied
mathematics and philosophy, then
traveled to Europe and attended
meetings of the Vienna Circle, a group
of philosophers and scientists committed
to anti-metaphysical philosophy, where
he met Rudolf Carnap. During World
War II he served as a naval intelligence
officer before returning to Harvard
University, where he remained until his
death. Quine continues to exert a huge
influence in Anglo-American philosophy
and taught some of its most important
figures, such as Hilary Putnam, Donald
Davidson, and Daniel Dennett.

ESSENTIAL TEXTS *From a Logical Point of
View*; *Word and Object*; *Ontological Relativity
and Other Essays*; *Quiddities: An Intermittently
Philosophical Dictionary*.

KEY IDEAS

Quine defended a strong form of
naturalism: everything that exists is part of
nature, and the only way of knowing
about the world is through science. He
applied these ideas to fundamental
questions about meaning and knowledge.

He attacked the distinction between
statements that are analytic (true in
virtue of their meaning)—such as "All
unmarried men are bachelors"—and
those that are synthetic (true because of
the way the world is)—for example,

"Snow is white" is true if and only if the snow is
white—Quine drew attention to a gray area in the
analytic/synthetic distinction.

"The cat sat on the mat." This
undermined philosophy's claims to
make distinctive contributions to
knowledge, and to provide knowledge
and science with foundations. Quine's
denial of such distinctions led the
Philosophical Lexicon to define the verb
"to quine" as "To deny resolutely the
existence or importance of something
real or significant." Although his thought
is complex and controversial, Quine
wrote with great clarity and style.

SEE ALSO ▸ Two ways of knowing (*pp.66–7*) •
Philosophy of science (*pp.178–89*) • Carnap (*p.330*)

Simone de Beauvoir

◉ 1908–1986 🏳 France

The feminist philosopher and novelist de Beauvoir had a lifelong association with Sartre (*p.336*). Her seminal *The Second Sex* (1949) deploys many of the conceptual tools of phenomenology and existentialism, while being alive to the social dimension of human existence. She explores how woman has always been relegated to a secondary role to man. In so doing, de Beauvoir proposes that biological sex (male/female) and socially constructed gender are deliberately confused by a male-dominated society, making it hard for women to break away from stereotypes and aspirations for their sex that were in fact created by men.

Donald Davidson

◉ 1917–2003 🏳 US

Davidson studied under Quine (*see p.337*) at Harvard and went on to a distinguished academic career at various American universities. He is unusual among major philosophers in never having produced a major book; his importance rests on his many short but incisive articles. In the philosophy of mind, Davidson held a materialist position, supposing each token mental event to also be a physical event. Still, he believed that the mental cannot be reduced to, or explained in terms of, the physical. He also denied that there are any laws connecting the two. With the Polish logician Tarski, Davidson argued that in order to be learned, a language must have a finite number of elements: the meanings of sentences must be a product of these elements and rules of combination.

John Langshaw Austin

◉ 1911–1960 🏳 England

Educated at Oxford, where he taught all his life, Austin was the leading figure in "ordinary language" or "Oxford" philosophy, which was fashionable in the 1950s. Avoiding the traditional philosopher's temptation to discourse on how language *ought* to treat an issue, Austin's approach to philosophical problems was to engage in rigorous and meticulous analyses of how language actually operates in ordinary usage. By examining our everyday talk about, for example, human freedom and agency, we can discover the subtle distinctions needed to resolve the most profound difficulties. An engaging and frequently amusing writer, his work is best known through the collections of papers and lectures collated after his death as *Sense and Sensibilia* (1962) and *How to do Things with Words* (1962).

Alfred Ayer

◉ 1910–1989 🏳 England

After graduating from Oxford, Ayer taught there, then at University College London. In 1959 he took the Wykeham Chair of Logic at Oxford.

His *Language, Truth and Logic* (1936) introduced logical positivism to the English-speaking world. In it, Ayer defends a version of the verification principle, by which meaningful statements must be sensitive to empirical evidence. Statements about physical objects can be reduced logically to statements about our actual or possible perception of them via the senses. An "emotivist" in ethics, he argued for the striking thesis that moral claims lack cognitive content, being mere expressions of emotional attitude (*see also p.115*).

Arne Naess

● 1912–   ⚑ Norway

A keen mountaineer, political activist, and Professor of Philosophy at Oslo University from 1939 to 1969, Naess is best known for his Gandhian ethics of solidarity, not just with our fellow humans but with the whole living environment.

Naess's "ecosophy" (from the Greek for "household" and "wisdom") advocates living wisely within our home, which is understood as the whole of nature. The emphasis on humanity's place within the whole ecological system ultimately means that there is no real distinction between us and every other living thing in the world.

Naess's thought was the inspiration behind the Deep Ecology movement, which he founded and named. He advocates non-violent resistance by direct action, and successfully opposed plans to build a dam by chaining himself, along with other demonstrators, to rocks at Mardalsfossen waterfall in 1970.

Recalling Spinoza, Naess focuses on the idea of self-realization but within the ecological whole, and argues that all living things have value and a right to flourish.

Louis Althusser

● 1918–1990   ⚑ France

A Marx scholar, Althusser argued that there is a radical difference, an "epistemic break," between Marx's early writings and the "scientific" period of *Das Kapital* (*see also pp.311–2*). Early Marx reflects the times with its focus on Hegelian concepts like alienation (*see pp. 302–3*), while in the mature work, history is seen as having its own momentum, independent of the intentions and actions of human agents. Thus Althusser's claim that we are determined by the structural conditions of society involves the controversial rejection of human autonomy, denying individual agency a role in history. Althusser was an important theoretical force within the French Communist Party.

Peter Strawson

● 1919–2006   ⚑ England

A philosopher of language at Oxford, Strawson notably, in "On Referring" (1950), took issue with Russell's theory of descriptions (*see p.323*), whereby a statement such as "The present King of France is bald" involves the claim that there exists a present King of France and is therefore false. Strawson argued that referring to something is not the same as asserting its existence, and while the sentence *presupposes* that there exists a King of France, the description's failure to refer means that the question of the sentence's truth or falsity doesn't arise. He later turned to "descriptive metaphysics," aiming to analyze the basic categories of our thinking about the world as reflected in ordinary language.

John Rawls

● 1921–2002 ⚐ US

Rawls's *A Theory of Justice* was the first sustained attempt since Kant to produce an alternative to utilitarian ethics and has become the touchstone for subsequent political philosophy in the Anglo-American tradition. It revives the social contract theories of Hobbes, Locke, and Rousseau.

LIFE AND WORKS

Educated at Princeton, Rawls joined the US Army, serving in the Pacific War; he visited Hiroshima after its destruction by the atomic bomb. He left the army and returned to academia, holding various lecturing positions before settling at Harvard in 1962, where he remained until his death. His early papers, such as "Justice as Fairness," reveal his interest in distributive justice, and *A Theory of Justice* attempts to place his findings into a systematic whole. The work was an immediate success and transformed political philosophy in the English-speaking world. While its major tenets have been criticized, it has determined the direction of political philosophy.

ESSENTIAL TEXTS *A Theory of Justice*; *Political Liberalism*; *The Law of Peoples*.

KEY IDEAS

Rawls argues that a just society is one that rational people would contract into if they were not biased by their own social situation. To determine what such a society would look like, Rawls asks us to imagine ourselves in a hypothetical "original position," ignorant of our circumstances in society. Rationally we would choose a society that does not favor particular groups or individuals, and our first priority would be to avoid anyone suffering undue restrictions of liberty or extremes of poverty.

To guarantee justice, Rawls suggests two principles: the "principle of liberty", by which everyone should be afforded equivalent liberty; and the "difference principle," whereby goods are distributed equally, unless unequal distribution benefits the least advantaged.

If you didn't know what position you would occupy in a society, said Rawls, what kind of society would you choose?

SEE ALSO ▶ The social contract (*p.165*) • Utilitarianism: be happy (*pp.102–3*) • Hobbes (*p.275*) • Locke (*pp.282–3*) • Rousseau (*pp.292–3*) • Kant (*pp.294–7*) • Mill (*pp.308–9*)

Thomas S. Kuhn

● 1922–1996 ⚑ US

Trained initially as a physicist, Kuhn questioned, in *The Structure of Scientific Revolutions*, the orthodox view of scientific progress as the gradual accumulation of knowledge. Instead he proposed that science develops through distinct periods.

Kuhn argues that there are periods of "normal science", in which scientists take for granted the presuppositions of the dominant theoretical framework of the time, or "paradigm". The paradigm—for example, Newtonian dynamics—dictates what kinds of problems there are and the methods scientists use to solve them. But at some stage the number of unsolved puzzles builds up, triggering a crisis and a revolutionary period in which new paradigms vie to take over from the old. Importantly, the new paradigm does not usurp the old because it is in any sense more true, for there is no neutral appeal to "facts" which could adjudicate between them. The radical conclusion is that scientific advance is determined by social change rather than impersonal reason.

The identification of Jupiter's circling moons was a factor in the Copernican revolution in astronomy, one of Kuhn's key "paradigm shifts" in science.

Jean-François Lyotard

● 1924–1998 ⚑ France

Lyotard was active in left-wing political circles in the early 1960s, but by the time of *Libidinal Economy* (1974) he had found much to oppose in orthodox Marxism. With *The Postmodern Condition* (1979), he rejected all "grand narratives" or systems of ideas, be they Christian or Marxist, that try to explain everything. This he did through a critique of modernism and the values of the Enlightenment. He introduced the term "postmodern" (*see also p.43*) to signal the rise of a new subjectivism and a distrust of human reason as the route to human salvation. In his critique of modernism Lyotard drew on both Wittgenstein's idea of language games (*see pp.326–7*) and Austin's speech acts theory (*see p.338*).

Gilles Deleuze

● 1925–1995 ⚑ France

Deleuze saw philosophy as a creative process for constructing concepts, rather than an attempt to discover and reflect reality. Much of his work has ostensibly been in the history of philosophy, yet his readings do not attempt to disclose the "true" Spinoza or Nietzsche. Instead they rework the conceptual mechanisms of his subject to produce new concepts, thus opening up new avenues of thought. Deleuze is best known for his collaborations with the psychoanalyst Félix Guattari, including *Anti-Oedipus* (1972) and *What is Philosophy* (1991), and for influential commentaries on film, literature, and art. After years of suffering from lung cancer, "chained like a dog" to oxygen cylinders, he took his life by jumping from his Paris apartment window.

Michel Foucault

◉ 1926–1984   ⚑ France

Foucault's work merges history and philosophy as he
investigates the complexes of beliefs that characterize
different cultural practices at different times, exposing
their deployment in social control and revealing the
historically conditioned nature of existing power relations.

LIFE AND WORKS

Foucault trained as a philosopher at the
Ecole Normale Supérieure in Paris and
held various academic posts before being
appointed Professor of the History of
Systems of Thought at the Collège de
France in 1970. His first major work,
Madness and Civilization, explores the
origins of the asylum and the history
of European attitudes to insanity. In
The Order of Things, Foucault investigates

current forms of knowledge and he
defends his early methodology in *The
Archaeology of Knowledge*. Important later
works are *Discipline and Punish*, his study
of the development of the prison system,
and his three-volume *History of Sexuality*.

ESSENTIAL TEXTS *Madness and Civilization*; *The
Order of Things*; *The Archaeology of Knowledge*;
Discipline and Punish; *History of Sexuality*.

KEY IDEAS

Foucault's work stems from his conviction
that the structures that organize the beliefs
of a culture are historically conditioned.
These "epistemes," historical constructs,
are determined by the social rules and
practices that regulate discourse. In the
Archaeology of Knowledge, he sets out his

method of investigation into the historical
emergence of such structures and the
systems of social control they engender.
But his purpose is to produce not mere
social history, but rather a "history of
the present:" a critical engagement with
current discourse and practice through
exploration of the processes
that produced them.

Foucault argues that the
emergence of the human
sciences in the 18th century,
subjecting human beings to the
scientific gaze, coincided with
the growth of systems of
disciplinary control. By
understanding how these have
developed, we can resist the
image conferred upon us by
the controlling order and
so forge new ways of living.

SEE ALSO ▸ Habermas *(facing page)*

Velázquez's *Las Meninas* (in which the
artist depicts himself painting) is
analyzed in *The Order of Things* as
representing the emergence of the
human subject as a category of thought.

Noam Chomsky

● 1928– ᴾᵁ US

Chomsky's landmark work, *Syntactic Structures*, has been profoundly influential within theoretical linguistics. Today he is better known as a political activist for his wide-ranging and detailed critiques of Western governments' policies.

Chomsky obtained his PhD in linguistics from the University of Pennsylvania in 1955, since when he has taught at MIT. In *Syntactic Structures*, he points out that children learn the grammar of their native languages with remarkable rapidity. Moreover they acquire this ability on limited evidence and without explicit training, facts best explained by assuming they have an innate language-learning disposition and a tacit knowledge of a "generative grammar." As this skill is universal, certain grammatical structures must be common to all languages.

A tireless campaigner, Chomsky works to expose the way powerful elites restrict the terms of debate within the media and manipulate the populations of democratic societies.

At a young age, children are capable of producing an infinite number of sentences using a limited number of words and a finite set of syntactical rules.

Jürgen Habermas

● 1929– ᴾᵁ Germany

Habermas is the most important living exponent of the Frankfurt School of critical theory. His brand of neo-Marxism resists the relativist tide in much of the discourse on "postmodernity," reaffirming the possibility of recovering the Enlightenment ideal of reasoned consensus.

Habermas studied at Frankfurt's Institute for Social Research under Horkheimer and Adorno (*see p.333*), and holds, in common with these thinkers, suspicions about the "instrumentalism" of our modern technocratic society. Technology, with its emphasis on understanding and control, is seen as the means to achieve social ends. Yet what is now lacking is an effective "public sphere" in which to conduct critical discussion of the nature and desirability of those ends. Hence Habermas developed a theory of social communication in opposition to this instrumentalism, in order to reinvigorate

the Enlightenment project. It is worth noting that while many contemporary intellectuals are accused of political quietism, Habermas has done as much as any, with the notable exception of Chomsky (*above*), to engage in meaningful debate over issues of international public concern, such as globalization and the role of religion in a secular society. Recent interventions have included criticizing US foreign policy toward Iraq.

Habermas's most important works include *The Structural Transformation of the Public Sphere* (1962) and *The Theory of Communicative Action* (1981).

Richard Rorty

● 1931–   ⚑ US

Trained in the Anglo-American tradition of "analytic" philosophy, Rorty is known for his critical take on many of the central concerns of that tradition, such as the possibility of objective knowledge and truth.

Educated at Chicago and Yale, Rorty has taught at Princeton and Virginia and is currently a professor at Stanford University, California. Influenced by Quine's critiques of empiricism (*see p.337*) as well as the American pragmatist tradition, his approach has affinities with the work of so-called "post-modern" thinkers.

Rorty's "anti-representationalist" theory of mind, developed in the late 1970s, led him to question the model of philosophy as a matter of coming to discover and describe the truth about reality. *Philosophy and the Mirror of Nature* (1979) attacks the possibility of a neutral stance from which an objective gaze may be cast on any topic. Since we have

access only to our own beliefs, and no neutral access to the facts as they are in themselves, we cannot hope to compare our beliefs with reality to ensure that they are accurate.

From pragmatism, Rorty inherits the idea that truth is a matter of what works rather than a correspondence between beliefs and facts, and thus he encourages us "to see knowledge as a matter of conversation and of social practice, rather than as an attempt to mirror nature." Rorty has consciously allied himself with various other "anti-representationalist" thinkers, from Nietzsche (*see pp.316–7*), Heidegger (*see pp.328–9*), and Derrida (*below*) to James (*see p.313*) and Wittgenstein (*see pp.326–7*).

Jacques Derrida

● 1930–2004   ⚑ France

Derrida is most associated with the term "deconstruction," a technique involving close readings of texts to open up the fluidity of meaning by focusing on seemingly incidental details and so uncovering their hidden or unthought aspects.

Derrida studied at the Ecole Normale Supérieure under Foucault (*see p.342*) and Althusser (*see p.339*), later teaching there and at other Parisian institutions.

Influenced by the structuralist account of meaning, Derrida denies that the sense of a term is determined by what it refers to: rather, it is the product of its differential relations with other terms in the language as a whole. Moreover, since our attempts to interpret a term or a text cannot step outside language, meaning can never be given definitively but is forever "deferred." Derrida introduces the neologism "différance," to signal the deferred/different nature of meaning.

The force of philosophical texts relies as much on figurative and rhetorical devices as strict argumentation. And on Derrida's reading, Western metaphysics has been organized by a metaphorics which prioritizes "presence:" that is, it is driven by a desire to bring fully and immediately to mind concepts such as essence, origin, substance, end, truth, and so on. In the inevitable frustration of the desire to anchor meaning in such terms lie the seeds of the text's own "deconstruction," a process Derrida sees as his task to trace. His work has had a significant impact on the English-speaking world, particularly within literary studies.

Saul Kripke

● 1940– ⚑ US

Kripke published the first of several papers on modal logic when just 19. Taking up Leibniz's idea that a necessary truth is one that is true in all possible worlds, they helped develop the research area known as "possible world" semantics.

Kripke takes the view that a proper name refers to the same object in every possible world in which it exists and, therefore, that true identity statements involving proper names, such as "Everest is Chomolungma," are metaphysically necessary. He claims that there are necessary truths which can only be discovered empirically, such as that water is H_2O. His most important works are *Naming and Necessity* (1980) and *Wittgenstein on Rules and Private Language* (1982).

Something of a prodigy, Kripke taught graduate-level logic at Massachusetts Institute of Technology (MIT) while himself still a student at Harvard (*right*).

Peter Singer

● 1946– ⚑ Australia

Singer is known principally for his work in applied ethics where his views have come under attack from pro-life campaigners and disability rights groups. Based for much of his career at Melbourne and currently Professor at Princeton, Singer has developed the utilitarian approach pioneered by Bentham and Mill in order to address a range of issues of contemporary concern, such as abortion, euthanasia, and social egalitarianism. Most renowned are his claims in *Animal Liberation* (1976) in which he condemns as "speciesist" the justification of our ill-treatment of animals on the grounds that they are not human. What is important are a being's capacities to suffer, reason, and have self-consciousness. The controversial implication here is that fetuses and some impaired human beings have a lower moral status than higher apes.

Julia Kristeva

● 1941– ⚑ Bulgaria

Considered the most influential contemporary feminist thinker, Kristeva was born in Bulgaria but moved to Paris in 1966. Although she holds a professorship in linguistics at the University of Paris VII, her thought is marked by its interdisciplinary approach. From the work of the French psychoanalyst Jacques Lacan she develops the idea that the unconscious is structured like a language, and distinguishes between what she terms the "semiotic"— that which is instinctive and sensual, originating in prelinguistic infant development—and the "symbolic" —the rule-governed system of signs of the mature language-user in which words correspond with meaning.

INDEX

Page numbers in **bold** refer to
main entries; numbers in *italics*
refer to illustrations and captions.

A

a priori knowledge 66–7, **70–73**
Abelard, Pierre **262**
"absolute idealism" 40–41, 306
ad hoc modifications, scientific
    theories 187–8
Adorno, Theodor **333**, *333*, 343
Aenesidemus 29
affirming the consequent **204**
Albertus Magnus 265
Alexander the Great 28, 29, 248,
    248, 250
allegory, Plato's Theory of Forms
    76–81
Althusser, Louis **339**, 344
analytic philosophy 43
analytic propositions 67
animal liberation 345
Anselm of Canterbury **261**, *261*,
    267, 279
    on existence of God 140, 141,
    261
anti-realism **91**
Antisthenes 28, 250
appeal to authority fallacy **201**
Aquinas, St. Thomas 33, **264–7**,
    265, *266*, 273
    on existence of God 141, 261,
    266–7
    Summa Theologiae 265
    Thomism 33, 265
Arendt, Hannah **176–7**, *177*
argument: definition 195
    reasoning 195, 196
Aristotle 24, 25, 28, 84, **248–9**,
    248, *287*
    Aquinas and 265, 266, 267
    on Atomism 241
    Boethius's commentaries on 258
    Christianity and 33
    on heavenly bodies 188
    Islamic philosophers and 32
    "Kalam argument" 260
    Metaphysics 232, 259
    on the mind 111
    and the philosophy of science
    179
    political philosophy 161, 172
    on virtues 108, 109
    on Zeno of Elea 240
artificial intelligence **132–7**
astronomy, Pythagoras and 234
Atomism 24, 29, 36, 241, 282
atoms, Locke's corpuscles 84–5
Augustine of Hippo, St. 30, **256–7**,
    256
    on existence of God 139
    on natural evil 155, 257
    Plato's influence 33
Aurelius, Marcus, Emperor *28*,
    29, 252
Austin, John Langshaw **338**, 341

B

authority, appeal to **201**
Averroes (Ibn Rushd) 32, 261,
    263, *263*
Avicenna (Ibn Sina) 32, *32*,
    259–60, *259*
Ayer, Alfred 17, 75, 115, *115*,
    338, *338*

Bacon, Francis 34, 37, **274**, *274*,
    332
Baconian method 274
Beauvoir, Simone de 336, **338**, *338*
Behe, Michael 148–9
beliefs: degrees of reasonableness
    222–4
    faith and reason 157
    foundationalism 60–61
    infallibilism 59
    "justified true belief" theory 62
    and knowledge 50, 60
    philosophical 14–15
    reliabilism 55, 63
    scepticism 50
Bell, Clive 221
Bentham, Jeremy 41, 102, **300**,
    300, 308, 309
Berg, Alban 333
Bergson, Henri **320**, *320*
Berkeley, George 38, 39, **288–9**,
    288
    and mind-dependence 85, 86–9,
    91, 289
Bible 36, 260, 280, 281
Big Bang *143*, 148
Bloch, Ernst 325
body, substance dualism 125, *126*,
    128, 279
Boethius **258**
brain: consciousness 124–9
    property dualism 127
    replicating 136–7
    see also mind
Brandsma, Titus **325**, *325*
Brentano, Franz 319
Bruno, Giordano **272**
Buddha *26*, **230–31**, 305
Buddhism 26
    enlightenment 230–31
    nirvana 231
    religious experience 151
    "third eye" *127*
    Zen Buddhism 321
Burke, Edmund 169, **299**, *299*

C

Calvin, John 36
capitalism 163, 312, 333
Carnap, Rudolf **330**, 332, 337
Cartesian geometry 278
categorical imperative, moral
    philosophy 106, 297
category mistakes 212, **225**
Catholic Church
    Aquinas and 265
    faith and reason 157
    Reformation 36
    religious experience 151
    Thomism 33

cause and effect 90–93
The Cave, Plato's allegory of **78–9**
certainty, knowledge and 58–9
Chinese Room thought-experiment
    134–5, 136
Chomsky, Noam **343**, *343*
Christianity: Augustine of Hippo
    256–7
    Dark Ages 30–31
    "The Fall" 155, *155*, 257
    influences 29, 81
    Nietzsche's criticisms of 316–17
    Reformation 36
    religious experience 151
    in Roman Empire 30
    Scholasticism **32–3**, 34
    see also Catholic Church
Cicero 34
Clifford, William 157
color, mind-dependence 82–4, 85,
    88, 91
common good **172–7**
Communism 43, 311–12, 339
communitarianism **172–7**
computers: artificial intelligence
    132–7
    future of 137
Comte, Auguste 40, 43, **306**, *306*
concepts: experience and 92
    and foundation of knowledge 61
    Hume on **93**, 290–91
conditional statements 88
confirmation, philosophy of
    science 179
Confucianism 26, 241
Confucius 26, *26*, 235, **236–7**, *236*
consciousness 123, **124–9**
Copernicus, Nicolas 35–6, 188–9,
    188, 269, 277, 297
Corpus Hermeticum 272
corpuscular theory of matter
    84, 282
cosmological argument, existence
    of God 142–3, 146
cosmology: Dante and 267
    and improbability of life 148
    Thales of Miletus's theory 232
counterexamples, method of 212,
    216–19
Crates 252
Croton 24, 233
cultural differences: moral beliefs
    112–13, 120–21
    religious experience 151
    virtue ethics 109
Cynics 28, 250, 252

D

Dante Alighieri 267, *267*
Dao De Jing 26, 235
Daoism 26, **235**
Darwin, Charles 147, 148, 320
Dasein 43, 329
Davidson, Donald 337, **338**
death: Buddhist view of 231
    Epicurus on 251
deconstruction 328, 344
deductive reasoning 180, 186,
    195, 198
Deep Ecology movement 339

degrees of reasonableness **222–4**
Deleuze, Gilles **341**
democracy *166–7*
  Plato's *Republic* 247
  Rousseau on 293
  social democracy 164, **170–71**, 176
  Spinoza and 281
Democritus 24, *46*, 240, **241**, *241*, 251, 311
Dennett, Daniel 337
deontology **104**, 110
Derrida, Jacques 328, **344**, *344*
Descartes, René 36, 43, 46, 67, 194, **276–9**, *277*
  on a priori knowledge 70
  category mistakes 225
  dualism 125, 279, 281
  Hobbes's objections to 275
  "I think, therefore I am" 36, 279, 329
  on the pineal gland 127
  and rationalism 37–8
  "trademark argument" **68–9**, 279
design: and existence of God 72, 147
  intelligent design 148
  natural selection 72, 147
desires, and freedom 174–5
dialectic 302–3
Diderot, Denis 37, 292, *292*
dilemma, false 203
Diogenes Laertius 232, 238, 251
Diogenes of Sinope 28–9, *29*, **250**, *250*
door puzzle 99
doubt, philosophical **51–4**
dreams 152
dualism: arguments for 128–9
  objections to 127–8
  property dualism 127, 128
  substance dualism 125, *126*, 128, 279, 281
Duns Scotus, John **268**, *268*
duty: conflicts of 104
  moral philosophy **104**

E

Eccles, John 332
Eckhart, Meister **268**
economics: Adam Smith's *Wealth of Nations* 298
  capitalism 163, 333
  Marxism 311–12
  social democracy and 176
ecosophy 339
educational theory, Rousseau 293
Einstein, Albert 15
élan vital 320
Eleatic school 239, 240
eliminative materialism 126–7, *127*
embryos, stem cell research **110–11**
Emerson, Ralph Waldo **307**, *307*
emotivism 72, 115
empiricism **38–9**, 49, 67
  and a priori knowledge 70, 71
  Berkeley and 289
  and mathematical knowledge 73
  on morality and God **71–3**

Encyclopédie 37
Engels, Friedrich 311
Enlightenment 15, **37–9**, 84, *287*, 292
enlightenment, Buddhism 230–31
enumerative induction 196
Epicureans 29, 34
Epicurus 21, 24, 29, **251**, *251*, 311
Erasmus 36, **269**, *269*
ethics: metaethics 101, **112–21**
  normative ethics 101, 102
  practical ethics 101
  virtue theory **108–9**, 111, 113
Euclidean geometry 38
evidence: and knowledge 50
  philosophy of science 179, 180
evil **153–6**
  evidential problem of 154
  and existence of God 147, 159, 257
  utilitarianism and 103
evolution 147, 148–9
existentialism 43, 316
  Heidegger and 329
  Jaspers and 325
  Kierkegaard and 310
  Ortega y Gasset and 324
  Sartre and 336
experience: and cause and effect 90–93
  and concepts 92
  and empiricism 67
  knowledge and 60–61, 66–7

F

facts, and values 113, 118
faith, and reason **157–9**
fallacies **198–211**
false dilemma **203**
falsificationism **186–9**
family resemblance 212, **220–21**
al-Farabi 32, **258**, *258*, 259, 260
Fermat, Pierre de 73
Feuerbach, Ludwig Andreas **307**, *307*, 311
Fichte, Johann Gottlieb 40, **301**, *301*
fideism 157, 159
Forms, Plato's Theory of 29, 75, **76–81**, 246–7, 249, 254–5, 305
Foucault, Michel 43, **342**, *342*, 344
foundationalism 60–61
Frankfurt School 343
free choice, liberalism 163, 164
free will 19, 154, 155, 320
freedom: communitarianism and 172–3
  future of 176–7
  liberalism 162
  negative freedom 162–3, 175
  political philosophy 161
  positive freedom 174–5
  rights **168–9**
  Rousseau on 293
  social contract 165
  social democracy 170
  social freedom 175
Frege, Gottlob 43, **318**, *318*, 319, 326, 330

French Revolution 37, 169, 299, 301
Freud, Sigmund 152, 187, *187*
fundamental questions 15

G

Gadamer, Hans-Georg **330**, *330*
Galileo *34*, **84**, *186*, 188
  on color 82–3, 85, 91
  heliocentric model of universe 35–6, 84
  and the Inquisition 277
gambler's fallacy **200**
Gassendi, Pierre 36
Gaunilo 140
Geist 302, 303, 306
genetic fallacy **205**
geometry 38, 73, 278
German Idealism 295, 301
Gettier, Edmund 62–3
al-Ghazali **261**, *261*, 263
God: and duty 104
  essence 266
  faith and reason **157–9**
  Leibniz on 285
  and morality **107**
  nature of 139
  perception of 267
  perfection 139, 140, *144*, 279
  philosophy and 16
  and Plato's Theory of Forms 81
  problem of evil **153–6**, 159, 257
  religious experience **150–52**
God, existence of 139, **140–49**
  Aquinas on 266–7
  Berkeley on 86–9, *289*
  degrees of reasonableness 224
  Descartes on 279
  empiricism and 19, **71–3**
  intelligent design 148–9
  Kalam argument 142, 260
  ontological argument 68, 140–41, 261
  regress problems 213
  Spinoza on 280
  trademark argument 68–9
Goldman, Alvin 55, *55*
goodness: and divine commands 107
  Form of the Good 81
  intuitionism 114
government *see* political philosophy
Greenfield, Susan 126, 136
Guattari, Félix 341

H

Habermas, Jürgen **343**
hallucinations, religious experience 152
Han Feizi 26, **253**, *253*
happiness, utilitarianism 71, 102–3
harm principle 163, 164
Hegel, Georg 40, 165, **302–3**, *302*
  criticism of social contract 165
  and social freedom 174, 175
Hegelianism 303, 307, 310, 311
Heidegger, Martin 43, 319, **328–9**, *328*
Héloïse 262

Heraclitus **238**, *238*, 239, 247, 252
Herodotus *232*
Hick, John 156
Hinduism *151*, 213, 305
history of philosophy **23–43**
Hobbes, Thomas 36, 165, **275**, *275*, 281, 283
Hölderlin, Johann Christian Friedrich 302
Horkheimer, Max 333, 343
humanism 34, *35*
Hume, David 38, 39, *67*, **290–91**, *290*, 292
  on a priori knowledge 70, 73
  on cause and effect 90–93
  on concepts *93*, 290–91
  and cosmological argument 142
  on foundations of knowledge 60–61, 290
  influence of 15, 295, 296–7
  objections to moral realism 118, 119, 291
  problem of induction 179, 180, **181–4**, 186, 332
  subjectivism 71
  teleological argument 147
Husserl, Edmund 43, **319**, *319*, 328, 336

I

Ibn Rushd *see* Averroes
Ibn Sina *see* Avicenna
idealism: "absolute idealism" 40–41, 306
  Berkeley and 86–9, 91
  German Idealism 295, 301
Ideas, Locke's theory of 86
identity, personal 123
illusions: optical 53, *53*
  Plato's Theory of Forms **76–81**
  and reality 89, *94*
  theatrical *59*
individualism 172–3
induction, problem of 179, **180–84**, 332
inductive reasoning **196**, 198, 274
inequality 163–4, 170–71
infallibilism *59*
"inference to the best explanation" 197
infinite regress 142–3
innate truths 67
intelligence, artificial **132–7**
intelligent design 148–9
intention, deontology 104
intentionality 123
  Husserl and 319
intuition *67*, 72–3, 114, 320
intuitionism 104, 114
Islamic philosophy **31–3**

J

Jackson, Frank **129**, *129*
James, William 307, **313**, *313*, *314*
  on faith and reason 157, 159
  influence of 320, 321
  on religious experience 150–51, *313*
Jaspers, Karl **325**

judgments: motivation and moral judgments 119
  self-evident judgments 114
justice, defining 171
justification: for beliefs 60
  "justified true belief" theory 62
  and knowledge 58–9
  problem of induction 181–4

K

Kalam argument, existence of God 142–3, 260
Kant, Immanuel 39, 40, 75, **294–7**, *305*
  on existence of God 141, 261
  Fichte and 301
  influence of Burke 299
  moral philosophy 105, 297
  objections to 106
Kierkegaard, Søren 41, 43, **310**, *310*
  on faith and reason 158, 159
kings, divine right of *283*
Kingsley, Charles 54
Kitaro, Nishida **321**
knowledge **49–73**
  a priori knowledge **70–73**
  foundationalism 60–61
  infallibilism *59*
  "justified true belief" theory 62
  mathematical knowledge 73
  Plato's Theory of Forms 77
  rationalism *67*
  reason and experience **66–73**
  scepticism **50–57**
  what is knowledge? **58–63**
  see also empiricism
Knox, Monsignor Ronald 86
Koran 32, 258, 259, 260
Kripke, Saul 129, **345**, *345*
Kristeva, Julia **345**, *345*
Kuhn, Thomas S. **341**, *341*

L

Lacan, Jacques 345
Laches *216*, 218–19
Laín Entralgo, Pedro 324
language: jargon 215
  logical atomism 322–3, 326
  "ordinary language" philosophy 338
  picture theory 326–7
Lao Tzu 26, *26*, **235**, *235*
Legalism 26, 253
Leibniz, Gottfried Wilhelm 38, 40, 272, **284–5**, *284*
Leibniz's law 208, 209
Lenin 43
Leucippus 24, 241
Lewis, C.S. *81*, *81*
Li Si 253
liberalism **162–71**
  future of freedom 176
  individualism 172–3
  and inequality 163–4
  rights 168–9
  social contract **165**, 168, 173
  social democracy 170
libertarianism 164, 170, 298

life: evolution 147, 148–9
  improbability of 148
  intelligent design 148–9
  right to life 110
Livy 270
Llull, Ramon **268**
Locke, John **282–3**, *282*, 288
  on color 83–4, 85, 88, 91
  concept of matter 282, 289
  empiricism 38, 39, 282–3, 289
  and the forest test 85
  on foundation of knowledge 60–1
  on mathematical knowledge 73
  theory of Ideas 86
logic 50, 195
logical atomism 322–3, 326
logical behaviourism 126
logical positivism 338
logical problem of evil 153–4
López-Aranguren, José Luis 324
love, and God's will 107
Lucretius 29, 34, 251
Luther, Martin 36, *36*
Lyotard, Jean-François 43, **341**

M

Machiavelli, Niccolò 253, **270–1**, *270*
machines, artificial intelligence **132–7**
Maimonides, Moses 32, *32*, **262**, *262*
Malebranche, Nicolas 288
Manicheanism 256, 257
Mao ZeDong *241*, 253
Marcuse, Herbert 333
Marías, Julián 324
market: libertarianism 164, 298
  social democracy and 176
Marx, Karl 303, 307, **311–12**, *311*, 333
  Communist Manifesto 41, 311
  influence of 33, 43
  Das Kapital 311, 339
  Popper on 187
  and social freedom 175, 176
Marxism *43*, 311–12, 325, 336, 341
masked man fallacy **208–9**
materialism 125–7
mathematics 73
  Descartes and 278
  Pythagoras and 233, 234
  Russell and 322
matter: corpuscular theory 84, 282
  Locke's theory of 282, 289
maxims, moral philosophy 105–6
meaning: Russell's theory of 323
  structuralism 344
Medici family 270
medieval philosophy **30–33**
memory 54, 123
Mengzi (Mencius) 26, 236, 253
metaethics 101, **112–21**
metaphysics 46, **75–95**
  mind-dependence **82–95**
  One-Over-Many argument 80–1
  Plato's Theory of Forms **76–81**
method of counterexamples 212, **216–19**

Milesians 24, 232, 238, 239
Mill, James 41, 308, 309
Mill, John Stuart 40–41, **308–9**, *308*, 322
  on a priori knowledge 70
  on moral knowledge 71, 309
  On Liberty 163
  and phenomenalism 88
  utilitarianism 102–3, 309
mind, philosophy of 46, **123–37**
  artificial intelligence **132–7**
  Chinese Room thought-experiment **134–5**
  consciousness 123, **124–9**
  Leibniz on 285
  mind-dependence **82–99**
  substance dualism 125, *126*, 128, 279, 281
mirror puzzle 75, **96–8**
modus ponens 204
Mohism 26
molecules 84–5
monads 285
monotheism *144*
Montaigne, Michel de **272**
Moore, Gordon 137
moral philosophy 46, **101–21**
  cultural differences 112–13, 120–1
  doing God's will **107**
  duty **104**
  empiricism on morality and God **71–3**
  moral realism 112–13, 118–19
  reason and **105–6**
  subjectivism 71–2
  utilitarianism **102–3**
  virtue ethics **108–11**
  what is morality? **112–21**
motivation, and moral judgments 119
Mozi 26, **241**
music, mathematical basis 234, *234*

N

Naess, Arne **339**, *339*
Nagel, Thomas 124, 125
natural philosophy 46
natural rights 168
natural selection 147, 149
naturalism 337
nature, laws of 179
Nazism 319, 322, 325, 328, 329, 333
necessary evil argument 154, 156
negative freedom 162–3, 175
neo-Marxism 343
Neo-Platonism 29
  Augustine of Hippo and 256
  Averroes and 32 263
  Avicenna and 32, 259–60
  Boethius and 258
  al-Farabi and 32, 258
  al-Ghazali and 261
  Plotinus and 29, 254
neurons 136–7
neutral state, liberalism 163
Newton, Isaac 37, 39, *39*, 284
Nicholas of Cusa **269**, 272

Nietzsche, Friedrich 41, 43, 307, **316–17**, *316*
  genetic fallacy 205
  on Heraclitus 238
nihilism 316, 317
nirvana, Buddhism 231
Nizamiyyah school 261
"noble savage" *293*
normative ethics 101, 102
normative reasoning 175
Norse people 151

O

Ockham, William of **269**
Ockham's Razor 269
One-Over-Many argument, Plato's Theory of Forms **80–81**
ontological argument, existence of God 140–41, 261
"ordinary language" philosophy 338
Ortega y Gasset, José 321, **324**, *324*
Orwell, George *215*
"Oxford" philosophy 338

P

paradoxes, Zeno of Elea 240
Parmenides 24, 25, **239**, *239*, 240, 241
particle physics *19*
Peano, Giuseppe 322
Peirce, Charles Sanders **313**, *313*, *314*, 321
perception 150–51
  Locke's theory of 282–3
  and philosophy of mind 123
  and reliability of senses 53
perfection, of God 139, 140, *144*, 279
Peripatetic School, Athens 248
perspectivism 317
pessimism 304, 316
phenomenalism **88**, 89, 91
phenomenology **43**, 319, 325
philosophes 37, 38, *292*, 299
philosophical reasoning 17, 19–20
physical objects, mind-dependence 85, 86–9, 91
physicalism 129
physics *19*, 84–5
picture theory, language 326–7
Plato 10, *10*, **244–7**, *245*, *287*
  Academy 245, *246*, 248
  in Dante's *Divine Comedy* 267
  dialogs 216, 220, 245
  Euthyphro 107
  influence of 25, 28, 33, 81, 248, 249
  influences on 238, 242, 245, 247
  mirror puzzle 96, 97
  and Parmenides 25, 80–81, 239, 240
  on perfection 139
  Republic 78, 161, 247
  Thaetetus 49, 53
  Theory of Forms 29, 75, **76–81**, 246–7, 249, 305
Plotinus 29, **254–5**, *254*, 257, 260

pluralism 163
political philosophy **161–77**
  communitarianism **172–7**
  Confucius on government 237
  genetic fallacy 205
  Hobbes and 275
  liberalism **162–71**
  Locke and 283
  Machiavelli and 270–71
  Rousseau and 292–3
  Spinoza and 281
Polycrates 233
Popper, Karl Raimund **186–7**, 189, **332**, *332*, 333
Porphyry 254, *263*
positive freedom 174–5
Positivism 40, 43, 306
post-hoc fallacy **202**
postmodernism 43, 316, 341, 343
post-structuralism 316
practical ethics 101
practical wisdom 109
pragmatism 313, 344
primary qualities 82–5
Proclus 240
property dualism 127, 128
propositions: analytic and synthetic propositions 67
  theory of knowledge 49, 50, 62
Protagoras 53
Protestantism 36
Proust, Marcel *320*
pseudoprofundity 212, **214–15**
psychoanalysis 152
psychology 123
Putnam, Hilary 337
puzzle solving 197
Pyrrho of Elis 29, **250**
Pythagoras 24, **233–4**, *233*, 239, 247

QR

Quine, Willard Van Orman **337**, *337*, 338, 344
rationalism 49, 67
  and a priori knowledge 70
  in the Enlightenment 37–8
  problem of induction **180–84**, 332
  rational intuition 72–3
  "trademark argument" **68–9**
  see also reasoning
Rawls, John 161, 165, **340**, *340*
realism 91
  moral realism 112–13, 118–19
reality: illusion and 89, *94*
  Plato's Theory of Forms **76–81**
reasonableness, degrees of **222–4**
reasoning 192, **194–7**
  deductive arguments 180, 186
  faith and **157–9**
  fallacies **198–211**
  knowledge and 66–7
  and moral philosophy 105–6
  normative 175
  philosophical reasoning 17, 19–20
  problem of induction **180–84**, 332
  virtue ethics 108–9

reductio ad absurdum 240
Reformation 36
regress 212, **213**
  infinite regress 142–3
  One-Over-Many argument 81
reincarnation 231, 234, 255
relativism: moral beliefs 112–13,
  120–21
  and tolerance 120
  virtue ethics 109
relativist fallacy **199**
reliabilism **55**, 63
religion, philosophy of 46, **139–59**
  doing God's will **107**
  faith and reason **157–9**
  philosophy and 16–17, *18*
  problem of evil **153–6**, 159
  Pythagoras and 234
  religious experience **150–52**
  substance dualism 125
  see also God, existence of
Renaissance 33, **34–6**, *287*
revolutions, and rights 169
rights **168–9**
  communitarianism and 173
Roman Empire **28–9**, 30, 151
Romanticism 40, *163*, 292, 307
Rorty, Richard **344**, *344*
Ross, W.D. 104
Rousseau, Jean-Jacques **292–3**,
  292, 299
  and social freedom 37, 175, 176
Russell, Bertrand 43, 318, **322–3**,
  322–3, 330, 339
  on philosophy 19
  Principia Mathematica 322, 326
  on the universe 142
Ryle, Gilbert 56, 225, **331**, *331*

S

Santayana, George **321**
Sartre, Jean-Paul 43, *228*, 334, **336**,
  336, 338
scepticism 49, **50–57**, 86, 278–9
Sceptics 29, 250
Scheler, Max **325**
Schelling, Friedrich Wilhelm Joseph
  von 40, 302, **306**
Scholasticism **32–3**, 34, 273
Schopenhauer, Arthur 41, 303,
  304–5, *304*, 316
science, philosophy of **179–89**
  Descartes and 279
  Enlightenment 37, *37*
  and existence of God 146
  falsificationism **186–9**
  inductive reasoning 196, 274
  and mind-dependence 85
  mirror puzzle 97
  naturalism 337
  philosophy and science 18–19
  problem of induction 179,
    180–84, 332
  Pythagoras 233
  Renaissance **34–6**
  scientific proof 224
  Thales of Miletus 232
Searle, John 134–5, 136, 137
secondary qualities 82–5, 91
Sellars, Wilfrid **61**

Seneca 29
senses: Berkeley and 289
  and empiricism 67
  and foundations of knowledge
    60–61
  Hume on 290
  Locke's theory of perception
    282–3
  Plato's Theory of Forms 77
  reliability of 53, 55, 278–9
Shank, Roger 134
Shelley, Mary 169
Siddhartha Gautama 26, **230–31**
Singer, Peter **345**
slippery slope fallacy **210–11**
Smith, Adam **298**, *298*, 306
social contract **165**, 168, 173
social democracy 164, **170–71**, 176
social freedom 175
society: Confucius on 236–7
  Rousseau on 292–3
sociology 306
Socrates 25, 239, **242–3**, *242–3*
  in Dante's *Divine Comedy* 267
  on family resemblance 220
  on importance of thinking
    philosophically 21
  influence on Plato 242, 245, 247
  Laches 218–19
  method of counterexamples
    216, 218–19
soul 16
  Aquinas and 267
  in embryo 110
  immortality of 255
  Plato's Theory of Forms 77
  substance dualism *126*
Spinoza, Benedictus 38, 40, 272,
  280–81, *280*
spiritual growth, evil and 156
state: libertarianism 164
  negative freedom 163
  rights 168
  social contract **165**, 168, 173
  social democracy 170–71
  see also political philosophy
stem cell research **110–11**
Stoics 29, 34, 252
Strawson, Peter **339**
"stream of consciousness" 313
structuralism 344
Suárez, Francisco **273**, *273*
subjectivism 71–2
substance, Leibniz on 285
substance dualism 125, *126*, 128,
  279, 281
suffering 230–31, 305
supercomputer hypothesis 51, *51*, 54
"Superman", in Nietzsche's
  philosophy 317
Swinburne, Richard 146, 147,
  148, 156
synthetic propositions 67

T

Tarski, Alfred 338
Taylor, Charles 161, **175**, *175*, 177
teleological argument: Aristotle's
  theory of substances 249
  existence of God 147

Thales of Miletus 24, **232**, *232*
theism 224
theodicies 154–6
theories, falsification of **186–9**
Theresa of Avila, St. 150, *150*
thinking tools 20, 192, **212–25**
Third Man Objection, Plato's
  Theory of Forms 80–81
Thomism 33, 265
thought, artificial intelligence
  132–7
thought-experiments 134–5
tolerance, and relativism 120
totalitarianism 301
"trademark argument", existence
  of God **68–9**, 279
Transcendentalists 307
truths: innate truths 67
  relativist fallacy 199
Turing, Alan **133**, *133*

UV

Unamuno, Miguel de **321**
unicorns *92*, 93
universe 18
  Atomism 241
  beginning of 142–3
  and existence of God 72, 146,
    147, 148
  intelligent design 148–9
  Leibniz on 285
utilitarianism **102–3**, 104, 110,
  300, 309
values, facts and 113, 118
Vedas 26
veil of perception problem 86
verification, principle of 115
Vienna Circle 337
virtue theory **108–9**, 111, 113
virtues, necessity for evil 156
vision, reliabilism 55, *55*
visions 150, 151
vitalism 324
Vitoria, Francisco de **272**
Voltaire 37, 284, 292

W

water, as ultimate substance 232
Whitehead, Alfred North 10,
  245, 322
Williams, Bernard 68
Wittgenstein, Ludwig 43, 75,
  326–7, *326*, 341
  on family resemblance 212,
    220–21
  on scepticism 56–7
  Tractatus 326
Wollstonecraft, Mary 169, *169*

XYZ

Xunzi 236, 253
Zen Buddhism 321
Zeno of Citium 29, **252**, *252*
Zeno of Elea 24, **240**, *240*
Zeus 151
Zhuangzi 26
Zoroastrianism *139*
Zubiri, Xavier 324

ACKNOWLEDGMENTS

Author's acknowledgments

Although Stephen Law is the main organizer, author, and editor of this work, it also contains contributions by Dan Cardinal (Orpington FE College), Michael Lacewing (Heythrop College), and Chris Horner (William Morris Academy). Stephen Law wishes to acknowledge the very fine writing of all three of these contributors, without which this volume would have been much the poorer. In addition, James Garvey, of the Royal Institute of Philosophy, provided enormously generous, incisive, and detailed feedback. Stephen Law would also like to thank Peter Gallagher, of Heythrop College, University of London, for his very helpful comments on several of the Who's Who entries. Dan Cardinal would like to thank Gerald Jones and Jeremy Hayward for their contributions to Chapter Two.

Publisher's acknowledgments

The publishers would like to thank: Carolyn Walton, Steve Setford, and Klara and Eric King for editorial assistance; Hilary Bird for the index; Charles Wills and Jenny Siklos for Americanization; Yukki Yaura for the Chinese lettering on pp.134–5; Nick Harris at Splinter Group for the illustration on p.98; and all those individuals and institutions that helped us to obtain photographs for the Who's Who in Philosophy chapter.

Picture credits

The publisher would like to thank the following for their kind permission to reproduce their photographs:

(Key: a-above; b-below/bottom; c-centre; f-far; l-left; r-right; t-top; rh-running head)

1 Alamy Images: Visual Arts Library (London) (t). 2–3 Corbis: Bettmann (c). 4 iStockPhoto: Lynn Chealander (c). 5 Science Photo Library: Mehau Kulyk (c). 6–7 Corbis: Ali Meyer (c). 8 Alamy Images: Dale O'Dell (br). 9 Corbis: Steve Raymer (c). Mary Evans Picture Library: Mary Evans Picture Library (t). 10–11 iStockPhoto: Daniela Andreea Spyropoulos (rh) 10 DK Images: Rough Guides (c). 11 iStockPhoto: John Grigg (c). 14–21 DK Images: David Malin/Anglo Australian Observatory (rh) 14 Alamy Images: Christian Darkin (b). 15 Corbis: Burstein Collection (tr). 16 The Art Archive (ca). 16–17 Alamy Images: Robert Fried (cb). 18 Corbis: Kazuyoshi Nomachi (b). 19 Science Photo Library: David Parker (tl). 20 Mary Evans Picture Library (c). 21 Getty Images: Matthias Clamer (c). 22–23 Getty Images: The Bridgeman Art Library (c). 24–43 DK Images: Rough Guides (rh). 25 iStockPhoto: Sandra von Stein (t). 26 Alamy Images: Mary Evans Picture Library (c). 27 Corbis: Punit Paranjpe/Reuters (c). 28 Corbis: Adam Woolfitt (b). Mary Evans Picture Library: Edwin Wallace (c). 30 Mary Evans Picture Library (c). 31 Corbis: Murat Taner/Zefa (c). 32 Alamy Images: Ben Ramos (bl). Corbis: Archivo Iconografico, S.A. (tr). 33 DK Images: Museo de Bellas Artes, Seville (br). 34 Corbis: Bettmann (c). 35 Corbis: Arte & Immagini SRL (t). 36 Mary Evans Picture Library (t). 37 Alamy Images: Visual Arts Library (London) (b). 38–39 Corbis: Bettmann (c). 41 The Kobal Collection: Renn Prod/France 2/D.D.Prod (c). 42 Corbis: Peter Turnley (c). 43 iStockPhoto: Arpad Benedek (c). 44–45 Getty Images: Altrendo Nature (c). 46–189 iStockPhoto: Jeffrey McDonald (rh). 46 Alamy Images: Mary Evans Picture Library (tc). 48 Mary Evans Picture Library: Harry Price (c). 49 iStockPhoto: Gloria-Leigh Logan (t). 50 Corbis: Historical Picture Archive (c). 51 The Kobal Collection: Warner Bros/Jasin Boland (b). 52 Corbis: Hulton-Deutsch Collection (br). 53 Alamy Images: Hideo Kurihara (b). 54–55 Alamy Images: Chris Howes/Wild Places Photography (bl). 55 Alamy Images: Phototake Inc. (ca). Rutgers State University of New Jersey: Alvin Goldman (c). 56 Corbis: Bettmann (ca). iStockPhoto: Ulrich Zillmann (fbl); (bl). 57 Corbis: H&S Produktion (b). 58 Getty Images:

Hulton Archive (b). 59 Corbis: Swim Ink 2, LLC (ca). 60 Mary Evans Picture Library (b). 61 Alamy Images: Visual Arts Library (London) (cla). iStockPhoto: Li Kim Goh (ca). 62–63 Corbis: Reinhard Eisele (b). 63 Corbis: Ronnie Kaufman (cra). 64–65 Jupiter Images: Lorenz/Avelar (c). 66 Science Photo Library: Bluestone (b). 67 Alamy Images: Classic Image (cr); Mary Evans Picture Library (cl). 68–69 Corbis: Richard T. Nowitz (c). 70 Alamy Images: Zak Waters (b). iStockPhoto: Vasko Miokovic (c). 71 The Kobal Collection: MGM (bl). 72 Corbis: Owen Franken (t). Mary Evans Picture Library (bc). 73 Alamy Images: Visual Arts Library (London) (ca). 74 Corbis: Louie Psihoyos (c). 75 iStockPhoto: Michael Puerzer (t). 76–77 Alamy Images: Philip Bramhill (b). 77 iStockPhoto: PhotographerOlympus (ca). 78–79 Jupiter Images: Ken Sherman (b). 79 Alamy Images: Mary Evans Picture Library (ca). 80 Alamy Images: Peter Horree (b). 81 The Kobal Collection: Walt Disney Pictures/Walden Media (t). 82 iStockPhoto: Peter Elvidge (bl). 82–83 Alamy Images: Phototake Inc. (tl). 84 Alamy Images: Mary Evans Picture Library (b). 85 Science Photo Library: Richard Megna/ Fundamental Photos (t). 86 Corbis: Zen Icknow (bl). 87 Corbis: Cooperphoto (c). 88 Alamy Images: Bert Klassen (b). 89 akg-images (tr). 90 iStockPhoto: Bonnie Schupp (bl). 91 iStockPhoto: Jose Antonio Nicoli Andonie (br); Maciej Stachowiak (t). 92 Alamy Images: Mary Evans Picture Library (ca). iStockPhoto: Andrzej Tokarski (t). 93 iStockPhoto: Dóri O'Connell (cr). 94–95 Getty Images: The Bridgeman Art Library / John William Waterhouse (c). 96 Alamy Images: Werner Otto (ca). Corbis: David Turnley (b). 97 iStockPhoto: Vasiliy Yakobchuk (t). 99 Corbis: Roger Ressmeyer (b). iStockPhoto: Enrico Fianchini (ca). 100 Corbis: Todd Gipstein (c). 101 Frances Twitty (t). 102 iStockPhoto: Daniel Goldwasser (c). 103 Alamy Images: Peter Horree (c). Corbis: Mark Peterson (t). 105 Corbis: Corbis Sygma (b). 106 Getty Images: Altrendo Images (t). 107 Corbis: Kapoor Baldev/ Sygma (b). 108 Corbis: Pierre Perrin/Corbis Sygma (c). 109 Corbis: Ted Streshinsky (cb). iStockPhoto: Duncan Walker (tr). 110 iStockPhoto: Alvaro Pantoja (cra). 111 Science Photo Library: Zephyr (b). 112 Getty Images: Orlando / Hulton Archive (b). 113 The Art Archive: Musée du Louvre Paris / Dagli Orti (t). iStockPhoto: Scrambled (cb). 114 iStockPhoto: Ljupco (b). Mary Evans Picture Library (ca). 115 Corbis: BBC (b). iStockPhoto: Morgan Mansour (ca). 116–117 iStockPhoto: Thomas Tuchan (c). 118 Corbis: James Robert Fuller (tr). 119 Getty Images: Taxi / Alan Powdrill (b). 120 Alamy Images: Black Star (b). 121 Alamy Images: Tim Graham (t); Mary Evans Picture Library (cb). 122 iStockPhoto: Johanna Goodyear (c). 124 NHPA: Stephen Dalton (br). 125 iStockPhoto: konradlew (b). 126 Mary Evans Picture Library (b). 127 Alamy Images: Mary Evans Picture Library (cb). iStockPhoto: Ralph Paprzycki (t). 128 Alamy Images: supershoo (t). 129 Frank Jackson (br). 130–131 The Kobal Collection: MGM (c). 132 Corbis: John Springer Collection (b). iStockPhoto: Kenneth C. Zirkel (c). 133 Science Photo Library: Pete Leonard/Zefa (b). 134–135 Corbis: David McCarthy (c). 136 Science Photo Library: David McCarthy (c). 137 Corbis: Bettmann (br); Gregor Schuster/zefa (t). 138 Corbis: Kazuyoshi Nomachi (b). 139 iStockPhoto: Ron Hohenhaus (t). 140 Alamy Images: Visual Arts Library (London) (c). 140–141 iStockPhoto: Mlenny (b). 141 Alamy Images: Mary Evans Picture Library (tc). 142–143 Corbis: Drew Gardner (b). 144–145 Corbis: Jagadeesh NV/Reuters (c). 146 Alamy Images: David Pearson (t). Richard Swinburne (bc). 147 Corbis: Bettmann (b). 148–149 Corbis: Randy Faris (b). 149 Science Photo Library: David Goodsell (t). 150–151 Mary Evans Picture Library (b). 151 Alamy Images: Visual Arts Library (London) (b). 152 Alamy Images: Visual Arts Library (London) (b). 153 Alamy Images: Westend61 (b). 154 Getty Images: Daniel Berehulak (t). 155 Alamy Images: Visual Arts Library (London) (c). iStockPhoto: Christian Wagner (b). 156–157 iStockPhoto: Shaun Lowe (b). 157 Alamy Images: Popperfoto (c). 158–159 Getty Images: Ken Fisher (b). 160 Alamy Images: Nicholas Pitt (c). 161 iStockPhoto: Vladimir Pomortsev (t). 162–163 Alamy Images: Network Photographers (c). 163 Alamy Images: Visual Arts Library (London) (tr). 164 Corbis: Joseph Sohm; ChromoSohm Inc. (b). 165 Corbis: Stefano Bianchetti (tc). 166–167 Mary Evans Picture Library: Mary Evans Picture Library (c). 168 iStockPhoto: webking (tc). 169 Alamy Images: Classic Image (tc). Corbis: Randy Faris (b). 170 iStockPhoto: Katie Winegarden (t). 170–171 Corbis: The Art Archive (t). 172 Corbis: Bernard Bisson/Corbis Sygma (bc); Ruggero Vanni (t). 173 Alamy Images: Greenshoots Communications (t). 174 Alamy Images: Visual Arts Library (London) (t). 174–175 Corbis: Diego Goldberg (b). Charles Taylor (tr). 176–177 Corbis: Peter Turnley (bc). 177 akg-images (tr). 178 Corbis: Bettmann (c). 180–

181 iStockPhoto: Matthew Scherf (bc). 182–183 Corbis: Carl & Ann Purcel (b). 183 Corbis: Hulton-Deutsch Collection (c). 184 Getty Images: Alexander Walter (bc). 184–185 Alamy Images: Mary Evans Picture Library (c). 185 Alamy Images: ImageState (c). 186 DK Images: NASA (bl). 187 Alamy Images: Arco Images (tc). 188 Alamy Images: Michael Hilton (bl). Mary Evans Picture Library (ca). 189 Corbis: Vincent/Zefa (b). 190–191 Getty Images (c). 192 Getty Images: FPG (c). 193 The Kobal Collection: Walt Disney/ The Kobal Collection/Pier Mountain (c). 195 Alamy Images: Pictorial Press (cra). iStockPhoto: Adrian Moisei (tl). 196 iStockPhoto: Andriy Doriy (c); (cr); Robert Kyllo (tl). 196–197 iStockPhoto: Adam Booth (b). 198–199 Corbis: H. Armstrong Roberts (b). 199 Alamy Images: Suzy Bennett (bl). iStockPhoto: Kai Krien (tl). Mary Evans Picture Library (cra). 200 Alamy Images: TH Foto (tl). Getty Images: Thomas Wiewandt (b). 201 Alamy Images: Mary Evans Picture Library (cra). Corbis: Bettmann (bl). iStockPhoto: Tom Grill (tl). 202 iStockPhoto: YangYin (tl). 202–203 Corbis: Rick Friedman (b). 203 Alamy Images: Popperfoto (bl). Corbis: Franco Vogt (cra). iStockPhoto: Nicholas Belton (tl). 204 Alamy Images: Suzie Packard (b). iStockPhoto: javaman3 (tl). 205 Alamy Images: Photowood Inc (cla). iStockPhoto: powershot (tl). The Kobal Collection: Lucasfilm/20th Century Fox/Frank Connor (br). 206–207 iStockPhoto: Ines Gesell (c). 208 Alamy Images: Content Mine International (tl). Corbis: John Van Hasselt (cl). 208–209 Alamy Images: Nigel Hicks (b). 209 Alamy Images: Pictorial Press Ltd (tr). 210 iStockPhoto: Julie Deshaies (tl). 210–211 Getty Images: Jason Hosking (b). 211 Corbis: Bettmann (tl). iStockPhoto: Tomasz Zajaczkowski (cr). 212 Corbis: H. Benser (b). 213 Alamy Images: Papilio (br/panda); Worldspec/NASA (br/earth). DK Images: Lindsey Stock (tr). iStockPhoto: Umbar Shakir (cla). 214 iStockPhoto: Cindy England (tl). 214–215 Corbis: Chris Rainier (b). 215 akg-images (cl). Getty Images: Tim Brown (tl). 216 iStockPhoto: Ralf Stadtaus (tl). Mary Evans Picture Library: Edwin Wallace (bl). 216–217 Getty Images: Dave Nagel (cr). 218 Corbis: CinemaPhoto (tl). 218–219 Alamy Images: Phil Talbot (br). 219 Alamy Images: Visual Arts Library (London) (fcl). Jamey Ekins (cl); Juan Jose Gutierez Barrow (cr); Keith Lamond (fcr). 220 Alamy Images: Marilyn Shenton (b); Stockfolio (tl). 221 iStockPhoto: Ramsey Blacklock (cra); Derek Dammann (tr); Nicola Gavin (tl); maodesign (cla); Adrian Moisei (tc); Ivan Stevanovic (ca). 222 iStockPhoto: Christos Georghiou (cl). 222–223 The Kobal Collection: Paramount/ Melinda Sue Gordon(b). 223 Corbis: Swim Ink 2, LLC (br). iStockPhoto: Creacart (tr); Lise Gagne (crb); Jose Antonio Nicoli Andonie (cra); Lee Pettet (cr). 224 iStockPhoto: Arne Thaysen (cr). 224–225 Corbis: Adam Woolfitt (b). 225 iStockPhoto: David Safanda (tl). 226–227 Corbis: Archivo Iconografico, S.A. (c). 228 Corbis: Hulton-Deutsch Collection (c). 229 Corbis: Massimo Listri (c). 230 DK Images: Rough Guides (tl). 231 Alamy Images: Ron Yue (r). 232 iStockPhoto: Henry Lucenius (cr). Mary Evans Picture Library (tl). 233 Alamy Images: Mary Evans Picture Library (tl). Getty Images: Fedor Andreevich Bronnikov (b). 234 Corbis: Tim Pannell (b). 235 Alamy Images: Mary Evans Picture Library (tl). Corbis: Kevin Fleming (b); (c). 237 Corbis: Dave G. Houser (br). 238 Corbis: Chris Hellier (cr); Corbis (tl). 239 Corbis: Mimmo Jodice (tl). iStockPhoto: Christian Wagner (b). 240 Alamy Images: Mark Sykes (tl); Mary Evans Picture Library (tl). 241 Alamy Images: Popperfoto (tl). 242 Corbis: Gianni Dagli Orti (tl). 242–243 Corbis: Francis G. Mayer (b). 244 Corbis: Peter Johnson (c). 245 Alamy Images: Visual Arts Library (London) (tr). 246 Corbis: Araldo de Luca (b). 247 Corbis: Bettmann (tc). 248 Alamy Images: North Wind Picture Archives (b). 249 DK Images: Natural History Museum, London (tc). 250 Alamy Images: Classic Image (tr). Corbis: Christie's Images (cra). 251 Corbis: Araldo de Luca (b). 252 Alamy Images: Classic Image (tl). The Kobal Collection: Paramount Television (bl). 253 Baidu Image Search Service: Baidu Image Search Service (tl). Corbis: Keren Su (c). 254 Alamy Images: Visual Arts Library (London) (tl). Mary Evans Picture Library (c). 255 Alamy Images: nagelestock.com (tl). 256 Alamy Images: Mary Evans Picture Library (tl). Corbis: Brooklyn Museum (b). 257 Getty Images: Ian Waldie (tl). 258 Alamy Images: Trip (bl). Corbis: Leonard de Selva (tr). 259 Alamy Images: Mary Evans Picture Library (tl). Corbis: Bettmann (tl). 260 Corbis: Kazuyoshi Nomachi (b). 261 Alamy Images: Mary Evans Picture Library (tl); Trip (cl). 262 Mary Evans Picture Library (tc). 263 The Bridgeman Art Library: Ms Lat 6823 fol.2 Averroes (1126–98) in Conversation with Porphyry (c.232–c.305) (pen & ink and wash on paper) (b/w photo) , Italian School, (14th century) / Bibliotheque Nationale, Paris, France, Giraudon / The Bridgeman Art Library (br).

Corbis: Roger Antrobus (tl). 264 iStockPhoto: Vaide Dambrauskaite (c). 265 Corbis: National Gallery Collection; By kind permission of the Trustees of the National Gallery, London (tr). 266 Alamy Images: Visual Arts Library (London) (bl). 267 Mary Evans Picture Library (cl). 268 Corbis: Gianni Dagli Orti (cl); Stapleton Collection (bc). 269 Alamy Images: Corbis (tr). Corbis: Archivo Iconografico, S.A. (br). 270 Alamy Images: AEP (tl). 271 iStockPhoto: Hedda Gjerpen (b). 272 Alamy Images: Mary Evans Picture Library (tr). 273 Alamy Images: Mary Evans Picture Library (b). John J. Burns Library (tl). 274 Alamy Images: Mary Evans Picture Library (tl). iStockPhoto: Caitriona Dwyer (tr). 275 Alamy Images: Pictorial Press Ltd (tl). Corbis: Bettmann (c). 276 Getty Images: Vanessa Berberian (b). 277 Corbis: The Art Archive (b). 278 Corbis: Stapleton Collection (b). 279 Corbis: Archivo Iconografico, S.A. (ca). 280 Corbis: Archivo Iconografico, S.A. (tl). 281 Alamy Images: Visual Arts Library (London) (tl). 282 Alamy Images: Classic Image (tl). 283 Alamy Images: Mary Evans Picture Library (b). 284 Alamy Images: Mary Evans Picture Library (tl). iStockPhoto: Jeff Dalton (b). 285 Corbis: Wolfgang Kaehler (tl). 286–287 Corbis: Ted Spiegel (c). 288 Alamy Images: Leslie Garland Picture Library (b); Mary Evans Picture Library (tl). 289 Mary Evans Picture Library (tr). 290 Corbis: Christie's Images (c). DK Images: National Maritime Museum (cl). 291 The Kobal Collection: MGM (t). 292 Alamy Images: Mary Evans Picture Library (tl). Mary Evans Picture Library (bc). 293 Corbis: Alexander Burkatovski (t). 294 Alamy Images: Fabrice Bettex. 295 Alamy Images: Lebrecht Music and Arts Photo Library (tl). 296 Getty Images: Richard Price (b). 298 Corbis: Hulton-Deutsch Collection (tl). 299 Mary Evans Picture Library (tl); (c). 300 Alamy Images: Mary Evans Picture Library (tl); Visual Arts Library (London) (tl). 301 Corbis: Bettmann (tl). iStockPhoto: David Virtser (b). 302 Alamy Images: Mary Evans Picture Library (tl). Mary Evans Picture Library (c). 303 iStockPhoto: Szabolcs Borbely (tl). 304 Alamy Images: Lebrecht Music and Arts Photo Library (tl). Corbis: Christophe Boisvieux (br). 305 iStockPhoto: Gintautas Tumulis (b). 306 Alamy Images: Visual Arts Library (London) (tl). DK Images: Judith Miller/Jo de Buck (bc). 307 Alamy Images: Lebrecht Music and Arts Photo Library (tl). Corbis: Jean Louis Atlan (cr). 308 Alamy Images: Mary Evans Picture Library (tl). Corbis: Catherine Karnow (c). 309 Corbis: Hulton-Deutsch Collection (tc). 310 Alamy Images: Mary Evans Picture Library (tl). Corbis: David Turnley (b). 311 Alamy Images: Lebrecht Music and Arts Photo Library (tl). Corbis: Swim Ink 2/LLC (bc). 312 Corbis: Peter Turnley (b). 313 Corbis: Bettmann (tl); (br). 314–315 Alamy Images: Les Polders (c). 316 Alamy Images: Lebrecht Music and Arts Photo Library (bc); Popperfoto (tl). 317 Corbis: Christies Images (bl). 318 akg-images (tl). iStockPhoto: Goran Mottram (c). 319 Alamy Images: Popperfoto (tl). 320 Alamy Images: Mary Evans Picture Library (tl). Corbis: Bilic/photocuisin (bl). 321 Corbis: Macduff Everton (c). 322 Alamy Images: Popperfoto (cr). Corbis: Bettmann (tl). 323 Corbis: Terry Cryer (b). 324 Corbis: Bettmann (tl); Christie's Images (b). 325 Corbis: Bettmann (bl). Nederlands Carmelitaans Instituut (tr). 326 Getty Images: Hulton Archive (tl). 327 Alamy Images: Arcaid (tr). Corbis: Brooks Kraft (b). 328 Corbis: Bettmann/ (tl); Peer Grimm/EPA/ (b). 330 akg-images: ullstein bild (bl). Alamy Images: Neil McAllister (br). 331 Getty Images: George Douglas/Stringer (tl). iStockPhoto: Bjorn Barton-Pye (b). 332 Corbis: G. Baden/zefa (b). Getty Images: Hulton Archive (tl). 333 Getty Images: Hulton Archive (tl). Mary Evans Picture Library (c). 334–335 Alamy Images: Christian Liewig (c). 336 Alamy Images: Popperfoto (tl). 337 Getty Images: Farhad J Parsa (b). Dr Douglas Boynton Quine (tl). 338 Alamy Images: Popperfoto (cr). Corbis: Bettmann (tl). 339 Sijmen Hendricks (tl). iStockPhoto: emily2k (cr). 340 Corbis: Everett Kennedy Brown/epa (b). Harvard University Gazette: Jane Reed (tl). 341 Getty Images: Bill Pierce (tr). 342 Corbis: Bettmann (tl). Getty Images: Diego Rodriguez de Silva y Velasquez (bl). 343 Corbis: Christopher Felver (tl). iStockPhoto: Elena Kouptsova-Vasic (cra). 344 Corbis: Richard Melloul//Sygma (bl). Getty Images: Time & Life Pictures/ Marty Katz (tl). 345 Alamy Images: Visions of America, LLC (cr). Getty Images: Jim Bourg (tl). Peter Waldvogel (tl). 346–352 iStockPhoto: Daniela Andreea Spyropoulos (rh).

Every effort has been made to trace the copyright holders. The publisher apologizes for any unintentional omissions and would be pleased, in such cases, to place an acknowledgment in future editions of this book.

All other images © Dorling Kindersley
For further information see: www.dkimages.com